P9-BIH-369

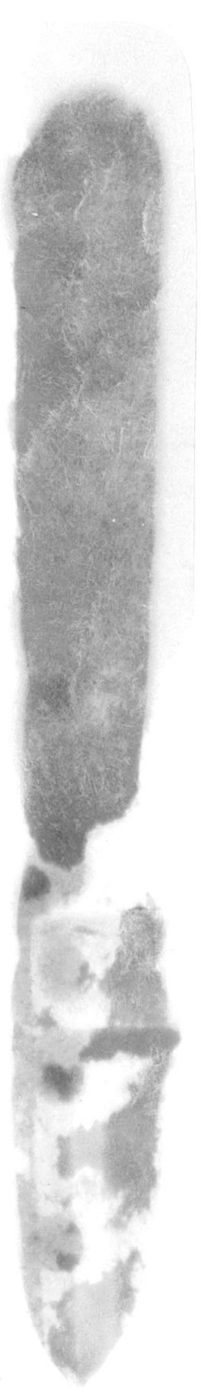

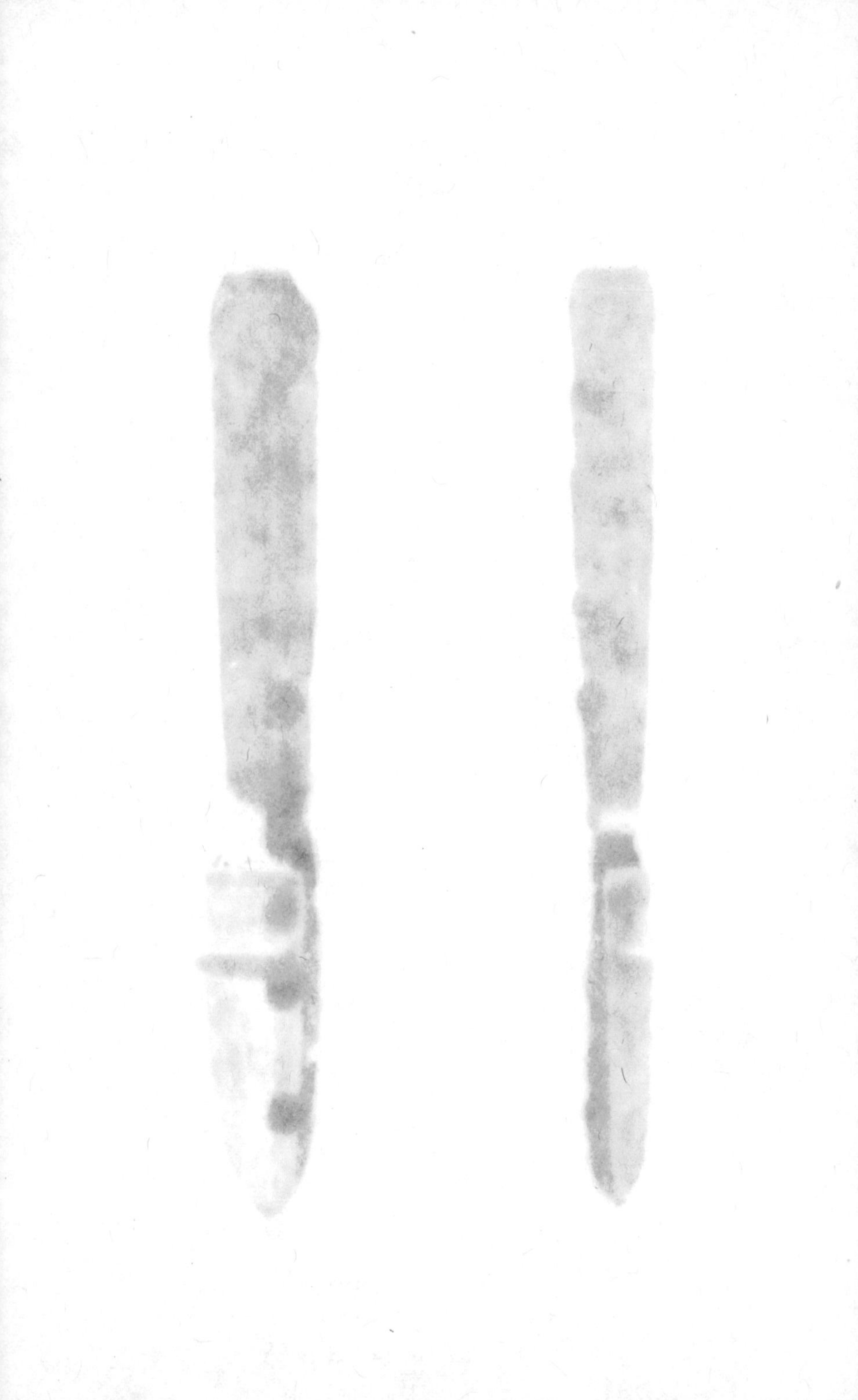

THE LITERATURE AND THOUGHT OF MODERN AFRICA

Claude Wauthier

THE LITERATURE AND THOUGHT OF MODERN AFRICA

A Survey

TRANSLATED BY SHIRLEY KAY

GREENWOOD PRESS, PUBLISHERS
WESTPORT, CONNECTICUT

Library of Congress Cataloging in Publication Data

Wauthier, Claude, 1923-
The literature and thought of modern Africa.

Revised version of the author's L'Afrique des Africains.
Reprint of the ed. published by Praeger, New York, in series: Praeger library of African affairs.
Bibliography: p.
1. Nationalism—Africa. 2. Africa in literature. I. Title.
[DT21.W313 1975] 320.9'6 75-14706 2·9·77
ISBN 0-8371-8228-X

This is a revised version of the original French edition,
L'Afrique des Africains: Inventaire de la Négritude,
published by Editions du Seuil, Paris, 1964

This edition originally published in 1967 by Frederick A. Praeger, Publishers, New York

Reprinted with the permission of Praeger Publishers, Inc.

Reprinted in 1975 by Greenwood Press, a division of Williamhouse-Regency Inc.

Library of Congress Catalog Card Number 75-14706

ISBN 0-8371-8228-X

Printed in the United States of America

To
the memory of
my sister and my father

CONTENTS

PREFACE TO THE ENGLISH LANGUAGE EDITION

THE CLOSING POINT for this study of African thought and literature is May 1963: the date of the conference at Addis Ababa which founded the Organisation of African Unity. Though the text has been up-dated to early 1966 in respect to major political events, I have thought it desirable to keep 1963 as the *terminus ad quem* for the main substance of the book.

Since this date there have been new developments in Africa, and the continent's writers and intellectuals, ever growing in numbers, have enriched its literature with new works. It is not possible in this Preface to give even the most important of them a cursory mention. Yet there is an African literary event which must be referred to: the publication of the speeches of Patrice Lumumba, edited by the Belgian journalist, Jean Van Lierde, with a preface by Jean-Paul Sartre. The fate of the first prime minister of independent Congo is described by Sartre thus: 'Dead, Lumumba ceased to be an individual man and became Africa, with its desire for unity, the multiplicity of its social and political systems, its divisions, its discords, its strength and its weakness. He was not, nor could he be, the hero of panafricanism: he was its martyr.'

Since May 1963, two notable African intellectuals, in conflict with their respective governments, have died in prison: Fily Dabo Sissoko of Mali, and J. B. Danquah of Ghana. Two others are under detention as I write: Mamadou Dia, accused of having plotted against President Senghor of Senegal, and Ndabaningi Sithole, in a camp for political detainees in Rhodesia.

Although even a brief outline of the continent's history over the last three years is beyond my scope here, it is necessary to say a few words about some of the problems which are singled out for attention in the text of this book.

The Central African Federation of Northern Rhodesia, Southern Rhodesia and Nyasaland has ceased to exist. From it have sprung two new and independent African states: Malawi (formerly Nyasaland) and

Zambia (formerly Northern Rhodesia). Southern Rhodesia has become Rhodesia *tout court.* A government seeking to maintain white supremacy there has replaced the political groups which were endeavouring to make the experiment of a multiracial state. Under its leader, Ian Smith, this government in November 1965 broke with Britain and declared Rhodesia to be an independent, sovereign state.

Shortly before the OAU conference in Addis Ababa in 1963, the Union Africaine et Malgache was dissolved. This seemed to substantiate the panafrican opposition to regional groupings, but only for a time, for the same states belonging to the former French West and Equatorial Africa were soon to regroup themselves in the Organisation Commune Africaine et Malgache. This admitted a new member to the grouping, Congo-Leopoldville, where Moise Tshombe made a remarkable return to power, becoming—until late 1965—prime minister of the united Congo after a long period in the wilderness.

In Nigeria, a fourth region (the Mid-West) was created at the expense of the Western Region. The Mid-West's first head of government, the poet Dennis Osadebay, attached himself to the NCNC, the party of Dr Azikiwe. The split in the Action Group—one section of which, led by Sir Samuel Akintola, became the Nigerian National Democratic Party (NNDP)—considerably complicated the political situation, not only in the Western Region but throughout the Federation. The federal elections of December 1964 saw the clash of two major groupings: the United Progressive Grand Alliance (a coalition of the NCNC and the Action Group), and the Nigerian National Alliance (a coalition of the NPC and the NNDP). This represented the breakdown of the old alliance between the Northern and Eastern Regions, while at the same time the Western Region was torn between two rival factions. This political situation was transformed by the military coup in January 1966.

Nigeria has not been alone among African countries in experiencing the removal of civilian government by the military. There was a veritable epidemic of revolution at the end of 1965 and the beginning of 1966. Army leaders seized power in Congo-Leopoldville, in Dahomey, in the Central African Republic, in Upper Volta and, finally, in Ghana, whose former president, Kwame Nkrumah, had to seek asylum in Guinea.

By the beginning of 1964, the military had already made their presence felt in the former British East Africa. The civil power managed to retain the upper hand, but the gravity of the situation—amounting, in the case of Tanganyika, to mutiny—constrained the governments of Kenya, Tanganyika and Uganda to appeal for British troops to restore order. In the spring of 1964, Tanganyika and Zanzibar—the sultan of which was driven out by a left-wing movement immediately after his country became independent—formed a new federal state: Tanzania. This is the third example, so far, of the fusion of two former colonial territories, the other two being Somalia and Cameroon.

We should note, finally, the meeting at Geneva in March 1964 of the International Conference on Trade and Development, which was of major concern for the Third World, and for Africa in particular. The main problem before the conference was to find a way to redress the growing imbalance of trade between the industrialised and the developing countries: an imbalance largely due to the low prices of primary materials exported by the Third World and to the high prices of industrial products from the northern hemisphere. This is one of the most agonising problems confronting former colonies.

C. W.
March 1966

PREFACE TO THE FRENCH EDITION

THE WORKS of some one hundred and fifty black African writers are cited in this book. Of these writers, the earliest were slaves, born in Africa, who had had the rare good fortune to study in Europe or America. The most recent are members of the intellectual elite formed under colonial regimes. Although I hope that no work of major importance has been omitted, I have in no way endeavoured to be exhaustive, even for the French-speaking countries of Africa. For, indeed, had I attempted to be, the present state of research in the subject would have made this impossible. African literature is, in fact, so 'new' that it has been relatively little explored. Although the struggle for emancipation from colonialism has now attracted attention to the works of African writers, this is still true even of the most recent period.

It would take several teams of research workers to compile a complete catalogue of African literature in the widest sense of the word, including the works of ethnologists, historians, theologians, jurists and economists. An inventory would be needed, not only of the collections in the great libraries of the former 'colonial' capitals, but of the libraries in Africa as well. Further, one would need to hunt among the stocks of publishers who have issued works at the authors' expense, since African writers who are little known frequently send their books for publication on these terms.

For French-speaking Africa, Joucla's voluminous *Bibliographie de l'Afrique française* (which, however, does not go beyond 1937) could serve as the starting point of such an enquiry. The initial steps towards a new inventory have, in fact, been taken by Africans; and two students at Northwestern University, Illinois, recently completed a general bibliography for the Liberian Republic. Until only the other day, illiteracy was the general rule in the continent. The number of African writers is still sufficiently limited for a new survey of their works to be covered by a relatively brief catalogue, but the situation is changing rapidly. Over the last few years, the output of African literature, currently enjoying a vogue, has increased by leaps and bounds. Doubtless in a few decades a bibliography of black African writers will fill a volume of considerable dimensions.

I have taken the present study up to the summer of 1963, to the morrow of the summit conference of the thirty-two independent African countries. This conference took place at a moment when the leaders of the new states had experienced their first few years of sovereignty; it embodied their opinions on the subject and will probably mark an important date in African history. In any case, it seemed a convenient point to terminate a literary history of Africa as seen from a political angle.

I have excluded from this study, with certain exceptions, all that part of African literature which forms the oral folklore tradition, such as has been preserved in the collections of European ethnologists like Frobenius or Labouret. My primary interest has been the modern trend of nationalist thought as expressed in the languages of the colonial powers.

Similarly, I have not attempted to study the works of Negro writers in Arabic since these are situated in a very different context from the one under consideration. Without going back to the university of Timbuktu, destroyed at the end of the sixteenth century by a Moroccan military expedition, or mentioning the Arabised fringe of eastern Africa, it suffices to recall that Arab culture enjoyed considerable popularity in Western Africa, particularly at the beginning of the nineteenth century in the Fulani emirates of what is now northern Nigeria. The historical chronicles of the conqueror and religious reformer, Dan Fodio, and of his son Bello, sultan of Sokoto, date from his period. The standard of culture at the court of Sokoto is nicely illustrated by an episode during the visit of the English explorer Clapperton in 1824. Sultan Bello asked him to obtain for him an Arabic version of the works of Euclid as his own copy had been destroyed by fire the preceding year; Clapperton fulfilled this request in 1826.

In order to keep within the strictly 'colonial' or post-colonial domain, I have excluded from the field of my research the literature of Liberia and Ethiopia. These two independent African countries escaped European domination, with the brief exception of Ethiopia during the period of Mussolini. The literature of Liberia, however, does present certain analogies with that of the former African colonies, if only as a result of the long struggle waged by Monrovia to preserve its tenuous existence in face of the appetites of the neighbouring powers, Britain and France. The work of the first great Liberian writer, E. D. Blyden—about whom I shall say only a few words—is an appeal for the rehabilitation of the Negro; it has a considerable influence on the first generation of English-speaking African intellectuals from the Bight of Benin. After Blyden, Liberian literature was further enriched by authors who sought to exalt national sentiment and to make Liberia better known; these included Abayomi Karnga (author of a history and an essay on African customs in Liberia), Ernest J. Yancy and Doris Banks Henries, who devoted one of her books to the Liberian heroes and heroines of the days when the first pioneers were encountering the hostility of the autochthonous tribes. This preoccupation is still to be seen in present-day writers, such as the journalist Henry B. Cole, author of *Meet the Liberians* and *Who are the Liberians?*, or the historian Ernest Eastman in his history of the State of Maryland. E. Reginald Townsend has published a collection of the speeches of the present president of Liberia under the title *President Tubman Speaks*. It should be noted also that those in charge of Liberian education insist that children should learn something of the literature of their own country; a textbook of Liberian authors has been published for their use which contains, besides an extract from the works of Blyden, tales from African folklore and the poetry of H. Carey Thomas.

Ethiopian literature, of which the principal works are written in Ge'ez, reached its culmination in the Middle Ages. However, it is frequently only a literature of translation, as has been pointed out by Sir E. A. Wallis Budge, keeper of Egyptian and Assyrian Antiquities at the British Museum, who was responsible for the translations of several Ethiopian manuscripts of primary importance which were brought to London at the end of the last century by a British expedition to that country. Thus, the famous *Kebra Nagast*, which recounts the story of Menelik (son of Solomon and the Queen of Sheba, from whom the present dynasty claims descent), was compiled by a Coptic priest in the sixth century, translated from Coptic into Arabic in the fourteenth century, and then retranslated into Ethiopian.

The History of Alexander is even less Ethiopian in origin: it is taken from the Greek story of the pseudo-Callisthenes and exists in Syrian, Arabic and Persian versions apart from the Ethiopian one. The real Callisthenes, a great-nephew of Aristotle, was historian at the court of the Macedonian monarch and among his works, which have not come down to us, was a life of Alexander. The pseudo-Callisthenes, who was of a far later date, made the conqueror of Darius into a christian hero; his story, which was clearly evangelistic in purpose, was widely read in a variety of versions at a period when, according to Budge, many people in the Middle East and Far East had adopted Alexander the Great as a compatriot. The same applies to *The Book of Baralam and Yewasef*, a legendary story with equally evangelistic intent, of which the original Greek version has long been attributed to Saint John Damascene; there are a good half-dozen later versions of this work in Arabic, Syrian, Persian, Armenian, Georgian and Hebrew, as well as the Ethiopian version. The story tells of the son of an Indian king who was converted to christianity. This edifying tale blends in a curious way buddhist traditions and recollections of a legendary visit to India by the Apostle Thomas; the earliest Portuguese explorers believed they had discovered relics of this visit in the keeping of a Nestorian sect which was still existent at the time of their arrival on the coast of Coromandel. An even more curious case is that of another great work of Ethiopian literature, the collection of *Miracles of the Virgin*. This book, according to Jean Doresse, was originally written in Latin in France, at the time of the twelfth-century plague; from there, he writes, it was taken to the East and translated into Arabic at Sadnaia in Syria, whence it crossed Egypt—amassing a collection of local tales on the way—before finally reaching Ethiopia, where it was adapted with remarkable skill.

It is superfluous to mention that this Ethiopian literature has remained the domain of but a handful of scholars. For a brief moment, Ethiopia was exposed to western influence, chiefly by the Portuguese who had gone in search of Prester John; but shortly after the expulsion of the Jesuits, who had tried to convert the Ethiopian kings to catholicism, the country withdrew once again into isolation. The seventeenth-century German scholar, Hiob Ludolf—the first great Ethiopian specialist in Europe—was never able to visit Ethiopia, and carried out his research in the Collegium Aethiopicum at the Vatican with the help of four Ethiopian monks who had been converted to catholicism and had left the country with the last of the Jesuits. At the end of the nineteenth century, a number of important manuscripts were brought back to Europe, mainly to London and Paris. The Italian conquest gave rise to a certain renaissance in Ethiopian studies, and the most recent of the very few general studies of Ethiopian literature is that of Enrico Cerulli. One of the, equally rare, recent studies in French on the subject is an article by Jean Doresse, "Littérature éthiopienne et littérature occidentale au Moyen Age", published in Cairo in 1962 in the *Bulletin de la société d'archéologie copte*. In Peggy Rutherfoord's anthology of African literature, *Darkness and Light*, there is a very brief extract from the *Kebra Nagast*, translated by Sir E. A. Wallis Budge. A study of contemporary Ethiopian literature has yet to be made.

I should like to express my gratitude to all those who have helped me to write this book. First to M. Robert Cornevin, D. ès L., director of the Centre d'Etudes et de Documentation sur l'Afrique et l'Outre-mer, whose encouragement has been particularly valuable, and without whose help there would have been some serious gaps in this text. M. Pierre Jean Oswald has kindly given me the benefit of his publishing experience. Mr Joseph Murumbi, minister in the Kenya government, and Mr David Williams, editor-in-chief of *West Africa*, both gave me access to their extensive libraries in London, the former on East African, and the latter on West African, countries formerly under British rule. Señor Julian Marcos, the Madrid film director, generously made available to me the documentation which he had collected for a film on the Negro question. M. Alioune Diop, director of *Présence Africaine*, has assisted with several biographical details on various African writers. M. Hampaté Ba and M. Brasseur, of the Institut Français pour l'Afrique Noire (IFAN), offered me their notes on the work of Ibrahima Mamadou Ouane and the empire of the Macina. M. René Parnaudeau recounted his memories of colonial literature in the early part of the century. M. Jean Duvignaud, director of the Centre de sociologie at the university of Tunis, M. Claude Tardits, ethnologist and research assistant at the Centre National de Recherches Scientifiques (CNRS), and M. Gilbert Ancian, expert on economic affairs for Africa at the Société d'Études pour le Développement Economique et Sociale, were among the first to read this manuscript and gave me the benefit of their helpful advice. Mme Coisel, librarian at the Centre d'Etudes et de Documentation sur l'Afrique, has saved me a great deal of valuable time by her competence and helpfulness.

INTRODUCTION

THROUGHOUT HISTORY, the demand for national independence has gone hand in hand with cultural revival. One of the most striking examples of this trend is to be found in the national movements of eastern Europe during the last century. There grammarians, historians and poets united in their struggle to revitalise the soul of their people: the grammarians, by forging a national language from a dialect; the historians, by substituting the history of a nation for that of a series of dynasties; and the poets, by exalting revolutionary struggle.[1]

The movement for emancipation in the former African colonies is no exception to this rule. Independence has been preceded there by a cultural activity which is all the more surprising in that illiteracy was the general rule in black Africa until the second world war. Twenty years ago, publication of a book by an African author was still an isolated occurrence; nowadays, hardly a month passes without some novel, ethnographic monograph, political pamphlet or study on political economics coming from the pen of an African writer. A genuine readership has been won in specialist circles by the poet Léopold Sédar Senghor; by novelists like Camara Laye, Ferdinand Oyono, Mongo Beti, Amos Tutuola and Peter Abrahams; by economists such as Mamadou Dia (former prime minister of Senegal); by theologians such as Father Alexis Kagame and Father Vincent Mulago (both graduates of catholic universities); by lawyers like T. O. Elias,* who was appointed in 1960 to the commission charged with drawing up the Congolese federal constitution; and by ethnologists such as K. A. Busia and J. B. Danquah. Other factors also indicate the extent of this springtide in African cultural life: regular publication of periodicals of a quality unknown heretofore on the continent, and the organisation of conferences whose repercussions can be judged by the interest which they have aroused in the press and among the governments concerned.

The most important periodical produced by the Negro intelligentsia

* T. O. Elias later became federal minister of Justice in his own country, Nigeria.

is undoubtedly *Présence Africaine*, launched by Alioune Diop of Senegal in Paris in 1947. It had reached its sixty-second issue by July 1963, and several of its special numbers have run to more than 400 pages. *Tam-Tam*, the organ of French-speaking catholic African students, is also published in Paris and has been in existence for several years. A group of Nigerian intellectuals produces *Black Orpheus* in Ibadan; this magazine was originally launched by two European specialists on Africa, Ulli Beier and Janheinz Jahn. The importance of *Présence Africaine* is shown by the quality of the European contributions it has attracted. These have included such well-known African specialists as Monod, Richard-Mollard, Balandier, Griaule and Herskovits; but, more significant still, André Gide, Emmanuel Mounier, Jean-Paul Sartre, Michel Leiris and Albert Camus welcomed its appearance with enthusiasm and agreed to become its patrons.

To appreciate the progress which has been made, one has only to recall the ephemeral existence of Negro intellectual periodicals produced in Paris between the two wars. *Légitime défense*, brought out by three young West Indians, Jules Monnerot, Etienne Lero and René Ménil in 1932, lasted only for one issue. In 1934, Césaire, Senghor, Damas and some others launched *L'Étudiant noir*, which brought Africans and West Indians together on its editorial board for the first time. However *L'Étudiant noir* did not last long either. *La Revue du monde noir*, which counted among its contributors the Haitian Price-Mars, the American Claud MacKay and the West Indian René Maran, survived for only six numbers. And the communist-inspired *Cri des nègres* was banned. (Number XLIII of *Présence Africaine* was seized in October 1962, the government ruling that some articles on Guiana and the West Indies were prejudicial to national security. It was the first time that this review had been seized.)

Présence Africaine soon became a publishing house also. Alioune Diop and his colleagues have published the works of many African writers (and some Europeans too), originally as special numbers of the review, later in various collections. This secondary role has been no less effective than the original one: Negro intellectuals, previously often reduced to publishing their works 'at the author's expense', have now found a publisher who specialises in making their works known.

The first conference of African intelligentsia was held at the Sorbonne in Paris in 1956, under the auspices of *Présence Africaine*. This first Congress of Negro Writers and Artists was followed by a second gathering in Rome in 1959. The Afro-Asian writers have also met several times: in New Delhi in 1956, in Tashkent in 1958 and in Cairo in 1962. More recently another conference was held at Kampala in Uganda for African writers of English tongue. As another example of international interest in the African cultural renaissance, we may cite the Society of African Culture which, founded by members of the *Présence Africaine* group, is now included by UNESCO among the organisations with consultative status.

Alioune Diop follows his predecessors of the inter-war years in his resolute commitment to the cultural and political struggle for African emancipation. The conferences of Paris and Rome were no less anti-colonialist. The Paris Congress was advertised with a poster designed by Picasso and had all the trappings of a major event. In an editorial taking stock of the occasion, *Présence Africaine* claimed: 'The congress has elucidated basic truths which can be briefly summarised as follows: 1. No nation without a culture; 2. No culture without a past; 3. No authentic cultural liberation without political liberation first.'[2] The general resolution adopted at the close of the Rome Congress was equally explicit; it proclaimed among other things that 'political independence and economic freedom are the indispensable prerequisites of fecund cultural development in underdeveloped countries in general and in the countries of black Africa in particular'.[3]

Times were changing: in 1956 it was a French university which offered its hospitality to the African intellectuals; in 1959, in Rome, this solicitude was shown by the highest authorities of church and state. There, before the opening of the sessions, the president of the Society of African Culture, Dr Price-Mars, Haitian ambassador to Paris, was received by the president of the Italian republic and by Pope John XXIII. In the meanwhile, Ghana and Guinea had attained independence. The conferences at Tashkent and Cairo were even more deeply affected than those of Paris and Rome by the political pre-occupations of their promoters. Sharaf Rashidov, president of the Supreme Soviet of Uzbekistan, welcoming the delegates in his inaugural speech to the conference at Tashkent, declared that the conference 'was directly inspired by the principles elaborated at Bandung'.[4] At Cairo, the general theme of the discussions was 'the study of ways of reinforcing the Afro-Asian personality and resurrecting national cultures' (according to a statement of the Tunisian delegate, Mohamed Mzali, on his return home).[5] However, debates of a political nature figured prominently; thus, the delegation from Uganda walked out of the conference in protest against 'the third commission's refusal to include in the resolution on imperialism a mention of communist imperialism by the USSR and China'.[6] Furthermore, a sharp controversy developed between the Chinese and Russian delegations over a resolution on disarmament.[7]

These brief comments on the conferences of the intelligentsia of Africa and the Third World suffice to show how deeply the cultural renaissance in these countries has become involved in the political struggle, and how at times political interests have tended to push cultural ones into the background. However, although black Africa has proved no exception to the rule that a nation aspiring to freedom will seek to reaffirm its original contribution in the domain of arts and letters, it is none the less true that in Africa this trend has taken on a very unusual appearance.

Africa's intellectual elite is a limited minority since the great majority of the population is still illiterate. This elite, moreover, has been educated almost exclusively in the languages of the colonial powers, and it is in these languages, almost without exception, that it has found expression. Finally, since its works are produced in French, English and Portuguese, this intelligentsia is writing for only a limited public: the narrow stratum of the population which is literate. In fact, the African elite is addressing its works as much to a European readership—and particularly to those of liberal opinion—as to its fellow countrymen. In this way the cultural renaissance in black Africa at the moment of independence is a very special phenomenon. It is quite different from comparable movements in countries that sought to shake off the yoke of the Austro-Hungarian empire, and even to those in Arab and Asian countries since these could draw on extensive past civilisations to furnish the raw material of cultural revival.

Surprising as it may seem, there is—as far as I know—no comprehensive work on this African cultural renaissance which has been one of the most original features of the emancipation of the black continent. Admittedly, the proceedings of the Congresses of Negro Writers and Artists (and particularly those of the second Congress when the roles of historians, ethnologists, lawyers, theologians and others were systematically analysed), give some idea of the thinking of Negro intellectuals on these various topics. But these proceedings do not constitute a synthesis of African writing; they are rather a succession of speeches by different personalities on the problems facing the African elite in their various fields.

This does not mean that the importance of the problem has been overlooked by students of African literature and politics. For the latter, the African cultural renaissance is clearly one aspect of the political revolution, while the former acknowledge that the political significance of this literature is certainly one of its most characteristic features. But both groups have usually limited themselves, in the study of this cultural renaissance, to its purely literary manifestations, and have scarcely considered the works of African lawyers, theologians, economists and ethnologists.

Several specialists in African political studies have pointed out the importance of the intellectuals and their works in the African revolution. As early as 1956, Thomas Hodgkin devoted a chapter to this in his *Nationalism in Colonial Africa*. Philippe Decraene in his book *Le Panafricanisme* also allots several pages to *Présence Africaine* and to the concept of 'negritude', the literary expression of 'panafricanism'. Among those who have studied African literature, Jean-Paul Sartre in his "Orphée Noir"—written as a preface to Léopold Sédar Senghor's *Anthologie de la nouvelle poésie nègre et malgache*—stresses the political preoccupations of the poets of black Africa. And Léon G. Damas, the black poet from Guiana, points out in his *Poètes d'expression française* the political significance of the break between the black surrealist poets of the present generation and the Parnassian traditions of their elders. The German scholar, Janheinz Jahn, on the other hand, in his book *Muntu*, has sought in modern African literature only the authentic Negro 'vein'—that is the resurgence of ancestral beliefs, which he takes to be the touchstone of all 'negritude'. He makes a long incursion into the domain of African metaphysics, but barely alludes to the political implications of the African cultural revival. On the other hand, Lilyan Kesteloot in her thesis on *Les Écrivains noirs de langue française*, puts great stress on the political aspect of the works of black writers. In her opinion, these writers 'have produced original works only when they have become politically committed'.[8] She points out that the black intelligentsia, and particularly the *Légitime défense* and the *Revue du monde noir* groups, feel undeniably the attraction of communism.

Even so, none of the above writers (Sartre, Damas, Jahn and Kesteloot) goes on to place the literary movement known as 'negritude' in the wider context of a cultural revival which includes anthropology, law, theology, history and folklore. This does not mean that they are unaware of it: merely that they make only brief references to it. They have deliberately limited themselves to the study of African literature; their concern is not with the far wider subject of that intellectual aspiration which has impregnated not only poetry and the novel in Africa but also African research in all the different human sciences. In this respect, the reticence of Jahn and Kesteloot towards such revealing works of contemporary African thought as those of the anthropologist Jomo Kenyatta or the historian Sheikh Anta Diop is surprising, even for studies of purely literary criticism. Yet African historians and ethnologists were invited to the first Congress of Negro Writers and Artists; and, by the time of the second Congress, the organisers were so convinced that 'negritude' was not just a purely literary movement that space was systematically given to their contributions beside those of the writers. The report of the papers given and of the resolutions adopted reflects their preoccupation in an almost arithmetic way; for every resolution on literature or on the arts there are seven more on as many different fields of study: on politics, linguistics, philosophy, sociology, theology, science technology and medicine.

The only overall enquiry into the reactions of cultivated Africans to colonisation is that of Peter Sulzer in *Schwarze Intelligenz*. In this, he not only analyses works of literature, but collects together passages from African writers on economics, politics and religion. He completes these extracts with accounts of conversations with educated Africans on these subjects. Unfortunately, his enquiry is restricted to South Africa alone.

Anthologies are now appearing on all sides. (By 1963 there were a good dozen, in addition to those of Damas and Senghor.)[9] Until very recently these have been of a purely literary nature, but by now the idea that it was a mistake to separate literature, economics and politics has finally prevailed, albeit circumspectly. A speech of Kwame Nkrumah's is mentioned, together with a passage from Kenyatta's writing, in Peggy Rutherfoord's *Darkness and Light*. The American Negro poet, Langston Hughes, includes texts of Kwame Nkrumah and Tom Mboya in *An African Treasury*, and in the French version of this anthology, produced by Christiane Reygnault, he adds extracts from the works of Sékou Touré, Mamadou Dia and Kenyatta.[10] This was also the concept of the Abbé Grégoire, a century-and-a-half ago, in *De la littérature des nègres*, in which he gave an account of the 'life and work of Negroes who had distinguished themselves in sciences, arts or literature'. It is no longer necessary, as it was in the days of the Abbé Grégoire, to give such a list of famous Negroes in order to prove the existence of 'their intellectual faculties, moral qualities and literature'.

However, for anyone wishing to understand more fully the process of emancipation of the African colonies it is useful—if not indispensable—to study the recent literature of the black continent, not in isolation, but in the more general context of the whole African cultural revival. I have tried to help fill this gap in our knowledge. This seems to me all the more important since African writers and research workers are linked by so many communal preoccupations and characteristics.

The first characteristic common to both is their political 'commitment', which holds true for nearly all of them. Side by side with a politically committed literature, there is in present-day Africa a committed history, a committed ethnology and a committed theology. The black historian aims to denounce the barbarity of the colonial conquest and to rehabilitate the African chiefs who opposed it; the ethnologist wishes to refute the prejudices which rate the African as a primitive savage; the theologian seeks to discover in the African tribal beliefs a more refined metaphysics, more closely akin to christianity, than that which the early missionaries thought they had found. Even the study of linguistics has become a field of battle for African intellectuals. Thus Sheikh Anta Diop has fiercely attacked the generally accepted theory that African languages are 'class languages' in which the nouns are divided into different categories according to the article which precedes them. He sees in these theses one of the manifestations of Lévy-Bruhl's theory on the prelogical mentality of primitive peoples: a theory which the African elite rejects vigorously. Sheikh Anta Diop writes:

> It has been thought that these articles corresponded to mysterious categories into which the prelogical mentality of the Negro *sui generis* divided beings and things. A great effort has therefore been made to distinguish categories of inanimate objects, intelligent beings, females, abstract ideas, etc. To say that these categories have been devised by a mentality which is impenetrable to the western mind is just a way of blocking further research with formulae which are even more impenetrable to the mind of man.[11]

This is not, however, a one-way commitment, a straightforward fight against colonialism and for the rehabilitation of Negro values; there are novelists in French-speaking Africa who have extolled the benefits of colonisation. Bakari Diallo from Senegal, in his novel

Force et Bonté, praised the two 'cardinal virtues' of France. There are also novelists and ethnologists—frequently christians—such as David Ananou, Quenum and Amon d'Aby, who have passed severe judgement on some of the fetishist practices. Some historical and geographical works, such as those of Akindélé and Aguessy on Dahomey, fall outside the colonial controversy. There is also a considerable literature in the vernacular from South Africa—pejoratively called by Janheinz Jahn *Zoeglingsliteratur* ('schoolboy writings')—which reflects the teachings of missionaries and colonial officials. Finally, there are African poets such as Birago Diop who have rejected the temptations of political claims. Moreover Maître Lamine Gueye, the veteran of African politics in French-speaking countries, has, in his time, been an ardent supporter of the *loi-cadre*. In short, there exists in Africa, beside a 'committed' literature, a 'pro-colonial' literature, a conformist literature and a neutral literature.*

Black Narcissus

There is another factor in this question, seen from the angle under consideration, which further stresses the artificiality of endeavouring to separate novelists and poets on the one hand from specialists in the social sciences on the other. This is the fact that virtually all Negro intellectuals, politically committed or not, christian or communist, have concentrated on one subject alone: Africa. This solicitude for the African homeland has gone so far that practically no African writers have tackled any other theme. One of the rare exceptions is R. E. G. Armattoe, an English-speaking writer from Togo, who has produced some twenty books, of which some (such as *The Swiss Contribution to Western Civilization*) are completely divorced from the African theme. But Armattoe is also, and I should say primarily, noted for his *Deep Down the Blackman's Mind*.[12]

The hero of the African novel is nearly always black, and if by chance he is white, as in *Le Regard du roi* by Camara Laye, the action at least is situated in Africa and the story deals with the contact with African mentality. The poet, for his part, sings of the African woman and the land of Africa, or denounces colonialism. There are as yet no

* While the black Angolan writers Mario de Andrade and Agostino Neto were taking an active part in a nationalist movement, their compatriot, the poet Oscar Ribas, was awarded in January 1963 the Order of Dom Henri by the Portuguese minister for Overseas Territories.

African sociologists who have analysed the structure of European society, no African ethnologists who so far have studied the primitive tribes of Central America or of Australasia. The same applies to the lawyers. Lamine Gueye has concentrated on the legal status of his fellow countrymen, Santos on the right to opt for French citizenship, Doudou Thiam on the extent of this citizenship in French overseas territories, Nikili Abessolo on dowry in the Cameroon, T. O. Elias and J. B. Danquah on the customary institutions of Nigeria. It is the same with the economists and, very noticeably, with the political theorists. The reasons for this 'narcissism' are probably mainly to be found in the urgent need felt by all these intellectuals to concentrate on the problems of their own countries, rather than in a desire to speak only of things that they know well.

This interpenetration of literature and the social sciences is also shown, almost physically (if one can use the term), by the frequent attempts of a number of authors to try their hands in several different fields. The ethnologists Amon d'Aby and Danquah have written plays, Quenum has produced folk talks and Hazoumé an historical novel. Sheikh Anta Diop classes himself an historian and linguist; Senghor is both a poet and a theorist of African socialism. But, above all—and this was only to be expected in a continent where the intellectual elite is still no more than a minute section of the population—many of the writers and research workers are also politicians. Among the ethnologists, Jomo Kenyatta is the first prime minister of Kenya; K. A. Busia and J. B. Danquah were leaders of the opposition to Nkrumah in Ghana;* Quenum was formerly a senator of the French Union; Hazoumé was formerly counsellor of the French Union; Boubou Hama is president of the National Assembly of Niger; Mbonu Ojike was once a minister in the Eastern Region of Nigeria; Mabika Kalanda was formerly foreign minister of the Congo-Leopoldville. The economists have produced Mamadou Dia, a former prime minister of Senegal, and Abdoulaye Ly, founder of the Senegalese Parti du Régroupement Africain and former minister. Among the prose writers and playwrights, Bernard Dadié is minister of Information of the Ivory Coast; Sheikh Hamidou Kane was former minister of the Plan for Technical Assistance in Senegal; and Seydou Badian Couyaté is minister of Rural Economy and the Plan in Mali. Nazi Boni of the Volta Republic, and Fily Dabo Sissoko, of the

* Busia went into exile until the fall of Nkrumah in early 1966; Danquah died in prison in Ghana.

Soudan,* are former French deputies, while the Congolese Jean Malonga was formerly a senator of the Section Française de l'Internationale Ouvrière (SFIO). Among the poets, Senghor is president of Senegal; Mario de Andrade and Agostino Neto are nationalist leaders in Angola; Keita Fodeba is minister of the Interior in Guinea; and Antoine Roger Bolamba was minister of Information and Tourism in Congo-Leopoldville.

Although this is no new phenomenon—one has only to recall Lamartine, Disraeli and, nearer our time, Mao Tse-tung—it has rarely been so prevalent. In black Africa close ties link writers, researchers and politicians. This is the strange destiny of the intelligentsia which we are proposing to study here. The kernel of the problem is unquestionably to be found in the reasons which drove this elite—which came, after all, from the social class closest to the colonists, both in culture and standard of living—to play (with few exceptions) a leading part in the movements for national independence. Most of this activity took place at a time when any hope of independence for Africa seemed still very distant.

The freeing of erstwhile colonies has been one of the most striking features of the history of the twentieth century. Its rapidity is an example of the 'speeding-up' of historical processes which seems to have considerable affinity with certain aspects of present-day life. For this reason alone the present survey seemed imperative. It should also serve to elucidate the reactions to be expected from the far greater number of African intellectuals in the next generation. Though free from the complexes of those who have lived under colonial rule, they will in all probability have been brought up on the literature of their elders.

I should point out that, though this book gives priority to the study of the intelligentsia of former French colonies, it deals also with the English-speaking and Portuguese-speaking African intelligentsia. This is a necessary recognition of 'panafrican spirit' which characterises the spirit of very many in the indigenous elite of the continent, despite the effects of the political and linguistic barriers following the European partition of Africa. Not that these effects should be lightly dismissed: Jomo Kenyatta's ethnological study, *Facing Mount Kenya*, first published in 1938, was not translated into French until 1960, yet there is not one African specialist who does not regard this book as being of primary importance. It would also be a serious mistake to isolate the history of

* To differentiate clearly between eastern (Nilotic) Sudan and the western (formerly French-governed) Sudan, the spelling 'Soudan' is used throughout for the latter.

African literature today from the powerful stimulus and vital contribution it received from the Negro elite of the West Indies. Aimé Césaire, one of the originators of the concept of 'negritude', was born in Martinique; George Padmore, the theorist of 'panafricanism', came from Trinidad. American Negro writers living in Paris during the 1930s—such as Claud MacKay, Langston Hughes and Countee Cullen, to name but three—also exerted a profound influence on the 'negritude' movement, as has been pointed out by Lilyan Kesteloot. And in the anthologies of Negro poetry from Latin America—the poetry, for example, of Emilio Ballagas and Ildefonso Pereda Valdes—or in Roger Bastide's studies of Brazilian Negro writers, one detects immediately the themes which have inspired the writers of black Africa. Finally, it must be noted that European intellectuals have also played a far from negligible role in the awakening of Africa; it would be unjust to forget this.

I should add that this study is limited in time, covering essentially the period from the beginning of the second world war to around 1963. However, this does not exclude occasional forays into the works of the pioneers of the African intelligentsia such as Ignatius Sancho, a slave taken into the patronage of Lord Montagu in England, or Elaudah Equiano, known as Gustavus Vassa, who presented a petition on the abolition of slavery to the English parliament. Both were eighteenth-century writers whose works appear in the invaluable anthology of the Abbé Grégoire. This anthology served as the basis for another, compiled fifty years later, by Wilson Armistead, also a fervent abolitionist. These two works make it possible to trace the earliest African intellectuals writing in European languages—though they did not restrict themselves to living languages: for example, the works of Amo, a lawyer educated in Germany, and of Capitein, a theologian who had studied in Holland, appeared in Latin. As far as I know, there are no comparable anthologies for the nineteenth century, and yet even here there are interesting discoveries to be made. There was James Africanus B. Horton, for instance, a doctor of medicine from Edinburgh University and corresponding member of the Paris Institut d'Afrique, who served as an army doctor during the first British expeditions to the Gold Coast; and there was Léopold Panet, who wrote 'native of Senegal' after his name when he signed the account of his secret mission across the Sahara on behalf of the French government in 1849. Perusal of these older texts sheds a sometimes unexpected light on the works of our own generation.

PART ONE

RETURN TO ORIGINS

Y a bailar venimo
de Tumbuctu y Santo Tome

LOPE DE VEGA *Canto de los Negros*

And we came to dance
from Timbuktu and São Tomé

I

LINGUA FRANCA

Sentez-vous cette souffrance
Et ce désespoir à nul autre égal
d'apprivoiser, avec les mots de France,
Ce coeur qui m'est venu du Sénégal?[1]

(Do you not feel my suffering and despair, which is beyond compare, to be forced to express in French this heart which comes from Senegal?)

ALTHOUGH they were written by an Haitian poet, these lines illustrate fairly clearly the basic dilemma of African intellectuals: the necessity of expressing themselves more often than not in a foreign language. Rabemananjara, the Malagasy poet, voiced the same dismay at the second Congress of Negro Writers and Artists: 'Truly our conference is one of language thieves. This crime, at least, we have committed ourselves. We have stolen from our masters this treasure of identity, the vehicle of their thought, the golden key to their soul, the magic *Sesame* which opens wide the door of their secrets, the forbidden cave where they have hidden the loot taken from our fathers and for which we must demand a reckoning.'[2] F. D. Sakiliba also emphasises, in his article "Présent et futur des langues africaines",[3] the 'paradox of nationalism expressed in English and French'.

These are just a few examples; the problem of a national language has proved one of the most intransigent for African intellectuals. Of course, it is not only black Africa that has been faced with this problem. Gandhi's reply to Macaulay's advocacy of education in English is well-known:

> Is it not a painful thing that, if I want to go to a court of justice, I must employ the English language as a medium, that when I become a barrister, I may not speak my mother-tongue and that someone else should have to translate to me in my own language? Is not this absolutely absurd? Is it not a sign of slavery? Am I to blame the

> English for it or myself? It is we, the English-knowing Indians, that have enslaved India. The curse of the nation will rest not upon the English but upon us.[4]

During one of the first sessions of the Algerian Constituent Assembly in November 1962, Ferhat Abbas, then president, exclaimed: 'I have known colonists' sons at school who could speak Arabic better than I. It is a fact that I, your president, am unable to express myself in Arabic as well as I should wish.'[5] This problem of a written national language has been of great concern, often leading to impassioned debate, particularly among intellectuals of the former French Africa. In fact, there is virtually no African literature in the vernacular in former French West and Equatorial Africa.

It is a different matter in the English-speaking African countries, and particularly in South Africa where works in Xhosa, Sesotho and other languages have been produced by writers and journalists such as Mopeli-Paulus, Mqhayi, Mangoela and Sekese. One of the greatest black South African novelists, Thomas Mofolo, author of the well-known *Shaka*, wrote in Sesotho. This flowering of vernacular literature in South Africa goes back several decades, however, and is now slowing down. At least this is what Peter Sulzer suggests in his *Schwarze Intelligenz*, where he remarks that the golden age of South African Bantu literature 'was followed by a low period after the 1920s'. Jahn adds the commentary that this setback coincided with the accession to power of the Boer Nationalist Party in 1924. All the same, South African vernacular literature is not dead today, and one of the best contemporary African novelists in the Republic of South Africa is A. C. Jordan, who writes in Xhosa.

However, even taking South Africa's contribution into account, African literature in the vernacular falls far short of the literary output in French and English. Much the same is true of African journalism. One of the first newspapers to appear on the continent under African direction was in Bantu: *Imvo Zabantsundu* ('Native Opinion'), published by Tengo Jabavu.[6] But most of the early newspapers in British Africa were in English. *The African and Sierre Leone Weekly Advertiser* was the earliest: its first number appeared in 1855. Despite being edited mainly by Africans, it was written in English and used numerous extracts from the British press, notably *The Morning Post* and *The Observer*. Its motto was 'Ethiopia shall soon stretch out her hands unto God' (here 'Ethiopia' signified the whole of the black continent). It appeared regularly for some fifty years. Sierra Leone played an important role in inaugurating an African press; the first university in black Africa had been founded at Fourah Bay, near Freetown, in 1827 by the Church Missionary Society, and this facilitated the formation of an African elite. Immigrants from the British West Indies also contributed to the development of journalism in Sierra Leone; these included F. A. Belgrave, founder of the *African Interpreter and Advocate*, and the lawyer W. Rainy, founder of the *West African Liberator*. These two papers appeared regularly during the 1860s and 1870s.

The first newspapers in the Gold Coast appeared almost as early as those of Sierra Leone. The *Accra Herald*, later called the *West African Herald*, was founded in 1857. The proprietor was Charles Bannerman, son of the famous James Bannerman, a half-caste of Scottish father and African mother, who was lieutenant-governor of the Gold Coast shortly after 1850. The freedom of expression enjoyed by the *West African Herald* is surprising for the period. For instance, in 1861 the paper came to the support of the proprietor's brother, Edmund Bannerman, who had been sentenced to seven years' imprisonment for embezzling public funds while working in the British colonial magistrature. The paper accused the colonial administration of racial discrimination in these words: 'Had he been a white man, we are certain that the governor would never have sanctioned these most extraordinary proceedings. There is no need to multiply the proofs as to the treatment here adopted towards coloured men and white men.' But it was only towards 1880 that the African press in the Gold Coast acquired genuine importance. Two politicians, who were also writers, were among the first generation of African journalists: Attoh Ahuma and J. E. Casely-Hayford. Attoh Ahuma, a founder of the Aborigines Rights Protection Society, one of the first nationalist organisations in the colony, was editor-in-chief of the society's organ, the *Gold Coast Aborigines*, started in 1898. J. E. Casely-Hayford, who was also one of the organisers of ARPS and later of the movement for the unification of British West Africa, was editor-in-chief of the *Gold Coast Echo* and afterwards of the *Gold Coast Leader*. David Kimble's remarkable work, *A Political History of Ghana, 1850–1928*, gives a great deal of interesting information on the Gold Coast press during that period.

Why should we find this almost exclusive use of European languages, both in literature and journalism? There were often imperative reasons.

The first is that a written language came to Africa only with the arrival of the Europeans. There were only two attempts to invent a written language for the dialects of black Africa: that of the Vai tribe in Liberia, an attempt which seems to date from the early nineteenth century, and the later effort of the Bamoun sultan, Njoya, begun at the time of the German colonisation of the Cameroon. Neither achieved practical range; both the Vai alphabet and the Bamoun alphabet were little used and rapidly became literally dead letters. Both these African attempts stemmed from contact with the European world.[7]

It seems that the Arabic alphabet applied to African languages has not produced the desired results. Sakiliba has pointed out:

> Kanuri, Hausa, Songhai, Bamana, Wolof and Fulani adopted the Arabic alphabet in a more or less long-lived and more or less superficial fashion. Unfortunately, the written versions of these rich and vital languages fell short of the exciting results which might have been expected. In the first place the low standard of education of the African scribes who adapted the Arabic letters to the local sounds meant that the adaptations were only relatively successful. Admittedly, the Fulani of the Fouta-Djalon were capable of completing the defective vowel structure of the imported Arabic and transscribing with the letter *b* the *pé* sound which existed only in their language. More serious was the fact that the few texts transcribed were exclusively religious and were of absolutely no use in revitalising African oral and folklore traditions.[8]

Lavergne de Tressan is of a similar opinion:

> The so-called scholars who used the Arabic characters were automatically muslims and the subjects dealt with were generally islamic religious texts in verse. The results are deplorable: bad transcription, a lexicology limited to abstractions with wholesale borrowing from Arabic, disfigured, shortened and inverted syntax, alien to the spoken tongue which, for all that it was not usually a written language, was nevertheless the normal mode of expression of the people. The comparison between the heavy pathos of the Arabic-Fulani so-called mystical religious songs and the light, rhythmic prose of the Fulani shepherd songs is particularly significant.[9]

Georges Balandier is even more categorical:

> The erudite *karamoko* of the Fulani or the Malinkes is a confirmed muslim and often uses Arabic characters in an entirely personal way in his transcriptions. But this transcription of the Koran could never

come into common usage. It serves only to preserve the religious text or the chronicles relating great deeds of the past. There is no question here of Negro literature transcribed with the help of Arabic characters.[10]

But for Fily Dabo Sissoko, on the contrary: 'The scholars of the Fouta-Djalon . . . have accomplished the miracle of adapting Arabic to Fulani phonetics, thus giving their language the impulse needed to raise it to the level of a literary language capable of rendering every shade of thought.'[11]

Henri Gaden, a former colonial governor, has translated into French one of these Fulani texts transcribed in Arabic, a *quacida* (a Fulani poem of the Fouta-Toro) by Mohammadou Aliou Tyam, which tells the life of al-Hajj Umar. Gaden rates this 'the work of an historian' but adds that the document was 'unique to the Fouta-Toro, both for the number of its lines and its historical value' (Tyam's manuscript has 1,200 lines). Whatever merit Fily Dabo Sissoko may have found in this literature, one must confess that it enjoyed only a very limited success.

The second reason for the use of European languages is the incredible multiplicity of African dialects. Out of some 2,000 languages in the whole world, specialists have counted between 700 and 1,000 in Africa alone.[12] Clearly, under the circumstances, any work written in an African language can have only a very limited readership, despite the fact that there are some important linguistic groups in the continent. However, these groups—such as the Hausa and Fulani languages, or commercial languages such as Swahili, which is spoken throughout former British East Africa—are the exceptions to the rule.

The third reason stems from the educational policy of the colonial powers, and particularly France. In the French colonies, use of the vernacular was forbidden in the schools, and teaching was carried out exclusively in French. This application of the doctrine of assimilation to education was extremely strictly enforced, and only Koranic schools escaped the general rule. (Bernard Dadié, in his novel *Climbié*, gives his impressions as a schoolboy when this edict was passed and pupils were forbidden to speak their mother tongue in school, even to each other. The edict was used to pick out the pupils who were to sweep out and clean the school, allegedly as a punishment.) In British territories and in South Africa, the ruling was different and primary education for Negro children was frequently carried on in the vernacular, particularly in the mission schools. (This was also true of the Belgian

Congo.) Teaching was frequently started in an African language and then carried on later in the English language, particularly in British West Africa.

It was necessary to adapt the alphabet somewhat in order to render African languages in writing, since most of these languages are tonal. This difficulty has been met with varying degrees of skill, depending on the authors involved; additional phonetic symbols have also been introduced. Hazoumé has said on this subject: 'We are waiting impatiently for a genius in our race who will give us a form of writing suited to our tone languages.'[13] Sakiliba maintains: 'The Latin alphabet is certainly best suited to enable the African languages to fulfil the role that awaits them in the evolution of 150 million Africans. When adapted to the needs of the borrowing dialects by the addition of diacritical marks, it can render faithfully the astonishing range of African vocal tonality.'[14] These efforts to extend teaching in the vernacular were greatly helped by the protestant missions and by the Bible Society, which, in 1950, had already published the Old and New Testaments in a hundred different African languages.[15] It would be no exaggeration to claim that the spread of literature and journalism in the vernacular is due largely to the protestant influence. This has been felt, of course, chiefly in the Anglo-Saxon colonies and in South Africa.

We should also note the considerable role played in this field by catholic missions—in British colonial territories no less than in French ones—which set up printing presses that have enabled a vernacular press to develop: for instance, in Togo, where the oldest newspaper is the weekly *Mia Holo*, published in Ewe and founded some forty years ago. In English-speaking Africa, the catholic influence was particularly lively in Uganda, despite the hostile efforts of King Mwanga who, in 1886, executed the young converts who were canonised recently by the Vatican. The first catholic newspaper in a native tongue was the monthly *Munno*, founded in 1911; today the existence of the Uganda Catholic Press Association is witness to the vitality of catholic journalism there. In South Africa, where admittedly the protestant influence is stronger, *Um Afrika*, the first catholic newspaper in Zulu, was published in 1888, a few years after the protestant paper *Imvo Zabantsundu*.

Teaching both in the language of the colonist and in the indigenous tongue has come under criticism from African intellectuals. 'Who can describe the swindle practised on young Africans who have a foreign language foisted on them as their mother tongue?' exclaims Albert

Tévoedjré, on the subject of education in French overseas territories.[16] Maghemout Diop, on the other hand, recalls that 'in the Belgian Congo each ethnic group was meticulously educated in its own language, which resulted in the continued isolation of these different groups and perhaps even served to widen the gap which separated them'.[17] Parmenas Githendu Mockerie (one of Kenyatta's companions in the independence movement) used the pretext of a journey in Italian Somaliland to bring up the problem: 'In every Italian port we visited, I found African porters speaking Italian. In British East Africa it is unlikely that you would find porters speaking English. Even if they had been lucky enough to go to school at all they would only have been taught in their native tongue.'[18]

Whatever the weaknesses—or merits—of teaching in the vernacular, this applied in any case only to primary education in British, South African and Belgian territories. Secondary education was given almost exclusively in the European languages, and it is now true to say, for the whole of Africa, that a real intellectual grounding can be acquired only through the medium of the colonial languages. Thus, French or English or Portuguese has become not only the language of all educated Africans in given areas but also the only means of communication between the different tribes. The role of these European languages is analogous to Latin in the Middle Ages: the role of *lingua franca*.

Léon G. Damas has pointed out this aspect of the problem for the French language, at the level of the French Union: 'French seemed an admirable vehicle for Negro expression, allowing for communication between all Negroes, Africans, West Indians and Malagasies, who all have different languages, complicated still further by an abundance of dialects and characterised by an almost total absence of written literature.'[19] The primary importance of the European language is also affirmed in British Africa, in spite of the system of mixed education (first in the vernacular, then in English) used in primary schools. F. D. Sakiliba reports that one of the most conclusive experiments in this field was carried out by the Nigerian political leader Nnamdi Azikiwe (later president of Nigeria) in 1937, when he founded a chain of newspapers in both English and the vernacular. 'Zik' soon discovered that a press in the vernacular was useless for one very simple reason: 'with the educational system of the day, people capable of reading and writing their own language would read and write primarily, and often far better, in English'.[20]

National poetry

Although African intellectuals admit the need to use a foreign language, this does not seem to them a definitive solution to the cultural and political aspects of their problem: the search for an authentic means of national expression. The intellectuals have put this question in much the same form as that evoked in Léon Laleau's poem: is it possible to create an authentic Negro literature and, more difficult still, a Negro poetry in a foreign language? This subject was discussed in a series of articles by Negro intellectuals in a 'debate on the conditions for national poetry' carried out in the columns of *Présence Africaine*.[21] It has also attracted the attention of Jahn and Sartre.

David Diop gives a negative, albeit somewhat qualified, reply to this question. In his opinion, the African writer 'knows that by writing in a language which is not that of his brothers he cannot genuinely translate the voice of his country. But, by contributing with his writing to the ending of the colonial regime, the French-speaking, creative Negro writer is assisting the revival of our national cultures.'[22] For others the surrealism of Negro poetry enables the poet to appropriate the French language (it was André Breton, the surrealist leader, who discovered Césaire and recognised him as one of his greatest disciples). In the words of Léon Damas, from a speech at Brazzaville in 1954: 'The miracle which results in the fusion of our intimate poetry with a language—of completely different origin—in which it is expressed reaches its most astonishing consummation in surrealism. It is here that the Negro poet finds the right to break with tiresome syntax and can hurl the words of France into a delirious torrent which belongs to the African race alone.'

For Janheinz Jahn, the language which the black poet uses is unimportant. It is the way in which he uses it which is either specifically Negro or not. He writes: 'It is just because the new African poet does not use European words as concepts, and because he disregards the meaning and imagery they have acquired in European languages, that African poetry written in these languages has such extraordinary freshness.'[23] For Jean-Paul Sartre, the use of the colonialists' language is a form of struggle. 'To the guile of the colonisers', claims Sartre in "Orphée Noir", 'the black poets reply with a similar but inverse guile. Since the oppressor is present even in the language that they speak, they will use that language to destroy him. The [surrealist] European poet of today tries, by dehumanising words, to return them to nature.

The black herald, however, will strip from them their Frenchness, will shatter them, will destroy their traditional associations and will juxtapose them with violence.'

Over and above the question of whether an authentic Negro poetry can exist in a foreign language, there remains the problem of language as a determining factor of human existence, on which the unity of a nation often depends, and this has worried African intellectuals very much.

'If Africa were freed by compulsion, no [African] writer would even consider expressing his feelings and those of his people in anything other than his own, rediscovered, language', affirms David Diop in *Présence Africaine*. It is interesting in this respect to note the movement which started some time ago in Haiti for the use of Creole as a literary language. This patois, derived from French, is the spoken language of the ordinary people, whereas French has remained that of the middle classes and the administration. It is a question of replacing 'a borrowed, official language, French', by 'our true mother tongue which we babble at our mother's knee, the language of our whole country', says Ernest Doyon, one of the protagonists of the movement, in the preface to a book on the *Philologie du Créole*. According to Morisseau-Leroy, another partisan of Creole, 'writers in Haiti have always felt the urge to speak to their people in Creole',[24] and in fact an Haitian literature in Creole does exist, of which the best-known writer is Oswald Durand whose poem *Choucoune* was published in 1884. There is, however, no unanimity among Haitian intellectuals. René Depestre, in particular, who started the open debate on Negro poetry in *Présence Africaine*, is a partisan of a new Haitian literature 'which would open the African shutters of Haiti'; but he wishes to maintain the supremacy of French, which is 'after all, an "haitianised" treasure'.[25] In the French West Indies, the movement in favour of Creole has not taken such a clear form as in Haiti. Gilbert Gratiant, a poet from Martinique who has written in Creole, thinks that the literature of his country should be bilingual: 'Naturally, French must not cease to progress. Every West Indian should learn to speak and write it better and better, but his loyalty to his other mother tongue, Creole, is not merely sentimental. This language is fused so firmly with West Indian life that it is true to say it illustrates better than any other the essence of our specifically West Indian civilisation.'[26]

In French black Africa, there is no equivalent to Creole. In their efforts to escape the servitude of the French language, African intellectuals have naturally turned to the vernacular languages. In English territories, and especially in Sierra Leone, a kind of bastard English mixed with Portuguese expressions and known as 'Pidgin' has developed. This is almost exclusively a spoken language and is used only by an uneducated social class in contact with Europeans. However, as far as I know, there is no real Pidgin literature.

All the same, several poets from the west coast have tried their hand at Pidgin. Among them is the Nigerian Dennis Osadebay in *Blackman Trouble:*

> Sometam I think about dis life
> And de trouble blackman see
> Poor blackman, he must face big strife,
> Or fall down on his knees,
> When he must get some little good,
> Or put for him belly scanty food. . . .[27]

Armattoe from Togo uses this language of the people to tell of Negro poverty in *The Negro's Coming: a Litany:*

> De black man ain't got nothin',
> Push him away.
> He ain't got a cent,
> Push him away.
> He ain't got brains,
> Push him away.
> He ain't got guts,
> Push him away. . . .[28]

The Pidgin of Osadebay and Armattoe is easy to decipher in comparison with older and more authentic examples, such as the following extract dating from 1824. This is a letter from the king of Bonny to George IV, in which he complains about an exploratory expedition by a British ship in the Niger delta:

> Brudder Georges . . . send warship look um what water bar ab got, dat good, me let um dat. Brudder send boat chopum slave, dat good. E no send warship, for cappen no peake me, no lookee me face. No, No, No; me tell you, No; Suppose you come all you mont full palaver, give e reason whye do it, me tell you, you peake lie, you peake lie, you peakeed-n lie. Suppose my fader, or my fader fader come up from ground and peake me why English man do dat, I no sabby um why.[29]

Despite all that has been said of Amos Tutuola's English, which is sometimes a little naïve, it is all the same very far from Pidgin.

There are other problems related to the use of African languages which have concerned black intellectuals. Some European linguists have pointed out the poverty of vocabulary of African languages, and concluded that they were not suitable to replace European languages, especially in the technical sphere. Although translation of the Bible into Yoruba and Xhosa poses no particular problems, since the life of African peasants is still very close to that of the shepherds of Judaea, translation of scientific works is quite a different matter.

African intellectuals have disputed the validity of this pretended 'poverty' of African languages. As early as 1853, the Abbé Boilat, a Senegalese half-caste and author of a Wolof grammar, had taken up their defence. In the preface of his *Esquisses Sénégalaises*, he thus concluded a long passage in which he examined and rejected popular prejudices about Negroes: 'How could a people devoid of education, grammarians, academy, even verbal conventions, have so much order, method, so many general rules in their languages? Many scholars have worked on this material and all have left many stones unturned. One thing is certain: these men are the descendants of Adam, created in God's image and saved by the blood of Jesus Christ.'[30]

Sheikh Anta Diop has studied this question at length in the second part of his *Nations nègres et culture*. After stressing the need to develop African national languages, especially for education ('education in the mother tongue would save years of delay in the acquisition of knowledge'), Sheikh Anta claims that there is no insurmountable obstacle to 'the introduction into African languages of expressions and concepts capable of rendering the scientific and philosophical ideas of the modern world'. He points out in particular that scientific terms based on Greek and Latin have roots whose meaning is often imprecise. Moreover, it is not necessary to have recourse to classical languages in order to create a word 'polygonal' for a figure with more than four sides; German has produced *vieleckig* from *viel* (many) and *eckig* (cornered). He devotes a whole chapter of his book to a French-Wolof scientific glossary in order to support his argument with concrete examples. He gives a translation into the Senegalese language of many scientific terms, ranging from elementary geometry to thermo-chemistry by way of thermo-dynamics and general chemistry. Finally, he has translated into Wolof several pages from a résumé of Paul Langevin's theory of relativity.

Egyptian humanities

Although this original 'defence and illustration of Wolof' (which Sheikh Anta Diop writes as 'Valaf') is concerned particularly with scientific vocabulary, it is also relevant to literature in the vernacular. 'A comparable development of [African] languages', writes Diop, 'is inseparable from a literature of translation of all kinds (poetry, songs, novels, plays, works of philosophy, mathematics, science, history, etc.). It is also inseparable from the creation of a modern African literature which will necessarily be educative, militant and essentially destined for the masses.'[31] Sheikh Anta Diop also devotes numerous pages to the relationship which, according to him, exists between Wolof and ancient Egyptian. He believes that the Pharaohs and their subjects were black, and that the Senegalese language is not the only African dialect with Egyptian roots. Hence he feels that ancient Egyptian is eminently suitable as the starting point for authentically African classical studies. 'The problem of Negro humanities', he writes, 'is thus solved; Africans from all over the continent now know that they can and should contribute to Negro studies in the humanities, based on ancient Egyptian. This basis is as legitimate for Africa as is the Graeco-Latin basis of humanities for the West.'[32]

Without quoting Diop, Senghor declared at the first Congress of Negro Writers and Artists: 'I believe that if the study of ancient Egyptian were today made obligatory in our schools and colleges, it would be as important for us as Greek and Latin, and maybe even more important.'[33] It is also Senghor who puts in the mouth of a prince of his country this implicit reproach to his western culture:

Enfants à tête courte, que vous ont chanté les koras?
Vous déclinez la rose, m'a-t-on dit, et vos ancêtres les Gaulois.
Vous êtes docteurs en Sorbonne, bedonnants de diplômes,
Vous amassez des feuilles de papier—si seulement des louis d'or
à compter sous la lampe, comme feu ton père aux doigts tenaces!
Vos filles, m'a-t-on dit, se peignent le visage comme des courtisanes
Elles se casquent pour l'union libre et éclaircir la race!
Etes-vous plus heureux? . . .

(Children of small head, what have the *koras* sung to you? You 'decline' the rose, I have been told, and your ancestors the Gauls.

Graduates of the Sorbonne, growing fat with degrees, you are amassing a heap of papers—if only they were golden coins to count under the lamplight as your late father did with his greedy fingers. Your daughters, I have been told, paint their faces like courtesans; they are all for free love and to whiten our race! Does this make you any happier?)[34]

This does not prevent Senghor's advocating the cross-breeding of cultures, as he himself explained at the first Congress of Negro Writers and Artists.[35] Although there is a tremendous thirst for a national language among many African intellectuals, they are far from wanting a break with western languages and culture. In the article already quoted, Sakiliba contends that 'everything recommends that, whatever the number of future states in Africa, French and English should be preserved as instruments of culture, diplomatic vehicles one might say, within an immense continent'. Tchidimbo says: 'We could not tolerate the solution of an Africa shut in on itself through teaching in the native languages. . . . We have every faith in the virtue of hybrid civilisations.'[36]

In his speech to the first Congress of Negro Writers and Artists, Paul Hazoumé expresses his concern that: 'Westerners seem today to regret having imposed the study of European languages. They are anxiously asking whether it would not be better to go back, as quickly as possible, on what they now take to have been an error on their part in the task which they had set themselves of educating the Africans, and to start teaching them from now on in their own languages.'[37] After underlining the difficulties in the use of African languages (multiplicity, transcription of sounds, etc.), the Dahomeyan ethnologist concluded: 'As an African, I cannot help wondering if the reasons used by westerners to justify the decision to teach Africans in their own language alone henceforward do not hide the real motives which they are ashamed to admit: motives of sordid personal interest, prestige, fear of competition which they dare not allow to grow in face of the rapid development of the African elite, brought up until now without distrust of the same humanism as themselves. Some partisans of education in the vernacular have even suggested, somewhat timidly, that their culture might produce social and even mental disturbances in Africans fed on it.'[38]

It can be seen that African intellectuals have attached great importance to this question of a national language. Now that all the French colonies have attained independence, it will be interesting to see how their policy evolves in this field. For the moment, at any rate, it does not look as though the position of French as the official language were in any danger, any more than that of English in African countries formerly under British rule. All efforts to unify related dialects attempted so far—admittedly under colonial rule—have failed. In the Gold Coast, in particular, the scheme to unite Fanti and Twi into one language, Akan, failed, according to Lord Hailey, because of national jealousies and the problems of transcription.[39] Israel's success with Hebrew has not led African intellectuals to forget the solution adopted by India, where English was kept as an official language after independence. At a seminar in Tunis in 1959 organised by the *Congrès pour la liberté de la culture*, graduates from several newly independent countries maintained that it would be impossible to use their national languages in the schools.[40]

The most pressing problem in Africa is to bridge the gap between English- and French-speaking Africans, and this has been recognised by the partisans of panafricanism. Following the recommendations of the first Africa Peoples' Conference at Accra in December 1958, Ghana and Guinea have taken the lead in introducing measures to intensify the teaching of French and English in their respective countries. Thus, the language of the colonists seems sure to keep its position as *lingua franca*, for the time being at any rate.

All the same, the search for a communal African language remains at the hub of the efforts of African intellectuals active in the cause of African unity. The linguistic resolution passed at the second Congress of Negro Writers and Artists puts this very clearly.[41] This resolution states first: 'The relationship between African languages is as strong and as clear as that between Indo-European languages. To give but one example, a relationship has been established between languages as far apart (geographically speaking) as Ronga from South Africa, Sara, Wolof, Diola, Fulani, Serer, Sarakole, [spoken in French West Africa] and ancient Egyptian.' Then it proposes:

(i) that free and federated black Africa should not adopt any European or other language as a national tongue;

(ii) that one African language should be chosen. This would not necessarily belong to a relative majority of peoples since the richness and character of a language are more important qualities linguistically. All Africans would learn this national language besides their own regional language and the European language of secondary education (English, French, etc.); the latter would be optional.

(iii) a team of linguists would be instructed to enrich this language, as rapidly as possible, with the terminology necessary for expression of modern philosophy, science and technology.

Finally, the same text suggests that the following languages, among others, would be suitable on account of their prevalence or cultural richness: Swahili, Hausa, Yoruba, Bambara, Mandingo, Fulani and Wolof.

In fact, Tanganyika adopted Swahili as an official language in 1963, and the Conference of African Heads of State at Addis Ababa in May 1963 allowed African languages as working languages of the new Organisation of African Unity alongside English and French, 'where possible'. The restriction implied in this 'where possible' meant, for the authors of the Charter of the OAU, that an African dialect, in order to qualify, must be a written language, and that the country wanting it to be used should supply qualified personnel for the task to the secretariat of the organisation.*

* This reference to the use of African languages within the organisation was added to the original text of the Charter (article 29) following a request by President Nasser that Arabic be allowed as well as French and English. The final version of the text of article 29 mentions African languages first, then the languages of the two former colonial powers, but makes no explicit reference to Arabic.

2

CUSTOMS AND TRADITIONS

'THE INHABITANTS of the black lands are bucolic people without reason, wit or skill and with no experience of anything at all; they live like brute beasts without law or order.' This picture of barbarous Africa, as painted by Leo Africanus in the sixteenth century, was one of the postulates of the civilising mission of colonisation for more than one European intellectual. It was supported by theories such as Gobineau's on the inequality of human races or that of Lévy-Bruhl on the prelogical mentality of primitive peoples. It was also to become the standard view of African society for the average European.

Inevitably, African intellectuals were cut to the quick by such a judgement, and this may help to explain why such a large number of them have become ethnologists. The nationalist wing of the African intelligentsia holds it a completely false view and a mere pretext for colonisation. Mbonu Ojike claims of the European: 'He assumes that the African has neither laws nor political organisations; that the society is therefore chaotic, living in a miasma of tribal disorder. . . . I wonder how much longer these fictions can blind the West.'[1] C. S. Tidiany sums up the problem as the need 'to justify colonial expansion, while imperialism went on to develop the theory of racial and cultural inferiority'.[2] Emmanuel C. Paul, teacher at the Institute of Ethnology at Port-au-Prince, Haiti, considers that ethnological studies in the nineteenth century, 'instead of redressing the mistaken views of the white nations on the black peoples and their culture, in fact provided a rational basis for colonialism by elaborating a veritable dogma of Negro inferiority'.[3] But a number of African ethnologists have rejected these extreme positions. Whereas some have exalted the virtues of African tribal organisation, there are others who have pointed out the degrading or harmful character of certain African rites. Half way between these extremes, the major preoccupation seems to be to explain (as a justification or otherwise) the African tribal institutions and customs.

*Kenya's fiery javelin**

The most interesting figure of African ethnology is still unquestionably Jomo Kenyatta. His political career was interrupted in 1953 when he was sentenced to seven years' imprisonment for his part (which he always formally denied) in the Mau Mau uprising. In 1961 he was freed and immediately took a leading place in the political life of Kenya. His book, *Facing Mount Kenya*, written in 1938, is devoted to the institutions of his own tribe, the Kikuyu (from whom practically all Mau Mau supporters were recruited). The passion with which he defends the coherence and logical bases of these institutions is striking.

Perhaps the most revealing passage in this respect is that dealing with clitoridectomy of girls. After recounting the indignant condemnation of this practice by British religious, governmental and medical authorities, Jomo Kenyatta simply writes:

> The real argument lies not in the defence of the surgical operation or its details, but in the understanding of a very important fact in the tribal psychology of the Gikuyu†—namely, that this operation is still regarded as the very essence of an institution which has enormous educational, social, moral and religious implications, quite apart from the operation itself. For the present it is impossible for a member of the tribe to imagine an initiation without clitoridectomy. Therefore the abolition of the surgical element in this custom means to the Gikuyu the abolition of the whole institution.
>
> The real anthropological study, therefore, is to show that clitoridectomy, like Jewish circumcision, is a mere bodily mutilation which, however, is regarded as the *conditio sine qua non* of the whole teaching of tribal law, religion and morality.[4]

Jomo Kenyatta does not attempt to pass over in silence the medical aspect of the controversy. He describes at length the methods used (special diet, cold bath, preparations of medicinal herbs, etc.) to prevent infection and dull the pain. He refutes energetically the accusation that clitoridectomy, on account of the scars it leaves, is the cause of difficult births and the numerous deaths of first-born. These cases are the exception, he claims, but for this reason have been treated in the

* Title given to Kenyatta: see Georges Balandier's preface to the French edition of *Facing Mount Kenya*.

† Kenyatta, in company with many linguists, prefers the form Gikuyu to Kikuyu as a more accurate rendering of the tribal name in the speech of the people.

hospitals of the colony, directed by Europeans, and have thus attracted attention. And, he adds, 'there are hundreds of first-born children among the Gikuyu and the writer is one of them'.[5]

Apart from the ethnographic study in *Facing Mount Kenya*, Kenyatta has a precise political objective in his book: he sets out to denounce what he considers the injustice of the distribution of the fertile land in the White Highlands to European colonists. This was the source of a contention which has dominated the history of his country ever since it was colonised. He states explicitly in his conclusion:

> When the European comes to the Gikuyu country and robs the people of their land, he is taking away not only their livelihood, but the material symbol that holds family and tribe together. In doing this he gives one blow which cuts away the foundations from the whole of Gikuyu life, social, moral and economic. When he explains, to his own satisfaction and after the most superficial glance at the issues involved, that he is doing this for the sake of the Africans, to 'civilise' them, 'teach them the disciplinary value of regular work' and 'give them the benefit of European progressive ideas', he is adding insult to injury, and need expect to convince no one but himself.[6]

Kenyatta's political career actually started on account of this dispute: he was chosen as the spokesman of his tribe to put their claims before the various British commissions of enquiry round about the 1930s.

Kenyatta's book is impregnated throughout with a nationalism which is never divorced from his attachment to the ancestral traditions of his tribe. The dedication of his work provides perhaps the best example of this: 'To Moigoi and Wamboi and all the dispossessed youth of Africa; for perpetuation of communion with ancestral spirits through the fight for African Freedom, and in the firm faith that the dead, the living, and the unborn will unite to rebuild the destroyed shrines.'

Christianity and democracy

African ethnologists have stressed two points in particular in their rehabilitation and explanation of their ancestral customs. The first is that African beliefs cannot be summed up as the worship of fetishes: on the contrary, African religions recognise the existence of God the creator. The second is that the political organisation of African tribes is just as democratic as European parliamentary institutions.

Emmanuel C. Paul points out that it was President de Brosses, the famous French jurist, who popularised the term 'fetishism' in his book *Du culte des dieux fétiches*, 1760. 'As a good christian', adds the Haitian ethnologist, 'this writer found gods everywhere among the "savages" and believed that revelation was the privilege of a few wise men. He contributed to the nineteenth-century view of Negro religions as crude polytheism, a combination of magic and sorcery.'[7]

In his *History of the Yorubas*, the Reverend Samuel Johnson notes that the name of the God of the Yorubas, *Olorun*, means 'lord of heaven'. 'They acknowledge him maker of heaven and earth, but too exalted to concern himself directly with men and their affairs; hence they admit the existence of many gods as intermediaries, and these they term *orisas*. They also believe in a future state, hence the worship of the dead, and they have a belief also in a future judgement.'[8] 'The Gikuyu believes in one God, Ngai, the creator and giver of all things', exclaims Kenyatta;[9] he also makes a fundamental distinction between worship of this God and ancestor worship.

The Abbé André Raponda-Walker also points out that the people of Gabon recognise a God, 'the supreme Being, the Great Architect of the Universe, Creator and Master of all things'. He continues however, 'but the people of Gabon place this God almost beyond what we usually think of as the "spiritual world" and on a very different, and infinitely higher plane. . . . The Gabonese pray only to their ancestors, the intermediaries between God and man. This has led some Europeans to conclude that Africans, generally speaking, "do not bother much with God".'[10] 'The African has always believed that there is a God, the Being to whom he attributes all creation', declares Mbonu Ojike.[11] In his work on the Songhai,[12] Boubou Hama stresses that 'there is not a single tribe in French West Africa which does not call on God', and he draws attention to the fact that 'the different names for God are related and derive from a common root; this would seem to be a proof that both the concept and the terminology go back to a distant past, before the advent of christian and muslim influences'.

Paul Hazo mé, in his study "L'Ame du Dahoméen révélée par sa religion", considers that John the Baptist's definition of God is close to the conception the animists of Dahomey have of the Supreme Being.[13] The Dahomeyan ethnologist pushes still further his parallel between the animist beliefs and the christian religion. Thus he sees in the *legba*—a grimacing statue with a huge phallus which is placed on the threshold of Dahomeyan homes—a representation of the Evil Spirit. He also reports the Dahomeyan's belief in 'the existence of the soul, in its perenniality, or in other words its immortality, and in the afterlife'. Hazoumé adds, however, that 'since the ancestors of the present populations had no writing and therefore left no written documents, it is not possible to verify whether their belief in the existence and immortality of the soul was original or whether it was due to the influence of monotheistic religions brought in from abroad, such as christianity and mohammedanism'.[14] Finally, he notes the belief in another world, in a city of the dead where they answer to their ancestors for deeds in this world.

Maximilien Quenum, also from Dahomey, thinks that the religion of his country was originally monotheistic, but that 'personification' of the forces of nature overlaid the original beliefs and confused the issue between God and his manifestations. However, according to Quenum, 'this evolution has not suppressed the idea of God',[15] and the concept of *Mahou* (the supreme being of the Fons) has remained very orthodox. Quenum also notes the Dahomeyan's belief in a non-material and immortal soul which is illustrated, as well as in other ways, by the human sacrifices made by the kings of Abomey to send servants after the shades of the dead.[16] In several proverbs he finds traces of belief in a judgement after death.

In *The Akan Doctrine of God*, J. B. Danquah of Ghana set out very clearly the relationship between christian and Akan notions of the Supreme Being. He also believed that this idea antedated the Europeans' arrival. His study is largely based on a philological analysis of the attributes of the supreme divinity of the Akan, *Odomankoma*, 'he who is uninterruptedly, infinitely and exclusively full of the manifold, namely the interminable, eternally, infinitely, universally filled entity'.[17] The author concluded his analysis thus: 'The system we have just examined in this work is evidence of the everlasting transmutation of the Holy Ghost in the world. In other words, the spirit of God is abroad, even in the Akan doctrine of the Gold Coast.'

However, all these writers are far from asserting a strict analogy between christian and African ontologies or even from recognising any true coherence in African metaphysics. Quenum, a fervent catholic, draws the line firmly: 'The cosmogonic ideas of this country, if one can call such a puerile collection of fairy tales by this name, cannot be arranged into any theory.'[18] Hazoumé, who is also a catholic, mentions that 'in the absence of tested, irrefutable evidence, the Dahomeyan indulges in philosophical speculations devoid of any scientific basis on the city of dead and on human destiny'.[19] Quenum is of the same opinion: if the idea of a judgement in after-life exists among the people of Dahomey, he writes, there is no 'precise information on the acts subject to punishment *post mortem*', and he remarks that lack of a positive moral standard is the essential proof of the inferiority of fetishism.[20] Boubou Hama, unlike Hazoumé, notes that the idea of God's goodness, of a beneficent God, is alien to African religions.[21]

Kenyatta and Ojike do not seem to have been worried overmuch by such problems. Neither of them is at all kind to the missionaries—Kenyatta especially, because of their fight against clitoridectomy. Ojike reproaches them more succinctly for having contributed to the disappearance of the initiation tests of virility, offering 'nothing half as effective to replace them'.[22]

Kenyatta and Ojike assert the democratic organisation of political power in African societies in almost identical terms. 'The Gikuyu system of government prior to the advent of the Europeans was based on true democratic principles. But according to the tribal legend, once upon a time there was a king. . .', writes Kenyatta.[23] 'Throughout Africa the political system is so highly democratised that no one feels that one's freedom is stifled', declares Ojike.[24] Both writers support their thesis by reference to the councils of heads of families at village level, which in their turn elect delegates to the assembly of elders at tribal level, etc. Kenyatta recalls that power was originally exercised by a despotic king, Gikuyu, the founder of the tribe. A popular uprising led to a more democratic regime; the rebels drew up a constitution which delegated power to a given age-group for a period of thirty to forty years, a system fairly widespread in Africa. (The 'relief' of the 'seniors' by the 'juniors' is evoked in a picturesque way by the Voltaic novelist, Nazi Boni, in *Crépuscule des temps anciens*.) Kenyatta regards the nomination of native chiefs by the British administration as a retrogressive return to arbitrary rule.[25] The same note is struck by Parmenas Githendu Mockerie, one of Kenyatta's colleagues, in *An African Speaks for his Own People*. He maintains that 'the Kikuyu country had been a democracy for centuries before it came under the European power'.[26]

The Lebu republic was, in the view of Sylla Assane, 'a democratic republic in every meaning of the word'.[27] This republic was founded in 1795, he recalls, following a revolt by the Lebu fishermen of the Cape Verde peninsula against the authority of the *damel* (king) of

Cayor. It was 'killed' by Captain Protet's expedition in 1857, when the French first established themselves at Dakar. Sylla Assane describes in detail the political organisation which consisted of a ministry and two houses. The prime minister, or *serigne n'dakarou*, was elected by an assembly of leading citizens, the *diambours*, who made up the upper house and whose members were older than those of the assembly of *fres*, or lower house, which wielded less power. Sylla Assane notes, however, that ministerial posts soon became hereditary 'and this had serious drawbacks'.

The defence of African democracy offered by Ndabaningi Sithole—an ordained minister and one of the leaders of the ZANU (Zimbabwe African National Union) party of Rhodesia—is the most original. In *African Nationalism*, he maintains that the African system of government was so democratic as to be paralysing: 'The people—the common people—are the basis of all properly constituted authority, although many European and American observers think that the chief is the basis of African authority. The real trouble with African institutions was that they were democratic to a fault, and this, in a way, has held the people down, since to carry out any programme required the sanction of the whole clan or tribe.'[28]

Why should African intellectuals be so keen to prove that the people of black Africa believed in a Supreme Being, and that tribal societies south of the Sahara respected democracy? The reasons seem self-evident. These two characteristics appeared to them the essential criteria of civilisation for the colonial powers, which are themselves christian democracies. The West, moreover, seemed to have been chiefly impressed by explorers' tales of despotism, petty Negro kingships, and fetish worship. (It is interesting to note that Gandhi did not think it necessary to establish the comparative values of Indian institutions and western democracy. In the wider context of his contempt for the material civilisation of Europe, he denounced, with considerable vehemence, the British parliamentary system as sterile and corrupt.)

Medicine and magic

Fetishism and sorcery pose problems that are not merely religious but also medical and psychiatric. Several African leaders and ethnologists have given these their attention. They are more or less unanimous on the efficacy of the herbal preparations used by healers in the African villages. Kenyatta,[29] Boubou Hama[30] and Fulbert Youlou[31] differentiate between these healers and the witch-doctors, who use their power in the service of evil. (But opinions diverge as to whether a strict separation can be made or whether the same individual may practice sometimes one and sometimes the other profession.) Interest in the pharmaceutical knowledge of African healers was the general theme of the contribution to the second Congress of Negro Writers and Artists by an African doctor, Fabien Ekodo-Nkoulou-Essama. His paper bore the title "La Médecine par les plantes en Afrique noire", and his conclusions were widely supported by quotations from the works of European specialists, especially Professor Perrot.[32] According to the author, these specialists 'consider that the fetishist may have acquired extensive knowledge through his own lengthy observations and those of his predecessors'. Essama then urged that African research workers should be trained to recover the secrets of traditional African pharmacopoeia. He noted that European workers in this field have complained that, more often than not, they have been checked by the suspicion of the African healers. However, as Essama pointed out, 'before this recent move preaching collaboration, witch-doctors were hunted down. We know from personal experience that in many cases the witch-doctors were pursued and imprisoned merely for having practised their art.'[33] Kenyatta before him had denounced similar cases, of which his grandfather had been among the victims, and for which he placed responsibility on the shoulders of the administration and the missionaries.[34]

In his chapter on "Medicine and Magic", Kenyatta barely mentions the virtues of medicinal herbs, but attacks resolutely the problem of so-called 'magic' practices. On the subject of love charms, he declares:

> From personal experience . . . it can safely be said that this is one way of transmitting thoughts telepathically from one mind to another. It seems that, through concentration, the magician or the possessor of love magic is able to penetrate into the mental mechanism of the person with whom he desires to establish communication. . . . If the functions and the methods of magic of this nature are studied carefully and scientifically, it will most probably be proved that there is something in it which can be classified as occultism, and, as such, it cannot be dismissed as merely superstition.[35]

Of curative charms (incantations, etc.) he says:

> This way of curing diseases can be attributed to the psychological

> influence of the magical beliefs on the patient's organism. The suggestions put to him by the magician penetrate to the conscious and unconscious mind. In this way belief in magical power as an instrument of supernatural healing is intensified. This influence helps the sick man, who is in a state of anxiety, to be cured, to create in his mind a picture of perfect health and avoid mentally seeing the manifestation of disease. I will venture to say here that treatment of this kind is associated with what is known in certain European quarters as 'Spiritual healing'.[36]

Mbonu Ojike also believes in the curative value of the medical practices of African healers, and says that Europeans see only the elements of sorcery enveloping them.[37]

Maximilien Quenum, however, thinks that intervention of the Evil Spirit, the Devil of the Bible, is the only hypothesis capable of explaining the tricks of the witch-doctors such as the *bô* (casting of spells) or the 'possession' trances common in the animist ceremonies of his country. Quenum reports several scenes of fetishism which he observed as a 'vigilant, incredulous and forewarned' witness, and eliminated three hypotheses which could explain them: hypnotism, autosuggestion and divine intervention since 'God is not extravagant and does not amuse himself making miracles all over the place'. The Dahomeyan ethnologist concludes: 'Why should we not consider the *bô* as a material condition inspired by the evil spirit to produce certain effects?'[38] Boubou Hama, on the other hand, has frequently advanced the hypothesis of hypnosis to explain the *zimma*'s (fetishist's) hold in cases of 'possession'.[39]

Possession, as is well known, is one of the most controversial subjects of ethnology. 'Voodoo' in particular has attracted a lot of attention from Haitian intellectuals. J. C. Dorsainvil gives an explanation of it, based on the work of Charcot, in *Vodou et névrose*, which came out in 1931, while Dr Price-Mars has presented the whole cult as a veritable religion. Frantz Fanon has suggested that dance and possession among colonised peoples are escapist phenomena: the frustrated, tense, colonial subject gets rid of his pent-up aggressiveness in a 'muscular orgy', while the schizophrenic duplication of personality enables him, by a trick of compensation, to forget his unhappy lot.[40] On this subject Jean Rouch's film, *Les Maîtres fous*, should also be noted for its inclusion of a new character in the traditional drama played by the possessed: this new character is the British governor of the colony.

One of the best studies of cases of possession in a country which has not been colonised (Ethiopia) is Michel Leiris' *L'Afrique fantôme*. Pierre Verger, eminent historian of the Afro-Americans, has some valuable photographs of scenes of possession in Dahomey and Brazil in his *Dieux d'Afrique*.

The same desire to rehabilitate African customs marks the approach of Negro ethnologists to several other subjects, among them the status of women. On this subject, Ojike maintains that 'the institution of bride-price does not mean that African wives are treated as chattels'.[41] Quenum considers that the African woman of the animist societies of Dahomey is by no means a 'slave'. As for the price of a dowry, it is only recently that it has reached such proportions that the young fiancé falls inevitably into heavy and lengthy debt, and thus encourages concubinage and prostitution. Kenyatta thinks that one advantage of polygamy is to spare the young mother all work during the very long nursing period prescribed by custom.[42] But Quenum, who is a catholic, speaks out strongly against polygamy, which he terms 'a regular bear-garden'.[43]

In another field, Hazoumé's monograph on "Le Pacte de sang au Dahomey" attempts to show the psychological and social causes of the blood pact and its usefulness in a given society. 'The mentality of the people of Dahomey shows a basic mistrust which is always on the look out for real or imaginary enemies, by whom every native feels himself threatened. It is easy to understand that, with this disposition, the natives of Dahomey should have surrounded themselves with defences and had recourse to the solidarity which is precisely what "sworn friendship" offered.'[44]

Without bothering to use it as any kind of justification, the Abbé Raponda-Walker explains simply and without comment the taboo which forbids the Benga to kill the *ndjombé* antelope: legend has it that one of these antelopes, generations ago, showed the fleeing tribe a ford which enabled them to cross the river and escape their pursuers. In gratitude the Benga decided never to hunt the animal which had saved them.[45]

Like many other writers, the Nigerian A. K. Ajisafe mentions the Africans' traditional courtesy and hospitality. 'The native custom in its purity is that no visitor or stranger on friendly terms must go unentertained with kola nuts and drinkables or food or free lodging. The kola nuts and the drinkables are taken together by the host and the guest. A man who will not entertain his visitor or stranger is believed to be mischievous, is shunned and treated with disrespect by the community.'[46]

Dr Hastings Banda, who led Malawi [Nyasaland] to independence, would like to defend what is valuable in African customs before it is too late. He wrote, in the preface which he and Cullen Young together prepared for *Our African Way of Life*, a work which incorporates three ethnological essays by Malawian writers:

> They [the three writers] are all conscious of the impact of a civilisation which considers itself superior, but they are none of them prepared at all points to admit that superiority. They are conscious that much of their community thought and communal life has been judged unfitting and detrimental to progress. Missions and government alike have striven to expound and enlighten, yet there is so much in the new culture that seems, not merely not better, but actually less good than what they know of the old, that they try—while yet there is time: while still the old they value is in being—to get through to the European mind some inkling of their African truth, their African scale of values, their African social ethic.

[The three essays in question are manuscripts presented to the African International Institute, which in 1930 inaugurated a prize scheme to encourage young African authors to write in the vernacular languages. By 1945, 399 manuscripts had been submitted to the Institute, in forty-one different African languages: twenty-three prizes had been awarded to the best of these manuscripts, of which only a dozen had been published.]

As we have just seen, however, African ethnologists have been moved more by the need to give an explanation, comprehensible at least if not logical, of practices at first sight contrary to common sense or our moral standards, than by a desire to praise the positive aspects of African customs. Some of them, such as Quenum, feel this is necessary for the promotion of better understanding between Africans and Europeans. 'All the mistakes which we deplore today in the history of colonisation have sprung from the fact that colonisers and colonised did not understand each other', he writes in the preface of his work *L'Afrique noire: rencontre avec l'Occident*. 'The efforts of French and Africans to establish a community between France and Africa are in danger of remaining sterile if the fundamental themes of Negro civilisation are ignored. Understanding these themes is the only basis for a real community.'[47] And Julien Alapini hopes that *Les Initiés*, his book on fetishist practices in Dahomey, will prove 'an instructive work for Africans as well as Europeans'.[48]

The critics

These efforts to promote a fuller understanding of the African world have not excluded all criticism. In several writers one can find, freely allied to praise for the civilising mission of the colonial powers, severe condemnation of some of the rites and customs of African peoples. Thus, Alapini points out the stupidity of judicial tests, resembling the medieval 'divine judgement', whereby witch-doctors claim to discover those guilty of crimes. These tests are, in fact, 'a noxious business, for many innocent people have been sacrificed for having given nothing to the charlatan'.[49] He also warns against the dangers of contagion in the ritual funerals of tuberculosis victims, where the witch-doctor sells the dead man's belongings. Hazoumé declares: 'Most of the people of Dahomey today are thankful for the French conquest which has brought a desire to end these barbaric customs' (ritual killing of deformed babies).[50]

Amon d'Aby, from the Ivory Coast, is a particularly harsh critic. He stigmatises the multiplication of religious festivals as conducive to idleness. 'We should take note . . . that the religious beliefs of the Agni, with their periods for work (*am'bé*) and their obligatory rest periods (*anaa*), have not failed to affect this people's aptitude for work. Throughout Sanwi, Indenie and Moronu, the days of *anaa* alone—not counting other holidays (for funerals and various ceremonies)—amount to nearly 200 obligatory days of rest each year in honour of the terrestrial gods.'[51] Further on he denounces the inhuman and retrograde character of some of the practices relating to the birth of deformed babies. 'The fact that, in recent years, some women abandon their "ill-fated" babies at birth or give them away to whomever will take them, instead of allowing them to be killed as is still the custom in the villages, does not detract from this criticism.'[52] He gives a particularly gloomy picture of the economic and social consequences of funeral rites.

> 'Funerals kill us, ruin us and prevent any work being done': these are the words with which villagers always begin an account of their news to townspeople. . . . Both the lengthy speeches over the corpse or the bier, and the humiliating treatment of the widow bear but a distant relationship to the peace of the soul in the land-of-

truth. Certain practices, such as the public or semi-public confessions, wearing of rags, exposure to the inclemency of the weather, prolonged daily weeping and obligatory fasting for weeks or even months, seem completely superfluous. . . . For the women it brings heavy toil since they have to look after hundreds of strangers who have insisted on coming to offer their respects to the memory of the deceased. Every time there is a death and a funeral in the village in one way or another everyone gets into debt and loses time.

The costs of putting up the guests are not the only expenses of a funeral. To get a closer idea of these one must add the cost of covers, loin cloth and wraps for the burial, the expense of entertaining dozens of relatives and above all the cases of bottles of alcoholic drink consumed by them, by in-laws, 'sons', local notables, dancers, visiting strangers, and all sorts of people. Everything is a pretext for drinking, and even the women will now only accept rum, gin or *koutoukou* (a spirit distilled clandestinely from *bangui*, a palm wine, with an average alcohol content of 30%) formerly drunk only by men. Nothing could be more likely to encourage turberculosis and the aggravation of hereditary weaknesses than this permanent state of physical exhaustion, under-nourishment and drunkenness. The effects are especially noticeable in the villages where there is a low birth rate and rampant tuberculosis, particularly among the women.

It is time to react vigorously in the face of this serious threat to the individual and society, and to free our brothers from the funerals which 'ruin and kill them'. It is not so much a question of condemning the religious bases of the rites as of attacking the current outward degeneracy with vigorous measures.[53]

Kenyatta's book was published in 1938, Amon d'Aby's in 1960. These dates are a valuable check to the historian who would distinguish between a first generation of ethnologists denouncing the retrograde character of African customs under the influence of colonialism, and a second generation fired with the results of the struggle for political emancipation, and inclined to vaunt an African precolonial 'golden age'. Certainly, some African intellectuals have swum with the current and succumbed to the one or the other temptation; their development is significant in this respect. But this has not been the general rule. African ethnologists have for the most part avoided a black-and-white attitude, and the views of Kenyatta and Amon d'Aby are examples of political courage and intellectual honesty which should be noted.

Patriarchies and matriarchies

Sheikh Anta Diop's ethnological study, *L'Unité culturelle de l'Afrique noire*, has a rather different perspective from those of the preceding authors. While Kenyatta, Ojike, Hazoumé, Quenum, Alapini and Amon d'Aby have concentrated on the structure of a specific and contemporary tribal group, Sheikh Anta Diop extends his enquiry to the whole of Africa, and especially to ancient Africa, where his poles of research are the Egypt of the Pharaohs and the Meroitic Sudan rather than the medieval empires of Ghana or Mali. As a result, he draws comparisons not with modern European society but with Assyria, ancient Greece, classical Rome, the Germanic tribes and the great invasions—even with Aryan India. The subtitle of his book is *Domaines du patriarcat et du matriarcat dans l'antiquité classique* (Areas of patriarchy and matriarchy in classical antiquity). The central theme of Diop's book is that there are two kinds of society—one suited to Africa and the other to the European world, whose structures differ on a wide range of points, starting from the fundamental difference between the African matriarchy and the European patriarchy. At the end of his book, he summarises the characteristic features of these societies by citing their antinomies:

> In conclusion, the southern cradle of society, particularly as confined to the African continent, is characterised by the matriarchal family, the creation of a territorial state as opposed to the Aryan city state, the emancipation of women in domestic life, xenophilia, cosmopolitanism, a sort of social collectivism whose corollary is quietism extending to heedlessness of the morrow, a material solidarity of rights for each individual which means that moral and material need is unknown to our day. These are poor people, but no one feels alone, no one is distressed by it. In the moral sphere, there is the ideal of peace, justice, goodness, and an optimism which precludes all thought of guilt or original sin from religious and metaphysical concepts. Favourite literary genres are the novel, short story, tale, and comedy.
>
> The northern cradle, confined to Greece and Rome, is characterised by the patriarchal family, the city state. (Fustel de Coulanges has said that between two cities there was a barrier more impassable than a mountain.) Clearly it is through contact with the south that the people of the north have widened their conceptions of

> a state to the level of a territorial state or empire. The special character of these city states, outside which man was an outlaw, developed internal patriotism as well as xenophobia. Individualism, moral and material solitude, world-weariness, all the stuff of modern literature which even in its philosophical aspects is merely an expression of the tragedy of a way of life inherited from the past: such are the attributes of this cradle. . . . An ideal of war, violence, crime and conquest, left over from the nomadic life, with the corollary of guilt and the concept of original sin giving rise to pessimistic religious and metaphysical systems, is characteristic of this cradle. . . . The outstanding literary genre is the tragedy.[54]

Diop postulates the following premise as a starting point for his study: Humanity has not known a universal transition from matriarchy to patriarchy; instead it has split into two geographically distinct cradles of mankind, one of which has favoured development of a matriarchy and the other a patriarchy.[55] To begin with, he refutes the theses of the German Bachofen and the American Morgan, who both consider the patriarchy as the culminating point and a more evolved organisation than the matriarchy; Engels also adopted this line in *The Origin of Family, Private Property and the State in the Light of the researches of Lewis H. Morgan*. Sheikh Anta Diop, who has never hidden his marxist sympathies, points out that his criticisms of Engels' theories 'are not an attack on the basis of marxism; it was merely a question of showing that, in the construction of one of his theories, a marxist had used material which had not been proved consistent'.[56]

Between the southern (Negro) cradle, and the northern (Indo-European) cradle, there are areas of confluence like Arabia, Phoenicia and Mesopotamia. The author also thinks the Semitic peoples in these areas are the result of the miscegenation of Negro and Aryan races in the distant past. Among his arguments of an historical, philosophical and sociological nature, he quotes Lenormant—even though, as he says in the preface, the latter may seem a writer of the past:

> Despite the value they attached to genealogy and superior stock, the Arabs, and especially the sedentary townspeople, did not keep their race pure . . . the infiltration of Negro blood, which has spread to all parts of the peninsula and seems destined one day to change the appearance of the race completely, began in a very distant past. It started in the Yemen, which was in continual contact with Africa on account of its geographical position. . . . The same infiltration

came slower and later in the Hejaz and the Nejd, but even there it took place at a far earlier date than is generally thought. Antar, the romantic hero of pre-islamic Arabia, was a half-caste through his mother, and yet his totally African appearance did not prevent his marrying a princess from one of the tribes proudest of its nobility; this melanian mixing was so common, and had long been accepted in the centuries immediately prior to Mohammed.[57]

African law

Legal provisions constitute one of the fundamental elements in the structure of a society, alongside religious customs and state institutions. Works on African common law by African lawyers will be reviewed in this chapter because of their ethnological interest.

In his doctoral thesis in law, *La Portée de la citoyenneté française dans les territoires d'Outremer*, Doudou Thiam, later to become minister of Foreign Affairs in Senegal, sketched among other things the outlines of a philosophy of African customary law and pointed out the differences between this and the bases of French statute law. To start with, French legislation is fundamentally secular in spirit, while the political institutions of African societies are stamped with religious mysticism: the sovereign is usually the high priest, and families are religious associations. This has important consequences in the conception of property laws: lands belonging to an African family cannot be sold or divided among the various heirs after the death of the head of the family. This is the direct opposite to French law, where, in fact, not only may landed property be sold or given away, but the law states explicitly that any of the heirs has the right to ask for the property to be divided between the heirs at any time after the death of the owner. Thiam thinks that this reflects the individualist viewpoint of French legislation in which the family as a group has no legal status. In black Africa, on the contrary, land is held by a family or by tribal common ownership and death of the father of the family or the tribal chief has scarcely any legal effect on the common ownership of the property: another father or another chief takes the place of the deceased. In the same way marriage, in African custom, is not merely an act of consent between two individuals; far more important, it is the entry of a new member into the family group.

English-speaking writers have made the customary law of their countries the subject of a fairly large number of studies. In 1903 one of them, Casely-Hayford, already with panafricanist intent, dedicated his *Gold Coast Native Institutions* to 'a unified West Africa'. He is not the earliest of African lawyers, though. As early as the eighteenth century, Antoine Guillaume Amo, a slave born in Guinea, came by chance to Germany where he made a university career for himself and wrote *De jure Maurorum*.[58] In Ghana, J. B. Danquah published *Akan Laws and Customs* in 1928, and, in Nigeria, A. K. Ajisafe published *The Laws and Customs of the Yoruba People* in 1924. More recent are the works of the Nigerian lawyer, Dr T. O. Elias, a graduate of London University; from our point of view the most important of them is *The Nature of African Customary Law*. Dr Elias has endeavoured to rehabilitate African customary law and to show that it constituted a coherent legal system. His chapter "Common errors about African law" is particularly explicit; one by one he reviews the prejudices of missionaries, ethnologists, judges and colonial officials on the subject. While he expresses only restrained criticism of the attitude of the last three categories, he is definitely hard on the first, 'especially those of the older generation [who] are accustomed to regard African law and custom merely as detestable aspects of "paganism" which it is their duty to wipe out in the name of christian civilisation'.[59]

African lawyers, like the ethnologists, are for the most part 'politically committed' intellectuals. Each has sought to rehabilitate all that seemed of value in African social institutions, and has disputed the validity of the naïve view, widespread in Europe both in scientific works and in popular opinion in England and France, that represents black Africa as a continent devoid of culture. We have seen the reservations in this effort at rehabilitation, particularly from the christian writers. All the same, the attitude of the African intelligentsia in the field of ethnology has in general been a reaction against the humiliation resulting from European scorn of African societies. Hence the need to draw certain parallels, even very approximate ones, to establish belief in a Supreme Being, the existence of a democratic system, an effective pharmacopoeia, a coherent legal system, etc. So much significant repetition of 'we too' is doubtless the upshot of the refusal to be culturally assimilated. This extensive taking up of positions is often merely a prologue to the demand for independence.

3

BACK TO THE SOIL

STORIES, LEGENDS AND PROVERBS have always been a source of literary inspiration. This is particularly true of black Africa, where many indigenous writers have drawn extensively on them. In French-speaking Africa, one can mention Bernard Dadié with his collections of stories, *Le Pagne noir* and *Légendes africaines*; Maximilien Quenum with his *Trois Légendes africaines*; Birago Diop with *Les Contes d'Amadou Koumba* and *Les Nouveaux Contes d'Amadou Koumba*; Fily Dabo Sissoko with *Harmakhis* and a collection of proverbs *Sagesse noire*; Dika Akwa with a collection of aphorisms called *Bible de la sagesse bantoue*; Julien Alapini with his *Légendes et contes du Dahomey*; Alexandre Adandé with a study of Dahomeyan proverbs "La Tradition gnomique"; and Joseph Brahim Seid with *Au Tchad sous les étoiles*—without taking account of a whole host of short stories published in various reviews which it would take pages to list. This absorbing interest in the treasures of their folklore is scarcely less marked in Negro writers from other parts of Africa. As early as the beginning of this century, Sir Apolo Kagwa, *katiriko* (prime minister) of Buganda for thirty-seven years, published in the vernacular a collection of the stories and proverbs of his country.

It should be remembered in any analysis of this attachment to the treasures of 'the soil'—as Sissoko calls it in the subtitle of his collection of poems, *Harmakhis*—that in Africa this source of inspiration is based on purely oral tradition. African writers, in their efforts to transcribe the stories and legends of the *griots**, are in a position far closer to that of Pisistratus when he commissioned scribes to set down in writing the songs of the *Iliad* and the *Odyssey* than to that of La Fontaine drawing

* A griot is both a guardian of tradition, a man who is often well-born and always respected, and a story-teller who entertains. Niane notes this double character, which today can lead to confusion between 'a caste of professional musicians living off others' and the venerable bards who are guardians of the tribal history of ancient Africa and now becoming extinct. Today, he notes, the griot is reduced to living from his musical art; formerly he was attached to some princely family.

on *Le Roman de Renart.* For them it is a question of writing down an exclusively oral folklore literature, saving it from the oblivion which threatens it when the Negro societies lose their own traditions through contact with western civilisation. If this cannot be done in the original language, it will undoubtedly be attempted in the foreign tongue of the colonists; the essential thing, surely, is to preserve this cultural heritage. This is certainly the aim of regionalist African writers. At the beginning of his study "Le Rôle de la légende dans la culture populaire des noirs d'Afrique",[1] Bernard Dadié claims that this is a real 'necessity', While there is certainly no nation where such preoccupations have not cropped up at some time or other, the interesting thing here is to analyse more deeply the reasons for this particular literary revival. In turning to the literary tradition of their ancestors, Africans have sought to show its worth and to give it a role which far transcends a simple curiosity for things of the past. By asserting the spiritual and moral richness, the didactic value and historical interest of their tales and legends, African intellectuals have also sought to reply to their detractors: to answer the charge that Africans are a people without literature or culture, merely because they had no written records.

It is typical that both Thiam and Bernard Dadié should have started their studies of the subject by expressing regret at European indifference and incomprehension of this aspect of the cultural life of the people of Africa. Thiam wrote:

> A stranger comes from some distant corner of Europe; his attitude is complicated. He may be prejudiced: he has read and heard a lot about Africa; he looks with pity on these 'primitive' people, then goes his way muttering 'the Negroes are just big children'. He may want to understand: he observes carefully, we translate some of our stories for him, but his mentality is such that he cannot always understand the rich but complex soul of Africa. Also, hearing praise of cunning and lies, he makes too hasty a judgement—'they are cheats and liars'.[2]

And Dadié has written:

> They have neon lighting while we still go by the light of a storm lamp. They have the telegraph and we the drum code; they have books and we have stories and legends by which our forebears transmitted their knowledge. These stories and legends are our museums, monuments and street names—our only books, in fact. This

is why they have such an important place in our daily lives. Every evening we leaf through them and despite the whirl of our present-day life, we cling to our past. This gives us strength. Over-hasty observers, unaware of these facts, have unfortunately not always penetrated further than the sordid appearance of our straw huts. They have not known how to read the hoary old men sitting at the threshold of these straw huts. People with no books, no monuments, and therefore of no value.[3]

African intellectuals frequently stress the richness of this oral folklore literature. Ahmadou Hampaté Ba is one of them; in a study of the Fulani poetry of the Massina, he praises the diversity of literary genres, their precise codification, the variety of musical instruments and dances accompanying them—all of which is indicative of the level of development reached by this poetry.

In a different but related field, the review *Black Orpheus* has published a vigorous refutation of the view that African folklore is virtually devoid of 'creation myths'. The anonymous author of the article recalls: 'The anthropologist Hermann Baumann actually claims that the Negro is "devoid of the gift for true myth-making".' And Paul Radin contends that 'the true creation myths are uncommon'. Most collections of African folklore are, in fact, limited to fables and 'fairy-tales'. Even Frobenius's book, *African Genesis*, is most disappointing in this respect, because all the creation myths therein come from north of the Sahara, while the Negro tales in the book are legends and fables rather than myths. 'Actually', concludes the author of the article, 'West Africa is as rich in creation myths as any other part of the world.'[4] (As an illustration he gives the Kono and the Ijaw accounts of the African version of the creation of man.)

Negro writers stress above all the three 'functional' aspects of this folklore: practical wisdom, moral range, and didactic value. The title of Fily Dabo Sissoko's collection of Malinke proverbs, *Sagesse noire* (Black Wisdom), is typical. In his preface, Sissoko points out that 'the stories, sayings, proverbs and rhythmic ritual songs are a reflection of this wisdom which is mostly preserved by the griots, its capable and vigilant guardians'.[5] 'The only merit of the present collection', he adds, 'is to apply the methods and principles of "anthropologie du mimisme" to the sayings and proverbs of the "Negro peasantry".' 'Proverbial tradition', writes Marcel Jousse, 'is a practical, incarnate science, which stems from everyday actions; it is the ethnic regulation of these actions and their lasting codification. It is an essentially "peasant" science in that it is based on the actions of the "peasant" in the ancestral homeland.' This proverbial science, springing from the trivia of daily life, may rise to dizzy heights by means of simple human bilateralism, 'just as the eagle soars towards the sun simply by beating his wings alterately'. (The work of Jousse, the theorist of 'anthropologie du mimisme', to which Sissoko refers, is *Père, Fils et Paraclet dans le Milieu ethnique palestinien*, Paris 1941.)

Alexandre Adandé, in his article on the proverbs of Dahomey, "La Tradition gnomique", points out:

> The ingenuity and strength of expression, often picturesque, in Negro proverbs . . . surprises many people. There are two reasons for this surprise: forgetfulness and ignorance. Forgetfulness, because such people do not generally remember that in most cases these proverbs were current in their own country in the most distant past; ignorance, in that they do not realise that human wisdom has no frontiers in time or space, that it is found, true to itself, among peoples of the most varied country, race and culture. In fact, our proverbs are directly comparable to those of other peoples.[6]

Prince Dika Akwa goes even further; the proverbs collected in his *Bible de la sagesse bantoue* illustrate *niambeism*, the philosophical and religious thought of the Negroes of the Cameroon (from the name of their supreme being, '*Niambe*, strength of strengths, generator of the cosmic energy which is the universe'). The author defines the guide lines of this philosophy in the preface to his collection. He compares it to the systems of Marx, Bergson, Nietzsche and existentialism, after first crossing swords with Lévy-Bruhl's theories of prelogical mentality. Thus, he finds the marxist 'law of contradiction', according to which 'in all things there is a certain element which sets what dies against what is born', mirrored in the Douala saying, 'young palm-trees grow on old palm-trees'. He interprets the Cameroon proverb, 'each man should live by his work', as forbidding any form of capitalist system in Bantu society. Similarly, the principle of interaction, which to Sartre means that 'the action of an individual will involve the world in which he is', finds its counterpart in '*Songa diwo di louse bonamasonga*' (one bad tooth infects the whole jaw).

African intellectuals draw attention also to the moral range of their stories, legends and proverbs. Bernard Dadié maintains that they are 'a lesson in prudence, generosity, patience and wisdom, indispensable to the guidance of mankind and the stability of society'.[7] Thiam points out that Leukh the hare's 'morality' is superior to that of his European counterpart, the fox of La Fontaine's fables. Both are mischievous and cunning but, writes Thiam, 'although the means are the same, the end is different. The fox is an egoist; he uses his knavery for his own ends, to flatter his base instincts. . . . The hare on the contrary uses his cunning to uphold the rights of others. He dispenses a sharp lesson to the wicked and the cheats.'[8]

In a way, then, this folklore has condensed the wisdom and ethics of the Negro peoples. Bernard Dadié carries his lesson one stage further, however: it is through the legends 'that the elders teach the young easily remembered lessons on the cosmogony, tribal history, social laws, origins of their various products, religious beliefs, social structure, economics, relations with other tribes, the lives of the heroes of fable, the evolution of civilisation (that is, invention of the caste system), the foundation of villages, the totemic relationship between an animal and a clan, and above all the cult of friendship carried to such extremes that a lion cub kills its mother to avenge the mother of its human friend'.[9] The young African receives a complete course of instruction listening to the griots and bards of his tribe. Indeed, the *Trois Légendes africaines*, collected by Maximilien Quenum—telling of the migration of the Baule from their ancient capital at Kumasi to the Ivory Coast, the historic rivalry between kings Sundiata and Sumanguru of the empires of Mali and Sosso, and finally the installation of a prince of the royal family of Allada on the throne of Abomey—are all lessons in African history, even if they are clothed in fantasy.

The most important aspect of this African oral literature is, then, its educational, or strictly functional, side. It is interesting to note that tradition forbade story-telling or listening to griots before nightfall, in order not to encroach on the day's work.[10] To this 'closed-circuit functionalism' within the tribal unit of former times, African intellectuals are now trying to add another function, in keeping with the needs of the Negro peoples of Africa today. When Alexandre Adandé asserts the 'pressing need for African museums', he is not thinking only of rescuing remains of the past. The up-to-date nature of his appeal is stressed by the fact that it is addressed to educated Africans: 'The care and taste shown in exhibiting collections will be taken by the illiterate as an example of government interest in local activities and traditions. For the educated, whose knowledge of the riches of their land is lamentable, the sight of the gold masks, the beautiful Baule weights for measuring gold, a bronze head from Benin, a glass bracelet cast in Nupe, exhibited in a public museum will not only be a revelation, but also an encouragement to know their country better and to respect its history and its assets.'[11]

Fily Dabo Sissoko feels that, in rescuing their cultural traditions from oblivion, Africans can assert their own cultural identity 'against the principle of assimilation'.[12] In a more subdued manner, Birago Diop, in dedicating his first collection of stories to his daughters, merely urges them to remember that 'the tree can grow only by sinking its roots into nourishing soil'. Joseph Brahim Seid, for his part, ends the preface to his collection of stories from Chad with the following remark, untroubled by any political afterthought:

> When night has fallen they [the people of Chad] love to gather in big groups to hear the old people telling beautiful stories which sometimes have no end and must be continued each evening by the light of the moon. These countless children of Chad invite you, gentle reader, to come and sit among them beneath a blue sky studded with stars, and listen to the voice of one of their own people telling their tales and legends, which contain more of the supernatural than the real. They ask only one thing of you: that you share with them their innocent and candid joy.[13]

Now this resurrection of their folklore, in which African intellectuals are engaged, is not intended merely to make their people aware of a cultural heritage of which they can be proud: it must also show that this culture is similar to that of other peoples in the world. Thus, the study of African folklore is two-sided: first it considers the African, then mankind in general. It is also to serve as a demonstration of the universality of the human spirit, beyond the barriers of race. This is what Bernard Dadié maintains in a paper entitled "Le Conte, élément de solidarité et d'universalité", prepared for the second Congress of Negro Writers and Artists. 'Are the dreams of other men so different from those of Africans?' he asks. 'The similarity between other people's stories and ours is such that it is difficult to speak of a black or a white soul. Souls are seen to be the same in their aspirations. The adventures of Tom Thumb resemble those of the young Soudanese Marandenboué; the tricks of the fox are like those of the hare; indiscretion is punished in the bee-woman of Borneo as in the yam-woman of the Ivory Coast; the bee and the toad of Senegal, and the fox and the stork of France play the same tricks on each other.'[14] In their respective collections, Fily Dabo Sissoko, Adandé and Dika Akwa have all compared European and African proverbs with the same meaning.

The regionalist novel

The regionalist 'vein' of black writers is not limited to stories drawn directly from folklore. Several African novels also take their subject from the soil: Malonga's *La Légende de M'Pfoumou Ma Mazono*, Camara Laye's *L'Enfant noir* and *Le Regard du roi*, Tchibamba's *Ngando*, Nazi Boni's *Crépuscule des temps anciens*, and many of Amos Tutuola's tales of fantasy.

L'Enfant noir was very well reviewed in France. 'There is an innocence which is the science of the heart', wrote Luc Estang. 'It enables a student of twenty-five to evoke his childhood in Upper Guinea; and it allows the reader to be touched by a simple tale which transcends custom, habit, and superstition and gives us the human quality, affection, seriousness, reserve, and religious spirit of the race.' More important for our context than the 'simple talent' and 'authentic taste' of the work, mentioned by Gerard d'Houville, is the effort to elucidate the ways and customs of the country, as Luc Estang has pointed out. Camara Laye strips the recipes and tricks of the witch-doctors of their supposed mystery; he shows, for example, that the roaring of lions which so terrifies the young about to be put to the test of circumcision is made with an ingenious wooden instrument waved like a sling. The author leads the European reader with ease into the strange world of age groups and virility initiation ceremonies. When Laye describes scenes concerned with African superstitions, such as his father's ritual incantations at the forge, or the fetishist cult of the serpent in his parents' house, he does so completely naturally, with disarming directness. After telling several anecdotes about his mother's gift of second sight, he goes on to reduce these 'proofs' of a mysterious power to mere childhood memories of which he is no longer too sure:

> I do not wish to say more and I have told you only what I saw with my own eyes. These miracles—they were miracles indeed—nowadays I think about them as if they were the fabulous events of a

> far-off past. That past is, however, still quite near: it was only yesterday. But the world rolls on, the world changes, my own world perhaps more rapidly than anyone's; so that it appears as if we are ceasing to be what we were, and that truly we are no longer what we were, and that we were not exactly ourselves even at the time when these miracles took place before our eyes.[15]

The impression which remains when we close this book—so charged with affection and filial love, giving a picture of a peasant community whose mentality no longer seems strange or primitive—is that the African is a man just like any other and his tribe is a society just like any other.

This first novel by Camara Laye is purely descriptive and autobiographical. On the other hand, the second, *Le Regard du roi*, is an imaginative work full of symbolism. But the difference goes deeper still. Throughout this second book, the author seems determined in a thousand different ways to suggest that Africa is impenetrable to the European mind. First there is the surf reef, a great belt of strong waves along the coast of Africa which for many years kept ships away, and which Clarence, the young European hero of the book, feels after he has landed he will never to able to cross over again. This is a symbol of the jealously guarded secret of Africa; the continent will not release foreigners who have discovered it. Then there is an explanation of the frescoes in the king's palace—and are they merely frescoes?—in which 'the king kills his most faithful vassals precisely because they are most attached to him'; and then the absurd, Kafka-like trial of Clarence accused of having taken back a coat which he had given away. There is also an endless journey into a mysterious forest in the company of an old beggar. Clarence loses all sense of time in the search for an unknown place: doubtless a representation of the life-rhythm and geography of an Africa without watches or maps. There is the contrast between two concepts of justice. Clarence demands and obtains a halt to the bastinado of one of his enemies, the master of ceremonies, which he considers too cruel; his pity wins him neither the gratitude of the victim nor the respect of the crowd. The master of ceremonies is prepared to suffer his punishment in silence, as a man. Clarence not only deprives him of a martyr's halo, but humiliates him further by forcing him to admit his generosity. The crowd, however, feels cheated of a spectacle it found amusing and frustrated to see a guilty man escape his just deserts. Finally, there are the young hero's conversations with the old beggar and with the blacksmith Diallo, in which Camara Laye systematically contrasts the European way of thinking and feeling with that of the African. The final impasse is reached at the end of an easy, friendly conversation with a young woman when the question (less culinary than one might think), 'Which is worse to eat, snails or locusts?', is, of course, never answered.

Jahn sees such conversations above all as an African lesson in humility for the European. He singles out for special note the passage where Clarence shows his surprise that the king has not been able to find a job for him, and remarks that he would have been content to be a simple drummer-boy:

> 'That is not a simple occupation', said the beggar. 'The drummers are drawn from a noble caste and their employment is hereditary. Even if you had been allowed to beat a drum, your drumming would have had no meaning. You have to know how; you see, you're a white man.'
>
> 'I know!' replied Clarence. 'There's no need for you to remind me of it all the time. I've known it longer than you. Oh, you get on my nerves!'
>
> 'Yes, but the white men think they know everything', went on the beggar. 'And what *do* they know, when all's said and done?'[16]

Jahn adds the commentary: 'The usual relationship of teacher to student between Europe and Africa is reversed. In this case it is the European who is the student.'[17]

The difference in tone, style and, doubtless, intention between these two books by Camara Laye is such that one is led to wonder whether they are really both by the same hand. However, Janheinz Jahn has picked out two passages, one from each book, which he feels illustrate the two fundamental and complementary aspects of the African conception of artistic creativeness. The first, from *L'Enfant noir*, is the scene where Camara Laye watches his father making a piece of gold jewellery in his forge and accompanying his work with ritual incantation:

> It occurred to me later on that my father could easily have relinquished all the work of smelting the gold to one or other of his assistants: they were not without experience in these matters; they had taken part hundreds of times in the same preparations and they

> would certainly have brought the work to a successful conclusion. But as I have told you, my father kept moving his lips! We could not hear those words, those secret words, those incantations which he addressed to powers that we should not, that we could not hear or see: this was essential. Only my father was versed in the science of conjuring the spirits of fire, air and gold, and of conjuring evil spirits, and that is why he alone conducted the whole operation.[18]

Jahn thinks that ritual incantation is the expression of belief in the omnipotence of the word, the *nommo*, a term which he has borrowed from Dogon cosmogony as described by Marcel Griaule in *Dieu d'eau*. The German writer equates this with 'The Word', the *Logos* which appears in Genesis. He writes: 'Camara Laye's father, the blacksmith, makes a piece of jewellery from a gold ingot with the help of the *nommo*, the word. He weaves a spell. The manual work is undoubtedly important but it is secondary; it is the word which is the decisive factor, the magic factor transmuting and changing one thing into another, and into precisely the thing which it ought to become.'[19]

The second passage, from *Le Regard du roi*, is the one in which Diallo the blacksmith explains to Clarence that the axe which he is forging is to be offered to the king who is due to arrive soon in the village:

> 'Will your axe be ready by the time he comes?' asked Clarence. 'Probably', Diallo replied. 'Anyhow, I hope it will be. But what is an axe? I have forged thousands of them, and this one will undoubtedly be the finest of them all; the others will have been no more than experiments I made in order to forge this one perfect axe. So that this will be the sum of everything I have ever learnt; it will be like my life, and all the effort I have made to live it well. But what does the king want with an axe? He will accept it; at least I hope he will accept it, and perhaps he will even deign to admire it: but he will accept it and admire it only in order to give me pleasure. After all, what sort of pleasure could he take in it? There will always be axes that are finer and more deadly, more murderously sharp than any I can fashion. . . . Yet I go on forging it. Perhaps I can do nothing else, perhaps I am like a tree which can bear only one kind of fruit. Yes, I am like that tree. And perhaps, in spite of having so many faults, perhaps because I am like that tree and lack the means to do anything but this; in spite of everything,

> the king will give me credit for my good will. But as far as the axe itself. . . .'[20]

Jahn considers that this passage expresses a second criterion of the African's conception of art: a work of art does not have an existence of its own; it has value only through the significance which the artist infuses into it. This is the contrast between the European point of view —that the work of art is created for the viewer—and the African view that it is valid only through the intentions of the artist (in the case of Diallo, the joy which the king's admiration would give him). In Africa a work of art is never a *kintu*, an object in itself; it takes on meaning only from the creative action. This creative action is the modal force, *kuntu*.

Jahn maintains that the European is unable to differentiate between these two notions of *kintu* and *kuntu*, notions which are absolutely distinct in African philosophy. According to Abbé Alexis Kagame, *kintu* and *kuntu* are two out of four fundamental categories, in an almost Kantian sense, of the Bantu-Rwanda philosophy of existence. This is described in his *La Philosophie bantu-ruandaise de l'être*, his doctorate thesis in philosophy at the Gregorian university of Rome, published by the Académie des Sciences de Belgique in 1956. Jahn has taken this research and that of Griaule as the basis for his outline of African philosophy whose themes he has tried to find in the work of the writers and poets of the 'négritude' movement. He summarises Diallo's thought in the following way:

> In Camara Laye's novel, the blacksmith spends his life forging axes, each sharper and more beautiful than the last, which he wants to offer the king. Hardly has he finished one axe than he starts another, sharper and more beautiful still. For the king who will come one day, he forges axe after axe. As for the axes which he has already forged, works of art now superseded, let the peasants take them. But the one on which he is working at the moment, the last of the line: that is for the king. It is not to have a special purpose, but merely to give delight.[21]

This aim—to show a kind of deep-seated incompatibility between the African and European mentality—which we credit to Camara Laye, is also to be found, under a different aspect, in the weird novel of Paul Tchibamba from the Congo. The author explained this in an interview with *Présence Africaine*: 'In *Ngandu* I have tackled the difficult problem of cause. Europeans and Africans do not think of this problem in the same way. For you the cause is responsible for the results which it engenders. We, on the other hand, admit that a man—even in his right mind—is not always responsible for his acts; at times the *ndokis*, or ill winds if you prefer, may intervene between cause and result, making the effects deviate from their intended goal.'[22]

Nazi Boni, in the preface to his *Crépuscule des temps anciens*, states firmly his intention of reawakening in Africans a taste for their ancestral culture:

> The invasion of the black continent by Europeans brought to a close the era of an Africa which was wholly African. The colonists imposed their rule. Africa felt this blow so keenly that it withdrew into itself, and before adapting to the new regime suffered a short but definite setback. Its culture was shaken, its demography vacillated. Then began a longish period of anomaly and decivilisation while the conqueror judged the conquered and forged his methods of colonisation in virtually total ignorance of the Negro spirit. There is barely time for a last, urgent appeal to our scholars to double their efforts if they do not want some of the cultural treasures of our old continent to be lost in the seas of oblivion. Soon it may be too late. . . . This book . . . is neither a code of customs nor a pharmacopoeia of magic recipes; it is an expression of the peasant way of life, the religion, wars and feelings of a living people before the period of colonisation. . . . Africa would not be itself if it were ashamed of a past of which it has only to be proud and from which it must draw the inspiration essential for revival.[23]

Amos Tutuola also has revealed the reasons which led him to write: 'I wrote for my own pleasure without thinking of publishing what I wrote. Also, I had nothing else to do in the evenings. Finally, it seemed necessary to write down the tales of my country since they will soon all be forgotten.' Tutuola is both a Grimm and an Edgar Allan Poe to Africa. The world of fantasy in which this Nigerian moves so easily is also that of the legends and mythology of the Yoruba country. In his *The Palm-Wine Drinkard*, there is a journey into the land of the dead where everything is topsy-turvy—a sort of African *Alice Through the Looking Glass*. Only rarely does one find a glimpse of the contemporary world, such as that extraordinary Eden-Palace installed in the trunk of a colossal white bombax tree, a sort of phalanstery with a dance hall.*

La Légende de M'Pfoumou Ma Mazono by Malonga, former socialist senator of the French Congo, is also well endowed with extraordinary tales. There is a river crossing on the backs of hippopotami summoned by a magic formula, and witch-doctors who expose themselves without injury to the bullets of the best shots of the village. This is not the main purpose of the book, however. The young hero embarks on a philanthropic political undertaking: 'to found a new city where the slave would be equal to his master and would rediscover his human dignity, where social supremacy would depend on intelligence alone. Those were the ideals of our young revolutionary.'[24] M'Pfoumou Ma Mazono was, moreover, an historical character, as Malonga tells us at the end of his book: 'Finally we should add that, thanks to the laws of M'Pfoumou Ma Mazono, slavery no longer existed, except in embryo state where it was possible to cheat the legal system then in force. This held from the accession of Hakoula's son until the arrival of the Europeans. Although the latter may still have had work to do in these humanitarian endeavours, they were certainly helped by an internal revolution.'[25] Malonga gives no further explanation of the intention of his book. Did he want to show that Negroes had not waited for the arrival of the white men to revolt against slavery? Probably. His other novel, *Coeur d'Aryenne*, is a fierce indictment of the 'colonials'.

An analysis of regionally inspired African literature, collections of proverbs, stories and legends, and novels of the soil, leads to conclusions similar to those drawn from the study of African ethnological writings: here is the same desire to rehabilitate African ancestral values. These must not be lost else the African of today will be in danger of becoming depersonalised, and Africa will be a continent with no culture of its own. This other aspect of the pilgrimage which African intellectuals

* A relatively high number of critical studies have been made of Amos Tutuola's works. There is a good summary of them in the section on Tutuola in Gerald Moore's *Seven African Writers.* The attention of literary critics has especially been drawn to the fact that the Nigerian's plots are often similar to those of the great legends of universal literature: for example, the hero returns to his homeland after winning dearly bought experience through a quest strewn with pitfalls. Gerald Moore does not concede to this analogy the importance which has sometimes been attributed to it; unless, as he ironically puts it, we agree that Tutuola took a crash course in world mythology before sitting down to write *The Palm-Wine Drinkard.* Moore's admiration for Tutuola's work is in no way diminished by the fact that he may have been influenced by the works of the Nigerian, D. O. Fagunwa, which were written in the vernacular.

are making to their origins is a new expression of their defensive reactions to the policy of assimilation. This can be read between the lines of Mamby Sidibé's introduction to the "Contes de la savane" which appeared in *Le Monde noir*, a special number of *Présence Africaine*:

> In a society with no alphabet and starting out with no written literature, oral folklore has absorbed the treasures which in other countries would have been confided to books: a whole exuberant tradition consisting of history, religion, amusing stories, moral instruction, satire and psychological observation. This rich store, handed down through the ages, ensures for Africa the permanence of its institutions and the indestructible solidity of its resources in a powerful originality which exotic trappings may sometimes hide but never destroy.[26]

4

TO EACH HIS OWN TRUTH

'Ever since the fifteenth century, the Negro peoples' history has been brutally twisted to the advantage of their white masters. . . . Our wish is to study our own history and to correct that which was drafted without us and against us.'[1] This is how Joseph Ki Zerbo, a university *agrégé*, defines the task of African historians. But this historical research should not be confined to the past. 'We know that the history of a country can have a determining effect on its future, according to the way in which it is presented', Abdoulaye Wade has remarked.[2] Sheikh Anta Diop considers that the purpose of a history of Africa written by Africans should be as follows: 'The Negro must be able to grasp the continuity of his nation's history and to draw from it the moral support he needs to recover his place in the civilised world.'[3] According to this Senegalese writer, the work of European scholars on the history of Africa is utilitarian and pragmatic. It is destined to put over a point of view 'which would serve the interests of colonialism'. 'Under the cloak of science, the aim is to make the Negro believe that he has never produced anything of value.'[4] In the presentation, by the publisher, of *African Glory*, by Charles de Graft-Johnson of Ghana, another weakness of African history as seen through European eyes is pointed out. 'It is hardly too much to say that there is a widely held belief that Negro history begins with the colonisation of lands inhabited by "savages" who had lived in the same primitive fashion from time immemorial. There will be no excuse for such ignorance now that this book is available.'

For others it is just a question of putting over a different—and purely African—point of view, to shed new light on the history of the black continent. This history can be given a double meaning at times, as Andriantsilaniarivo of the Malagasy Republic has explicitly said, à propos of the conquest of his country: 'Then came the defeat. For if the conquest of 1895 was a victory for France, it was certainly a disaster for Madagascar. Events of this sort cannot be interpreted in one way only.'[5]

These few quotations are representative of the main guide lines of African historical research. They are clearly closely related to those of the ethnologists and the folklore writers.

It is instructive in this context to see African Negro attitudes in the light of similar preoccupations among writers from other former colonies. One of the most striking examples of this is the Algerian, Amar Ouzegane, who was a minister in Ben Bella's government. In *Le Meilleur Combat*, he takes up arms against the interpretation of the legend of Roland as 'the epic of a good christian continuing the arabophobic crusade of Charles the Hammer'. He writes: 'The battle of Roncevaux was *not* as depicted in the popular prints in which the French "humiliated the Saracen" by the sword and their fabulous exploits, and triumphed by the strength of their arms and courage against odds of one to a hundred—when it was not one to a thousand! In fact the sordid truth is that Charlemagne's nephew was no martyr of the christian faith, but a professional foreign soldier defeated by christians in the defence of their own country. The battle of Roncevaux was only one episode in a cruel, merciless war of plunder waged by the barbaric north against the christian people of Euzkadie, the Basques.' He quotes Gil Reicher's book, *En Pays basque*, in support of his argument: 'It is well known that the Basques avenged themselves by attacking the French rear-guard in the valley of Roncevaux, the Orriaga of the Basques. . . .' Ouzegane concludes: 'The legend of the *Chanson de Roland* was a psychological smoke-screen put out to obliterate even the memory of this sublime action. The Saracens had crossed the Pyrenees, not as invaders, but in answer to an alarm call from their neighbours, the christian Basques. To unveil the true character of the battle of Roncevaux is to recognise that the chivalrous spirit of Saladin the Great was not just unusual personal nobility but the very basis of the moral superiority of Islam.' (pp. 50 ff.)

*The griots**

Just as African folklore writers have asserted the cultural interest of their oral literature, so African historians have stressed the value of the oral historical sources and traditions of Africa. They have criticised European historians for their contempt of such sources which has resulted, among other things, in African history's being seen only through the accounts of European missionaries and explorers. As a

* For definition of 'griots', see p. 63 above.

first step, therefore, African historians have sought to refute the claim that the historical tales and dynastic poems handed down from generation to generation of griots are of little or no value.

As early as 1897, the Reverend Samuel Johnson succeeded in cross-checking legendary and written sources on the origin of the Yorubas. He wrote: 'This shows that there is nothing improbable in the accounts as received by tradition.'[6] Some sixty years later, Djibril Tamsir Niane, in the preface to his *Soundjata ou l'épopée mandingue*, stated even more categorically:

> Unfortunately, the West has taught us to despise the oral sources of history. Everything that is not written in black and white is considered to be without foundation. There are even plenty of African intellectuals narrow-minded enough to despise these 'talking' documents, the griots, and to believe that for lack of written documents we know nothing, or virtually nothing, of our past. Such people simply prove that they know their country only from the white man's point of view. The words of the traditional griots deserve something better than scorn.[7]

Niane gives an example of this: his *Soundjata* is none other than a faithful translation of a griot's tale. In fact, most African historians have drawn more or less extensively on oral historical traditions. The use each author has made of them, however, has varied according to his aims and the sort of book he was writing. When Akindele and Aguessy recount the legends on the founding of the kingdom of Porto Novo, they do so as any other European or African historian would do. When Niane transcribes the account of the life of the Mandingo emperor with all the turns of phrase and apostrophes of the griot, omitting none of the fantastic or supernatural episodes, he is doing the job of an archivist. And Ibrahim Issa's evocation, in *Grandes Eaux noires*, of the history of the people of the Niger loop, is a legend hung on the peg of the historical expedition of the legionaries of Septimus Flaccus against the Garamantes.*

This said, I should point out that African historians are perfectly well aware of the relative reliability of oral sources, which cannot be used without a great deal of caution. Joseph Ki Zerbo, who (like

* This legend is not entirely free of political intent: the author contrasts the generosity of the Negro chiefs, who give a safe conduct to the lost Roman soldiers, with the brutality of the Roman column.

Niane) hopes that these oral traditions will be exploited, defines the extent to which they may be used:

> The griots are living archives; they are annalists endowed with prodigious memories, a source of African history to be used with the necessary precautions. Sometimes they establish a correct but incomplete line of succession: the kings come in the correct order but may have been separated by others which the griots have not learnt or have forgotten. Moreover, since the sensational element is most in demand by the audience, there is a danger of bias towards the detail which hits the jack-pot and a willingness to inflate this detail. With these reservations, however, cross-checking between the tales of several griots, according to appropriate critical methods, can enable a valid historical sequence to be built up from the verse chronicles of the Negro troubadours.[8]

Abbé Alexis Kagame, in a brief introductory study to the 'war poetry' of his country, also warns against the inaccuracies and omissions of the dynastic songs.

> There are two distinct branches of war poetry: one lyrical, called *Ibyivugo* (warrior odes); the other heroic, called *Ibitekerezo*. The latter is none other than a history of the conquests of Rwanda and the military expeditions of olden days; its poetic style comes from the exalted deeds and warrior odes of the heroes, which are embedded in the tale. The warrior bards have left us some highly developed poems, often divided into cantos, which the Court has preserved as 'classics'. . . . One must not think, however, that each poem necessarily corresponds to some real exploit. The Court bards were continually composing such poems and included in them fictitious heroic deeds. It was, after all, poetry, and a work of imagination.[9]

Saburi O. Biobaku from Nigeria also insists on the care with which he used oral history in the preparation of his work *The Egbas and Their Neighbours, 1842–1872* (a comparatively recent period).

> In addition to written sources, material for this study was obtained from oral evidence and traditional accounts, especially for the introductory chapters. The history of a non-literate people is essentially remembered history, which is transmitted from generation to generation. By interviewing knowledgeable persons in an informal atmosphere, valuable oral evidence may be obtained. Such

evidence must be checked and cross-checked and then rigorously analysed if it is to yield historical material. The use of oral evidence in the introductory chapters of this book has enabled me to complete the picture delineated without being dogmatic.[10]

Negro Egypt

One of the books which has caused a great stir in African nationalist circles is *Nations nègres et culture*, in which (as has already been mentioned) the Senegalese historian, Sheikh Anta Diop, tries to prove that the inhabitants of Egypt of the pharaohs were black, and that consequently humanity owes one of its oldest civilisations to the Negro race. An amazing inspiration animates and sustains this exposition which covers 253 pages packed with quotations and references. The chapter headings include "Birth of the Negro myth" and "The modern falsification of history", to prick the conscience of European historians. In order to defend his thesis, which runs directly counter to the generally accepted theories of Egyptologists, the author of *Nations nègres et culture* has attempted to be exhaustive, and has drawn his arguments from all fields of history, ethnology and linguistics.

The Bible is one of the first texts studied by Diop. He gives an original explanation of the curse on the sons of Ham: it was the Egyptians (who were black) that the Jews wished to curse after the persecution which made them decide to leave the kingdom of the pharaohs. It is here, and not in the legend of a drunken Noah, that one must look for the reasons for the biblical curse hanging over the Negro race and the negrophobia found in the Holy Scriptures, a trait which, Diop point out, does not appear until after the Exodus. The author backs up this emotional argument with a philological one on the origin of the word Ham: Moses took it from Egypt, called by the Egyptians *Kemit*, meaning 'black' in ancient Egyptian, just as *Kam* does in Hebrew. Diop draws the following conclusions:

> From this point, all the obvious contradictions fade away and the logic of events becomes transparent. The Egyptians, symbolised by their black colour, *Kemit* or Ham in the Bible, will be cursed in the literature of the people they have oppressed. Thus we see that the biblical curse on the descendants of Ham has a completely different origin from the ostensible one given it today and for which there is not the slightest historical basis. What is difficult to understand is

> how *Kemit* or Hamite which means black, ebony, even in Egyptian, has come to stand for a white race. Ham is cursed, blackened, and made the ancestor of the Negroes when needs dictate; but he is whitened when the origins of civilisation are in question, since there he was inhabiting the first civilised country in the world. It is then that the idea is cooked up of eastern and western Hamites; this is nothing but a convenient invention to deprive the Negro of the moral advantages of the Egyptian civilisation and other African civilisations as well, as we shall see.[11]

This is merely a starting point for the author of *Nations nègres et culture* who, throughout the book, undertakes to refute the notion of 'Hamite' to which, he says, 'absolutely no historical, geographical, linguistic* or ethnic facts can be made to correspond'.[12] Hence he rejects Champollion's interpretation, based on examination of a stele discovered near Thebes, according to which the Egyptians had 'dark red' skin. Diop considers that 'the colour of the Egyptians, referred to as dark red, is none other than the natural colour of the Negro'.[13] On the stele in question (which was found on a tomb in the Valley of the Kings), Champollion found a mention of the four races recognised by the Egyptians: first the Egyptians (whose colour was dark red), then the Negroes, then the Asians (of a swarthy yellow colour), and finally the

* In fact, the meaning and even the spelling of the word is not always very clear. In his *Histoire des peuples de l'Afrique noire*, Robert Cornevin has this to say about it: 'Writers have used Chamite, Hamite and Khamite somewhat indiscriminately. These are three spellings of the same term coming from the name Ham, son of Noah. African linguistics, the work of missionaries, are strongly impregnated with biblical references. Since the true pronunciation was Hamite, the word was given a rich variety of spellings in French works. Denise Paulme, following Seligman, spells it "kamite"; Labouret writes "hamite"; Poirier draws a distinction between the Chamites, who left Egypt and occupied eastern Africa, and the Hamites, whom he classes as proto-Berbers who followed the North African coast and occupied the whole Maghrib. This is one way of distinguishing between eastern and northern Hamites, for it should be remembered that the term Hamite comprises two major linguistic groups: 1. the eastern Hamites (ancient Egyptian, Beja, Galla, Somali, Danakil); and 2. the northern Hamites (all the Berber dialects from Tripoli to Morocco, and the languages of the Tuareg and Tubu of the Sahara, as well as the ancient Guanche of the Canaries).

The term Hamite, which had a purely linguistic meaning to start with, has come to include the anthropological and cultural characteristics of all the ethnic groups speaking Hamite dialects and inhabiting the zones into which the Hamites spread. It is certainly rather odd that Ham, the only one of Noah's sons who was black, should be cited as the ancestor of peoples of white race as the result of a chain of reasoning which is irregular to say the least. It is obviously desirable that an international congress of anthropologists should define clearly what is meant by these terms.' (pp. 70–1.)

white race. Diop thinks it is clear that 'from these very early times the Egyptians differentiated between the two groups of their race—civilised Negroes of the valley and the Negroes from regions in the interior of Africa—in such a way that there could be no confusion with the white and yellow races of Europe and Asia'.[14] Later, commenting on a book by Baumann, the Senegalese historian writes: 'One notices, incidentally, that Baumann has even gone so far as to whiten the kings of the Sudan. He follows a well-known Nazi procedure which would explain away every African civilisation as the efforts of a white race or the offspring of one, and he is even prepared to claim that there are "black" white people and "dark red" white people, etc., all lumped together under the convenient title of Hamites.'[15]

Sheikh Anta Diop, who believes the Semitic people are the result of interbreeding, refers to the works of two Greek historians, Herodotus and Diodorus Siculus, to prove that the Egyptians were originally black—as, since the Persian conquest in 525 BC, they have always been ruled by foreigners: Macedonians under Alexander, Romans under Julius Caesar, Arabs in the seventh century, Turks in the sixteenth century, and so on.

> Herodotus remarked several times on the Negro character of the Egyptians; he even mentioned it indirectly in other contexts. . . . To prove that the Greek oracle is of Egyptian origin, Herodotus used the following argument, among others: 'When they add that this dove was black, they mean that this woman was Egyptian.' . . . Diodorus Siculus [of Sicily] reported the Ethiopians as saying that the Egyptians were one of their colonies which was established in Egypt by Osiris.[16]

The Senegalese historian also quotes more recent historians in support of his thesis. He takes this comment on the Copts from Volney, who visited Egypt at the end of the eighteenth century.

> They all have the puffy face, swollen eyes, flattened nose and thick lips of the real half-caste. I was inclined to attribute this to the climate when a visit to the Sphinx gave me the key to the enigma. On seeing this head, which in every detail is typical of the Negro, I remembered the remarkable passage of Herodotus in which he says: 'I consider the Colches to be an Egyptian colony because, like them, they have black skin and crinkly hair.' In other words, the ancient Egyptians were true Negroes like all the peoples of Africa. Since

> then their blood has mixed for centuries with that of Greeks and Romans and has lost the intensity of its original colour, but they have retained the cast of their early features.[17]

According to Diop, it was only after Napoleon's expedition to Egypt and Champollion's discoveries that the viewpoint changed and the infant science of Egyptology began to assert that the Egyptians were white. What were the reasons for this change? Diop thinks that, spurred on by imperialism, it was becoming increasingly 'inadmissible' to accept the theory of a Negro Egypt which until then had seemed obvious.

> The birth of Egyptology was therefore characterised by the need to destroy utterly, at all costs, and in all minds, the memory of Negro Egypt. Henceforth, the common denominator in the theses of Egyptologists, their intimate relationship and deepest affinity, can be summed up in their desperate attempt to refute the concept of a Negro Egypt. Practically all Egyptologists state, a priori, the falsehood of the thesis of a Negro Egypt.[18]

The stand of the Senegalese historian naturally leads him to take sides in the great classical controversies of Egyptology. He is against the partisans of the 'Delta supremacy', who assert that Egyptian civilisation originated in Lower Egypt; on the contrary, he supports those who believe the cradle of civilisation to have been Upper Egypt, and that it came from the high plateaux of Ethiopia. He regards the former theory merely as a 'devious way of establishing a Mediterranean and white origin for Egyptian civilisation'.[19] He also takes sides in the controversy concerning Egyptian chronology. Some historians date the beginning of the civilisation of the pharaohs as several thousand years ago; others would have it go much further back. The former are advocates of the so-called 'short' chronology and the latter of the 'long' chronology. According to Sheikh Anta Diop, the 'short' chronology enabled an Asiatic origin to be advanced for the civilisation of the Nile valley, while the 'long' chronology established the Egyptian civilisation as anterior to all others, and particularly to the neighbouring civilisation of Mesopotamia. He continues:

> It is clear from these texts that the urge to synchronise Egyptian and Mesopotamian history stems from the realm of ideas and not of facts. The prevailing idea at the moment is to explain Egypt by way of Mesopotamia—that is, from Western Asia, cradle of the Indo-

> Europeans. All I have said shows that if one keeps strictly within the limits of conclusive fact, one is obliged to see Mesopotamia merely as a belated offspring of Egypt.[20]

He then gives 'the various factors proving the Negro origins of the Egyptians'.[21] These are the analogies which he finds between ancient Egypt and traditional Africa: circumcision (and he quotes Herodotus); ritual killing of the king when his strength declines; cosmogony (and he quotes Masson-Oursel who, he says, 'stresses the Negro character of Egyptian philosophy'); matriarchy, which 'is the basis of social organisation in Egypt as in black Africa'; the relationship between the Meroitic Sudan and Egypt; and finally, language. He spends a long time on this last point, devoting two chapters to his comparative study of the Egyptian and Wolof grammar and vocabulary. He rejects the German hypothesis of Egyptian as a Semitic language. 'It is as difficult to uphold, and naturally even more so to prove, the relationships between Egyptian and the Indo-European and the Semitic languages, as it is easy to prove the profound unity of Egyptian and the Negro languages.'

In his last chapter, the author eliminates the theories which seek a cradle outside Africa for the Negro race. He then endeavours to show how the different Negro peoples living there all originated from the high plateaux of Ethiopia. At the end of his long exposition, he concludes: 'So one sees that the coloured man, far from being incapable of initiating any skills, was the very one to have originated them in the first place, in the person of the Negro. . . .' But his final remark is a warning against 'the excesses of nazism in reverse': the Egyptian civilistion which the Negro could claim in evidence 'might have been created by any other human race—in so far as one can speak of a race—which had found itself in so favourable and unique a spot'.[22]

Sheikh Anta Diop's theories on the relationship between African languages and ancient Egyptian, and on the Negro race of the pharaohs' subjects, have been greeted with great reserve in scientific circles. The French historian, Suret-Canale, whose opinions are less open to reservation since he is resolutely anti-colonialist, has written:

> If Sheikh Anta Diop jeers with reason at such European 'scholars' who, through unadmitted racial prejudice, have tried to 'whiten' ancient Egypt at all costs, then he himself falls into the same trap in seeking to 'blacken' at all costs, and to give a 'Negro' origin to the civilisations of the Sumerians, Carthaginians . . . and Bretons. The

truth is that the Egyptian population in antiquity was, anthropologically speaking, no different from what it is today; thousands of perfectly preserved mummies, as well as skeletons, leave no doubt at all on this point! No serious evidence of a modern 'whitening' of the Egyptian population has been produced (the Arabic contribution has been numerically insignificant). The truth is that in the past, as today, there was more or less pronounced miscegenation with the black population of the Upper Nile (such interbreeding also takes place in the opposite direction via the infiltration of white elements into Nubia). There are, and there always have been, Negro elements in Egypt, and even possibly Negro dynasties ruling over a white population. The ancient Egyptians, like the Arabs after them, were happily free of any colour prejudice! The theory of the Egyptian origin of Negro-African languages was proposed a short time ago by Mlle Homburger. This linguist's main argument was that the evolution of ancient Egyptian (down to its final version, Coptic) has led to a structure and morphological characters very similar to those of Negro-African languages. But, if these facts are true, they could well be interpreted in another way: that the evolution of Egyptian was influenced by the Negro-African languages spoken in the Nile valley. In any case, as I have said, mingling the fundamentally different concepts of race and culture can lead to the most dangerous confusion. The Egyptian civilisation had close links with the civilisations of the Eastern Mediterranean and the Asian Middle East, but its influence in Africa beyond the valley of the Nile and the Sahara regions was extremely limited. Compared with it, the civilisations of black Africa show original characteristics which it is neither necessary nor convincing to attribute to exterior influence, unless one is going back to the a priori hypothesis of the inferiority of the people of black Africa.[23]

African glory

Charles de Graft-Johnson of Ghana is clearly as eager as Sheikh Anta Diop to give back to Africans a pride in their past. The title of his book is significant in this respect: *African Glory—The Story of Vanished Negro Civilisations*. The author sets out to show the power and degree of civilisation achieved by Africa south of the Sahara in the middle ages. William Conton of Sierra Leone has set himself a similar task in his *West Africa in History*. 'I have tried to capture for you a little of that greatness and to show how it was temporarily lost and how it has now been regained.'[24]

The three great medieval African empires which Charles de Graft-Johnson singles out for special study are, in chronological order, the empires of Ghana, of Mali and of the Songhai. He stresses the aspects in each which reveal among the African people those qualities which racist and colonialist literature has denied in Negroes. To the picture of the savage, uncultured Negro living from hand to mouth, he contrasts that drawn from the accounts of Arab historians—Ibn Haukal, Al Bekri, Al Idrisi, Ibn Batuta, Ibn Khaldun and others—of the riches of the empire of Ghana, the splendours of the great Kankan Musa and his astonishing pilgrimage to Mecca, the importance of the university of Timbuktu and the fame of its scholars, the exploits of the great conquerors such as Sundiata and Askia the Great. The defeat of the Songhai empire by Sultan Al Mansour's Moroccan army marked the end of the great Soudanese empires of the middle ages. De Graft-Johnson also remarks on the intellectual loss which this meant to West Africa.

> The losses suffered by the Moroccan soldiers caused their leaders to adopt harsh measures against the city dwellers of the Songhai empire, particularly against the scholars of Timbuktu. All the scholars, lecturers, professors, jurists and theologians were driven in chains to Morocco. All their books were also transported to Morocco. Among those deported was Professor Ahmed Baba, the distinguished historian of Sankore University* so frequently quoted in the *Tarikh es Sudan* and other works. Professor Ahmed Baba was not released from his Moroccan prison until 1607, and in that same year he returned to Timbuktu to die.[25]

The Ghanaian historian adds: 'We get a picture of the importance attached to learning in the Songhai empire from a statement made by Professor Ahmed Baba while a prisoner in Morocco. He is reported to have said; "Of all my friends in the Soudan it was I who owned the smallest library, but I possessed 1,600 volumes".'[26]

This picture of the 'African empires of the past' is completed by a relatively brief study of the kingdoms of the Congo and Monomotapa, based on the accounts of Portuguese explorers such as Duarte Lopez, Damiac de Goês, de Barros and Father Dom Gonçalo da Silveira. De

* The mosque around which the university of Timbuktu was founded. (See de Graft-Johnson, *African Glory*, p. 98.)

Graft-Johnson stresses the rich gold mines and splendid palace of the king of Monomotapa. He does not restrict himself to the Negro empires; he goes back to their origins and also takes sides in the controversial question of the origin of the Negroes. He contests the theories of South African anthropologists who hold that the Negro race is of relatively recent origin, and that the Negro is a newcomer and stranger in Africa.* 'These are the bases for a *Herrenvolk* theory worse than any that Hitler ever disseminated.'[27]

Abdoulaye Wade attacks in similar fashion Delafosse's theory on the subject: 'In the face of two equally hypothetical possibilities, that of an Australian origin for the natives of Africa or vice versa, Delafosse has opted for the former. This is an easy choice but not justified: it presents the Negro as a stranger to Africa, with all the ulterior deductions which such a postulate involves.'[28]

One of the most interesting aspects of *African Glory* is its 'pan-Negro' concept of the history of the African continent. De Graft-Johnson eliminates, so to speak, the geographic and racial frontier of the Sahara. In the first place, he also is not far from thinking that the Egyptians were black. On this subject he quotes the opinion of Sir Ernest A. Wallis Budge, Keeper of Egyptian and Assyrian Antiquities at the British Museum: 'There are many things in the manners and customs and religions of the historic Egyptians, that is to say, of the workers on the land, that suggest that the original home of their prehistoric ancestors was a country in the neighbourhood of Uganda and Punt.'[29] But the Ghanaian goes even further:

> In Africa, where the Negro is found completely at home, it has been noted that his distribution at one time covered Egypt, Morocco, Tripolitania, Tunisia, and Algeria. The appearance of other races in North Africa modified the predominantly negroid character of the population, but even in the modification, to repeat a phrase from Sir Harry H. Johnston, 'both in nigrescence and in facial features the

* It is well known that this problem is of major political importance in South Africa. This is how H. Maclear Bate puts the European point of view in *South Africa Without Prejudice*. When Jan van Riebeeck reached the Cape in the seventeenth century, he found only a few scattered tribes of Hottentots and Bushmen, not Bantus. 'It was not until 130 years later, in 1779, that the Europeans came into violent contact with the Xhosas who crossed the Fish River 400 miles east of Cape Town which was an agreed boundary. This began a period of South African history of special significance. Every South African schoolboy knows that the Bantu is as much an invader in South Africa as the white man.' (p. 46.)

ancient negroid strain has never been completely eliminated in these lands'. If even the Egyptians have Negro blood in their veins, then it is safe to assume that a study of the history of any part of the African continent is also a study of Negro history.[30]

De Graft-Johnson claims many well-known figures as 'Africans'. In his book we see the pharaohs of Egypt; the suffetes of Carthage; the Roman emperor Septimus Severus, born at Leptis Magna; Tertullian, born at Carthage; St Augustine, born at Targaste in Numidia—all enter the pantheon of great Africans. The author emphasises the complete absence of racial prejudice among the Romans to explain the high positions held by these men; he also stresses their attachment to their native land, as in the case of Septimus Severus.[31]

One long chapter of *African Glory* is devoted to slavery, and describes its consequences for Africa as well as its horrors:

> Tribal life was broken up or undermined and millions of detribalised or decentralised Africans were let loose upon each other. The increasing destruction of crops led to cannibalism in certain areas.... Tribes had to supply slaves or be sold as slaves themselves.... Violence, brutality and ferocity became the necessities of survival.... The stockades of grinning skulls, the selling of one's own children as slaves, the unprecedented human sacrifices, were all the sequel to this grand finale, the rape of African culture and civilisation.[32]

De Graft-Johnson supports the estimate of Dr W. E. B. DuBois—the American Negro sociologist generally regarded as 'the father of panafricanism'—that the slave trade cost Africa some 100 million inhabitants. The Ghanaian author does not fail to pay tribute to the efforts of the English abolitionists, but he does attack 'the impression [which] prevails in certain quarters that the Negro under slavery was a docile being who never struck a blow in defence of his own cause or in defence of his own freedom; but this is an utterly false impression', and he recalls the slave revolts in Haiti and Santo Domingo. There is a considerable Haitian literature with an analogous viewpoint, devoted to Toussaint Louverture and the other heroes of the war of independence in that large West Indian island. In the same vein, George Padmore recounts the risings of 'chestnut' Negroes, rebel American slaves, some of whom made up one of the parties of immigrants sent to Sierra Leone.[33]

In his last chapter, de Graft-Johnson gives an account of the resistance by tribes and chiefs to British penetration of the Gold Coast. In his motion for independence to the Gold Coast Legislative Assembly in 1953, Kwame Nkrumah devoted a long section to the 'valiant wars against the British, the banishment of Nana Prempeh the First to the Seychelles Islands. . . . Then the Fanti Confederation—the earliest manifestation of Gold Coast nationalism . . . and the Aborigines Rights Protection Society, so many landmarks in a glorious history of national resistance.'[34]

Several of the themes developed by de Graft-Johnson recur in two articles by Joseph Ki Zerbo, "L'Économie de traite en Afrique noire ou le pillage organisé"[35] and "Histoire et conscience nègre".[36] Ki Zerbo also stresses, in the first of these articles, the immense importance of the 'demographic drain' of slavery. Taking his figures from several other works, he concludes that during four centuries the slave trade cost Africa 100 million individuals, without counting a further 50 million taken for the Middle Eastern slave trade. He points out as well that it was the fittest who were deported, and quotes an anonymous order of 1760 to the slave traders for men 'without wrinkled skin, dangling wizened testicles, narrow chests, staring eyes, or imbecile expression' and women without 'protruding nipples or flabby breasts'. In his second article, Ki Zerbo evokes the grandeur of the Soudanese empires, and describes the 'gold rush across the Sahara by a motley horde led by avaricious and ignorant Spanish renegades' which brought the Songhai empire to an end. He underlines the brutality of the European conquest and quotes General Dubosc's *Épopée coloniale*, as well as others, in support. (In a footnote he gives the evidence of a missionary on the appalling atrocities committed in the Belgian Congo. Similarly, Sithole draws on a European's account of the horrifying condition of Negroes requisitioned by the Belgians as bearers. International denunciation of these, and worse, excesses compelled Leopold II to send out a commission of enquiry.* In Fily Dabo Sissoko's book, *Savane rouge*, there are several terrible pages on the repression of a

* An Englishman, E. D. Morel, was among the first to arouse public opinion in Europe, and in Britain in particular, against the methods of the Belgian administration in the Congo. He founded the Congo Reform Association, which, in 1903, launched a vigorous campaign of protest. The novelist Joseph Conrad came back from a stay in the Congo in 1890 and gave a moving description of the atmosphere there in his *Heart of Darkness*. In *Congo Disaster*, Colin Legum puts forward the hypothesis that Conrad was thinking of Leopold II when he created Kurtz, the schizophrenic hero of the novel. Kurtz represented a leading company engaged in the ivory trade and combined a brutal attitude towards the Negroes with professions of faith in the civilising mission of the white man.

Tuareg rising during the first world war, and the no less painful measures taken by the French authorities afterwards.)

From this outline of several centuries of African history, Ki Zerbo draws the following conclusions: the theory that the present backward state of Africa springs from its centuries-old isolation, a result of its geographical position, is false. The reason, on the contrary, is historical: 'ever since the fifteenth century men of prey, the thieving scum of the ports of Europe and the Maghreb, often themselves under sentence of death, have accosted the Negro peoples with the sole aim of destruction and depredation for base commercial gain'.

Caste and class

In another of his books, *L'Afrique noire pré-coloniale*, Sheikh Anta Diop studies the great medieval empires of the Soudan. A careful analysis of the *Tarikh al Fettash* and *Tarikh es Sudan* has enabled him to show the level of economic development in Africa south of the Sahara at that period. Not only had money replaced barter, but the sovereigns of these realms were minting their own coins (according to the *Tarikh es Sudan*, Askia Daud was the first to commission coin depositories). There was a monetary exchange at Timbuktu (the *Tarikh es Sudan* mentions that the poverty resulting from the Moroccan occupation brought the exchange rate down to 500 cowries), and credit in the form of notes-of-hand was also known. (Ibn Haukal mentions a written IOU for 40,000 dinars from an inhabitant of Sijilmasa to one from Awdaghost. This represented a miktal of gold, the miktal being a unit of measure corresponding to about 4.5 grammes of gold dust.)[37]

However, the book is primarily a vast comparative study, rather more sociological than historical, of medieval African institutions and those of medieval Europe, of ancient Greece and Rome, and also of India. The author's object is to explain why the evolution of Africa, which knew a brilliant civilisation at the time of the Soudanese empires, should have come to an end and been overtaken by Europe. African historians had already attributed this backwardness to two causes: the geographic isolation of the continent (the desert barrier of the Sahara and the surf barrier which kept ships away for so long), and the demographic drain of the slave trade. Sheikh Anta Diop, from his analysis of the structure of African society, adds a third reason. Africa was spared revolutions because all social classes enjoyed a tolerable existence, including even the least fortunate, such as the slaves. This very stability led to stagnation and explains African technological backwardness. To put it in a nutshell: progress and revolution are synonymous for the Senegalese historian. For lack of social upheaval, Africa before the conquest did not develop.

Diop remarks that, in Africa, all castes—including slaves—were associated with power. Thus in the Mossi country, although power was hereditary, it was not automatically transmitted from father to son. The emperor must belong to the family of the Moro Naba but he was chosen from among the possible candidates by a college of dignitaries presided over by the prime minister. The latter was not noble: he must come from the people. The chief of cavalry also was always a member of one of three ordinary Mossi families. Diop adds the following comment:

> So the ministers who assisted the emperor, instead of coming from the aristocracy, were systematically chosen outside this class, from among the proletariat and slaves. . . . Such was the spirit of this constitution. To grasp its full originality, one must imagine that in the middle ages in the West (1352-3 was the date of Ibn Batuta's voyage to the Soudan, the time of the Hundred Years' War) the king of France or England—not just some provincial lord—chose to share his power, electively, with country serfs tied to the soil, free peasants, town craftsmen organised in guilds, and merchants. . . . Neither the middle classes nor the peasants in the West would have had the revolutionary virulence which has characterised them in the past, and the history of Western Europe would probably have been quite different. The non-absolute character of the [Mossi] monarchy is shown by the fact that ministers, once invested, could not be dismissed by the king.[38]

Regulations concerning landed property also led, according to Diop to different developments in Aryan and African societies. In Rome, ancient Greece and India, landed property was exalted for religious, reasons, and the proletariat and untouchables were excluded from it:

> Exalting property is an Aryan custom: in Rome, Greece and India it led to the rejection from society of a whole category of people without family, hearth or home, and without the right of possession. Everywhere they made up a poverty-stricken class which could only aspire to riches with the advent of money, that profane wealth not foreseen in the traditional and sacred laws regulating possession which

> the Aryans' forebears had drawn up. It is through the desire for possessions and material wealth that the genius of the Aryan race imposed its stamp on the caste system.[39]

To illustrate his proposition, Diop recalls the 'laws of Manu' in India, which define minutely the objects which each caste may possess. In Rome and in Greece, there were strict links between the ancestor cult and landed property, which was reserved for the well-born and the patricians. But in Africa, says Diop, 'restrictions . . . never concern material goods'.

> On the contrary, one can be sure that each time this is so, the opportunities for enrichment for members of the designated categories are enhanced, since—by some sort of spirit of compensation and sense of justice immanent in society—not only may they keep all their belongings but even increase them by 'demanding' those of others.[40] . . . [The result is that] the social system of castes gives more permanence and stability to society than the class system created by the Aryans in Greece and Rome.[41]

This class system is one of the factors of social upheaval unknown in Africa. 'The underlying causes of the transformations and revolutions in ancient society should be sought in this alienation without compensation of the proletariat, which had become numerically the preponderant section of the populace. This was the opposite to the golden rule of African societies.'[42] The author adds that Fustel de Coulanges also sees 'in the entry of this lower class into the city' a 'revolution which dominated the history of Greece and Italy from the seventh to the fifth centuries BC'.[43]

Then Diop lists the 'accidents of European history which led to systematic expropriation of the peasants'.[44] First there was the emergence of the feudal system of land ownership in the middle ages under the threat of the Nordic invasion. The peasant handed his land to the lord in exchange for protection. Later came the end of land tenure by free peasants; their arable holdings were expropriated by the nobility for sheep-rearing following the development of the wool industry. These despoiled peasants became the urban proletariat. From that time on, says Diop (who is following Marx's analysis throughout the whole of this part of his book), 'the situation was ripe for the birth of capitalism'.[45]

Nothing like this happened in black Africa: 'The king and the local lordling knew that they had slaves and reigned over a whole country whose extent was well known to them and whose inhabitants paid a fixed tax. But they had no feeling of owning the land. The position of the African peasant was therefore diametrically opposed to that of the European serf, tied to the soil and belonging, with the land he cultivated, to an overlord.'[46] Further on, he adds: 'Expropriation of land such as took place in Europe from the sixteenth century would have been inconceivable in precolonial Africa.'[47]

Hence, African economic life remained at the craftsman stage, guaranteed by the caste system, and tied to an agricultural economy. In this preface, Diop asserts that his study enables one

> no longer to be surprised by the stagnation, or rather the relatively stable balance, of precolonial African societies. As this analysis of politico-social structures reveals the stability factors of African society, backwardness in technical and other spheres can be seen as the result of a different evolution, springing from completely objective basic causes. So there is no longer any need to be embarrassed about it.

Ahmadou Hampaté Ba's "L'Empire peul du Macina" and Ibrahima-Mamadou Ouane's *L'Énigme du Macina* cover a more limited field than the works of Sheikh Anta Diop and Charles de Graft-Johnson. Both recall the life of al-Hajj Umar and the fight of the Tukuler, led by the great muslim warrior—later overthrown by the French, aided by the Fulani of Massina whom he had subjugated. Hampaté Ba, who is Fulani, traces the history of the reigns of the Massina kings, Cheikou Amadou and his son.

Ouane, who is a direct descendant of al-Hajj Umar, combines historical account, general opinions on French colonisation and a personal appeal. He was, in fact, deported to the Sahara by the French authorities under the Vichy government. There, he says, 'I worked under the whiplash and baton blows on a starvation diet'.[48] Although he was rehabilitated in 1949, he was still refused the right to open a Koranic school and was not readmitted into the French colonial administration. But his bitter memories and demand for reinstatement at the time when he wrote his book (it appeared in 1952) have not prevented his frequent assertions of affection for France. This is no blind admiration, however: Ouane is critical too. He particularly resents the fact that Negroes who fought for France are not treated as free men.[49] In his preface he says: 'Africa must not become a pallid imitation of

France; it must rise with the help of France.' All the same, he dedicates his book to Aguibou, younger son of al-Hajj Umar, who elected to fight at the side of Archinard against his older brother Ahmadou. This dedication is doubtless allied to his defence of chieftainship which occupies several pages of the book. The book should also be read in the context of relations between Fulani and Tukuler; it seems likely that the author's insistence on the common Egyptian origin and close relationship of the two peoples stems from a desire to reconcile victor and vanquished.

The hero cult

Arbab Djama Babikir's book, *L'Empire de Rabeh*, is primarily an enthusiastic biography of the Negro chief of Chad, who was defeated by the French in 1904. Not only does Babikir consider that 'in the history of the continent Rabeh will rank among the most illustrious leaders'[50] but he also asserts that his hero was a reformer with strict moral standards. He 'ardently desired to put a stop to the licence of the times' and 'banned alcohol';[51] finally he 'led the most simple life, an affectionate father and helpful friend'.[52] This is a rather different portrait from that drawn by the French official, Bretonnet, reviewing his troops before the battle of Kousseri in 1899, and reported by Babikir: 'This petty chieftain Rabeh . . . is a common slave trafficker whom M. Gentil created for his own glory, just as de Brazza invented Makoko.'[53] Babikir's book is symptomatic of one of the most characteristic features of the role undertaken by African historians: the rehabilitation of African chiefs who led the resistance to the European conquest.

Fily Dabo Sissoko paints a glowing portrait of al-Hajj Umar in *Les Noirs et la culture:* 'I should go so far as to say that al-Hajj Umar, like Hannibal, was a giant among men. Like Hannibal he possessed to a supreme degree a will of iron, unshakeably set on a specific goal: the propagation of a religious doctrine [tidjanism] and the founding of a state to this end.'[54] Abdoulaye Wade, for his part, not only endows these chiefs with military skill and patriotic virtues; he also sees them as 'politicians', fired with the ideal of African unity which was prevented only by colonisation.[55]

This exaltation of the African hero has been most clearly manifested in the field of literature. Shaka, a Zulu conqueror of the nineteenth century, stands out among these heroes; he seems to have exerted a real fascination on several African writers. The first to have devoted a book to Shaka was the South African writer, Thomas Mofolo. His book has been translated from Sesotho into English, French and German. It is well known that Shaka was a pitiless chief, and Pastor V. Ellenberger, who translated the book into French, sees in his fate 'the story of a human passion, an uncontrolled and then uncontrollable ambition which grew and developed fatally, as though fanned by some implacable Nemesis. Gradually it enveloped the whole personality, consuming all before it, until it led to the moral destruction of the character and inevitable punishment.'[56] Mofolo, a fervent christian, saw the tragic death of Shaka, assassinated by his brothers who were weary of tyranny, as a just punishment for his sins and paganism.

This paganism is personified by the witch-doctor Isanusi, who teaches him, from his adolescence, the magic formulae of power. Shaka becomes a great chief, extending his power over tribes and territories. He marries the beautiful Noliwe and this is the period of reforms which make him a loved and respected sovereign, founder of a new nation, the Zulus, 'people of heaven', forged from the tribes he had subjugated and unified. But the thirst for power was stronger. Neither love nor pity can have any place in the warrior's heart. Isanusi, the soothsayer who had taught him the first secrets of success, reappears and summons Shaka to choose: 'Which dost thou choose—Noliwe or absolute power?' And Shaka answers, 'Absolute power.'[57] The witch-doctor's face lights up. Shaka is of the stuff of heroes whom nothing will stop. Isanusi can confide to him the last magic formulae of omnipotence. Then Shaka plunges into a welter of blood and death: he kills Noliwe and his mother; then, suspecting his warriors, makes one regiment annihilate another. Like Caesar, he dies without attempting to defend himself, from the assegai thrusts of his brothers. But before breathing his last, he hurls this curse at them: 'It is your hope that by killing me ye will become chiefs when I am dead. But ye are deluded; it will not be so, for the Umlungu [white man] will come and it is he who will rule, and ye will be his bondmen.'[58] In spite of this welter of blood—and here perhaps is Mofolo's greatest strength—the character of Shaka remains fascinating throughout. To such an extent, indeed, that according to Jahn, the missionaries who employed Mofolo refused for many years to publish his manuscript for fear of awakening the flicker of some unknown pagan response. Mofolo had to wait twenty years for his book to be published.[59]

Senghor sees Shaka as a forerunner of African unity, a visionary who wanted to prepare for the fight against the white invader. Noliwe's murder is the decisive test: henceforth Shaka will be pitiless and the unity of the nation will be steeped in blood. Senghor's dramatic poem is dedicated to the 'Bantu martyrs of South Africa'. He begins with a charge levelled by a 'white voice':

Chaka, te voilà comme la panthère ou l'hyène à-la-mauvaise-gueule
A la terre clouée par trois sagaies, promis au néant vagissant.
Te voilà donc à ta passion. Ce fleuve de sang qui te baigne, qu'il te soit pénitence.

(There you lie, Shaka, like the panther or the evil-mouthed hyena, nailed to the ground by three assegais, promised to the wailing emptiness. There you are then at your passion. May this river of blood which bathes you be a penitence for you.)

Shaka answers first for the murder of Noliwe:

Je l'ai tuée, oui! d'une main sans tremblement
Un éclair d'acier fin dans le buisson odorant de l'aisselle . . .
Je ne l'aurais pas tuée si moins aimée.
Il fallait échapper au doute
A l'ivresse du lait de sa bouche, au tam-tam lancinant de la nuit de mon sang
A mes entrailles de laves ferventes, aux mines d'uranium de mon cœur dans les abîmes de ma Négritude
A mon amour à Noliwé
Pour l'amour de mon Peuple noir.

(Yes, I killed her. With a steady hand, a flash of fine steel in the scented bush of her armpit. I should not have killed her had I loved her less. I had to escape from the doubt, from the inebriating milk of her mouth, and the fierce thudding of the night of my blood in my loins of boiling lava, from the uranium mine of my heart in the depths of my blackness, from my love for Noliwe to love of my black people.)

Then the white voice replies:

Ma parole Chaka tu es poète . . . ou beau parleur . . . un politicien!

(On my faith, Shaka, you are a poet . . . a fine speaker anyway . . . a politician.)

And Shaka replies:

Des courriers m'avaient dit:
'Ils débarquent avec des règles, des équerres, des compas, des sextants
'L'épiderme blanc, les yeux clairs, la parole nue et la bouche mince
'Le tonnerre sur leurs navires.'
Je devins une tête, un bras san tremblement, ni guerrier ni boucher.
Un politique tu l'as dit—je tuai le poète—un homme d'action seul
Un homme seul et déjà mort avant les autres, comme ceux que tu plains.
Qui saura ma passion? . . .
Je voyais dans un songe tous les pays aux quatre coins de l'horizon soumis à la règle, à l'équerre et au compas
Les forts fauchés les collines anéanties, vallons et fleuves dans les fers.
Je voyais les pays aux quatre coins de l'horizon sous la grille tracée par les doubles routes de fer
Je voyais les peuples du Sud comme une fourmilière de silence
Au travail. Le travail est saint, mais le travail n'est plus le geste
Le tam-tam ni la voix ne rythment plus les gestes des saisons.
Peuples du Sud dans les chantiers, les ports, les mines, les manufactures
Et le soir ségrégés dans les kraals de la misère.
Et les peuples entassent des montagnes d'or noir, d'or rouge—et ils crèvent de faim.
Et je vis un matin, sortant de la brume de l'aube, la forêt des têtes laineuses
Les bras fanés le ventre cave, des yeux et des lèvres immenses appelant un dieu impossible.
Pouvais-je rester sourd à tant de souffrances bafouées? . . .

(Messengers had told me: 'They land with ruler, set-square, compass, and sextant; men of white skin, light eyes, naked word and narrow lips, with thunder on their ships.' I became a head, a steady arm, neither warrior nor butcher. A politician you have said—I killed the poet—a man of action alone, a man alone and already dead before the others, like those you pity. Who can know my passion? . . . In a dream I saw all the lands to the four corners of the horizon subjected to the ruler, the set-square and the compass, their forts destroyed, their hills flattened, valleys and rivers in chains. I saw the lands to the four corners of the horizon beneath the grid of the twin tracks of iron, I saw the people of the South like a silent ant-heap at work. Work is sacred, but work is no longer a gesture, drum and voice no longer intone the songs of the seasons. People of the South in the yards, ports, mines and factories, in the evening segregated into kraals of misery. And the people were piling up mountains of black gold and red gold—and they died of hunger themselves. I saw one morning, rising from the mists of dawn, the forest of woolly heads, withered arms and hollow bellies, immense eyes and lips calling on an impossible God. Could I turn a deaf ear to so much flouted suffering? . . .)[60]

Mofolo and Senghor are not the only African writers to have been inspired by Shaka, the 'black Napoleon of South Africa', as Sithole from Rhodesia calls him in *African Nationalism*.[61] An English-speaking South African writer, H. I. E. Dhlomo, has written a *Shaka* for the theatre. Recently Seydou Badian Couyaté, a minister in Mali, also wrote a play about the Zulu conqueror. A rehabilitation of Shaka is the symptomatic opening of *Let My People Go* by Chief Albert Luthuli, leader of the African National Congress in the Republic of South Africa. Nevertheless there is one discordant note in this chorus of praise: the black South African, S. M. Molema, in *Bantu Past and Present* rates Shaka as just another Attila.[62]

Africans seem to have made drama their first choice in their efforts to reawaken the memory of their heroes. Thus, Anatole Coyssi from Dahomey has evoked the legendary figure of the famous princess Ahouili-Ponouwa in "La Honte plus meurtrière que le couteau". Her witticisms have become proverbial and are still remembered by the Fons today. Plays by students of the William Ponty School at Dakar—attended by many present-day African leaders such as Hamani Diori and Modibo Keita, presidents of Niger and Mali respectively—have often taken as their protagonists African historical figures such as Sundiata or the *damels* (kings) of the Cayor in Senegal. This African theatre experiment was mainly due to the initiative of one of the pre-war directors of the high school, Charles Béart. For end-of-the-year celebrations students were encouraged to write and perform plays based on the folklore or history of their own countries. The William Ponty theatre reached its heyday with the 1937 production at the Champs-Élysées Theatre in Paris of *Sokamé*, a collective work by students from Dahomey, which tells the story of an African Iphigenia.

These legendary heroes are evoked by the poets clearly as an example and a call to action. For instance, E. E. Yondo in *Lève-toi*:

Quel est ton nom
Qui es-tu
Serais-tu
Ce cavalier à la monture de feu

Dont l'ombre victorieuse
Hanta hier
Les flancs des volcans en éruption
Comme un monstre sacré
Qui es-tu si ce n'est
Ce grand combattant qui s'ignore
Toi ce fier guerrier
Petit-fils de Priso-Priso
De la lignée des Samory
Qui luttèrent dent contre dent
Souffle contre souffle
Durant des saisons
Pour arracher l'Afrique maternelle
Au vent d'étincelles du brasier
Et à la caravane des razzieurs. . . .

(What is your name? Who are you? Can you be that knight with the fiery steed whose victorious ghost yesterday haunted the flanks of erupting volcanoes like some sacred monster? Who are you if not that great fighter who is unaware of himself; you the proud warrior, grandson of Priso-Priso of the line of the Samory who fought tooth and nail during many seasons to wrest Africa, their homeland, from the blast of the furnace, and from the raiders' caravan?)[63]

The great figures of contemporary African nationalism will soon have their chroniclers too. Pierre Bamboté has dedicated his *Chant funèbre pour un héros d'Afrique* to Patrice Lumumba, the Congolese prime minister assassinated in Katanga. This long poem in free verse is a passionate denunciation of colonialism. It is punctuated with passages from Vigné d'Octon's book, *La Gloire du sabre*, written in 1900, in which the French member of parliament told with indignation of the brutality of military expeditions to Africa.

Several Negro authors have felt the need to recall their famous men, in retort to the contempt with which their race has been treated. In the Gold Coast in 1905, Attoh Ahuma drew on Wilson Armistead in praise of West African intellectuals like Cugoana and Amo. His book *Memoirs of West African Celebrities* was intended, in his own words, 'to awaken a passionate patriotism in the breasts of our fellow-countrymen'.[64] Some thirty years earlier, James Africanus Horton from Sierre Leone had used the same sources for *A Vindication of the African Race*, his attack on the dogma of the fundamental inferiority of Negroes. Fily Dabo Sissoko proudly recalls Aesop and the two Dumas;[65] de Graft-Johnson gives a portrait of the legendary Negro general who served under Peter the Great in Russia—one of Pushkin's ancestors;[66] and Mbonu Ojike, in an appendix to *My Africa*, gives a list of great Negroes (among whom Shaka occupies a prominent position) which he calls an *African Who's Who*. Before him, the great American Negro intellectual, W. E. B. DuBois, had published an *Encyclopedia of the Negro*, giving the names of white defenders of the black race, such as the Abbé Grégoire, side by side with famous Negroes. An original expression of the African hero cult, which is also interesting with regard to the history of the press, was the strip cartoon of the legend of Sundiata which appeared some years ago in *L'Essor*, organ of the governing party of Mali.

Not all works of African historians are marked with the same nationalist ardour as those of Sheikh Anta Diop and Charles de Graft-Johnson. Paul Hazoumé's historical novel *Doguicimi*, which relates episodes of an expedition by the kings of Abomey against the Mahi tribe by way of the adventures of a Dahomeyan princess, finishes in fact on a note of homage to France. Addressing himself to his heroine, the author ends with these words:

> Doguicimi, I have imagined also that when the European delegation was received at the court of Guezo you looked forward to the arrival of the *Zojagués* [French]. They would have seemed to you to have the qualities necessary to put an end to the incessant wars of the kings of Dahomey, the black slave trade and human sacrifices which were ruining the country rather than enriching it. The elders assure us that the dead take an interest in all that happens in this world. No doubt then you are happy to see that where the diplomacy of the *Glincis* [English] was ineffectual, the French flag, a century and a half later, was destined to succeed fully: that it has brought peace, freedom and humanity to Dahomey.[67]

Babikir also in his foreword addresses 'the homage of [his] ardent gratitude and the expression of [his] loyal devotion to chivalrous and magnanimous France'.

African politicians have not been unaware of this picture of Africa which the historians have been elaborating. On the contrary, it has been a direct source of inspiration for many of them. As early as 1937,

Nnamdi Azikiwe, future president of the Republic of Nigeria, wrote in *Renascent Africa*:

> Educate the renascent African to be a man. Tell him that he has made definite contributions to history. Educate him to appreciate the fact that iron was discovered by Africans, that the conception of God was initiated by Africans, that Africans ruled the world from 765 to 713 BC, that while Europe slumbered during the 'dark ages', a great civilisation flourished on the banks of the Niger, extending from the salt mines of Therghazza in Morocco to lake Tchad . . . narrate to him the lore of Ethiopia, of Ghana, Melle, Mellestine, Songhay. Let him relish with the rest of the world that, while Oxford and Cambridge were in their inchoate stages, the university of Sankore, in Timbuctoo, welcomed 'scholars and learned men from all over the moslem world', as Sir Percy puts it.[68]

Even earlier than this J. E. Casely-Hayford, one of the greatest figures of African nationalism in the Gold Coast, had specifically demanded in 1911, in *Ethiopia Unbound*, the creation of a Gold Coast university with a chair of African history. He added: 'The kind of history that I would teach would be a universal history with particular reference to the part Ethiopia has played in the affairs of the world. . . . Africa was the cradle of the world's systems and philosophies, and the nursing mother of its religions.'[69]

The motion for independence presented by Nkrumah to the Gold Coast Legislative Assembly in 1953, now known in Ghana as the 'motion of destiny', also contained an historical résumé:

> In the very early days of the Christian era, long before England had assumed any importance, long even before her people had united into a nation, our ancestors had attained a great empire, which lasted until the eleventh century, when it fell before the attacks of the Moors of the North. At its height that empire stretched from Timbuctoo to Bamako, and even as far as to the Atlantic. It is said that lawyers and scholars were much respected in that empire and that the inhabitants of Ghana wore garments of wool, cotton, silk and velvet. There was trade in copper, gold and textile fabrics, and jewels and weapons of gold and silver were carried. Thus may we take pride in the name of Ghana, not out of romanticism, but as an inspiration for the future.[70]

A few days before Guinea's independence in 1958, Sékou Touré recalled the greatness of the medieval empires of Africa. The future first president of the Republic of Guinea quoted several passages from Al Bekri and the *Tarikh al Fettash*, and stressed European scorn for African history; he concluded: 'In this way a terrible inferiority complex was systematically instilled into the colonised peoples. The colonisers were given a superiority complex which led them to despise and even hate the men whom their ancestors were alleged to have dragged from a barbaric state, and to consider as unpardonable ingratitude the slightest pretension to any dignity whatsoever on their part.'[71]

Today the ancient names of Ghana* and Mali have reappeared on the map of Africa, and Rhodesian African nationalists have given their party the name of the famous ruins of the ancient mysterious capital of Zimbabwe. So, in the words of the Somali poet Syad, African politicians also have:

une oreille penchée
vers des siècles somnolents
sur le chemin obscur des temps

(one ear bent to the sleeping centuries along the dark road of time).[72]

* It was Dr Danquah, ethnologist and political opponent of Nkrumah, who first thought of giving the name of Ghana to the Gold Coast, several years before its independence.

5

THE RETURN REVIEWED

THE LESSON to be learnt from this survey of the works of African ethnologists, novelists of the soil and historians is self-evident: all of them have sought to give back to Africa a pride in its past, to assert the value of African cultures, and to reject a cultural assimilation which would have suffocated the Negro personality. Perhaps no one has summarised these objectives more clearly than Césaire in his speech to the first Congress of Negro Writers and Artists when he recalled the history of the colonisation of Hawaii:

> Some years after Cook's discovery of these islands, the king died and was succeeded by a young man, Prince Kamehamela II. Influenced by European ideas, the young prince decided to abolish the ancestral religion. It was agreed between the new king and the high priest that a great festival would be arranged during which the taboo would be solemnly broken and the ancestral gods destroyed. On the day arranged, at a sign from the king, the high priest threw himself on the images of the god, trod them underfoot and smashed them, while a great cry went up from the people: 'The taboo is broken.' Naturally several years later the Hawaiians welcomed the christian missionaries with open arms. . . . The rest is well known. It is part of history. In any case this is the simplest and most thorough example which we know of cultural subversion preceding subjugation. I ask you then, is it such a renunciation by a people of its past and its culture which is wanted of us? I tell you flatly, there is no Kamehamela II among us![1]

Although Césaire's rejection of cultural assimilation coincides with that of the other writers whom we have just studied, their ways diverge in their justification of this. Césaire had assumed and categorically stated the Negro's lack of technical skill in his *Cahier d'un retour au pays natal*:

> *Ceux qui n'ont inventé ni la poudre ni la boussole*
> *ceux qui n'ont jamais su dompter la vapeur ni l'électricité*
> *ceux qui n'ont exploré ni les mers ni le ciel*
> *mais ils savent en ses moindres recoins le pays de souffrance*
> *ceux qui n'ont connu de voyages que de déracinements*

ceux qui se sont assouplis aux agenouillements
ceux qu'on domestiqua et christianisa
ceux qu'on inocula d'abâtardissement . . .

(They who invented neither powder nor compass, they who could never control steam or electricity, they who explored neither seas nor sky, but who know the remotest corners of the land of suffering; they who have travelled only when driven from their homes, they whose exercise has been grovelling, they who were domesticated and christianised and infected with degeneracy. . . .)[2]

African intellectuals were not content with the glorious humility of the West Indian poet. Pride in their past is to be their first weapon. Their reasoning has been: if the coloniser bases his rights of conquest principally on a civilising mission, dogmatically presupposing the Negro's cultural inferiority, then he must be fought on his own ground and shown that the Negro is in no way his intellectual inferior. This is the underlying theme of all African research in the fields of ethnology and history, as well as of the efforts to revive her oral literature. The pilgrimage back to the origins of African culture is often just another aspect of the fight for independence.

The development of the work of Negro intellectuals can be summarised as a kind of dialectic progression: the first step was to show the equal worth of African and European civilisations; the second was to determine a difference of essence between the two civilisations; the third is the rejection of assimilation. They begin by showing that, as in Europe, African society was democratic; that African religion is dominated by a belief in one God, the creator and omnipotent; that African folklore is the expression of a rich oral literature; and that the African empires of the middle ages were no less grand than those of Europe at that time. They then go on to discover that African society is communal (as opposed to Europe's individualism); that the literary tradition of Africa is diametrically opposed to the Aryan tragedy; and that the African caste system has not produced the class warfare of the classical city states and India. Hence, any policy of assimilation is based on false premises.

This refusal of assimilation does not, however, signify that African intellectuals intend to follow a narrow isolationist path; this, they consider, would be an impoverishment. Senghor, in particular, convinced as he is of the need to return to Negro roots, is all the same a keen advocate of a mixture of cultures. At the Paris Congress he said:

'I also think that all the great civilisations resulted from miscegenation—objectively speaking: take the Indian, Greek, French civilisations, etc. In my view, and objectively, this cross-breeding is necessary. It springs from the contact between civilisations.'[3]*

It was in the field of education that the African intellectuals' quarrel with the policy of assimilation was destined to break out. Sékou Touré, to take one example, criticised French education in Africa very severely in his message to the Rome Congress: 'Our textbooks in colonial schools teach of the wars of the Gauls, Joan of Arc or Napoleon, the departments of France, the poems of Lamartine and the plays of Molière, just as if Africa had no history, past, geography or culture. . . . Our pupils are praised only for their aptitude at this wholesale cultural assimilation.'[4] Today the boot is on the other foot. In the independent countries of Africa, textbooks are appearing conforming to the aspirations of African nationalism, or simply just to an African viewpoint. Djibril Tamsir Niane, in collaboration with Suret-Canale, has written an *Histoire de l'Afrique occidentale*, Assoi Adiko an *Histoire des peuples noirs*, and Andrée Justin has edited an *Anthologie africaine des écrivains noirs d'expression française*. The next generation in Africa will undoubtedly know more of the reign of Sundiata than of Charlemagne, more of Senghor's poetry than Verlaine's. They will have learnt in advance in the classroom how to reply to their detractors who stick to the stereotyped view, expressed in the past by Lope de Vega, of the Negro as being just good enough to dance.†

* Senghor's view is not accepted unanimously. Thomas Mélone takes him to task for it in no mean fashion in the conclusion to his study, *Le Négritude dans la littérature négro-africaine*: 'Senghor has defined negritude as the "cross roads of give and take". He has even compared Eurafrica—an osmosis of Negro and western civilisations—with "a concert where Europe is the conductor and Africa the drummer". This modest study will have served to show up the ambiguity and deception hidden in this double assertion. We can state historically that in the career of the African Negro there was never any "sense of giving"; that had been systematically inhibited by the activities of the colonial powers.' (p. 129.)

† Senghor himself has said: 'We are the dancing peoples . . .' He obviously was not giving a pejorative meaning to the statement, unlike the Spanish playwright who uses an ironical Spanish Pidgin in his *Canto de los negros*. The Senegalese poet is merely stressing the sense of rhythm, excitability and intuitive understanding of nature, which he considers special gifts of the black race. This analysis of the Negro character has at times earned Senghor the reproach of his compatriots. Professor Busia, for instance, opposes Senghor's definition of negritude according to which 'emotion is Negro'. The Ghanaian author considers that this cannot be taken as the privilege of the black race alone (*The Challenge of Africa*, p. 45). But as early as the eighteenth century Gustavus Vassa had written: 'We are a nation of dancers, musicians and poets.'

PART TWO

REVOLT

I cry you mercy, then:
I took you for that cunning whore of Venice
That married with Othello.

6

THE POLITICAL KINGDOM

'Seek ye first the political kingdom.' This parody of Christ's injunction is by Kwame Nkrumah, leader of the Convention People's Party which led the Gold Coast to independence under the name of Ghana. It defined their goal. Their method was generally to become more and more demanding as the reforms conceded by the colonial power followed each other helter-skelter under the increasingly rapid pressure of events. In this context, 'reformism' became one of the main targets of African nationalism. Nkrumah issued a warning against the 'reformist' danger to the militant elements of the Convention People's Party on the morrow of the 1951 constitutional reform: 'There must be no fraternisation between our Party members in the Executive Council and the European officials, except on purely official relations, for what imperialists have failed to achieve by strong-arm methods, they will hope to bring off by cocktail parties.'[1]

The succession of constitutional stages through which the Gold Coast and Nigeria went before reaching independence parallels—and was almost as rapid as—the evolution of the former French territories: French empire, the 1946 constitution and the French Union, the *loi-cadre* of 1956 which offered a sort of autonomy to overseas territories, the constitution of 1958 which established the French Community, and the Act of June 4, 1960—now fallen into disuse—which instituted the so-called renewed Community. In Nigeria there was a series of constitutions, each bearing the name of a governor or minister: the Clifford Constitutions of 1922, the Richards Constitution of 1946, the Macpherson Constitution of 1951, and the Lyttelton Constitution of 1954. There followed the granting of autonomy to the three regions and, finally, of independence in 1960.[2] In the Gold Coast, the first reform of the Legislative Council came in 1925; further reforms were implemented during the second world war, in 1942. Then came the Burns Constitution of 1946, to be followed in 1951 with a reorganisation of the Executive Council, on which three senior British officials still sat as ex officio members. In 1954 parliamentary government was introduced, though the conduct of foreign affairs and of defence was still in the hands of the governor-general as the Crown's representative. Finally, in 1957, the Gold Coast colony became independent Ghana, a self-governing and sovereign member of the Commonwealth; the last traces of theoretical control by the Crown were soon to disappear with the proclamation of the Ghanaian Republic.

The pace of political developments quickened considerably thereafter in the other English-speaking African territories. It pressed forward at such a rate that Lancaster House in London, where Commonwealth constitutional conferences are held, was hardly ever empty. The proceedings of these long-drawn-out meetings have by now acquired their own 'ritual'. The minority report of a royal commission of enquiry; the walk-out by representatives of the party not content with the way things are going; protests by minority groups not granted the right to participate—these have now become routine matters for officials of the Colonial and Commonwealth Relations Offices.

The criticisms which have inevitably accompanied the reforms, both in French-speaking and English-speaking Africa, have found their basis and background in condemnation of the principle of colonialism. For those dissatisfied with any new reform introduced, this condemnation is still valid, since the new ruling will not in any way have affected the basic problem. And, when independence comes, there are still the sequels of colonisation to eliminate—among other things, the military bases of the former colonial power—and the dangers of neocolonialism to avoid, in particular the control resulting from economic and financial aid treaties. A tiresome procedure, Europeans may say: necessary vigilance, Africans will reply.

Nnamdi Azikiwe had already condemned the very concept of colonialism in 1937 in his *Renascent Africa*. In the struggle between the 'haves' (the powers who acquired colonies) and the 'have-nots' (those who were left out of the division of Africa), wrote Azikiwe in his preface, the Africans 'constitute an extraneous element, so far as European imperialism is concerned. The raw materials [of Africa] mean more to Europe than their existence . . . their manpower seems only valuable for the machinery of European imperialism and militarism.' And he asserted that 'the indigenous black Africans are not destined to accept the old idea of imperialism . . . that the twentieth-century African is bound to be renascent, and that this renascent Africa must be reckoned with as a concrescent factor of the world'. Nkrumah took a no less categorical position of principle in *Towards Colonial Freedom*, when he replied to a speech by the then secretary of state for the Colonies, Oliver Stanley, who had affirmed that British presence alone prevented 'disastrous disintegration in her colonies'.

> But it is the same supposedly altruistic 'British presence' that in 1929 mowed down by machine-gun fire poor defenceless Nigerian women for peacefully and harmlessly protesting against excessive taxation. . . . Indeed, it is 'British presence' that has compelled poor African workers to toil day in and day out in mines and on plantations for a mere pittance of ninepence (18 cents) a day of over ten working hours. It is 'British presence' that has persecuted and jailed and deported colonial labour leaders, only for having dared to organise labour in the colonies. It is 'British presence' that has brought war, oppression, poverty and disease and perpetuated mass illiteracy upon colonial peoples. It is 'British presence' that bleeds them white by brutal exploitation in order to feed the 'British lion' with red meat. These are the achievements of 'British presence' in the colonies. This is the 'disintegration' which 'British presence' is nobly preventing in the colonies.[3]

Césaire was no less trenchant in his famous *Discours sur le colonialisme:*

> Colonisation and civilisation? The commonest curse is to be the trusting dupe of a collective hypocrisy, highly skilled in mis-stating problems to legitimise the odious solutions which are being found for them. This brings us back to the point that the essential thing here is to see clearly, to think clearly—that is, dangerously—to reply clearly to the innocent initial question: What is colonisation in principle? We must agree on what it is not: neither evangelism nor a philanthropic undertaking, neither a desire to roll back the frontiers of ignorance, sickness or tyranny, nor the extension of the word of God or of law. It must be admitted once and for all, without flinching at the consequences, that the decisive action here is that of the adventurer and the pirate, the wholesale grocer and the armourer, the gold digger and the merchant, greed and force, and following them the baleful shadow cast by a form of civilisation which, at a moment in history, found itself obliged for internal reasons to give its antagonistic economies world-wide rein for their rivalry.

When Sékou Touré had to choose between the 'Yes' and 'No' of General de Gaulle's overseas referendum in 1958, he referred to this text, which had become one of the classics of the French-speaking

African intelligentsia. And he went on: 'Césaire's clear, precise argument is irrefutable. It leads us naturally to ask the question: Is decolonisation historically possible? Certainly this neologism on the lips of armchair, left-wing Europeans hides a dangerous deception.'[4]

A statue to Hitler

Naturally, nationalist leaders of black Africa drew moral inspiration from the emancipation of India, the defeat of Dien-Bien-Phu, the Bandung conference, the independence of Morocco and Tunisia, Egypt's moral victory at Suez, and Mao Tse-tung's success. The Rhodesian Ndabaningi Sithole in his *African Nationalism* quotes Gamal Abdel Nasser's *Egypt's Liberation: the Philosophy of the Revolution*; Nkrumah becomes a disciple of Gandhi; Senghor refers to the Tunisian minister, Ahmed Ben Salah, in *Nation et voie africaine du socialisme*; Mao Tse-tung takes his place among African marxist writers, by the side of Lenin; and so on.

For all this, it is quite clear that it was the second world war which was the starting point for 'decolonisation' in Africa. A decisive push in this direction was given by the contributions of manpower demanded from the colonies of the time, and by the explanation that the war was a struggle against Nazi racialism. African intellectuals are perfectly well aware of this. It was expressed in the most forceful terms by Albert Tévoedjré, former editor-in-chief of *L'Étudiant d'Afrique noire* (who was charged in this capacity in 1957 with prejudicing the external security of the state), and later the secretary-general of the Afro-Malagasy Union. In *L'Afrique révoltée*, Tévoedjré writes:

> In private conversation, many Africans make no secret of the fact that, when Africa is independent, they will have to raise a monument to a man accursed in history: Hitler. Of course, such a remark may seem paradoxical or shocking, but Europeans are not perhaps sufficiently aware that the last world war meant a sharp awakening of African awareness. It opened wide the external world and made Africans very conscious of certain injustices. . . . No one can pretend any longer that they do not know, or have forgotten, the famous apostrophe of a black deputy at the French National Assembly: 'In helping you to extricate yourselves from the Hitler mess, we tasted the bread of freedom. Do not think that you can now take the taste away from us.'[5]

The same note is struck by Sithole: 'After the second world war, various movements were made by Africans to end British and French dominance in Africa. . . . You said it was wrong for Germans to rule the world. It is also wrong for the British to dominate Africans.'[6] It was, in fact, war veterans who provoked the 1948 incidents in Accra. The effect of these was far-reaching and, indeed, they can be considered one of the most important incidents in the independence movement of the Gold Coast.

The use of colonial troops in European wars, and even more that of Senegalese riflemen in the Algerian war, has been criticised by more than one African leader. The former Senegalese minister, Abdoulaye Ly, devotes a short and extremely sharp pamphlet to the position of these 'black mercenaries' as he calls them. In particular, he attacks General Mangin who appears, to him at least, the theoretician of the use of black African troops, on account of his book *La Force noire* and various articles and lectures on the same subject. Abdoulaye Ly assures us that General Mangin looks upon the Negro soldier above all 'as useful for economising in whites'.[7] All the same, it is probably not so much the involvement of black troops in the two world wars as their use in 1948 by Jules Moch, then minister of the Interior, to break communist-instigated strikes in France which rouses Abdoulaye Ly's ire. He recalls the intervention of several Negro parliamentarians on this subject. Hamani Diori, now president of the Republic of Niger, condemned this move by 'those who use Negroes for a job unworthy of our race'. Félix Tchicaya, deputy for Mid-Congo at the time, declared: 'They are soldiers who are being turned into murderers.' Ly is even more indignant at the epithet 'black gangsters' which was used at the time by the left-wing press in France, and at the description of them as 'black traitors to their class' coined by the communist deputy, André Dufour.

Sékou Touré believes that no 'colonial organism drew such a vigorous and exacting distinction between black and white as the colonial army'.[8] He is particularly indignant at the use of black forces in colonial wars after 1945: 'Just recently you have had to face situations under the French flag involving agonising questions of conscience (in Morocco, Tunisia, Vietnam and Algeria). You had to keep silent, to obey unquestioningly, to act without thinking.'[9] Léopold Sédar Senghor dedicated a collection of poems, *Hosties noires*, to the Senegalese riflemen. This is the most political of Senghor's poetic work; his indignation is expressed to the full in the *Poème liminaire:*

Vous Tirailleurs Sénégalais, mes frères noirs à la main chaude sous la glace de la mort
Qui pourra vous chanter si ce n'est votre frère d'armes, votre frère de sang?
Je ne laisserai pas la parole aux ministres, et pas aux généraux
Je ne laisserai pas—non!—les louanges de mépris vous enterrer furtivement.
Vous n'êtes pas des pauvres aux poches vides sans honneur
Mais je déchirerai les rires Banania sur tous les murs de France. . . .

(Senegalese riflemen, my black brothers whose hand is warm under the icy clutch of death, who should sing of you if not your brother in arms, your blood brother? I shall not leave it to the ministers or generals, no! I shall not allow contemptuous praise to bury you furtively. You are not the poor going empty-handed without honour; and I shall tear down the laughing Banania [advertisements] from all the walls in France.)[10]

The injustice shown to war veterans, who fell victim to racial discrimination again on their return home, was used in Northern Rhodesia by the African National Congress as one of the main themes of its propaganda during the 1950s. Kenneth Kaunda remarked in *Zambia Shall Be Free* that the story of the demobilised askari, kept out of hotels and restaurants reserved for whites only, was one of his 'most popular' subjects.[11]

One has to go back to the period between the wars to find a Negro defender of military service in the French army. The Mossi writer, Dim Delobsom, in his *Les Secrets des sorciers noirs* attacks witch-doctors who give future conscripts charms to obtain their discharge and add a slow poison which makes them fall ill when they reach their unit and so get sent home. 'It would be advisable to take firm action against the witch-doctors whose practices are prejudicial to French activity', he concludes, after noting, however, 'the Mossi's repugnance for military service' and pointing out that this gave rise to an exodus of young men to surrounding countries, particularly the Gold Coast.[12]

The native code

In the French empire before the second world war, when only a few selected Negroes represented the native population in the consultative administrative councils (in which the Europeans formed the majority) of each African colony, the statute for Africans was defined in a collection of texts known as *Code de l'indigénat*. One of its main provisos was the introduction of a system of compulsory duties which African intellectuals have usually classed as 'forced labour'. This has been the target of much criticism. 'It is a very versatile method of exploitation', says Joseph Ki Zerbo in his study "L'Économie de traite en Afrique noire". He gives specific examples:

> Requisitions for public works, particularly on the roads and for porterage; compulsory contracts with settlers; taxes in kind; compulsory cultivation as practised widely by the Belgians in the reservations (copying the methods of the Dutchman, Van den Bosch, in Java); collective rents in kind . . . [all] led to a terrible mortality. The notorious tragedy of the Congo-Ocean railway should not be forgotten. Out of 4,500 men working on it from January 1890 to May 1892, 900 died, and by June 1892 they had laid only 9 kilometres. So this first stage cost one human life for each 10 metres of track.[13]

The Native Code also gave the colonial administration penal powers, fiercely denounced by Abdoulaye Wade in the number of *Présence Africaine* devoted to Negro students.

As for political franchise, in Senegal it was effectively restricted to four communes (Saint-Louis, Rufisque, Dakar and Gorée) whose inhabitants had French citizenship. But this special status did not escape criticism from the Senegalese intelligentsia either. Maître Lamine Gueye, who is today undoubtedly the doyen of African politics in French-speaking countries and currently president of the Legislative Assembly of Senegal, devoted his doctoral thesis in law in 1921 to the subject, *De la situation politique des Sénégalais originaires des Communes de plein exercice*. Gueye argues that the status of French citizen granted to the Senegalese, on account of a decree of 16 *Pluviôse* of Year II of the First Republic (i.e. February 1795) abolishing slavery, engendered many legal conflicts between this statute and muslim legal custom. The author criticises the jurisprudence of the French colonial tribunals and the limited reach of the decree of *Pluviôse* because of the restrictions and impediments to the application of the principle of equality and assimilation which had inspired the Convention. He has been motivated by the same concern throughout his political career. The two 'Lamine Gueye laws' which he promoted in parliament are evidence of this. The first, of May 7, 1946, states that all nationals of French overseas territories shall have the same class of citizenship as nationals of the French homeland: this was the basis of article 80 of the

1946 constitution. Thomas Hodgkin has called it the 'Caracalla edict' of the French Union.[14] The second, of 1950, stipulated that French and African officials should enjoy the same rights; this regulation caused a lot of heart-burning at the time since it meant that polygamous African officials were thenceforward to benefit from the same family allowances as their French colleagues.

In 1943, also in a doctoral thesis in law, Maître Anani Santos, one of the nationalist leaders in Togo, commented on the 'natives' right to choose French law'. Already then, Santos had rejected the idea that the solution for the future lies purely and simply in an extension of the legislation of metropolitan France to the colonies. 'Assimilation as a solution is both false and dangerous', he writes. For Santos, 'to colonise is to create a new society with its own institutions and civilisation';[15] the best thing to do is to prepare for a future where settlers and native inhabitants will be ruled by a legislation based on their respective traditions. He explains this in the conclusion to his book:

> Colonial legislation should develop to such a pitch that Europeans also will exercise their right to choose it in the future. That is the dream of a still distant future, but we must look to it today as the only desirable solution. . . . Colonisation is a social fact: the contact between two peoples. This contact was rough at first but is tending to become more and more normal. Henceforth we should resolutely envisage a marriage of the two elements in which neither absorbs the other, where both are aware that they have been chosen to create a new form of humanity which they will have endowed with all their life force and which will lead to a better civilisation.

The 1946 constitution was based, so far as French overseas territories were concerned, on the recommendations of the Brazzaville conference of 1944, of which General de Gaulle was chairman. This created the French Union, and among other things abolished forced labour and granted consultative assemblies to the African territories as well as parliamentary representation in France.

Maghemout Diop, who a few years later founded the Parti Africain de l'Indépendance, the marxist leanings of which became increasingly apparent, considered this reform negative. In 1953 he wrote in *Présence Africaine*:

> Evidently we shall be told that the rough stage of colonisation is

> long since over; that, in the face of their growing responsibilities, Europeans have made amends and tried to redress the wrong they had done—if that were still possible; that colonists and colonised have together decided, in condemning the colonial system, to join forces to build a better future. In theory, yes. In practice, nothing has changed. . . . The Commonwealth and the French Union are not, and cannot be, fundamental innovations. They are mere modifications of form.

Maghemout Diop concluded that independence was 'indispensable'.[16]

Abdoulaye Wade is less direct in his judgement; he admits that 'the French colonial system seems relatively liberal beside the Belgian one, for example', and that the French Union may be considered 'a victory, albeit a fragile one, for the colonised peoples over the colonists, a step towards independence'.[17] Albert Tévoedjré analyses the institutions of the French Union under the chapter heading "Is colonialism dead?" He believes the nature of the colonial system changed after the war. First he mentions this resolution of the Brazzaville conference: 'The aims of French civilising efforts in the colonies do not include any idea of autonomy, or of any evolution outside the French bloc: the eventual institution of self government for the colonies, even in the distant future, is to be avoided.' Then he points out that, although the 1946 constitution allowed territories parliamentary representation in France, 'in practice we see that an African deputy often represents 700,000 constituents while his colleague from Toulouse, for example, represents about 50,000'. Tévoedjré quotes a European writer for an explanation of this numerical limitation on African deputies and senators: 'If representation were made proportional to the population, recent citizens could hold the balance between parties in the homeland, overthrow the majority and perhaps soon hold the majority themselves. In the last resort, the French Civil Code would be voted for by a majority of polygamists and—to make the picture blacker still—the Penal Code would be voted for by sons of cannibals.'[18]

It fell to Lamine Gueye, who at that time was serving in the directive organs of the Section Française de l'Internationale Ouvrière (SFIO) in Paris, to present the defence of the French Union. In his book, to which Guy Mollet—then secretary-general of the SFIO—wrote the preface, and which came out just before the *loi-cadre*, Gueye does not consider the 1946 constitution as the final stage. Although he expresses his faith in the French Union and France—the 'inventor of liberty'—he also proposes reforms tending to give Africans a greater share of power. Furthermore, he suggests the creation 'at the national level, of an assembly to study the major problems of overseas territories and endowed with suitable powers, and of a specialised parliament where the presence of an elected majority from overseas would give rise to fewer difficulties of a political or emotional nature: the present Assembly of the French Union, for instance, would serve if its statute were suitably modified'.[19] Finally, Gueye rejects the solution of independence adopted by Holland for Indonesia and by Britain for the Gold Coast. He asserts: 'The only thing asked of France is a strict equality of treatment in the application of its own laws.'[20] (This suggestion was ignored in the *loi-cadre* but is close to that of the Senate of the Community in the 1958 constitution.)

The results of this 1946 reform were examined from another point of view by Doudou Thiam. He defined closely the 'extent of French citizenship in overseas territories'. While for Lamine Gueye this extension of French citizenship was an immense step forward on the path of assimilation, it is the difficulty of its application which is stressed by Thiam, in order to show that this doctrine of assimilation is itself impracticable. This does not mean that Thiam is hostile to the French Union. On the contrary, he sees in colonisation, in spite of the 'errors' and 'deviations', an 'intercommunication between the values of the different civilisations' and stresses its positive aspect.[21] He refuses to regard the reform as a mere electoral law. It cannot fail, he says, to go beyond this narrow concept, especially since the dividing line between public and private law is fairly fluid at times. These difficulties over one particular problem only serve to illustrate a more general truth for this writer: the danger of transferring legal concepts wholesale from a given society to another quite different one. He enumerates several cases of jurisprudence where legal traditions in France and Africa were at loggerheads and where the decision was made in favour of French law, following the theory that the necessity of maintaining public order in the colonies over-rides any local customs. Doudou Thiam's thesis can be summarised as an appeal against assimilation. He is therefore delighted that the preamble to the 1946 constitution creating the French Union mentions explicitly that it 'consists of nations and people who pool their resources and efforts for the development of their *respective civilisations*'. The author emphasises the use of the plural here; it was adopted after a rough passage through the French parliament. He ends with these words:

> Following all these debates, the constitution conceded the cultural plurality which is fundamental to the concept of the French Union. Until that time a simple ethnological fact, the existence of civilisations overseas became henceforth a legal fact too. Respect for these civilisations was raised to the level of a constitutional principle out of the reach of the legislator. . . . Today those concerned have realised that it was impossible to transpose French citizenship *mutatis mutandis* to the colonies.[22]

*Balkanisation**

The *loi-cadre*, known by the name of Gaston Defferre who was minister for Overseas Territories in Guy Mollet's cabinet in 1956, introduced a system of relative internal autonomy for overseas territories. Each had a local government—the governing council—presided over by the governor but composed of African ministers. Furthermore local consultative assemblies were granted legislative powers.

Albert Tévoedjré was opposed to this *loi-cadre*, without wishing 'to denigrate those who believed, in drawing it up, that they were saving France from further dramas in Africa'. He felt that, from the first decree on its application, the law reasserted one of the fundamental principles of the French colonial system: integration or assimilation. It spoke of 'upholding the solidarity of the various elements of the Republic' and never questioned French political and economic domination. In fact, it was the central power, the French government, which managed the services controlling the life of the colonies since 'national defence, foreign affairs, commerce, economic planning, credit, currency, telecommunications, ports, customs, railways, inter-territorial roads, security, police, justice, higher education, etc., are strictly reserved to the French state'.[23] The emancipation of Ghana weighed heavily on the reform of the French Union, and Tévoedjré does not fail to point out that:

> At the moment when the Gold Coast becomes a state on a par with Belgium, France or Great Britain, can't they understand in Paris that the *loi-cadre* is not only a step backwards but also at times goes against the historical trends through which the world is passing today? . . . Before gaining independence, Ghana also went through

* I think it was André Blanchet, African correspondent of *Le Monde*, who first applied this expression to Africa.

> the trial period of internal self-rule. But Dr Nkrumah and his people knew that this was only a stage which would end on March 6, 1957.[24]

Sékou Touré considers that the main fault of the *loi-cadre* was to have 'balkanised' Africa. Defferre's reform effectively overlooked the existing federal structures of French Equatorial and West Africa,* and granted internal self-rule only at territorial level. However, the Guinean leader did see the law as 'a step towards a complete autonomy, which will enable the country to associate freely with France and to discuss common problems on equal terms'.[25] This passage, which dates from January 1958, was a statement of Sékou Touré's moral and political position as secretary general of the congress of the Parti Démocratique de Guinée. The Guinean political leader did not at that time want to break with France.

The Community

The 1958 constitution created the Community. Internal self-rule was considerably extended, and affairs common to France and the new African republics came henceforth under the competence of an executive council (composed of the African heads of government and presided over by the French head of state), and of a senate of the Community. The powers of these Community organs remained vague; but the new constitution gave each African territory the right of secession. This path was chosen by Guinea at the referendum of September 1958. Sékou Touré again reproached the French legislator for wishing to 'balkanise' Africa and he gives this as one of the main reasons for Guinea's 'No' at the referendum. Perhaps the clearest statement on the subject was his broadcast speech of August 28, one month before the referendum, in which the key words were 'balkanisation' and 'African unity':

> Is it necessary to recall over again that the Grand Council of French West Africa has passed resolutions against the 'balkanisation' of Africa? The Rassemblement Démocratique Africain (RDA) has shown,

* The Federation of West Africa (capital: Dakar) comprised the colonial territories of Mauritania, Senegal, Guinea, Upper Volta, Ivory Coast, Niger, Soudan and Dahomey; the Federation of Equatorial Africa (capital: Brazzaville) comprised Gabon, Middle Congo, Ubangi-Shari and Chad. Each federation had a governor and a federal assembly responsible for federal matters.

> at the Bamako conference and in many resolutions passed by its parliamentary group, the same desire to maintain the African federations. This African choice has been ignored by the draft constitution which will lead to arbitrary division and check all chances of economic, social, cultural and political development in Africa. . . . And so I say that if the French government answers 'No' to the legitimate aspirations of Africans, if its draft constitution does not take these propositions into account, the people of Guinea will choose independence on September 28, and will ask to negotiate contractual agreements with France. If this is refused Guinea will decide straight away to follow another course which will enable her to continue more effectively the struggle for emancipation and African unity. . . .[26]

On August 4, 1960, the Community's constitution was revised to allow independent African states to remain members. Philippe Decraene wrote in *Le Monde* that 'this modification acceded, after a delay of twenty-one months, to the request put forward by Guinea at the time of its constitutional referendum of September 1958'.[27]

What had been happening in the meanwhile? Mali had come into being as a federal state uniting Senegal and the French Soudan. In autumn 1959, Mamadou Dia, vice-president of the Federation of Mali, had told *Le Monde* of Mali's hope that the Community would become a multinational confederation linking France and the independent African states. In 1960 the four states of the Conseil de l'Entente—Ivory Coast, Niger, Upper Volta and Dahomey—also chose independence and decided to leave the Community, but nevertheless signed agreements of co-operation with France. At the constituent congress of the Parti de la Fédération Africaine in July 1959, Senghor endeavoured to show that French interest did not lie in the 'balkanisation' of Africa:

> That the reconstitution of the former federation of French West Africa on new bases should be in the political interest of Africans, springs from our basic concept of a nation. . . . That the reconstitution of the former federation is in the political interests of France, is clear to whoever follows the extension of the cold war to North Africa. . . . Francophone states are in danger of sliding one by one towards the Commonwealth or the People's Democracies. What else can Dahomey do, sandwiched between Nigeria and Ghana? How can you expect the people of Niger, poor and oppressed by a

feudal regime, to resist the attractions of a rich, democratic Nigeria, with 35 million inhabitants to boot? . . . I am afraid that the 'balkanisation' of black Africa will lead the Community to another Bandung unless a remedy is found soon. . . . The eight former French West African states will lose economically through 'balkanisation'. So will France. As I have said elsewhere, experts have calculated that unless the former French West African common market is re-established France will have to devote 7,000 million CFA francs annually to counteract the budgetary deficit of the poorer countries, over and above the credits from the Fonds d'Aide et de Coopération.[28]

Epitaph to indirect administration

Abolition of the traditional chieftaincies appeared to Sékou Touré to be one of the necessary conditions of political emancipation in his country. For him it was an indispensable *Prelude à l'independence*, as he called one of his books (published by *Présence Africaine*) which tells how he set about this task. Sékou Touré's attitude to the chiefs is, indeed, typical of most of the African nationalist parties. They regard the chiefs generally as a conservative, not to say retrograde, element which has too often influenced the African electorate in a direction favourable to continued colonial rule.

In West Africa, these chiefs were particularly powerful in the interior of the country, in strictly peasant communities, whereas in the large coastal towns the contacts between different populations, the power of the trade unions and the level of development of the inhabitants all worked against the chiefs' authority. This was so in Guinea, with the Fulani chiefs of the Fouta-Djalon mountains. The situation was very similar in Sierra Leone, where the chiefs of the protectorates of the interior were hostile to the descendants of slaves from the colony of Freetown. In Ghana, the traditional king of the Ashanti joined the opposition to Nkrumah; in Togo, Sylvanus Olympio's opposition party, the Comité de l'Unité Togolaise (CUT), had hardly any support among the Bassari and Kabre tribes. Above all, in Nigeria, the great Fulani emirs of Kano, Katsina, Sokoto, etc., have been playing—until the military coup of 1966, at least—a major role in the political life of the country. It is by no means a foregone conclusion that their future influence will be negligible. And in South Africa also, it is among the chiefs of the tribal reserves that the administration has found its support, and it is with their agreement that the Verwoerd government is intending to construct independent black states, or Bantustans.*

In most cases, the prestige of the chiefs depends on maintaining the tribal structure, and African nationalist parties have often identified 'tribalism' with chieftainship. In this context, it was clear that the chiefs must become the advocates of a certain degree of regionalism; and, in fact, their interested conservatism has often made them the champions of federalism. Thus, the Northern Region of Nigeria was the last to claim independence, and the Kabaka of Buganda was a staunch partisan of a federal structure for Uganda. This phenomenon was particularly widespread in British territory as a result of the British colonial system of indirect rule, which left the traditional hierarchy intact and gave it the widest possible authority. Lord Lugard first introduced this celebrated system in Nigeria. (In French Africa, the schools for chiefs' sons launched by Faidherbe are evidence of a similar policy, but they were short-lived. Actually neither the Almamy of the Fouta-Djalon nor the great traditional Mossi sovereigns, like the Moro Naba, played such an important role as the emirs of Nigeria or the Kabaka of Buganda.)

It is not surprising, under the circumstances, to find English-speaking African nationalists condemning in turn indirect rule, chieftainship, tribalism and the federal system. George Padmore, theoretician of 'panafricanism' and political adviser on African affairs to Nkrumah, roundly denounced chieftainship and tribalism in the chapter on Nigeria in *Panafricanism or Communism?* In a general fashion, the West Indian writer becomes the advocate of Nnamdi Azikiwe's centralist and unitary policies and opposes those of Obafemi Awolowo, the former prime minister of the Western Region and, with his book *Path to Nigerian Freedom*, theoretician of Nigerian federalism. The different views of Azikiwe and Awolowo can be understood if one remembers that Yoruba chieftainship is strongly structured in the Western Region, which is heir to the historic kingdoms of Ife, Oyo, etc.; on the other hand it is almost non-existent in the Eastern Region, the country of the

* It is interesting to note that, back in 1920, a black South African writer, S. M. Molema, had demanded the creation of separate black states. However, in his book, *Bantu Past and Present*, he envisaged these Bantustans in a very specific context: he saw them as a means of escape for the Negroes from Boer rule. His whole book is impregnated with hostility for the Dutch element in the population of his country. He was far less averse to the English element which he hoped, despite many deceptions, would not betray the liberal traditions of Britain. Moreover, he saw these separate black states only as a solution to fall back on if the white man continued to refuse to treat the black population on terms of equality. 'But', he added, 'first and foremost, the separation must be equitable.'[29]

dominant Ibo tribe and homeland of Dr Azikiwe. Moreover, Awolowo himself comes from a family of chieftains. Padmore writes: 'Mr Awolowo is definitely committed to tribal separatism', and he recalls this significant remark by the Nigerian leader: 'Nigeria is not a nation. It is a mere geographical expression. There are no Nigerians.'[30] Both the power inherent in, and the problems arising from, the traditional, separatist character of the chieftainship can be seen from Nigeria's political development since independence. The National Council for Nigeria and the Cameroons (NCNC) allied itself with the Northern People's Congress, led by the Fulani aristocracy in the north, to present a front against the Action Group. This alliance of the most progressive and the most conservative parties was not without surprises. By 1963, Chief Awolowo, leader of the opposition (Action Group) in the federal parliament, was accused of mishandling public funds. Azikiwe, leader of the NCNC, became president of the Republic of Nigeria, but personal and tribal animosities within regions and between one region and another put the federal constitution in jeopardy. The political demoralisation of the country was one of the main issues in the manifesto of the leaders of the military coup of January 1966, which was aimed particularly at breaking the influence over the federal political system of the traditionalist Fulani rulers in the Northern Region.

Judgement is passed on Lord Lugard's methods by Ntieyong U. Akpan* in his book, *Epitaph to Indirect Rule*. After recognising the positive aspects of the system, he comments: 'It led in real practice to a sort of quasi-apartheid policy in the colonial territories . . . where the Europeans always looked upon the natives as inferior races, fit for hewing wood and drawing water.'[31] J. Godson Amamoo, for a time Ghana's ambassador to Hungary, in his history of the years preceding the independence of his country, also shows African nationalists' distrust of chieftainship and indirect rule. He traces the origins of the Accra riots of 1948, and writes: 'All important appointments in the Government were held by British officials, who relied for support, not on [the] politicians, but on the chiefs, and the suspicion had grown that the chiefs were in league with the British to stifle the political aspirations of the people.'[32] Further on he states: 'It was through them

* Akpan is from the Eastern Region of Nigeria: the first British colonial territory in Africa to undergo an experiment in local democratic administration in place of the usual system of native administration or indirect rule. The purpose of his book is to study this reform.

that the British administered the Gold Coast. This system of indirect rule alienated many of the people from their chiefs.'[33] The African nationalist leader, Kenneth Kaunda, now president of Zambia, in many respects shares this distrust of the traditional authorities. In 1962, he wrote: 'Some day I should like to write a book with the old Congress files at my elbow to tell the wretched story of how the Provincial Administration tries to use the Chiefs to crush the Congress in the rural areas.'[34] He justified his opposition to a draft constitution, which stated that all electoral candidates should be approved by two-thirds of the chiefs of the constituency, with the following words: 'We all knew that the Chiefs were in the pockets of the Administration.'[35]

In Ghana, several of the parties in opposition to Nkrumah's CPP originally had a regional base: for example, the National Liberation Movement (supported by the Asantahene, king of the Ashanti), the Northern People's Congress and the Togoland Congress. Their style was cramped by a law of 1957 which prohibited associations of a religious or tribal character: they had then to amalgamate within the United Party, which was soon to demand, unsuccessfully, a federal constitution.* In *The Position of the Chief in the Modern Political System of Ashanti*, Dr Busia, the Ghanaian opposition leader who eventually went into voluntary exile for the duration of the Nkrumah regime, is working in the main trend of most African nationalists in his analysis of the progressive decline of moral and legal authority among the traditional chiefs as a result of indirect rule. But, he says, the Ashanti still regard themselves as a united people through their allegiance to the Golden Stool, the sacred symbol of Ashanti royalty. Busia, indeed, praises the action of the Asantahene, especially in his role as president of the Council of the Ashanti Confederation: an institution grouping the Ashanti chiefs which was re-established by the British administration in 1935.

It is hardly surprising that the late Sir Ahmadu Bello, prime minister of the Northern Region of Nigeria until his murder in the coup of January 1966, should have been a keen supporter of indirect rule. As the Sardauna of Sokoto (a very aristocratic title), Sir Ahmadu was a

* On this law, see Kwame Nkrumah, *Africa Must Unite*, p. 74. It is interesting to compare it with Sékou Touré's measures to end political regionalism. Legislative elections in Guinea are carried out by ballot on a national level, which means that a party may not put up candidates in a few constituencies only; it must offer a national list, with as many names as there are seats to fill in the whole country. (Article 4 of the Guinean Constitution.)

direct descendant of the great muslim reformer and Fulani conqueror, Usman Dan Fodio, who, in the latter part of the seventeenth century, gave the signal for revolt against the Hausa kings, following which the Fulani seized power and founded emirates still existing today. Sir Ahmadu was thus one of the most important and authentic representatives of that aristocracy whose supremacy gave Lord Lugard the idea of indirect rule. In his autobiography, *My Life*, he wrote:

> Lugard saw the administrative genius of the Fulani Rulers and their staffs; he utilised it as the mainspring of the Native Administration system, that he called 'Indirect Rule', and it has worked well since then. The only difficulty from his point of view was that the Fulani system did not cover the whole country. An attempt was made by the British to produce an imitation of Fulani Rule in what were then known as the 'pagan areas' and this failed completely.[36]

The secession of Katanga furnished nationalist African intelligentsia, who had denounced federalism, with a perfect example which corresponded in almost miraculous fashion to the definition of the retrograde forces opposing African emancipation. The support offered to Tshombe seemed to African nationalists a flagrant illustration of the methods of 'imperialist divide and rule'. Kwame Nkrumah stresses this point in *Africa Must Unite*: 'The Congo offers perhaps the most striking example of how tribal dissensions and political careerism are exploited in order to fragment united territories and exacerbate divisions. The aim of the marionette control of local careerists like Moise Tshombe, besides the maintenance of economic power, is to cut across the African determination to secure continental unity in full independence.'[37] In a similar context, African nationalists have objected to the methods of colonial administration by which one ethnic group was set against another—that is, arousing ethnic antagonism where, according to them, it did not exist before. The Congolese, Mabika Kalanda, in *Baluba et Lulua, une ethnie à la recherche d'un nouvel équilibre*, sets out to show how the Belgian administration in Kasai had encouraged dissension between the two tribes and, particularly in 1959, had roused the Lulua against the Baluba. The author follows his exposé of the machinations of Belgian administrators with an ethnologic study in which he asserts the essential relationship of the two groups (the Lulua being an offshoot of the Baluba). Finally, in *Le Meilleur Combat*, the Algerian Amar Ouzegane criticises the French strategy of separating the different ethnic groups in his country, and denounces 'colonialists, historians or lawyers who deny the unity of the Algerian people and differentiate on paper between Arabs, Kabyles and Mozabites'.[38]

The federalists

Dr Awolowo's advocacy of federalism, which went against the generally accepted ideas of African nationalists, was based above all on the fear that one regional group could dominate the others within a unified state: in his case this was the Northern Region which had a larger population than the Eastern and Western Regions together. At the time of the 1958 constitutional conference, after predicting a crushing victory for the Northern People's Congress, the party in power in the north, at the federal elections planned for the advent of independence in 1960 (a prediction which, indeed, proved true), he pointed out that this region, with 174 seats out of 312 in the federal parliament, 'would only require a few political satellites from the south to enable it to control the affairs of the federal government'.[39] To avoid such a dangerous state of affairs, Awolowo suggested a new division of Nigeria into a greater number of regions, coinciding more exactly with the different ethnic groups in the country. He asserted, in substance, that the ethnic diversity of Nigeria was the best defence against a dictatorship. To these general arguments he added another *ad homines*: 'The policy-making elements of the NPC, which now dominates the affairs of the federal government, are strong believers in the sacrosanct nature of the feudal system from which they draw their inspiration and main support.'[40]

In fact, at that time, most of the Nigerian political leaders, including Azikiwe, were more or less in agreement on the need for new regional delimitations. Indeed, a procedure to this effect had been provided for at the 1958 constitutional conference. However, their views diverged considerably on the practical terms of such a reorganisation which could have a profound effect on the interests of the three major political parties in existence: the NCNC controlling the Eastern Region, the NPC holding the Northern, and the Action Group with a majority in the Western.* Awolowo's distrust of the chiefs in the Western Region was not as strong as that which he expressed à propos of the emirs of the

* The government of the Northern Region wanted a delay which would enable officials to be trained; Sir Ahmadu Bello and his colleagues did not speak of the 'africanisation' but of the 'northernisation' of their administration. See Bello, *My Life*, p. 140 in particular.

north. He recalled that when he came to power as prime minister of the Western Region in 1952:

> I had to reckon with the Obas and Chiefs who were very jealous of and extremely sensitive about their traditional rights and privileges. In spite of agitation here and there against this or that Oba or Chief, the institution of Obaship and Chieftaincy was still held in high esteem by the people. But the traditional rights and privileges which the Obas and Chiefs wished to preserve were antithetic to democratic concepts and to the yearnings and aspirations of the people. . . . The problem which faced me, therefore, was that whilst I must strive to harness the influence of the Obas and Chiefs for our purposes, I must, at the same time, take the earliest possible steps to modify their rights and abrogate such of their privileges as were considered repugnant, to an extent that would both satisfy the commonalty and make the Obas and Chiefs feel secure in their traditional offices.[41]

Violence and non-violence

Emancipation movements in the Commonwealth and the French empire have been marked by a different stamp. One need only consider the debate at the Accra conference of African peoples in 1958: here partisans of non-violence, almost without exception English-speaking and imbued with the example of Gandhi, opposed the advocates of violence from the French colonies, including such men as Frantz Fanon, delegate of the provisional government of the Algerian republic, and Félix Moumié, delegate of the Union des Populations du Cameroun. In his autobiography, Kwame Nkrumah explains his conversion to Gandhi's ideas:

> At this time I devoted much energy to the study of revolutionaries and their methods. Those who interested me most were Hannibal, Cromwell, Napoleon, Lenin, Mazzini, Gandhi, Mussolini and Hitler. I found much of value to be gleaned and many ideas that were useful to me later in my own campaign against imperialism. At first, I could not understand how Gandhi's philosophy of non-violence could possibly be effective. It seemed to me to be utterly feeble and without hope of success. The solution of the colonial problem, as I saw it at that time, lay in armed rebellion. How is it possible, I asked myself, for a revolution to succeed without arms

> and ammunition? After months of studying Gandhi's policy, and watching the effect it had, I began to see that, when backed by a strong political organisation, it could be the solution to the colonial problem. In Jawaharlal Nehru's rise to power I recognised the success of one who, pledged to Socialism, was able to interpret Gandhi's philosophy in pratical terms.[42]

The example of the Indian nationalists also inspired Kenneth Kaunda: 'I was determined to combine Gandhi's policy of non-violence with Nkrumah's positive action.'[43] It should also be noted that it was in this field that he was attacked by the white settlers, particularly after his speech in February 1961 in which he said: 'Should Welensky and the British government continue to frustrate the legitimate aspirations of the African people of Zambia, a mass rising might result in Northern Rhodesia which would make Mau Mau seem a child's picnic.'[44] In *Zambia Shall Be Free*, Kaunda denies that these words were intended to be a call to revolt. He asserts that he only wished to attract attention to the serious consequences that might follow a policy hostile to the recognition of African rights. On the contrary, he points out several times that he had always urged the African population not to have recourse to violence to achieve their ends. But, sixty years before Nkrumah, Casely-Hayford, one of the pioneers of Ghanaian nationalism, had warned the British authorities that the possibility of armed combat should not be overlooked: 'The careless observer may think that the fear of British guns and Maxims has hitherto kept the Gold Coast free from disturbances. A greater mistake could not be made.'[45]

And in Kenya, one of Kenyatta's companions, Mbiyu Koinange, in *The People of Kenya Speak for Themselves*, replied in these words to accusations of atrocities during the Mau Mau revolt, the most important armed uprising in post-war Africa:

> Talk of Mau Mau atrocities is designed to obscure the issue of liquidation of Africans and win the sympathy for the settlers as representative of civilisation. I have not wanted to introduce atrocities in this pamphlet because, for every 'atrocity' that it has been proved the African insurrectionists committed, I can match a score committed by the settlers, the army, the police, and the Home Guard. The army set up score boards to chalk 'kills' of Africans.[46]

A few years later, his fellow-countryman, Tom Mboya, echoed the same theme in *Freedom and After*, and came to the conclusion that

Gandhi's methods could not be applied in Africa. 'If one can draw a general rule, it is that in any colony where there has been considerable white settlement, violence has become inevitable, although it was not the original policy of the nationalist party.'[47]

The cracking myth

In 1953, Maghemout Diop, by far the most intransigent of the Africans who had contributed to the special number of *Présence Africaine* devoted to students' views, wrote as a conclusion to his article "L'Unique Issue: l'independance totale": 'Every African must be convinced of the legitimacy of our independence and must believe it possible and essential in his generation.'[48] History moved faster than he had dared hope. The independence of Ghana precipitated events to such an extent that within ten years of the publication of Diop's article (1953), the whole of black Africa was free, with the exceptions of the Portuguese strongholds of Angola and Mozambique, the Federation of Rhodesia and Nyasaland, and the Republic of South Africa (roughly speaking, the southern tip of Africa).

Sithole has taken a striking comparison from Shakespeare to illustrate how 'the myth—of European superiority—is cracking': 'The now politically conscious African reminds us of Shakespeare's Caliban who mistook the new-comers to the island for gods, and immediately pledged his loyalty to them. . . . What a thrice-double ass was I, to take this drunkard for a god, and worship this dull fool.'[49] The Rhodesian author does not mention *Prospero and Caliban* by O. Mannoni which offers a study of the colonial situation via the story and characters of *The Tempest*.

7

THE COLONIAL PACT

'WE PREFER POVERTY as free men to riches as slaves', said Sékou Touré in his speech welcoming General de Gaulle to Conakry on August 25, 1958. This was one month before the referendum of September 28 by which Guinea alone of all French overseas territories of the day chose independence. This remark by the president of Guinea clearly expresses the attitude of African nationalists faced with the argument of their need for the economic and financial aid which the European countries gave their colonies. This aid took various forms, from the customs protection given under the system of Commonwealth preferences to the direct aid from the French government through the Fonds d'investissement pour le développement économique et social (FIDES). But many nationalists considered this aid as just another way of keeping them enslaved—a new form of 'colonial pact'. Indeed, all the theoreticians of African nationalism have taken the kernel of their arguments from a study of the economic links between the colonies and the colonial powers.

For Kwame Nkrumah, this is the crux of the problem; political emancipation is just the means: the end is liberation from economic exploitation. On the first page of his booklet *Towards Colonial Freedom*, he says:

> Colonial existence under imperialist conditions necessitates a fierce and constant struggle for emancipation from the yoke of colonialism and exploitation. The aim of all colonial governments in Africa and elsewhere has been the struggle for raw materials; and not only this, but the colonies have become the dumping ground, and colonial peoples the false recipients, of manufactured goods of the industrialists and capitalists of Great Britain, France, Belgium and other colonial powers who turn to the dependent territories which feed their industrial plants. This is colonialism in a nutshell. The basis of colonial territorial dependence is economic, but the basis of the

solution is political. Hence political independence is an indispensable step towards securing economic emancipation.[1]

From sugar economy to colonial pact

According to Nkrumah, colonialism is essentially an economic phenomenon, if not in character at least in origin. In this theory he was principally influenced by Lenin's *Imperialism, the Highest Stage of Capitalism. Towards Colonial Freedom* was written just after the second world war and shortly after the Pan-African Congress held in Manchester in 1945. It is a small booklet of thirty-six pages. The ideas set out here were later developed by several African economists, and not only those with marxist leanings.

In order to understand this economic hold more clearly and to find the deep-rooted causes of it, African historians have felt the need to 'take to pieces' the mechanism of European expansion from its beginning and to reconstruct the history of the system known as the 'Colonial Pact'.

Abdoulaye Ly has devoted a substantial book, *La Compagnie du Sénégal*, to one of the early episodes in this story. In it he traces the history of the company and studies the development of the sugar economy in the West Indies and its corollary, the import of African slaves. Why? Because, says Abdoulaye Ly:

> Modern capitalism cannot be understood without sugar. From the cultivation of the cane, through the industrial machine, to the maritime transport and the finished product, immense sums of capital are at stake and splendid profits are acquired in a setting of distinctly capitalistic businesses. . . . The labour force was provided by slaves, themselves the object of an intensive capitalistic traffic linking the supply depots of Africa with the plantations of the new world in a unique economic complex; this followed the lines of what the Dutch had tried to establish in the first quarter of the seventeenth century when they seized sugar-producing north-east Brazil and Angola, reservoirs of Negro labour, from the Portuguese.[2]

Thus, the sugar industry and the slave trade are for the Senegalese historian and economist two of the principal sources of revenue leading to the accumulation of capitalist wealth. This was of major importance since it preceded and made possible the industrial revolution. Ly defines the basic characteristics of this economy:

1. Cultivation of one crop: the plantations of sugar cane rapidly eliminated other cash crops such as tobacco, and overtook the production of foodstuffs to such an extent that at times famine raged and beef had to be imported from Ireland to feed the slaves;

2. Large estates: small family holdings of poor settlers, always uncommon, disappeared altogether and gave place to veritable latifundia;

3. An exploited proletariat: the extremely cheap slave labour force discouraged the arrival of white workers;

4. A monopolistic character: the Compagnie du Sénégal always had a complete or partial monopoly in the trade.

Then he gives a long account of the history of the company, its plans to found a settlement in Senegal in the eighteenth century, and finally the setbacks which led to its liquidation and threw open the doors to a period of liberal economy characterised by free competition, 'the era of the slave-traders'. Ly concludes:

> This was the significance [of the Compagnie du Sénégal] in the life of France: one facet, one moment in the development of capitalism in the framework of profiteering of the age of Louis XIV.* A moment also in European expansion. . . . There are, however, similarities between the past and today which exist outside any historical links and despite obvious differences, and which it is not for me to underline. May the living profit from them if they can.[3]

Ideas very similar to those of Abdoulaye Ly are expressed by the Nigerian writer, K. Onwuka Dike, in *Trade and Politics in the Niger Delta*:

> In the eighteenth century economists reckoned that the wealth of the Indies was one of the main supports of the contemporary British empire. This wealth was largely the product of African labour. It is now known that the triangular trade—that is the trade between Britain, West Africa, and the West Indies—provided one of the many streams from whence emerged the capital that financed the industrial revolution.[4]

But this industrial revolution was to become, in its turn, another reason for Europe to expand beyond its frontiers. According to most of the nationalist authors from underdeveloped countries, it was one

* Ly mainly studies the period from 1673–95.

of the principal causes of the colonial conquests of the nineteenth century. The Algerian leader, Ferhat Abbas, wrote:

> The colonial crime is above all a crime of the wealthy. Of course there had been conquistadors and evangelising expeditions in the fifteenth and sixteenth centuries; certainly the colonial adventure antedates the rise of the middle classes. But this adventure did not take on the character of a ferocious, rational exploitation until backed by capitalist interests. The expansion of Europe into Asia and Africa is directly related to industrial development and the machine age. To ensure and increase their profits, for centuries capitalist Europe destroyed, assassinated, despoiled and deported without restraint.[5]

The Indian historian K. M. Panikkar has remarked that the European concern for a monopoly in the spice trade eventually gave way to a desire to import textiles, tea and other goods. With the industrial revolution, Britain sought an outlet in Asia for its manufactured goods, and then an opportunity for capital investment.[6] African intellectuals in general are in agreement with this analysis. Mamadou Dia, for instance, having discussed the economic and demographic consequences of the slave trade for Africa, defines the main outlines of the structure of capitalism in the last century: 'Europe's negative role does not stop there. This work of destruction aimed at the very bases of African economy continued with increasing violence despite the abolition of slavery in the second half of the nineteenth century. It was pushed forward by western imperialism, as a result of the great industrial revolution of the day.'[7]

The exploitation of Africa

So much for history: the picture is not bright. It will be no better in the present period. The basic characteristics of African economy resulting from the colonial pact, as outlined by the African economists, are not without analogies with those which Ly had attributed to the sugar industry of the West Indies. Indeed the author's aim was to set out clearly the lesson of the past, and the similarity seems clear enough for a table of 'agreements' to be drawn up, These, approximately, are:

1. For the single crop cultivation of sugar in the West Indies we have, in present-day Africa, the priority of certain cash crops, also to the detriment of necessary foodstuffs;

2. For the great estates we have a concentration of capital in the hands of a few very powerful firms;

3. For the monopoly there is a whole battery of protective tariffs and fiscal advantages;

4. For the exploitation of the slave there is that of the workman or African peasant whose wages or income remain abnormally low.

A resolution presented by the West African delegates to the Pan-African Congress in Manchester in 1945 (in which Nkrumah played an important role), concentrated on one of these points: 'That when a country is compelled to rely on one crop (e.g. cocoa) for a single monopolistic market, and is obliged to cultivate only for export while at the same time its farmers and workers find themselves in the grip of finance capital, then it is evident that the government of the country is incompetent to assume economic responsibility for it.'[8]

Mamadou Dia mentioned the following points as typical of African economy during the colonial period:

> Capital, which during this period of liberalism was above all private capital, was invested in sectors where all the profits were assured in advance to the dominating economies and conspicuously to the particular interests of the non-African shareholders. . . . In agriculture there is a recession in the production of foodstuffs, in favour of cash crops such as coffee, cotton, ground-nuts and castor oil plants, to mention the main ones if not the whcle lot. Planting and picking on a small scale give way to extensive exploitation on the plantation scale. In this way a peasant subsistence economy is being replaced by a capitalist economy which is not even sensible enough to integrate Africa into the world economy of today. Instead it has chosen to remain a trading economy concerned only to promote to the full the accumulation of capital and high dividends.[9]

Dia emphasises the dangers of this exclusive concentration on a few cash crops: an insufficiently diversified economy, erosion and exhaustion of the soil, undernourishment of the Negro peasant. Ly analyses the same phenomena and also stresses the 'vicious circle' in which the African farmer finds himself: taxes in hard cash force him to cultivate one cash crop whose sale is his only way of obtaining currency.

Maghemout Diop and Albert Tévoedjré point out the considerable profits accruing to the large firms. These profits, they maintain, are largely the result of certain concessions which, while not amounting to the sort of monopoly granted in the past to a single agricultural company, nevertheless afford an often decisive protection against foreign competition. Tévoedjré remarks that the large companies' share in the taxes is minimal in relation to that of the African peasant:

> In the Soudanese budget for 1953 we see from the official figures that: (1) Taxes applying directly and exclusively to natives (personal or contract taxes, taxes on livestock, taxes on firearms) provide 55 per cent of the national budget; (2) The contributions of the settlers and their companies is infinitesimal in relation to their capacity to contribute: industrial and commercial profits, which we know to be very high, furnish only 3.4 per cent of the budget.[10]

However, the most important protection is that afforded by the tariff regulations, which prevent foreign competition. Tévoedjré quotes the following extract from *La Vie française*, April 16, 1954, as sufficient proof of this: 'Nationals of overseas territories are obliged to import at high prices since cheaper goods from abroad are mostly kept away. Thus, the price of corn imported from France is 80 per cent higher than that of foreign suppliers, sugar is 100 per cent higher, printed cotton fabrics 35 per cent higher.'[11]

The British system of imperial preferential tariffs is also energetically denounced by Kwame Nkrumah:

> The slogan 'Buy British and trade imperial' is used to stimulate the maintenance of higher prices for British manufactured goods. 'Preferential tariffs' (higher customs duties and lower quotas) are applied on foreign manufactured goods. . . . Tariffs are usually applied to protect domestic economy, but this is not so in the colonies. For there tariffs are applied for the protection of British trade and profits.[12]

A similar opinion is expressed by Abdoulaye Ly, who remarks that 'imports are sold at monopoly prices, inflated by taxes on turnover and customs dues which not only protect the goods of the colonial powers against foreign competition but also swell the governments' budgets'.[13] He considers that the enormous profits of European companies in Africa really stem from a 'technological' income; this is assured to the industrial countries by their superior productivity 'resulting from integration in the economic patterns of zones where the forms and means of production are still archaic'.[14] While French-speaking authors denounce the various forms of protection which enable European enterprises to make large profits, Kwame Nkrumah concentrates on the British chocolate industry's monopoly—protected by a governmental organisation, the Cocoa Marketing Board. For the author of *Towards Colonial Freedom*, this is just an illustration of a general rule: 'The introduction of capitalism into the colonies does not take the "normal" course it took in western countries. Free competition does not exist, and monopoly control of all the resources of the colonies demonstrates the perversion of finance capitalism.'[15] What is the position of African workers and peasants in this context? Nkrumah thinks the state to which they are reduced is extremely 'degrading'.

> Since the advent of capitalism into the colonies colonial peoples have been reduced to the level of labourers and contract bondsmen, and are unable to organise effectively due to government and monopolist combine interference. The philosophy of European capitalism in the colonies is that colonial subjects should labour under any foreign government with uncomplaining satisfaction. They are supposedly 'incapable' of developing the resources of their own country, and are taught to labour and appreciate European manufactured goods so as to become 'good' customers. The meagre stipend given to them as a wage by the European capitalist is spent on spurious imported manufactured goods—the only kind they get. Curiously enough, the same coin that is given to the 'native' as a wage by his exploiter eventually returns to the pocket of that wily exploiter.[16]

Albert Tévoedjré also devotes a large number of pages in *L'Afrique révoltée* to the deplorable condition of the African wage earner; his meagre earnings are one of the reasons for the exceptional profits of the European companies and firms operating in the colonies. Tévoedjré thinks that 'racial discrimination in the colonies finds one of its most fertile fields in the wage differential between Europeans and Africans'. He is also concerned at the increase of alcoholism in the colonies, a by-product of this situation. He points out that, in 1954, 'with the agreement of the French Ministry for Overseas Territories and the complicity of the African governments, subsidies were granted for the export of wine to the colonies. . . . It is usually the field of health which is quoted to support Europe's "civilising mission" overseas. Without denying this work one must admit that it is notoriously insufficient and seriously compromised by a materialistic view of the natives and by the deliberate introduction of alcohol into the black continent.'[17]

Mamadou Gologo is just as categorical when he asserts, at the end of his autobiographical novel *Le Rescapé de l'Ethylos*, that: 'Africa must overcome alcoholism, its inheritance from the colonial period.'[18]

The land and all that lies below

Mamadou Dia has tried to find the reason for the exodus of African peasants to the towns where their conditions of work, if they can find any, have a dangerous 'proletarianising' effect. The most important reason is the expropriation of native land; then there is the need to earn enough money to pay the taxes; finally comes the attraction of the big city. Dia takes Kenya as an example of wholesale land expropriation leading to a rural exodus which inevitably ended badly: 'Thus, the wholesale expropriation of the natives' lands has led in some countries to bloodshed and strife. The occupation of the White Highlands by three thousand British settlers, to the exclusion of four million Africans, is at the basis of a popular movement which, after simmering for thirty years, has now broken out as the Mau Mau rebellion.'[19]

Criticism from English-speaking writers is no less harsh. Nkrumah devotes two pages of his booklet to it: 'Hence it becomes a mockery to speak of colonial lands as belonging to the colonial "subjects", who only possess "surface rights" when valuable minerals are found on such lands.'[20] He exposes the trick of reserving certain regions for reafforestation when actually they conceal mineral resources. He also remarks that the British authorities throw the onus of proof of property rights on to the Africans in cases of expropriation. The latter thus unjustly suffer the consequences of the lack of any land survey before the arrival of the Europeans. Finally, Nkrumah quotes the example that 'in February 1944, the governor of Nigeria, in spite of strong opposition, passed a bill through the local legislature giving the British government in Nigeria the right to take possession of all minerals discovered on land in the possession of Africans'.[21]

This question of land ownership is naturally fully covered by African nationalists in Kenya also. Apart from Kenyatta, who introduces it indirectly in his ethnographic study, *Facing Mount Kenya*, Parmenas Githendu Mockerie has also studied the problem in *An African Speaks for his Own People*. Mockerie criticises the whole system imposed by Britain. He recalls the reduction of African wages in 1921 following the 'convention of association', and the restrictions on the movements of Africans within the country arising from a system of permits (the *kipandi* system), both of which contributed to the outbreak of the 1922 strikes under the leadership of Harry Thuku, head of the East African Organisation. (The demonstrations which followed his arrest caused twenty-five deaths.) He points out that the 'native lands trust ordinance' of 1930, which stopped the expropriation without compensation of African lands by settlers, was not respected in 1932 when a concession was granted to private European companies to exploit the gold mines of Kakamega, etc.

The problem of land appropriation by Europeans has been particularly crucial for a long time now in South Africa. One of the first protests against it by an African was that of the novelist, Sol T. Plaatje. He had been entrusted by the African National Congress, the first major black nationalist party in the Union, to carry out an enquiry into the disastrous consequences of the 1913 Land Act which forced black labourers to leave to the Europeans the lands which hitherto they had been cultivating.* Plaatje denounced this forced emigration in *Native Life in South Africa*, a very bitter book published in 1916.

From the FIDES *to the grant*

It was immediately after the second world war that the European powers decided to embark on a more active policy of economic and social development in their overseas territories. Plans were drawn up and institutions set up to increase the volume of investment, create new industries, advance education and intensify medical aid. For the French colonies this was the period of the FIDES, Fonds d'investissements pour le développement économique et social, and for the English colonies the Colonial Development and Welfare Acts. Similar institutions were established in the Belgian and Portuguese territories. There is no doubt that, in the minds of its promoters, this new policy was intended to make good certain omissions of the past and to give generous aid destined above all to promote the 'colonial man'. Politicians' speeches, which, in the past, had analysed the respective merits of the 'colonial doctrines'—assimilation by France, indirect rule by Britain, miscegenation for Portugal and apartheid in South Africa—now gave way

* The Act permanently prohibits Africans from buying or even renting land outside their own scheduled areas and confines their property rights to an area roughly one-eighth of the surface of South Africa. (See Colin and Margaret Legum, *South Africa: Crisis for the West*, pp. 10 f.)

imperceptibly to the economists' comparisons of the volume and methods of public investment overseas by the colonial powers.

How was this economic aid greeted by the African intelligentsia? However satisfied many African political leaders may have been to see such efforts on their behalf, which moreover they themselves had requested, there was plenty of criticism from the economists. Nkrumah, in his *Towards Colonial Freedom*, had already put his fellow countrymen on guard against the new policy of economic aid to the colonies.

> We learned also of a fund called 'Aid for Colonial Development and Welfare', which provides £120,000,000 sterling in grants to the colonies. A little arithmetical reflection, however, shows that when the population of the colonial empire is taken into consideration the amount works out at eighteen pence (thirty-six cents) per inhabitant per year. During the first year and a half after the passage of the said Act the amount spent was twopence (four cents) per inhabitant per year. Nor is this all. The benefits of the Colonial Development Fund are largely illusory, since the £120,000,000 is not in the safe keeping of a Bank of the British Empire as such, where any colonial territory can apply for the money it may need for its 'welfare development'. To simplify the issue: supposing, say, Nigeria needs £40,000 for its 'welfare developments', the British Government in Nigeria then goes to Barclays Bank, which advances the £40,000 to the people of Nigeria at six per cent interest. On this basis the people of the 'colony' of Nigeria eventually find themselves in perpetual debt to the very agencies which are supposed to be concerned with their 'welfare development'.[22]

The French-speaking economists' analyses of the FIDES are less summary but none the less critical. Abdoulaye Ly believes that the FIDES has not changed anything and that colonial exploitation goes on just as in the past. Hence he asserts that:

> From 1946 to 1949, during the period of political revolutions in colonial affairs, to which we shall return, the reconversion of a wartime economy (the war effort beneath the Vichy cudgel followed by that of de Gaulle) to a peace-time economy (the normal economy within the imperialist system) went through easily without any setbacks. In this way the surplus products of African labour was drained away by the new 'privileged African companies' of which

> the most important are the international trusts (the most powerful being the Unilever group, currently Anglo-American, formerly Anglo-Dutch). There have been hardly any tentative schemes by African members of parliament to make these firms invest some of their profits in Africa. It is only to a slight extent that, recently, and as a consequence of this drainage of profits, there has developed a small amount of African capital.[23]

To back up his argument, Abdoulaye Ly quotes at length from an article by François Walter in *Le Monde*.

> What is peculiar to French overseas territories, besides the extent of French financial assistance and the slow growth rate, is the small amount of private investment and the immense preference granted to goods coming from France. Here one thing stems from another. A moderate preferential system would not be unreasonable. But our overseas territories are enveloped in a network of rights and restrictions to such an extent that France provides two-thirds of their total imports and five-sixths of their European imports. Such an exorbitant privilege is very expensive. The colonies are obliged to import at high prices, since cheaper goods from abroad are mostly kept away. Their real income is reduced proportionally and hence the resources which they can take from it for their own investment. Encouraged once more to rely on our favourable laws rather than on its own dynamism, French industry, which is largely in control of the colonial markets, feels little temptation to finance the development of any industry there . . . particularly since it might suffer from the competition. Thus, despite the extensive work financed by our public funds, total investment in these countries remains insufficient. France and the balance of payments of the franc zone vis-à-vis other countries are no better off for it. Our exportable products are drained off into the easy markets of the colonies instead of making their own way on the foreign markets. What are the end results of this? The French budget is heavily loaded, development in the colonies is slow, and an indirect subsidy saves French industry from making the effort to become competitive.[24]

Thus it is not so much the principle of economic aid which Ly is condemning, as the context in which it is given. He considers that the FIDES operation is bound to fail since the structure of the colonial pact has remained unchanged.

In *Réflexions sur l'économie de l'Afrique noire*, Mamadou Dia stresses the decisive importance of the turning point in the colonial economy just after the second world war. The policy of aid and investment seems to him to herald the decline of the colonial pact economy. He emphasises the extent of investments made through the FIDES, the American Point-4 Aid Programme, the International Bank, the Colonial Development Corporation, etc., all of which indicate that a policy of 'grants' has been resolutely undertaken. However egotistical the motives behind this development may have been, Dia feels that this 'grant' economy cannot be considered as 'a mere extension of the colonial pact'.[25] But this does not prevent his expressing considerable reservations on the subject. Its essential characteristic, he says, is that it should take effect through the intermediary of public power. But 'public power has abandoned practically everywhere its role as a distributor of credit to mixed companies in which there is a government shareholding where private interests easily become dominant'.[26] Moreover, the new investment policy has not altered the dependence of African countries on a few cash crops—ground nuts, cocoa, coffee, etc.—and their economy is even more sensitive than before to fluctuations in world prices.[27] Finally, the rapid increase in production has not always benefited the African worker, whose purchasing power has actually decreased slightly. In Senegal, for instance, the peasant who sold 100 kilos of ground nuts in 1938 could buy 57 kilos of rice in exchange; in 1955, sale of the same quantity of the oil-yielding nuts would allow the purchase of only 42.5 kilos of the cereal.

So criticism is still stringent. Dia suggests this programme:

> A complementary economy, first of all within the continent, between the great production areas of Africa organised into large economic units by reshaping the frontiers according to geographic lines instead of the arbitrary political delineations of the Europeans. Also a complementary economy with regard to the West, in the sense of a truly bilateral solidarity so that Eurafrican co-operation would be something other than the association of the giant and the dwarf.[28]

A false dilemma

One of the major problems for any investment policy is to choose the sectors in which the major effort is to be made. Mamadou Dia belabours one of the 'false dilemmas' which some economists and geographers are trying to foist on Africa: should priority be given to agriculture or industry? Should one of them even be abandoned in favour of the other? He advocates a balanced economy in place of either alternative, and attacks some of the geographers who have maintained that Africa's role is chiefly agricultural, thus condemning it in advance to prolonged underdevelopment. In reply to Pierre Gourou, who suggests in *Les Pays tropicaux* that industrialisation should be relegated to the distant future on account of local conditions, particularly the low density of the population, Dia comments: 'Here we can see a certain paternalism rearing its head and, under the mantle of science, constructing a theory of the strictly agricultural role of Africa, a perennial source of agricultural product for the world market.'[29]

In a speech to the second Congress of Negro Writers and Artists, another West African economist, Mamadou Touré, also crossed swords with those who wished to make out that agriculture should remain the chief resource of the black continent. He ended his analysis with these words: 'Whatever their ideological attachments, the people of under-developed countries refuse to accept a solution whose consequences would condemn them to stagnation and poverty.'[30]

The most striking aspect of this controversy is that non-communist writers, such as Tévoedjré (a militant catholic), are often in agreement with colleagues such as Dia, Ly and Maghemout Diop who go along with marxist ideology to varying degrees.

8

POLITICALLY COMMITTED LITERATURE

'AFRICAN LITERATURE is politically committed', declared Léopold Sédar Senghor at the first International Congress of Negro Writers and Artists at the Sorbonne in 1956. Indeed, African poetry and novels do appear on the whole to be conditioned by the colonial situation; African poets and novelists have usually regarded their work, as Césaire did, as 'miraculous weapons' to defeat their 'omniscient and naïve conquerors'.

African poets have followed in the footsteps of the Pleiad of West Indian poets, among whom Léon G. Damas was one of the first to assemble a collection of poems in his anthology *Poètes d'expression française*, published in 1947. Damas, author of *Black Label* and *Pigment*, pointed out that the time was past when a black West Indian writer 'made it a point of honour that a white man could read his book without guessing at his colour'.[1]

> Today it is no longer a question of being conscientious, of trying hard not to break the rules, to keep the metre, to work on impeccable sonnets. The heirs of Leconte de Lisle, François Coppée, Sully Prudhomme, Catulle Mendès, and Léon Dierx have lived, and lived well, on their inheritance. The time of repressions and inhibitions has given way to a different age: one where the colonial subject realises his rights and duties as an author, novelist, short story writer, essayist or poet. Poverty, illiteracy, the exploitation of man by man, social and political racism weighing on the black and yellow races, forced labour, inequality, lies, resignation, tricks, prejudices, complacency, cowardice, responsibilities shirked, crimes committed in the name of liberty, equality and fraternity: these are the subjects of this native poetry expressed in French.[2]

And Damas concludes: 'More than ever before politics and literature are becoming interwoven and their synchronism is becoming more and more obvious in the works of representatives of the new school.'[3]

Fifteen years later, Henri Kréa resurrected this formula as the title of a collection of Algerian poetry: *La Révolution et la poésie sont une même chose*. The same year, Mario de Andrade, one of the leading lights of Portuguese Negro poetry, said: 'There is no need to comment on the attitude of the new black African poets; this is expressed unequivocally in their works. In all of them the central theme is arranged around the fight to dispel the dark night of colonial oppression.'[4] Francesco Nditsouna expressed this militant concern in one sentence: 'I am not a poet, I want to be a fighter', he said at the beginning of his collection, *Fleurs de latérite*.[5]

The poets

Revolt against colonial rule, resentment at racial discrimination and also the terrible bitterness left by memories, however distant, of the slave trade, inspired African poets in the first place. In fact, slavery is still one of the main themes of Negro poetry. How could it be otherwise? In 1773, one of the first Negro poetesses, the American Phillis Wheatley, who was born in Senegal, wrote in a poem *To The Right Honourable William, Earl of Dartmouth, His Majesty's Secretary of State for North America:*

Should you, my lord, while you peruse my song,
Wonder from whence my love of Freedom sprung,
Whence flow these wishes for the common good,
By feeling hearts alone best understood,
I, young in life, by seeming cruel fate
Was snatched from Afric's fancied happy seat:
What pangs excruciating must molest,
What sorrows labour in my parent's breast!
Steeled was that soul, and by no misery moved,
That from a father seized his babe beloved:
Such, such my case. And can I then but pray
Others may never feel tyrannic sway?[6]

The Brazilian Luis Gama, half-caste son of a white father and slave mother, and a self-educated lawyer, hurled this avenging cry a century later at the Brazilian aristocracy, already of largely mixed blood, in response to their disdain:

Se os nobres desta terra empanturrados,
Em Guiné têm parentes enterrados;
E, cedendo à prosápia, ou duros vícious,

Esquecem os negrinhos, seus patrícios;
Se mulatos de côr esbranquicada,
Já se julgam de origem refinada.
E curvos à mania que os domina,
Desprezam a vovó que é preta-mina;
Não te espantes, leitor, da novidade,
Pois que tudo no Brasil é raridade!

(If noblemen here, puffed up with vanity, have ancestors buried in Guinea, and, giving way to pride and vice, forget the Negroes who are their brothers: if half-castes whose colour has lightened already judge themselves of refined origin and, bowing to the craze to keep up appearances, despise their old grandmother who is a negress, do not let such novelty surprise you reader, for in Brazil all is eccentric.)[7]

Nowadays, the black Cuban poet, Nicolás Guillén can introduce himself to his readers in just three lines:

Yo soy también el neito,
bisnieto,
tataranieto de un esclavo.

(I am the son, the great grandson, and the great-great-grandson of a slave.)[8]

What is more surprising is that the subject of slavery should be just as common today. Sartre gives the following explanation of this in his "Orphée noir":

> It was during the centuries of slavery that Negroes drank the cup of bitterness to the dregs. Slavery is a fact of the past which neither present-day authors nor their fathers knew personally. But it is also a gigantic nightmare from which even the youngest are not certain they have awakened completely. The Negroes, divided by the languages, policies and histories of the colonial powers, have this one collective memory in common, from one end of the continent to the other. This is not surprising when one remembers that in 1789 the French peasants were still obsessed by panic-stricken fears whose origins went back to the hundred years war.[9]

Certainly, Senghor's anthology—to which "Orphée noir" is the preface—dates from 1948 and brings together more West Indian than African writers. But Sartre's analysis is still true of the youngest generation of African poets, like the Congolese Martial Sinda who cannot escape from this 'memory'. His poem *Clarté de l'aube* is evidence of this:

Négrier,
Plaie incurable au poignet de l'Afrique . . .
L'odeur des chicottes;
L'odeur des cordes au cou
Suffoque les vagues furieuses de ma pensée . . .

(Slave trader, unhealable wound in Africa's wrist. . . . The smell of clubs; the smell of ropes round the neck stifles the stormy waves of my thoughts. . . .)

Tchicaya U'Tamsi has an equally lengthy memory:

La mer obéissait déjà aux seuls négriers
des nègres s'y laissaient prendre
malgré les sortilèges de leurs sourires
on sonnait le tocsin
à coups de pied au ventre
de passantes enceintes
il y a un couvre-feu pour faisander leur agonie.

(Already the sea obeyed the slave traders; the Negroes let themselves be taken despite the spell of their smiles; the alarm-bell was sounded with a kick in the bellies of pregnant women passing by; there is a curfew to draw out their death agony.)[10]

After all what difference is there between the slave and the colonial subject? The Malagasy Rabearivelo* does not distinguish any:

Le vitrier nègre
dont nul n'a jamais vu les prunelles sans nombre
et jusqu'aux épaules de qui personne ne s'est encore haussé,
cet esclave tout paré de perles de verroterie . . .

(The Negro glazier whose countless pupils none has ever seen, to whose shoulders no one has yet raised himself, this slave decked out with pearls of glass.)[11]

* Jean Joseph Rabearivelo committed suicide in 1937. The literary critic, Armand Guibert, sees this suicide as the culmination of a tragedy, analogous to that which tormented the Kabyle writer Jean Amrouche: that of the African intellectual torn between his love of France and French culture, and his love for his colonised homeland. Rabearivelo's suicide, says Guibert, was a decisive shock to the development of Amrouche. See *Dialogues*, No. I, May 1963.

These reminiscences are only one aspect of the more general theme of the Negro's condition. Bernard Dadié also writes of his misery:

Je vous remercie mon Dieu, de m'avoir créé Noir
D'avoir fait de moi
la somme de toutes les douleurs . . .

(I thank you God for having made me black, for having made me the sum of every sorrow. . . .)[12]

The Angolan poet, Agostino Neto, paints the anguish of the exploited Negro:

Nous les enfants nus des 'sanzalas' de la brousse
les gosses sans-école qui jouent avec un ballon de chiffons
sur les terre-pleins à midi
nous-mêmes
les loués pour brûler notre vie dans les champs de café
les hommes noirs ignorants
qui doivent respecter le blanc
et craindre le riche
nous sommes tes enfants des quartiers des nègres
où n'arrive pas l'électricité
les hommes ivres morts
abandonnés au rythme des tam-tams de mort
tes enfants
qui ont faim
qui ont soif
qui ont honte de t'appeler maman
qui ont peur de traverser les rues
qui ont peur des hommes . . .

(We are the naked children of the 'sanzalas' in the bush, the kids with no schooling who play with a rag ball in the open spaces at midday. We are the ones hired to burn out our lives in the coffee fields, the ignorant blackmen who should respect the white man and fear the rich. We are your children from the Negro districts which the electricity does not reach; the dead drunks abandoned to the rhythm of the tom-toms of death; your children who are hungry and thirsty and ashamed to call you mother, who are afraid to cross the road, who are afraid of men.)[13]

David Diop harps on the litany of insults to his race in *Un Blanc m'a dit:*

Tu n'es qu'un nègre!
Un nègre!
Un sale nègre!
Ton cœur est une éponge qui boit
Qui boit avec frénésie le liquide empoisonné du Vice
Et ta couleur emprisonne ton sang
Dans l'éternité de l'esclavage.
Le fer rouge de la justice t'a marqué
Marqué dans ta chair de luxure.
Ta route a les contours tortueux de l'humiliation
Et ton avenir, monstre damné, c'est ton présent de honte.

(You're a nigger! A nigger! A dirty nigger! Your heart is a sponge which sucks up, frantically sucks up, the poisoned liquor of Vice, and your colour imprisons your blood in slavery in perpetuity. The red hot iron of the law has marked you, marked your lewd flesh. Your road takes the tortuous route of humiliation and your future, damned, monster, is your present of shame.)[14]

But the Negro poet is not resigned to his fate. His revolt is the 'Negro gesture' whose outlines Sartre had noticed in several poems in Senghor's anthology, a gesture that seeks to tear the Negro from the stereotyped image of submission. The Haitian poets, fellow countrymen of Toussaint Louverture, were the first to attempt this. Jacques Roumain sees the Negro as a 'hawker of rebellion'.[15] Jean F. Briere reminds his fellow Negroes of their endless fight against European domination in the following terms:

Cinq siècles vous ont vus les armes à la main
et vous avez appris aux races exploitantes
la passion de la liberté.
A Saint-Domingue
vous jalonniez de suicides
et paviez de pierres anonymes
le sentier tortueux qui s'ouvrit un matin
sur la voie triomphale de l'indépendance.

(Five centuries have seen you with arms in your hands. You have taught the exploiting races the passion for freedom. In Santo Domingo you blazed the way with suicides and paved with anonymous stones the tortuous path which opened one morning on the glorious road to independence.)[16]

But Pierre Bamboté is already forecasting the Negro peoples' revenge:

Ils ont assassiné encore nos frères, le Docteur Malan avec leurs hommes buvant tous les jours du café, du thé au lait
on nous assassine, on continue
sur les mains et sur les genoux, nous avançons, Peuple noir,
Courage.
On nous entend. On arrivera.
Nous crions ton nom Soleil Liberté
Chaque aube qui se lève a chaque aube, nous rampons sur les feux ardents. Justice, la voici notre aube à toucher du doigt avec la force des embuscades, avec nos poignets. . . .

(They have murdered our brothers again, Dr Malan with their men, always drinking coffee and tea. We are being killed, we continue on our hands and knees, but we are advancing. Courage, black people. We can be heard. We shall arrive. We call on your name, sun of freedom, each dawn which rises, each dawn we crawl on the scorching fires. Justice: that is our dawn to touch with the finger, with the force of ambushes, with our fists. . . .)[17]

Europe's 'civilising mission' is also often the target of Negro poetry. This is the 'colonial epic' in brief for Amadou Moustapha Wade:

Voici venir les 'civilisateurs'
le canon, la Bible braquée
sur le cœur africain
la terre fut gorgée
de sang
ses fils s'étaient levés
pour défendre l'aurore . . .

(Here come the civilisers, the cannon, the Bible aimed at the Negro heart; the land ran with blood, its sons had risen to defend the dawn. . . .)[18]

R. E. G. Armattoe, the poet from Togo, favours irony rather than the cry of suffering or indignation. Sarcastically he dedicates his poem, *The White Man's Tomb*, to 'Sir Francis Galton, founder of the Galton Laboratory at London University, who hoped the yellow races might exclude the coarse, lazy, black races from the metal bearing regions at least of tropical Africa'.[19] However the same *leitmotiv* of Negro suffering and revolt runs through his whole poetic work. The Nigerian

Wole Soyinka also takes irony as his weapon in the *Telephone Conversation*, in which he mocks with ferocious humour an English landlady who asks him the colour of his skin when he answers over the telephone an advertisement for a flat.[20]

Running parallel to this denunciation of the colonial regime is a defiant hymn of praise sung by the African poets to the grandeur and beauty of Africa, their true homeland. Martial Sinda evokes his country—slandered (as in *Hymne à l'Afrique*):

Afrique pourquoi es-tu . . .
le pays des contes déformés
à la manière de bon conteur blanc.

(Africa why are you . . . the land of stories twisted as though by a white story teller.)

And conquered (as in *Tam-Tam, tam-tam-toi*):

Afrique de jadis
Afrique domptée
O, Afrique, ohoe, notre Afrique . . .

(Africa of former times, Africa subdued, O Africa, Oh! our Africa. . . .)

Bernard Dadié's *Couronne à l'Afrique* has the imprint of an almost mystical fervour:

Je te tresserai une couronne
de douce lueur
avec l'éclat de la Vénus des Tropiques
Et dans l'orbe du scintillement fiévreux
de la voie lactée
J'écrirai
en lettres
de feu
ton
nom,
O, Afrique.

(I will weave for you a crown with a gentle glow, with the flash of a tropical Venus, and in the orb, feverishly sparkling, of the Milky Way, I will write your name in letters of fire, O Africa.)

Davidson Nicol discovered what his African homeland meant to him on his return from a long stay in Britain:

> I know now that is what you are, Africa:
> Happiness, contentment, and fulfilment,
> And a small bird singing on a mango tree.[21]

The theme of African emancipation has naturally taken its place in Negro poetry during the last few years. For Michael Dei-Anang, the independence for which he had been longing ever since 1949 would be a golden age of light, following a gloomy past of strife:

> When the dawn
> of independence breaks
> upon this golden shore
> oh, let it break
> upon a land
> wherein the beauteous glow
> of liberty
> has chased away
> the gloom of greed
> and the clouds of strife.[22]

The homeland freed at last is also a source of inspiration for Paulin Joachin, even if he does sound anxious as he greets 'Africa freed and taking off':

> *Je salue l'Afrique à l'envol rendu libre*
> *c'est l'expiration de ta peine ô ma Mère et j'exulte*
> *ils ont érigé leurs fortunes et leurs empires sur ton*
> *innocence et ta timidité . . .*
> *ô Seigneur choisis pour ce peuple de bons bergers*
> *et non pas de frénétiques ambitieux qui ne travailleront*
> *que pour leur promotion au rang d'idole*
> *je salue l'Afrique libre.*

(I greet Africa, freed and taking off; this is the end of your affliction, my mother, and I am exultant. They have built their fortunes and empires on your innocence and timidity. . . . O Lord, choose good shepherds for these people, not men of frenzied ambition who will work only for their own promotion to the place of an idol. I greet you, free Africa.)[23]

The time soon comes when the African poet glories in his blackness, like the Ghanaian poet F. E. Kobina Parkes in *African Heaven:*

Give me black souls,
Let them be black
Or chocolate brown
Or make them the
Colour of dust—
Dustlike,
Browner than sand.
But if you can
Please make them black,
Black.[24]

However, there is also a Negro poetry which is not politically involved. Subjects from African folklore take pride of place in Birago Diop's work, as in *Souffles:*

Écoute plus souvent
les choses que les êtres,
la voix du feu s'entend,
entends la voix de l'eau
écoute dans le vent
le buisson en sanglots.
C'est le souffle des ancêtres . . .

(Listen more often to things than to people. The voice of the fire is heard, listen to the voice of water, hear the wind, the bushes sobbing. This is the breath of your ancestors. . . .)[25]

Folklore also inspired the Nigerian Adeboye Babalola with his *Personnages de Village*, and the Ghanaian Efua Morgue with her *Ashanti History*, which begins like a fairy story: 'Once upon a time coconuts were rare . . .'[26] This non-commitment may sometimes stem from a desire to avoid the ire of the colonial authorities. In any case this is what David Diop believes to have found in the poetry of the Congolese writer, Antoine-Roger Bolamba: 'Is it prudence (we know the extraordinary . . . severity of the royal administration) which leads Bolamba to avoid themes that are too dangerous? For it is not possible that he should have seen no more of his country than appears in his works. I also have the impression that in his poem *Lokolé* he allows us to guess at the depths of his thoughts:

Lokolé
J'entends hurler la défaite aux abois
j'entends les râles
de l'égoïsme
Place à l'esprit
Il trône dans mon cœur
Dans mon cœur sonnent les trompettes
de la victoire
Victoire de Lokolé
Ma victoire, Notre Victoire.'

(*Lokolé*,* I hear defeat howling at bay; I hear the death rattle of egoism. Make room for the spirit, it reigns in my heart, in my heart sound the trumpets of victory. The victory of *Lokolé*, my victory, our victory.)[27]

It is without rancour, and intensely seriously, that the Malawi poet, James D. Rubadiri, describes the historic meeting between Stanley and the Negro king Mutesa:

The gate of reeds is flung open,
There is silence
But only a moment's silence—
A silence of assessment.
The tall black king steps forward,
He towers over the thin bearded white man
Then grabbing his lean white hand
Manages to whisper
'Mtu mweupe karibu'
White man you are welcome.
The gate of polished reeds closes behind them
And the West is let in.[28]

Negro poets have welcomed the reconciliation. Dei-Anang pays homage to Queen Elizabeth, as head of the Commonwealth, during whose reign his country achieved independence:

Queen of vast continents and seas
whose loyal sons
diverse in race,
are one in unity,

* *Lokolé* is a gong used in the past to send news by traditional sounds.

the world acclaims
your majesty.[29]

The refusal to hate and willingness to forgive have not waited for decolonisation to find expression. As early as 1939, in the *Cahier d'un retour au pays natal*, Césaire had said:

. . . mon cœur, préservez-moi de toute haine
ne faites point de moi cet homme de haine pour qui je n'ai
que haine car pour me cantonner en cette unique race
vous savez pourtant mon amour tyrannique
vous savez qui ce n'est point par haine des autres races
que je m'exige bêcheur de cette unique race
que ce que je veux
c'est pour la faim universelle
pour la soif universelle
la sommer libre enfin . . .

(. . . my heart, save me from all hatred, do not make me that man of hate for whom I have only hatred. You know my ruling passion to restrict myself to that race alone, you know that it is not for hatred of other races that I strain to work so hard for that race alone. It is because of the universal hunger of mankind, the universal thirst, that I wish to see it free at last.)

Félix Tchicaya U'Tamsi echoes Césaire's pathetic cry with a more haughty demand:

Je ne verrai plus mon sang sur leurs mains
j'oublie d'être nègre pour pardonner cela au monde
C'est dit qu'on me laisse la paix d'être congolais.

(I shall no longer see my blood on their hands, I forget that I am black, in order to forgive the world for that. That's all, may I be left in peace to be Congolese.)[30]

It is above all in Senghor's poetry that the great catholic pardon is found: it is the *Prière de paix* (prayer for peace) preceded by the exergue *Sicut et nos dimittimus debitoribus nostris*:

Seigneur la glace de mes yeux s'embue
Et voilà que le serpent de la haine lève la tête dans mon cœur, ce serpent que j'avais cru mort . . .

Tue-le Seigneur, car il me faut poursuivre mon chemin, et je veux prier singulièrement pour la France.
Seigneur, parmi les nations blanches, place la France à la droite du Père.
Oh! je sais bien qu'elle aussi est l'Europe, qu'elle m'a ravi mes enfants comme un brigand du Nord des bœufs, pour engraisser ses terres à cannes et coton car la sueur nègre est fumier.
Qu'elle aussi a porté la mort et le canon dans mes villages bleus, qu'elle a dressé les miens les uns contre les autres comme des chiens se disputant un os.
Qu'elle a traité les résistants de bandits, et craché sur les têtes-aux-vastes-desseins.
Oui Seigneur, pardonne à la France qui dit bien la voie droite et chemine par les sentiers obliques.
Qui m'invite à sa table et me dit d'apporter mon pain, qui me donne de la main droite et de la main gauche enlève la moitié.
Oui Seigneur, pardonne à la France qui hait les occupants et m'impose l'occupation si gravement.
Qui ouvre des voies triomphales aux héros et traite ses Sénégalais en mercenaires, faisant d'eux les dogues noirs de l'Empire.
Qui est la République et livre le pays aux Grands-Concessionnaires.
Et de ma Mésopotamie, de mon Congo, ils ont fait un grand cimetière sous le soleil blanc.

(Lord the mirror of my eyes clouds over and there is the serpent of hate raising his head in my heart, the serpent whom I had believed dead. . . . Kill it, O Lord, for I must continue on my way and I want to pray particularly for France. O Lord, among all the white nations, place France on the right hand of the Father. Oh! I know she is also part of Europe, that she has stolen my children as a robber from the north takes cattle, to enrich her lands with sugar cane and cotton, for the Negro's sweat is manure; that she also brought death and the cannon into my blue villages; that she set my people one against the other like dogs fighting over a bone; that she treated resistance as banditry, and spat on the heads that dreamt of greatness. Yes Lord, forgive France who preaches the straight path but takes the crooked one herself; who invites me to her table yet tells me to bring my own bread, who gives to me with the right hand but takes half away again with the left. Yes Lord, forgive France who hates occupiers yet imposes occupation so heavily on me; who opens the triumphal gates to heroes and treats her Senegalese as mercenaries, making them the black watch dogs of the Empire; who is a

Republic yet places the country in the hands of big companies. And of my Mesopotamia, of my Congo, they have made a great cemetery beneath the white sun.)[31]

The novelists

'Here at last is an African novel which has no political motive.' This was the sigh of relief of the French publisher who brought out, in 1957, the novel *Mission terminée* by the Cameroon writer Mongo Beti. The remark was all the more justifiable since the author's first two books, *Ville cruelle* (under the pseudonym Eza Boto) and *Le Pauvre Christ de Bomba*, were both particularly critical of the colonialists. However, *Mission terminée* did not signify a new departure in Mongo Beti's work, and in his fourth book, *Le Roi miraculé*, there is the same sarcastic tone as in the first two when he is discussing the civilising work of the colonial powers and the christian missionaries. African novelists are just as politically committed as the poets: denunciation of the colonial regime is the main theme of a whole series of African novels. Here again West Indian writers, such as René Maran, had blazed the trail. The latter had had to leave the colonial administration after writing his well-known *Batouala* during a spell in Ubangi-Chari.

The African 'protest' novel is sometimes given a contemporary political setting: the most striking example of this in French-speaking Africa is undoubtedly the latest novel of Sembène Ousmane, *Les Bouts de bois de Dieu*. This work is dedicated to black African trade unionists and tells of the strike on the Dakar-Niger railway in 1947-8. It is a long story in which the reader follows the action from town to town all along the railway line. The book takes the form of a distilled account of the experiences of a veteran trade unionist in black Africa. It shows all the problems connected with workers' movements: control of the militants who are quickly discouraged, solidarity between territories, support from other professional trade unions and from the metropolitan union headquarters, and the collection of strike funds. The daily reactions of the population are followed: reservations at times from the elderly, uneasiness among the women whose support will be decisive in the long run, a lack of class consciousness in some of the educated, collusion between the colonial administration and some black parliamentarians and the muslim religious authorities. Finally, we penetrate into the enemy camp, the upper ranks of the administration, who try out every possible diverting tactic: from creating an alternative union, bribing the leaders, false conciliation moves and forbidding Syrian tradesmen to give credit to the starving families of the strikers, to the final blood conflict between civil guards and the populace.

The struggle of African trade unionists and nationalists is also evoked in Bernard Dadié's novel, *Climbié*. Climbié finds himself in prison for having criticised in a newspaper article the injustice of colonial administration. When he is judged by a European magistrate far younger than himself, his disillusionment shows in the reflection that: 'He was only starting his career while Climbié and his friends all had at least 15 years' service behind them. But they had to stay at the bottom of the ladder, their position in life.'[32]

The classic of this genre is probably *A Wreath for Udomo* by the South African Peter Abrahams. This tells of the rise of a young Negro student who came to power in his country 'Panafrica'. He dies, assassinated because he betrayed the cause of nationalism by handing over another African leader, Mendhi, who had asked for his support, to the police of a neighbouring country, 'Pluralia', where the Europeans had stayed in power. This was the price of white financial aid and technical co-operation. Abrahams' novel re-creates splendidly the atmosphere of Labour meetings in London to which Negro students were invited, but it also shows political activities in Africa. We see the printing of the daily bulletin, which can hardly be called a newspaper but which gives the signal for the strike; we rub shoulders with the African market women led by Selina, whose support was a decisive trump card for the nationalist movement; we follow the career of the West Indian Negro, Tom Landwood, who worked for years to build up his theory of African nationalism in miserable lodgings in London, became a minister in Africa, and was then swept aside without compunction. Finally we see the 'new wave' of British colonial administrators in the person of a new governor with liberal ideas, and the conservative African leaders who are unwilling to take any risks. The book ends with the quasi-ritual murder of Udomo, alone in his brand-new palace, horrified to hear in the night the beat of the tom-tom announcing his execution and waiting like some cornered beast for the knife of justice to strike. It was Selina who ordered the execution of the man she had brought to power.

Peter Abrahams' novel caused a considerable stir in the Gold Coast in 1956. Appearing a few months before independence, it looked like a gloomy prediction, since similarities between Udomo's career and the early career of Nkrumah had not escaped notice. The president of Ghana had indeed been helped by the support of the women of his country, who control the small-scale retail trade as is usual on the west coast of Africa. He had been influenced by the works of the West Indian, George Padmore, a theoretician of African nationalism, whom he invited to Accra as his advisor immediately after independence. Padmore recalled the character of Landwood. Sir Charles Arden-Clarke, governor-general at the time, was a man of liberal ideas, like the governor in the book. The 'false' alert was given, in a way, by the *Daily Graphic** of Accra in July 1956; in a long critique devoted to Peter Abrahams' book, the following comment appeared: 'The link with events in the Gold Coast is clear.'

In South Africa, racial discrimination and apartheid have provided Negro writers with the setting, if not the subject, for a large number of novels. Most of Peter Abrahams' other books re-create the social climate of this country of racial segregation. The South African writer, with his *Mine Boy*, *Tell Freedom* and *The Path of Thunder*, is in many ways the Richard Wright of Southern Africa.

Ezekiel Mphahlele's autobiographical story, *Down Second Avenue*, is in the same vein. It includes two episodes which are typical of Negro life in South Africa: the police round-ups in search of shops selling illegally-distilled alcohol, and the compulsory evacuation of a Negro district, during which the police open fire and kill a child. In *African Image*, Ezekiel Mphahlele gives a long list of South African Negro literature of 'protest': beside Peter Abrahams he ranges H. I. E. Dhlomo, who expressed the despair of his oppressed race in a long poem, *Valley of a Thousand Hills;* Alfred Hutchinson, one of the accused in the famous treason trial,† who in *Road to Ghana* denounces the stifling climate which drove him into exile; news and short story writers such as Richard Rive, Alex La Guma and Bloke Modisane, who published a poignant autobiography, *Blame Me on History;* and a number of others. *Drawn in Colour*, a novel by Noni Jabavu, daughter of a Xhosa teacher, also gives a bitter description of apartheid: this is a book which Dr Verwoerd should be made to read, remarked the London *Observer* critic.

* The *Daily Graphic* belongs to the British newspaper chain of Cecil King, who also owns the London *Daily Mirror*, a paper with Labour sympathies.

† This interminable trial of some hundred intellectuals, whose only guilt was to disagree with apartheid, finally fizzled out with the acquittal of all the accused, the last ones in 1961. The trial had started in 1956.

Exploitation of the African peasant or worker under the colonial system has also provided the subject for several novels. Mongo Beti's first book, *Ville cruelle*, hinges on two economic events: first a European employer underpays his African labourers, then a young African peasant is refused sale of his cocoa harvest by the administration. The European employer is killed during a scuffle with his workmen who have come to claim their wages: Koumé is to blame for this. The police set off after him. He is helped in his flight by a young peasant, Banda, who has just been given a rough handling by the police because he protested against the marketing board's declaration that his 200 kilos of cocoa beans, the fruit of a year's labour, were unfit for consumption. Banda had been imprudent enough to disagree with the inspectors. In *Afrique, nous t'ignorons!* Benjamin Matip denounces the exploitation of the Negro peasant by white tradesmen; his hero, Samba, also attacks the elder generation of small scale black planters who passively accept colonial rule. Jean Ikelle-Matiba, also from Cameroon, puts in the dock forced labour in Cameroon between the two wars in *Cette Afrique-là*. Penal labour, beatings and imprisonment overwhelm the hero who made the mistake of not being willing to serve the French authorities after the departure of the Germans, who had given him the opportunity to continue his studies, and under whose rule he had started on a brilliant career which was interrupted by their defeat. In Sembène Ousmane's book, *O pays, mon beau peuple*, the hero Oumar Faye opposes the monopoly of European companies (who buy the industrial crops at low prices) by forming a co-operative. He comes up against the indifference of the authorities and is murdered by killers hired by the companies, worried at seeing their privileges threatened.

Prison, rough treatment, and racial humiliation are constant themes of the African protest novel. In each of Ferdinand Oyono's two books the prison episode is the climax of the drama: in *Une Vie de boy*, Toundi —the young servant accused of a theft he has not committed—dies of exhaustion trying to escape from the hospital to which he had been admitted following a brutal interrogation. In *Le vieux Nègre et la médaille*, the consequences are less serious. Meka is arrested in a round-up on the very day that he received an exemplary conduct medal from the colonial administration. He is knocked about, beaten and spat upon before being recognised, but he has lost all faith in white friendship for life. The scene of the beating-up in *Land of Sunshine: Scenes of Life in Kenya before Mau Mau* is taken from real life. Muga Gicaru tells how two European officers, accompanied by African police, interrogated eight Negroes arrested during an enquiry into a theft: truncheon blows rain, but there is also torture, applied to the genitals. The narrator is released because he is young and not yet circumcised.

Some of the most recent evidence on prisons and detention camps in Africa appears in Josiah Mwangi Kariuki's account of his own experiences. He was in fourteen successive camps in seven years, from 1953-60, suspected of being a Mau Mau sympathiser. A striking photograph of the informers dressed in long hooded robes revealing only their eyes, who decided the classification of detainees into unrepentant hard core, heavily infected but not unreclaimable, and clear or rehabilitated, is an illustration of the psychological methods used by the penal authorities. These agents were themselves Africans, attracted by the offer of gain or tranquillity or, says, Kariuki, just common thugs. The author also tells of maltreatment of prisoners which in several cases led to their deaths, as in the Hola camp where there were eleven victims. Kariuki gives a dead-pan description of beatings followed by detention in the cells, which on each occasion provided the substance of messages smuggled out to Labour members of parliament such as Barbara Castle; they served to arouse public opinion in Britain, and several times provoked debates in parliament. The author of *Mau Mau Detainee* estimates that 80,000 Kenyans had experience of the camps set up by the British colonial authorities in their fight against the nationalist movement.

Finally, the drama of the Negro's position is expressed in the accounts of milder humiliations to which he is daily subjected. These are the insults—and blows too—which the settler eagerly heaps on the shoulders of his boys and employees. The backwoods population are also subjected to the whims of bored administrators, such as the Belgian official who trained a more or less tame leopard to terrorise Africans in his district, as Mopila relates in his autobiography.[33] It is seen in its most naïve form in the story of the little boy who has never seen a black man and who wipes his hands after shaking hands with Fara, the hero of *Mirages de Paris*, by Ousmane Socé.

(In *Peau noire, masques blancs* the West Indian Frantz Fanon gives a long analysis of racism. The hegelian concept of 'existing for others' serves him as the point of departure, while Jean Paul Sartre's *Réflexions sur la question juive* provides him with interesting comparisons. Sartre writes à propos the Jews that 'they have allowed themselves to become poisoned by other people's opinion of them and live in fear that their actions should not conform to this; thus we might say that their conduct is perpetually predetermined from the interior'. Fanon comments:

> But the Jew may be overlooked as such. He is not wholly what he is. One can wait and hope. He is a white man and, apart from a few very debatable characteristics, he can pass unnoticed. He belongs to a race that has never known cannibalism. What an idea to eat one's own father! It is clear that one only has to be not black. Of course the Jews have been bullied, driven out, exterminated, burnt, but those are minor family troubles. The Jew is not liked from the moment he becomes vulnerable. But with me everything is different. I am not given any chance. I am predetermined from the exterior. I am not a slave of the 'idea' that others may have of me, but of my appearance.[34]

And Fanon adds: 'If Sartre's studies on the existence of others are true —to the extent, it should be remembered, that *L'Étre et le Neant* describes a deprived, alienated mind—their application to a Negro mind is false. This is because the white man is not the other person, but the real or imaginary master besides.')

Negro Jews

Among this literature of protest, there appears one of the most amazing books to have been published under an African-sounding signature: *An African Savage's Own Story* by Lobagola. Although it is made out to be an autobiographical novel, there is no doubt that most of it is, in fact, fairly hair-raising fiction. The Africa described by Lobagola, for all the precise geographical references, is highly improbable. This might lead one to wonder whether in fact it was an African who wrote it at all: the precautions taken to prove it—two photographs of the author and facsimiles of his passport and military record—have the opposite effect and actually arouse suspicion. Many passages are completely incredible. These include a nightmarish and hallucinatory account of the capture of the hero and his guide by cannibal dwarfs who make a porridge of the brains of their captives after splitting their skulls. Yet this description of appallingly primitive customs is not intended to exalt by contrast European civilisation. Lobagola defends some African institutions, such as polygamy, and judges European society without indulgence. It was in Europe, he says, that he learnt lying and hypocrisy. The chapters set in Europe and the United States are highly critical of racial discrimination, and Lobagola accuses the West of having made him a hybrid rejected by both Africans and Europeans.

However, the strangeness of the book stems from another source: the author asserts that he is a member of a tribe of Negro Jews lost in West Africa '600 miles to the north of Abomey Calavi, formerly the capital of Dahomey'. (This is not correct: the ancient capital of the kings of Dahomey was Abomey. Abomey Calavi is also in Dahomey but it is a lakeside village on the Cotonou lagoon, right beside the coast, whereas Abomey is some 70 miles inland.) Lobagola gives the following account of the origins of his tribe:

> How did Judaism come into my obscure land, in the middle of Africa, far south of Timbuktu, surrounded by heathenism and savagery? In about twenty villages two thousand souls, all black, believe they are of Jewish origin and call themselves 'B'nai Ephraim'. The other natives call them 'Emo-Yo-Quaim', or 'the Strange People'. My people, 'the children of Ephraim', have part of the Hebrew Torah, written in the script of Aramaic, brought with them when they came into their country over eighteen hundred years ago. Our Torah is not written in ink, but burned into the parchment by a hot iron.[35]

The rather 'shame-faced' preface (whose anonymous writer admits that the author has 'embroidered' his tale a little) includes some quotations from the *Encyclopaedia Britannica* and Maurice Fishberg's *The Jews: A Study of Race Environment*. These mention the presence of Jews in Africa and refer to Jewish settlements north of the Sahara such as the Mzab, the Falasha Jews of Ethiopia and those of the Loango coast.

The Negro Jewish community of Loango, like that of São Tomé, are descendants of Spanish Jewish children who were forcibly baptised and then deported by the Inquisition. One group of Jews expelled from Spain fled to Portugal, whence King John II sent some of them to Africa, and in particular 2,000 children to the island of São Tomé in 1493. The Falasha of Ethiopia, who claim descent from Menelik, son of Solomon and the Queen of Sheba, are not thought to be originally Jews. As for the Jews of the northern fringes of the Sahara, the *Tarikh al Fettash* mentions the existence of a Jewish minority in the Niger loop, and Askia Mohamed, one of the Songhai emperors, brought Moroccan Jewish gardeners from the Tuat to improve agricultural productivity. Among the many theories on the origins of the Fulani, Delafosse has upheld that of their Jewish origin. According to him the Fulani were the descendants of Jews who were deported from Egypt by order of one of the Ptolemies and who originally went to Cyrenaica. Persecuted by the Romans, they emigrated to the Fezzan, thence to the Air and finally to the Massina. This theory is challenged today by most specialists. However, Germaine Dieterlen and Hampaté Ba have found several references to Solomon in the initiatory texts of Fulani shepherds.[36]

John Henderson Soga, a black South African ethnologist, has also been struck by certain similarities between Jewish customs and those of tribes in southern Africa. In his book, *The Ama-Xosa: Life and Customs*, he suggests that a possible explanation may be Ethiopian influence on these tribes before their migration to the south, or perhaps Arab influence from the ports on the eastern seaboard of the continent. However this may be, it is interesting to note that the separatist African churches in South Africa identify themselves closely with the Old Testament.

Mauny, a professor at the Sorbonne, has reviewed the whole question in his article "Le Judaisme, les Juifs et l'Afrique occidentale".[37] He expresses astonishment at the 'mistaken idea' of nineteenth- and twentieth-century European historians who have sought a Jewish origin for African populations each time they were found to have 'whiter skins than the neighbouring races'. In the same context he thinks J. J. Williams' theories more than rash; the latter, in *Hebrewisms of West Africa* suggests that animism is merely another form of Judaism. 'This is taking holy exegesis rather far', Mauny comments ironically. As for the novel of Lobagola, 'only those who have never been to Africa could take it seriously'.

Lobagola's autobiography was published in London in 1930 and translated into French in 1932. Whether or not it was written by a black man, and in spite of its being not very true to life, it is nevertheless no mere literary 'curiosity': over and above the fantastic story and generally apocryphal description of Africa, it is a significant piece of evidence. The man who wrote this book wished to associate the hapless destinies of two persecuted races—the Negroes and the Jews—in one symbolic character.[38]

Portrait of the European

What kind of portrait of the European do Negro writers give their readers? The picture is often sinister or caricatured: drunken, debauched, dishonest and brutal settlers, coarse and violent police, self-satisfied and ridiculous administrators—these are the Europeans described in novels by Ferdinand Oyono, Jean Malonga and Mongo Beti. However, the friendly white man is rarely altogether absent. In *O pays, mon beau peuple*, there is Pierre, sickened by the cupidity of the great European companies; in *Climbié*, Targe, whose brotherly letter is the conclusion to the book; the teacher, Salvain, who is exasperated by his fellow-countrymen's scorn for the black people in *Une Vie de boy;* the inspector general of education who rescues Mambéké from the hands of the police in *Cœur d'Aryenne*. In Aké Loba's *Kocoumba*, it is Barge, the administrator, who saves the hero from the poverty into which he has sunk in Paris. In Sheikh Hamidou Kane's book, *L'Aventure ambiguë*, it is Pastor Martial's family. Finally, there is 'Doc' Bailleux, a white man whose exceptionally warm heart won him a place beside the famous warriors of Mandingo folklore, as is reported by Keita Fodeba, former director of the African Ballet and currently minister in Guinea, in his *Poèmes africains*.

Olympe Bhely-Quenum has tried to balance out his representation of the white man in *Un Piège sans fin*. Of two European warders in the Dahomey prison where his hero ends up, one is sympathetic, just and without racial prejudice, while the other is narrow-minded, irritable and scornful of Negroes. Like Césaire and Senghor, the Fulani novelist, Sheikh Hamidou Kane, casts out the hatred of the white man which wells up in his heart. This hatred is painful: it comes from 'repressed love'.[39] Frantz Fanon, the pure revolutionary who sided with the FLN, also overcame his resentment. In *Peau noire, masques blancs*, he says: 'I have not the right as a coloured man to hope that white people will develop a sense of guilt about the past of my race. I have not the right as a coloured man to worry over ways of stamping out the pride of my former masters. I have neither the right nor the duty to demand redress for my domesticated ancestors.'[40] In concluding an account of the merciless French repression of a Tuareg rebellion, Fily Dabo Sissoko recalls in his *La Savane rouge* the words spoken at an international conference in Gland, Switzerland, in 1927: 'We are beginning to understand that the country's troubles should not be blamed on France, but on a few Frenchmen.'[41] Jacques Howlett sees in the following lines by Joseph Miezan Bognini the expression of the poet's interior struggle with his feelings towards the white man, 'the strangers who brought emptiness';

> *Porter la haine au dedans de soi*
> *n'est pas chose facile à détruire.*

(It is not easy to destroy the hatred borne within.)[42]

Mamadou Gologo who, in his novelistic autobiography, is often acrimonious on the subject of the French administration, is capable of giving warm praise to some colonial officials such as one director of the William Ponty School (referred to by the initials C.B.—probably Charles Béart) or the doctor who founded the Dakar medical school whom he calls, without naming him, 'a true servant of France in Africa'.[43]

One of the most striking expressions of the desire to control all feelings of resentment towards the colonialists is to be found in Nwafor Orizu's book, where it has even provided the title, *Without Bitterness*. The young Nigerian prince, a disciple of Nnamdi Azikiwe, wrote this long work in 1943 while a student in the United States. The 400-odd pages of this fairly acid indictment of colonialism end thus: 'Africa must not train the rising generation to hate Europeans because of the evils wrought by imperialism in the past. Our fight must be for principles, not against peoples.'[44]

From its very beginnings, African nationalism was no less careful to suppress its rancour. One of the very first African intellectuals from the British colonies of the west coast, Dr Aggrey,* coined this striking comparison to illustrate the need for co-operation between races: in music the black and white notes are indispensable to each other, so in life, black and white people must come to an agreement. However naïve this formula may appear today, it nourished and inspired the first generation of nationalists in British West Africa between the wars.

Nevertheless, African criticism is not just one-sided: Aké Loba's novel, *Kocoumba, l'étudiant noir*, gives a totally uncomplacent picture of the life of African students. In *Crayons et portraits*, Fily Dabo Sissoko also gives a warning to his fellow countrymen. His favourite target is the pseudo-educated Negro, like his black *Bourgeois gentilhomme*.

> This type is very common. Completely illiterate, or barely able to read and write, he makes an impression all the same by his manner

*Kwame Nkrumah was a pupil of Dr Aggrey.

> and bearing. A subscriber to the Ligue des Droits de l'homme et du citoyen, to the official newspaper of the colony and to his local 'Party' paper, he likes to stretch out on his chaise-longue in the evening and be read to. He is a great newsmonger. He knows how Abd-El-Krim was defeated, how Galandou Diouf beat Maître Lamine Gueye. He knows that the Negus is dreaming revenge on the 'Duce'. Franco is at the gates of Madrid: that sets him in a flutter! He knows the financial intentions of M. Vincent Auriol! When he is doing business he gets his information directly in legal jargon, or has it got for him. He makes a display of the law and his rights. The duplicated letter from an MP or a general, or even a simple visiting card, throw him into such ecstasy that he is quite out of countenance. He is a naturalised Frenchman or is working to become one: he would give his whole fortune for that. His daughter will marry only a cultured man. So his life flows by. Good living and a good bed in the sort of fatuity which is the antipode of culture.[45]

In *Tante Bella*, it is ancient African institutions, grown increasingly dangerous in recent years, that Joseph Owono decries: in this case, dowry. The author first undertakes a long enquiry into the position of women; this covers both the life of prostitutes and the economic and social consequences of the fantastically high price which the dowry has reached. In the second part of the book, he tells the story of his pre-1914 heroine, who gave her name to the title. She was promised in marriage at the age of two, but the death of her future husband meant that she was passed like a bundle of goods from bed to bed by successive husbands. In short, this is a lengthy appeal for the emancipation of African women, which attacks custom and contemporary ways alike. And lastly, in *Jagua Nana*, Cyprian Ekwensi presents a scarcely flattering picture of Nigerian political morality.

The town

Even the non-committed novel is largely determined by the colonial situation. It is striking that the town, creation of the European in Africa, should be chosen as the setting for many novels. It is the town, with its pleasures and temptations, which Karim discovers in Ousmane Socé's first book.[46] Weighed down with debts from trying to impress his girl friends, Karim leaves Dakar and his European clothes and returns to his village and traditional garb. It is also the town which takes her fiancé away from the little peasant girl, Maimouna, in Abdoulaye Sadji's novel of the same name. Again it is the town which is the protagonist, one might almost say, of *Peoples of the City*, the first novel of Cyprian Ekwensi from Nigeria. He tells of the tribulations of a young African journalist in the teeming city, of his perpetual and fruitless hunt for lodgings which would give him the bourgeois stability he lacks on account of his numerous amorous adventures. But there is nothing tragic about this clutching city; the clever description overlooks the hovels and dens of the shanty towns of Lagos, and makes it seem a fascinating destination.

How different is Tonga, the *Ville cruelle* of Mongo Beti, where all is headstrong, deceitful strife. The towns in *Simbi and the Satyr of the Dark Jungle*, Amos Tutuola's last book, are cruel too. Simbi, the daughter of a very rich mother, is the most popular dancer in the village, but she chooses to leave her narrow, backwoods horizons to get to know 'poverty' and 'punishment'. She leaves the family home and pays heavily by a thousand trials for her spoilt whim in the course of an extraordinary journey, during which she has a miraculous escape from the satyr. The two towns she comes across on the way are both hostile to her. In the first the people are dyed many colours: their racial prejudices are such that Simbi has to flee to escape death. In the second, where she marries a carpenter, she has to sacrifice her newborn child to a pitiless god. (The episode of the 'town with multicoloured inhabitants' is one of the few political allusions in this Nigerian author's works.)

So in African literature the town has become a symbol of contact with the West, with its blemishes and attractions. The 'shock' of the invasion of European civilisation into tribal African society has been dealt with even more explicitly. Several African writers have found it a fine subject for a novel. First, there is the Nigerian Chinua Achebe, with *Things Fall Apart*. This is the story of the decay of the social structure of an Ibo village under pressure from administrators and missionaries. The suicide of the hero, Okonkwo, after he has taken part in burning down the missionary school and killing a British official with his own hands, is an admission of his impotence to stop the course of history as much as a final gesture of rebellion against the new order. He chooses to die rather than submit. This writer's second novel, *No Longer At Ease*, is also a story of failure. This time it is Okonkwo's grandson who is led to dishonour by the endless difficulties which face an African university graduate whose family refuse to allow him to marry a girl of a lower caste. The South African Archibald Jordan, in his *Ingqumbo Yeminyana* ("the wrath of the ancestors"), tells the story of an advanced traditional chief and his wife whose attempt to introduce civilisation to their tribe comes to a tragic end. *Blanket Boy's Moon*, a novel by Mopeli-Paulus, written in Sesotho and adapted by Peter Lanham, is one of the best illustrations of the conflict between tradition and urban detribalisation. The hero, Monare, after having lived in Johannesburg, goes back to Basutoland and, out of respect for tribal order, takes part in a ritual murder prescribed by the chief. But the novel is more than a simple account of the conflict between European and African civilisation: it is above all an indictment of apartheid.

Thus African novels and poetry have been in the forefront of the political struggle. So great has been the conviction that this is essential that the journal *Présence Africaine* has twice taken Camara Laye to task because his novels were not set in the context of the fight against colonialism. About *L'Enfant noir* the *Présence Africaine* writer said: 'Laye resolutely shuts his eyes to the most crucial realities, those which we have always been very careful to reveal to the public here. Has this Guinean, of my own race, who it seems was a very lively boy, really seen nothing but a beautiful, peaceful and maternal Africa? Is it possible that not once has Laye witnessed a single minor extortion by the colonial authorities?'

Présence Africaine was equally hard on *Le Regard du roi*. Their critic considered the dedication to the high commissioner of the republic in French West Africa ridiculous. But that was only a venial sin:

> Whatever Camara Laye does, however hard he tries, his work will never find a place outside the shelf of Negro literature. And seasoned critics, who woo him as a young Ephebe, are aware of this, are grateful to him for introducing them to the terrible rites of the brotherhood of Lions, and for allowing them an indiscreet peep through the chinks in the savage's hut. But mere picturesqueness is not enough to explain this suspect courtesy from the critics. J-P. Sartre said somewhere that new ideas are inevitably displeasing since they disconcert and even shock. If Camara Laye pleases easily this is because he is reassuring: nothing that he has to say is really new. So he should be classed among those docile and ambiguous clerks of

whom we were speaking above; he is also probably not the first of these intransigent writers with enough temperament and talent to succeed in spite of the combination of hostile circumstances.[47]

Sartre and "Orphée noir"

Here then, in these two articles, is a definition of what African literature should be. Sartre considers that this has in fact been the basis of the 'negritude' poetry, above all a cry of rebellion by the black proletariat. The author of "Orphée noir" writes: 'It is no mere chance that the most ardent poets of the negritude movements are also militant marxists.'[48] (I should point out that the Negro poets whose works Sartre studies are mostly West Indians or Haitians. Senghor's *Anthologie de la nouvelle poésie nègre et malgache*, to which "Orphée noir" is the preface, includes—apart from the Malagasy poets—only three Africans: Senghor, Birago Diop and David Diop. One should also bear in mind that Césaire and Damas have had a considerable influence on African poetry after 1948, the date when Senghor's anthology was published.)

Sartre observes that for West Indian Negro poets surrealism was a weapon. He supports Senghor's views on the review *Légitime défense*, founded by Etienne Lero and a few other West Indian intellectuals just before the war:

> *Légitime défense* was a cultural movement rather than just a review, said Senghor. Starting from a communist analysis of society in the islands, it found that the West Indian was the descendant of African Negro slaves who for three centuries had been kept in a stultifying proletarian state. It maintained that only surrealism could free him from his taboos and express his whole personality.[49]

Sartre points out all the same 'the abyss which lies between white surrealism and its use by a Negro revolutionary', and he takes Césaire's poetry as an example of this: 'Césaire's originality lies in the expression of his narrow, potent anxiety as an oppressed, militant Negro in a poetry which is highly destructive, free, and metaphysical at a moment when Eluard and Aragon were failing to give their verse political content.'[50]

Sartre describes in these words the turning point, where the negritude poet identifies himself with the proletariat, where 'race is transmuted into historicity':

'Recently it was on the grounds of ethnic qualities that the Negro claimed his place in the sun. Now he bases his right to live on his mission, and this mission, like that of the proletariat, springs from his historical situation. Because he, more than others, has suffered from capitalist exploitation, he, more than others, has the feeling of revolt and love of liberty.'[51]

Muntu

Without overlooking the political commitment of Negro poets and novelists, Janheinz Jahn sets out to define the non-political criteria of negritude. He finds these criteria in the philosophical conceptions of Africa which, according to him, are the underlying themes of authentically African prose and poetry. He starts by 'reconstructing' a Bantu philosophy from African ancestral beliefs as shown in the works of both European and African writers. Father Placide Tempels had examined the ontological system of the Baluba tribes of the Belgian Congo in *La Philosophie bantoue*, Marcel Griaule studied the cosmogony of the Soudanese Dogon in *Dieu d'eau*, Abbé Alexis Kagame wrote a thesis on *La Philosophie bantu-ruandaise de l'être* at the Gregorian University of Rome. Jahn works out the main lines of the Negro philosophical system, which are not only common to the whole of Africa but survive in the Haitian voodoo cults, beneath the veneer of christianity. He then discovers traces of this system in the works of contemporary Negro writers and picks them out as the touchstones of neo-African culture.

The first of these touchstones is the belief that living and dead belong to the same category of beings (*muntu*, says Kagame, means not only men, but also ancestors and gods). Between them there is a constant interplay which enables them to communicate the particles of that 'vital force' which Tempels takes as the cornerstone of Baluba philosophy. Jahn finds echoes of this belief in Birago Diop's poem "Souffles", whose *leitmotiv* is the refrain 'the dead are not dead'; in Amos Tutuola's *The Palm-Wine Drinkard*, where the hero goes off in search of his palm-wine tapper to the land of the dead; and in Senghor, who asks the 'dead who have always refused to die' to protect the roofs of Paris.[52]

A second basic element is the African conception of the universe, as described by Kagame: all beings, people as well as things, are so many 'related' forces which are all part of the *ntu*, the being itself, the universal cosmic force. This belief in a sort of intimate coherence of the universe enables the African poet to identify himself with the whole of nature. Jahn finds it in Senghor, when the Senegalese poet writes: 'Here come the days of the very distant past, unity rediscovered, the reconciliation of the lion, the bull and the tree.' It is even more explicit in Césaire's *A Perte de corps*, where the poet expresses the wish to:

jusqu'à me perdre tomber
dans la vivante semoule d'une terre bien ouverte . . .
alors la vie j'imagine me baignerait tout entier
mieux je la sentirais qui me palpe ou me mord.

(Fall until I lose myself into the living grain of an open country . . . then I imagine life would bathe me all over. I should sense it more clearly as it touched me or bit me.)[53]

The last touchstone is belief in the 'magic power of the word'. Jahn equates this with the *nommo* of Dogon cosmogony, which is 'word, water, seed and blood' all at once, according to Ogotemmêli, the sage whom Marcel Griaule questioned. In African metaphysics as Jahn explains them, 'all transformation, creation and procreation is made by the word', which is also the life force and controlled only by the *muntu*. The word is all-powerful in Africa and man alone is master of the word, says Senghor. 'The unshakeable belief that everything, including the poet himself, can be transformed by the *nommo* pervades the revolutionary art of a Césaire just as much as the profound irony of a Tutuola', writes Jahn. And he continues that the great Negro cry of Césaire 'that will shatter the foundations of the world' is only a memory of traditional African belief in man's power to conjure the forces of nature (on this occasion, to destroy the colonial world). To put it shortly, this is again the *nommo*, so close to the 'Word' of the Bible.[54]

Jahn concludes that it is not enough to be black and revolutionary to belong to the new neo-African culture. The work of Richard Wright, for instance (who himself had said in *Black Power*, his reportage on Ghana, 'I was black and they were black but that did not help me at all'[55]) is in fact part of American literature. An author's work is authentically 'Negro' only when it expresses a specifically African way of thought, drawn from the deeps of the African conception of the world. For the same reasons, Jahn opposes annexation of the 'negritude' poetry by the surrealists. He feels that 'while the surrealist poet abandons himself to the power of words, which he hopes will take control of him in a state of almost subconscious trance, the African poet remains master of the word which in turn gives him authority over the material world'.[56]

For Jahn, moreover, the African concept of art is different in its very essence from that of the West. One is communal, social, functional, utilitarian; the other is individualist, egoistic, seeking after pure beauty, art for art's sake. This subject is also developed very fully by African intellectuals, writers and exponents of the fine arts: for instance, Bakary Traoré's book on the black African theatre.

Sékou Touré, 'communocracy' and culture

This idea is also cherished by the politicians. Sékou Touré took it up in his speech to the second Congress of Negro Writers and Artists. The president of Guinea approaches the problem from the opposite point of view: his own, that of the statesman, the 'political leader considered as the representative of a culture'.

> Africa is fundamentally communocratic. The collective life and social solidarity give it a basis of humanism which many peoples might envy. These human qualities also mean that an individual cannot imagine organising his life outside that of his family, village or clan. The voice of the African people is faceless, nameless, devoid of any individualistic note. Now who has not noticed the advance of personal egoism in circles contaminated by the settlers? Who has not heard a defence of art for art's sake, poetry for the sake of poetry, each man for himself? Our anonymous artists are the wonder of the world, and requests for our dances, music, songs and sculpture come in from all parts where people are interested to know their deeper meaning: yet some of our young intellectuals think they need know only Prévert, Rimbaud, Picasso or Renoir to be cultivated and carry our culture, art and personality on to a higher plane. They can appreciate only the outward appearance of things; they can judge only through their complexes and their colonialised mentality. For them our popular songs have no value unless they fit harmoniously into western modes; they are unaware of their social significance. Our painting! they would like it to be more classical. Our masks and sculpture! merely aesthetic. They do not realise that African art is essentially utilitarian and social. . . . Intellectuals or artists, thinkers or researchers, their ability is valid

> only if it coincides with the life of the people, if it is basically integrated into the activity, thinking and hopes of the populace.[57]

So for Touré, African art should be above all militant: then it will rediscover its basic characteristics from the days of African tribal society. Art for art's sake will have no place in the new Africa.

The trial of negritude

Starting from an analysis of the functional role of African art, two Negro writers, both ardent nationalists, have gone against the generally accepted view and levelled a charge against the negritude movement. They are Frantz Fanon and Ezekiel Mphahlele.

Fanon understands and, up to a certain point, approves the reaction of the colonised intellectual who, by going back to the origins of his race, seeks a defence against assimilation and reasons for rejecting the dogma of European cultural superiority. He sees it as a desperate effort to renew contact with the people, with the life force of the nation. He asserts, however, that 'this plunge is not specifically national'.[58] And he continues 'this historical obligation on the African cultural elite to make their claims racial, to speak more of an African culture than a national culture, will lead them to a dead end'.[59] Obviously, says Fanon, American and African Negroes must fight side by side against the contempt of the white man 'who was accustomed to lump all Negroes together'; however, 'American Negroes have become increasingly aware that the problems of existence facing them did not touch on those of the Africans'.[60] To support his remarks, Fanon recalls that, at the time of the second Congress of Negro Writers and Artists in Rome in 1959, the American Negroes noticed that the 'objective problems were basically heterogeneous'[61] and decided to form their own society of American people of African culture, distinct from the Society of African Culture founded by Alioune Diop and his friends after the first conference.

Fanon agrees that negritude is a necessary stage for the intellectual of the colonies, who otherwise runs the risk of becoming stateless and rootless. However, 'although this step may lead to great heights in the realm of poetry, in life itself it often leads the intellectual into a blind alley. When the intellectual has reached the climax of his infatuation with his people, as they are and as they were, and decides to return to everyday life, he comes back from his excursion with material which is very unproductive. He praises their costumes, traditions, and appearance, and his forced, unhappy search recalls only a banal quest for the exotic.'[62] In place of negritude, and despite the advantage that it engenders intellectual freedom from colonisation, Fanon proposes a literature which is integral to the revolutionary struggle. He gives the example of Keita Fodeba's poem, *Aube africaine*, which tells the story of a Senegalese rifleman, decorated for his conduct in the front lines during the second world war, who was killed in the repression of the Tiaroye incident on his return home to Africa. At the end of his chapter on national culture, from which the above quotations were taken, Fanon sharply criticises Rabemananjara and Senghor because the Malagasy and Senegalese governments did not vote as the provisional government of the Algerian Republic (GPRA) wanted them to during the UN debates on the Algerian question. The author of *Les Damnés de la terre* takes this as a regrettable illustration of the vanity of negritude.*

In order to minimise the role of the negritude movement, Frantz Fanon stressed the difference between the concrete objectives of American and African Negroes, objectives which stem from their respective situations. Ezekiel Mphahlele starts from a similar argument, but applies it only to the continent of Africa, to express his doubts on the value of an African cultural renaissance as a means of solving the problems of Africa as a whole. He stresses in the first place that there is no single political context for Africa. It would be better, he thinks, to draw an essential distinction between those regions of Africa where a large number of white settlers (and Indian tradesmen) have come to stay, and those areas where the white population is in a small minority. Even clearer would be a differentiation between those parts of Africa with a multiracial society, and those which have remained almost exclusively Negro: that is, between Kenya, Southern Rhodesia and South Africa on the one hand, and the rest of the black continent on the other.

The positions of writers and artists in these two parts of Africa seem to Mphahlele to be antithetical. Having quoted the poetry of Senghor, Damas and Jacques Roumain, with their nostalgia for ancestral Africa, Mphahlele puts the problem of negritude in this way:

> Much of the poetry is sheer romanticism, often it is mawkish and strikes a pose. . . . Lately, *Présence Africaine* has, unfortunately, been

* Rabemananjara, several of whose poems appear in Senghor's anthology, was a minister in the Malagasy government at the time.

too preoccupied with anthropological creepy-crawlies to devote enough attention to the problems of the artist in his present predicament. It worried me a lot that such a useful institution did not seem to be aware of cultural crosscurrents that characterise artistic expression in multiracial societies. They seemed to think that the only culture worth exhibiting was traditional or indigenous. And so they concentrated on countries where interaction of streams of consciousness between Black and White has not taken place to any significant or obvious degree, or doesn't so much as touch the cultural subsoil. A number of these enthusiasts even became apologetic about the western elements in their own art. So on my way back to Nigeria from Britain, in November 1959, I stopped in Paris to exchange ideas with the men of *Présence Africaine*. Where do *we* come in—we, who are detribalised and are producing a proletarian art? Has the Society of African Culture no room for us? This is what I wanted to know. . . .

We met Thomas Diop, Rabemananjara, Paul Niger from Guadeloupe, and Dr Misipo, the Cameroonian scholar. During our talk Sekoto and I tried to bring home to our friends the problems facing culture in multiracial communities like those in South Africa. I shall try to make myself clear presently in this chapter. Our choral and jazz music, literature, dancing in South Africa have taken on a distinctive content and form which clearly indicate a merging of cultures. And we are not ashamed of it. Particularly is this so in our serious music. They couldn't understand why our classical music should not be purely indigenous. Rabemananjara argued that there could be no conscious merging of cultures until we had attained political independence. But then the artist never waits for that kingdom to come: our vernacular and English writers had been producing work since about 1870—long before organised political resistance took shape in 1912.[63]

Mphahlele, like Fanon, denounces the exoticism which all too often is the end result of negritude. Hence he criticises *The African* by William Conton of Sierra Leone. Mphahlele admits that this 'is a beautifully written and highly polished book and it shows a keen sensitivity'. But:

It is also a good example of how political slogans, if made a principle of art, can destroy the impact a work of art might have had. He is all the time advertising the African way of life to the foreign reader, with an air of discovery. His hero does say he is rediscovering the

> African in himself. The purity and innocence of Africa . . . naked feet . . . a girl soaping her body and laughing in the rain. The damnable old cliché that we have come to associate with the colonial or the European who comes to Africa with that back-to-the-womb expression on his face. A number of experiences Mr Conton's hero goes through in order to rediscover his Africa, to 'project the African Personality' are contrived, and this is the stance that spoils the author's good writing. Must the educated African from abroad come back to recolonise us? Must he walk about with his mouth open, startled by the beauty of African women, by the black man's 'heightened sensitivity'? It's all so embarrassing.[64]

Mphahlele also points out that it is no mere chance that the negritude movement was launched by writers in the French colonies, where cultural assimilation was pressed upon them, and not in the English colonies, under indirect rule.[65]

All the same, his judgement of negritude is not entirely negative. He recognises that some valuable aspects of traditional African culture must be saved and, although he thinks the hunt for an African personality is not politically useful, he admits that it is worthwhile in the sphere of art, on the express condition that it is not built up into a 'mystique'.[66] If the Negro writer embarks on a search for his personality he will, not unnaturally, find that it is African. But if this search is only a posture his art will suffer from it; such is the conclusion of the author of *The African Image*. 'I personally cannot think of the future of my people in South Africa as something in which the white man does not feature. Whether he likes it or not, our destinies are inseparable. I have seen too much that is good in western culture—for example, its music, literature and theatre—to want to repudiate it.'[67]

Mphahlele's political views are in accord with his cultural convictions. While he is sickened by the apartheid regime (he was exiled in 1957 for protesting against the Bantu Education Act which provides for separate education through the vernacular medium for Africans at the school level), he looks forward all the same to a multiracial society, which would be egalitarian and in which there would be no oppressed racial minority. He expresses his convictions generously: 'If nationalism is the antithesis of tribalism, then I am a nationalist. But if, in a multiracial society, a nationalist's object is to replace white dictatorship with black fascism, to replace, say, Afrikaner tribalism with black chauvinism, then I can't go along with him.'[68]

Revolt and negritude

Fanon's and Mphahlele's criticisms of writers of the negritude movement concentrate on the articulation of the Negro intellectuals' struggle for African independence, through the distinction they draw between the call to revolt and the exaltation of Negro values. Fanon, in a way, prefers literature to be a direct incitement to action, since for him the immediate problem is to stand shoulder-to-shoulder with the people in their fight. The rehabilitation of ancestral Africa is an affair of interest to the colonised intellectuals above all. It can only be a secondary and partial feature of the struggle. Mphahlele thinks the pilgrimage back to traditional African origins runs the risk of proving sterile from several points of view. In detribalised southern Africa, it has already been overtaken by a proletarian art mingling the different cultural influences in novel fashion. It is negative because it excludes enrichment from external sources; it is ineffective because it has taken refuge in memories, when African writers should be tackling first and foremost the situation of the colonial subject.

These criticisms may appear unjust. In the first place, it is artificial to separate the literature of protest from the exaltation of Negro values as categorically as the West Indian and his South African colleague have done. Often an African author has been a poet of negritude and a revolutionary writer at the same time. The rehabilitation of Negro values was envisaged as one more aspect of the fight against colonialism. Moreover, the dangers of withdrawing into themselves have not escaped intellectuals of the negritude movement: on the contrary they have urged the need for a cross-pollination of cultures. When that has been said, the similarity between the ideas of these two writers, from the West Indies and South Africa, calls for attention. Far from being fortuitous, it springs from the pressure of situations and events which are remarkably alike in the two cases. Both men are or were the spokesmen for two peoples—the Algerians and the South Africans—who have experienced such deep-rooted European cultural influence that a return to the values of their ancestors would not have the same significance for them that it has in territories free of settlers. Above all, however, at the time of writing those two authors were both subject to particularly brutal European domination (in Algeria, the war; in South Africa, apartheid), while all—or almost all—the rest of Africa was free. Their third point in common was distrust of the bourgeoisie. Mphahlele points out that in South Africa all the better jobs are strictly reserved for the white man; as a result the Negro intellectual there has remained a member of the proletariat, whereas in Ghana and Nigeria a diploma has become the certain and sought-after stepping-stone to middle class officialdom. The whole of Fanon's work is shot with scorn for the 'national bourgeoisie' who are too ready to appropriate the advantages of independence at the expense of the peasant masses who, according to him, are the true proletariat.

Thus both writers have felt the need, in the dramatic situation of the people to whom they belong or with whom they identify themselves, of a particularly active solidarity in the real and blazing terrain of daily combat. For them, when the blood ran in Sharpeville and Algeria, an academic pilgrimage back to their Negro origins was less indispensable than efficiency in the fight and in the field of protest.*

**Présence Africaine* published a criticism of *The African Image* in its number XLIV. In it, Abiola Irele replied to several of the points made by Mphahlele. He thought the South African 'had shown a surprising insensibility to the nature of the dilemma which had faced French-speaking Negro intellectuals during the years of assimilation'. But 'rather ironically, his book is a direct descendant of the general movement for the rehabilitation of Africa and its people, which is the basis of negritude'. Irele concludes: 'His insistence on the vitality of the new proletarian culture is possibly valid, but what is to be gained by his apparently utter indifference to our traditional and vital culture?'

— 9 —

THE NEW DESDEMONA

PERHAPS you have read in the press recently of the misadventures of the black rabbit in an American children's book, who married a white rabbit by moonlight. The vigilance of the whites in the state of Alabama succeeded in condemning these rabbits for subversive intent and banning them from the libraries. What was good for rabbits might become the same for people, wrote the racialist newspapers. If a black man happened to marry a white woman, where should we be? A few days previously French newspapers had reported that the Negro writer Oyono was guilty of precisely this, going for a walk with a white woman; he was attacked and knifed in the middle of the *Quartier Latin* beneath the indifferent eye of passers-by. That is racism: Nazi, Yankee or French, it is always stupid and deadly.[1]

M. Etiemble, professor at the Sorbonne, thus stigmatised racism in a speech at the UNESCO headquarters in Paris on May 31, 1959, in the course of a day devoted to peace and against racialism and anti-semitism.

Racism finds one of its most obvious outlets in the field of sexual relations. It is expressed in different ways according to the circumstances; these range from mere social disapproval of miscegenation to legal measures forbidding it. In French-speaking territories, there has never been any legal interdict on this point. On the contrary, there is specific anti-racialist legislation, particularly the law of July 29, 1881, which provides for imprisonment (of a month to a year) and a fine for press libel of persons of a specified race or religion, when such libel is intended to arouse hatred between citizens.

In Portuguese territory, miscegenation was an integral part of colonial policy. It is one aspect of the *luso tropicalismo*, says the Angolan poet, Mario de Andrade.

Some people, such as the Brazilian sociologist Gilberto Freyre, say that tropical countries under Portuguese rule and christian direction

> (Brazil, Africa, India, Madeira, the Azores) now show a unity of feeling and culture. This unity, in his view, is a logical result of the methods and conditions of Portuguese colonisation, the cordiality and characteristic friendliness of the Portuguese people, 'the most christian of modern colonialists in their dealings with so-called inferior peoples'. As a result of his contacts with the Arabs, the Portuguese would seem to have an hereditary aptitude for life in the tropics and a predisposition for sexual adventures with coloured women beneath the sign of a brown Venus. . . . Freyre also credits the Portuguese, 'the civilisers of the tropics', with a certain originality, a form of biological and social adaptability.[2]

In South Africa, not only are mixed marriages illegal but all sexual relations between persons of different race are prohibited. Usually South African courts show leniency towards European sailors who go on a spree with the black prostitutes; however, reports in the Johannesburg and Cape press give the impression that these legal arrangements have become, if not an instrument of blackmail, at least a sure way of discrediting those who appear guilty in the eyes of South African law. According to official statistics, the number of those found guilty under the South African Immorality Act amounted to 5,252 between the promulgation of the law in 1950 and June 1964; *Europeans*: men 2,614, women 118; *Africans*: men 119, women 1,208; *Coloureds*: men 76, women 1,072; *Asians* (mainly of Indian origin): men 17, women 28. Sexual relations between persons of African, Coloured and Asiastic origin are not forbidden by law. The existence of one and a half million Coloureds, living for the most part in Cape Province, bears witness to the change in inter-racial relations which has occurred three centuries after the arrival of the first Dutch colonists at the Cape—a change symbolised formally by the law of 1950. Shortly after his arrival at the Cape in 1652, van Riebeeck besought the Dutch East India Company to send 'some strapping farm girls'; but few arrived, and the leader of the first Dutch colonists eventually authorised mixed marriages. Indeed, he himself acted as witness for one of the first of these marriages—that of the celebrated Eva, a Hottentot whom he had had baptised, with Pieter van Meerhof, a Dutch surgeon. Eva gave birth to the first two Cape Coloureds, two children born before her marriage with van Meerhof.

In Rhodesia the law drew a distinction between the sexes: relations between a white man and a black woman were legal whereas those between a white woman and a black man were illegal and punishable by law. The law in question, the Immorality and Indecency Suppression Act, dates from 1903 when Rhodesia was administered on behalf of Britain by Cecil Rhodes' British South Africa Company. The penalty prescribed for an African who had sexual relations with a white woman was five years' hard labour. No penalty was prescribed for cases in which a European male had sexual relations with an African female: cases frequent enough in the early days of colonisation in Rhodesia. Shortly before the first world war, Sir Aubrey Woolls-Sampson, a British colonel visiting Rhodesia, summed up his impressions thus in an address in Salisbury: 'I am convinced that the crimes of the natives against white women are largely influenced by the infamous behaviour of a considerable class of white men in their relations with Kaffir women. . . . In Matabeleland, the number of white men living with native women is positively appalling.'[3] According to *The Politics of Partnership* by Patrick Keatley, the Commonwealth correspondent of the *Guardian*, it would seem that sexual relations between the two races has all along been one of the predominant problems in the political life of the country. Indeed, Sir Charles Coghlan, the first prime minister of Rhodesia and by origin a South African, did not hesitate to approve of the lynching of Africans guilty of rape against a white woman.

Among the efforts made to abolish the law of 1903, mention must be made of the proposal of Max Buchan, a member of the Rhodesian parliament, in 1957. He suggested the adoption of legislation similar to that in force in South Africa, which had, in his opinion, the merit of equal treatment of the races in this field. Buchan said of the first colonists and their successors: 'The conqueror considered, in many cases, that one of the fruits of victory was the woman of the conquered race. . . . While strong, lusty and victorious men are not likely to be subject to what one might term biological inhibitions, it remains for those who follow on to endeavour to stabilise the position as soon as possible.' Another effort, this time more liberal in character, was made by Garfield Todd, a former prime minister of Rhodesia, who was a protagonist of the 'multiracial' experiment of the Federation. He failed in his endeavour, and Patrick Keatley considers that this initiative of his was one of the reasons why his party, the United Federal Party, replaced him by Sir Edgar Whitehead as head of government. Todd's ideas were considered too 'advanced' by his political colleagues. Even so, the law of 1903 was eventually abrogated—in 1961.

A few years after the second world war, the unexpected political implications of a relatively banal love affair focused public opinion on racial prejudices in Southern Africa. This was the affair of Seretse Khama, heir to the chief of a tribe in Bechuanaland, a British protectorate hemmed in by the Union of South Africa. He was banned from succession because he had married an English girl.

In the southern states of the USA, legislation against sexual relations between races varies from state to state. As was to be expected, the different aspects of sexual racism have frequently provided the subject for poems and novels by black writers, and this is particularly true of the United States, where Richard Wright and Chester Himes (in his novel *If He Hollers, Let Him Go*) have exploited it. One cannot help being struck by the fact that in most of these novels the plot is remarkably similar. In almost every case, the rape of the white woman by the Negro, followed by the lynching of the latter by the European crowd or his execution by the Ku Klux Klan, are the two principal episodes. A stereotyped image of the two protagonists is frequently one result of this: the Negro is irresistibly attracted to the white woman—the greater the risk, the more tempting the stake. But memory of the humiliations of his race chokes him at the very moment he seeks to efface them by conquest of a white woman, and his exasperated desire is accompanied by the thirst for murder. The white woman is criminally coquettish. She too is attracted to the Negro, but once her desire is satisfied she is quick to cry rape. In short, there are few literary subjects where crime and love, blood and sex are so morbidly interwoven.

The *Ballad of Pearl May Lee* by the American Negress Gwendolyn Brooks is symptomatic of this conception of the two characters: it is the desperate cry of revenge by the black mistress, abandoned for a white woman who denounced her Negro partner of the moment for rape:

> . . . At school, your girls were the bright little girls.
> You couldn't abide dark meat.
> Yellow was for to look at,
> Black for the famished to eat.
> Yellow was for to look at,
> Black for the famished to eat.
>
> You grew up with bright skins on the brain,
> And me in your black bed.

Often and often you cut me cold,
And often I wished you dead.
Often and often you cut me cold.
Often I wished you dead.

Then a white girl passed you by one day
And, the vixen, she gave you the Wink.
And your stomach got sick and your legs liquefied.
And you thought till you couldn't think.
    You thought,
    You thought,
You thought till you couldn't think.

I fancy you out on the fringe of town,
The moon an owl's eye minding;
The sweet and thick of the cricket-belled dark,
The fire within you winding . . .
    Winding,
    Winding . . .
The fire within you winding.

Say, she was white like milk, though, wasn't she?
And her breasts were cups of cream.
In the back of her Buick you drank your fill.
Then she roused you out of your dream.
In the back of her Buick you drank your fill.
Then she roused you out of your dream.

'You raped me, nigger', she softly said.
(The shame was threading through.)
'You raped me, nigger, and what the hell
Do you think I'm going to do?
    What the hell,
    What the hell,
Do you think I'm going to do?

'I'll tell every white man in this town.
I'll tell them all of my sorrow.
You got my body tonight, nigger boy.
I'll get your body tomorrow.

Tomorrow.
Tomorrow.
I'll get your body tomorrow.'[4]

Richard Wright showed his originality in seeking to escape these clichés in *Native Son*; Bigger Thomas does not rape Mary, he accidentally kills her. But he kills her because he knows the all-powerful myth which will inevitably lead him to rape or murder. Bigger Thomas is the Negro chauffeur of a rich white heiress, Mary, who as much from a desire to be modern as from conviction, and influenced by her fiancé Jan, finds it amusing to brave racial prejudice. Both of them treat Bigger in a very friendly way. One evening Bigger helps Mary, who is extremely drunk, to get back to her room and into bed. Just as he is about to leave the room, Mary's blind mother comes in: terrified, Bigger covers Mary's mouth with a pillow because she is groaning in her drunken state. He waits, paralysed with fear lest Mary's mother should guess he is there, but the old lady is convinced by the silence that her daughter is not yet home and leaves the room. Meanwhile Mary has died of suffocation. Bigger knows that no one will believe his story: he will finish in the electric chair.

The theme of sexual relations between white and black takes on another orientation when one leaves the USA for the West Indies and Latin America. Indeed, social custom regarding racial relations is very different there. While in the USA even the lightest, borderline half-caste is still regarded as Negro, immediately over the frontier in Mexico subtle distinctions are noticeable according to the darkness of the skin, and these end up as a form of social etiquette. So much so that George Padmore thinks that Marcus Garvey's theories on defending the purity of the Negro race can be explained by his Jamaican origins. Garvey produced these theories in the United States just after the first world war. Padmore writes of him:

> Garvey thought of himself as the Moses of the Negro race, and since a chosen people cannot be defiled, Marcus Garvey naturally pontificated that only those who were one hundred per cent negroid could hold office in the organisation, and thus carried his all-black world to its logical conclusion—racial purity. Accordingly, he admonished both whites and blacks that the purity of the races was being endangered. 'It is the duty of the virtuous and morally pure of both the white and black races', he declared, 'to thoughtfully and actively protect the future of the two peoples by vigorously opposing

> the destructive propaganda and vile efforts of the miscegenationists of the white race, and their associates, the hybrids of the Negro race.' The fanatical racialism of Garvey brought him into head-on conflict with American Negro political, religious and social uplift leaders, especially their doyen and leading propagandist, Dr W. E. B. DuBois. Dr DuBois was the 'father' of Pan-Africanism, the rival political ideology to Garvey's Black Zionism. Rejecting co-operation with the light-skin American leaders, whom he denounced as 'the Hybrids of the Negro race', Garvey, because of his racial doctrine, rather welcomed the aid of two notorious negrophobists, E. S. Cox of the Ku Klux Klan and John Powell of the Anglo-Saxon Clubs. They frequently addressed Garvey's meetings, extolling his Back to Africa Movement, with its emphasis on 'racial purity'.

Padmore remarks that Garvey's hatred for half-castes sprang from the fact that in Jamaica they represented the middle class and got all the jobs which the whites did not want themselves. The blacks, on the other hand, were 'the despised masses, the lower class of workers in the towns, peasants and day labourers on the sugar plantations'.

> In a country where 'white' is synonymous with power and wealth, it is inevitable that gradations of colour were of paramount importance, and that the poorest were the blackest—like Garvey. The 'brown men' strenuously kept out those who strove to enter their ranks from below. The blacks regarded them as the gendarmes of white privilege and power. They aped the white folk, and the black folk hated them. That was the pattern in Jamaica in Garvey's day. . . .
>
> The situation in America is entirely different. There the white majority has no need of the services of the mixed blood Negroes to keep the black masses 'in their place'. All Negroes—black and light skin—are the same. They are all 'just niggers' to the American white man. Consequently, American Negroes of both light and dark skin work together for the betterment of their race.[5]

The stratification of society was just as apparent in the islands under Spanish or French rule, and in the Portuguese colonies, as it was in Jamaica. The Cuban Negro, Fernando Ortiz, makes a systematic analysis of the vocabulary of the first centuries of colonisation, in his *El engaño de las razas*: 'The Spanish subdivided half-castes into white half-castes, light half-castes, black half-castes, brown half-castes,

Moorish half-castes, negroid half-castes, wolfish half-castes and even wolf-like half-castes.' Moreau de Saint-Mery, in 1797, in his famous *Description topographique, physique, civile, politique et historique de la partie française de l'île de Saint-Dominique* set out to distinguish between 'all the shades produced by the different combinations of white with black, and black with Caribs or savages or West Indians'. The vocabulary of the Portuguese in Brazil was just as refined as that of the Spanish, reports the American Negro James W. Ivy. But above all 'the Brazilians were persuaded that Africans gave out a smell, *catinga*, like that of the goat'. Macedo de Soares noted that 'this metaphor [of the goat], of Portuguese origin, came from the unpleasant smell peculiar to those of African race and comparable to the smell of goats'.[6]

In the West Indies and Latin America, we enter a world where miscegenation has become the rule and where the sequence 'rape and lynch' is no longer the main-spring of Negro poetry and prose. But prejudice still exists and here social taboos provide the literary theme. James W. Ivy wrote in *Présence Africaine*:

> Even if he does not admit the African relationship, many a Negro writer from Latin America has felt a secret anguish at being born half-caste. The Brazilian Machado de Assis was such a one. Although it is not explicit in his works, it was this which coloured his view of life and provided the morbid themes of so many of his novels. An example of this was *A Palida*, 'the pale woman', in his volume of stories edited by R. Magalhaes, Junior, entitled *Cantos sem data* ("timeless songs"). A young man is rejected by his love until he inherits $300,000 from his godfather. Since he does not find her light-skinned enough, he begins to hate her and sends her away. From then on he pursues the quest of an even fairer woman, and abandons many on the way. The woman who best lives up to his ideal is in the last stages of tuberculosis, and dies two weeks later.
>
> Lima Barreto, one of the greatest Brazilian novelists, who was half-caste, was so keenly aware of his social position that he wrote in his diary for January 24, 1908: '*E triste nao ser branco*' ('It is sad not to be white!').[7]

Dark Venus

The themes found in Anglo-Saxon and Portuguese American Negro prose and poetry also occur in the works of French-speaking poets. But there are some others which reflect the particular nature of their position. Hence, the 'anguish' which James W. Ivy found in Machado de Assis is absent from the short poem *Silhouette*, by the Haitian Léon Laleau:

La dame qui vient de Rotterdam
En route pour sa saison à Cannes,
Songe, en arpentant le macadam,
Aux Antilles, à ses champs de cannes,
A sa cousine créole Ruth
Qui parle encore de ce pique-nique
Où ses chairs éprouvèrent le rut
D'un mulâtre de la Martinique.

(The lady from Rotterdam, on the way to her season in Cannes, is thinking, as she strides along the road, of the West Indies and its fields of sugar cane; and of her Creole cousin Ruth who still talks of that picnic when her flesh had felt the rut of a half-caste from Martinique.)[8]

Another Haitian, Jean F. Brière, addresses his Negro brothers in *Black Soul* with the words:

Je vous ai rencontrés dans les ascenseurs à Paris.
Vous vous disiez du Sénégal ou des Antilles.
Et les mers traversées écumaient à vos dents, . . .
A bord des paquebots nous nous sommes parlé.
Vous connaissiez les maisons closes du monde entier,
Saviez faire l'amour dans toutes les langues.
Toutes les races avaient pâmé
Dans la puissance de vos étreintes.

(I have met you in the lifts in Paris. You said you were from Senegal or the West Indies. And the seas you had crossed were foaming at your teeth. . . . On steamers we talked to one another. You knew the brothels throughout the world, you could make love in every language. Every race had swooned in your strong embrace.)[9]

It is remarkable that this claim of sexual prowess in the Negro male, which both Laleau and Brière take up, is also one of the clichés of European racism which—according to Frantz Fanon—fosters 'fear of the Negro's sexual powers'. The West Indian writer in *Peau noire, masques blancs* attributes this to the fact that 'the civilised white man retains an irrational nostalgia for extraordinary periods of sexual licence, orgiastic scenes, unpunished rape, unreproved incest. . . . Projecting his own dreams on to the Negro, the white man acts as though they really were the Negro's own.'[10] Moreover, for Fanon, the white woman's attraction for the black man is the expression of the latter's desire to 'whiten' himself at all costs. He writes ironically:

> From the blackest part of my soul, up through the streaky zone, arises all of a sudden this wish to be white. I do not want to be taken for black, but for white. Now—and this is a recognition that Hegel has not described—who can do this except the white woman? In loving me she proves that I am worthy of white love. I am loved as a white man. I am a white man. . . .
>
> Some thirty years ago, a Negro of the finest colour, in the middle of copulation with a blonde 'bombshell', shouted at the moment of orgasm, 'Long live Schoelcher'. When it is known that it was Schoelcher who made the Second Republic adopt the decree abolishing slavery, the necessity of dwelling at some length on the possible relations between white and black can be appreciated.[11]

Léon G. Damas from Guiana, however, now wants to know only the women of his own race:

> *Rendez-moi mes poupées noires*
> *qu'elles dissipent*
> *l'image des catins blêmes marchandes d'amour*
> *qui s'en vont viennent*
> *sur le boulevard de mon ennui*
> . . . .
> *Rendez-les-moi mes poupées noires que je joue avec elles*
> *les jeux naïfs de mon instinct . . .*
> *Rendez-les-moi mes poupées noires*
> *mes poupées noires*
> *poupées noires*
> *noires.*

(Give me back my black dolls to dissipate the memory of the pale whores touting love who come and go on the boulevards of my boredom. . . . Give them back to me, my black dolls, that I may play with them the naïve games of my instinct. . . . Give them back to me, my black dolls, my black dolls, black dolls, black.)[12]

In the same way as memories of slavery continue to haunt them, so the lynchings of Negros in the southern states of the USA still find an echo among poets of the negritude movement. This is noticeable, in the first place, among francophone poets of the West Indies and Guiana, like Damas whose searing refrain in *Black Label*—'He was hanged this morning at dawn, a Negro guilty of wanting to cross the line'—runs through the whole poem, but it is also to be found among the Africans. The lynching of Emmett Till, a young fifteen-year-old Negro, in Money, Mississippi, in 1955, for daring to whistle after a white girl—and the acquittal of the two white youths who killed him—are the subject of a poem by David Diop from Senegal, *A un enfant noir:*

Quinze ans
Et la vie comme une promesse un royaume entrevu
Dans le pays où les maisons touchent le ciel
Mais où le cœur n'est pas touché
Dans le pays ou l'on pose la main sur la Bible
Mais où la Bible n'est pas ouverte
La vie à quinze ans apaise la faim des fleuves
La vie des peaux d'enfer des nom-de-Dieu de nègres
L'enfant noir un soir d'août perpétra le crime
Il osa l'infâme se servir de ses yeux
Et son regard rêva sur une bouche sur des seins sur un corps de Blanche
Ce corps enfant noir que seul aux sex-parties
Le Blanc peut saccager au rythme de tes blues
(Le nègre quelquefois sous des murs anonymes)
Le crime ne paie pas te l'avait-on assez dit
Et pour que justice soit faite ils furent deux
Juste deux sur les plateaux de la balance
Deux hommes sur tes quinze ans et le royaume entrevu
Ils pensèrent à l'aveugle fou qui voyait
Aux femmes éclaboussées
Au règne qui trébuchait
Et ta tête vola sous les rires hystériques
Dans les villas climatisées
Autour des boissons fraîches
La bonne conscience savoure son repos.

(Fifteen years. And life like a promise, a glimpse of a kingdom in the land where houses touch the sky, but where the heart is not touched; in the land where the hand is laid on the Bible but the Bible is not opened. Life at fifteen satisfies the hunger of rivers, the life of those with devil's skins, the goddam niggers. The black child one August evening perpetrated the crime, infamously he dared to use his eyes and his look dreamt of a mouth and the breasts and the body of a white woman. That body, black child, that only the white man can play havoc with at sex-parties to the rhythm of your blues (sometimes the Negro, beneath anonymous walls). Crime does not pay, hadn't you been told often enough, and in order that justice be done they were two. Just two in the scales, two men against your fifteen years and the kingdom you had glimpsed. They thought of the blind madman who could see, of the fallen women, of the tottering reign. And your head burst amid the hysterical laughter. In the air-conditioned villas, round the cold drinks, a clear conscience enjoys its repose.)[13]

Several years later the Congolese Tchicaya U'Tamsi also evoked this memory in one of the poems in his collection, *Epitomé*:

Quelles fleurs tresser
pour Emmett Till
l'enfant dont l'âme dans mon âme est sanglante.

(What flowers shall I wreathe for Emmett Till, the child whose soul bleeds in my soul.)[14]

For the poets of the negritude movement, colonisation in Africa meant not only political dominion or economic exploitation: it was also sexual humiliation. The coloniser had overall sexual rights. The West Indian, Paul Niger, in his poem *Je n'aime pas l'Afrique*, claims that this ancient seigniorial privilege was the result of his 'buying power'. If the white man 'loves Africa', this is because he finds there not only 'food, obedience and chickens at four sous' but also 'women at a hundred'.[15] For David Diop this sexual humiliation is the central panel of the triptych summarising his view on colonisation:

Le Blanc a tué mon père
Mon père était fier
Le Blanc a violé ma mère
Ma mère était belle
Le Blanc a courbé mon frère sous le soleil des routes
Mon frère était fort
Le Blanc a tourné vers moi

Ses mains rouges de sang
Noir
Et de sa voix de Maître:
'Hé boy, un Berger, une serviette, de l'eau!'

(The white man killed my father, my father was proud. The white man raped my mother, my mother was beautiful. The white man beat my brother beneath the sun on the roads, my brother was strong. The white man turned to me, his hands red with black man's blood, and in his domineering voice said to me: 'Hey boy, a Berger,* a towel, water!')[16]

But the Senegalese poet recovers his serenity in singing of the beauty of the Negro woman in *Rama Kam—chant pour une négresse:*

Me plaît ton regard de fauve
Et ta bouche à la saveur de mangue
Rama Kam
Ton corps est le piment noir
Qui fait chanter le désir
Rama Kam
Quand tu passes
La plus belle est jalouse
Du rythme chaleureux de ta hanche
Rama Kam
Quand tu danses
Le tam-tam Rama-Kam
Le tam-tam tendu comme un sexe de victoire
Halète sous les doigts bondissants du griot
Et quand tu aimes
Quand tu aimes Rama Kam
C'est la tornade qui tremble
Dans ta chair de nuit d'éclairs
Et me laisse plein du souffle de toi
O Rama Kam!

(Your look of a wild animal and your mouth tasting of mangoes delight me, Rama Kam. Your body is the black pimento which makes desire hum, Rama Kam. When you pass by, the most beautiful woman is envious of the warm rhythm of your hips, Rama Kam. When you dance, the tom-tom, Rama Kam, the tom-tom stretched

* *Le Berger* is a French aperitif.

like triumphant sex gasps under the griot's leaping fingers; and when you love, when you love, Rama Kam, it is the tornado trembling in your flesh of flashing night, and I am left steeped in your breath. O Rama Kam!)[17]

West Indian poets also have sung to the dark Venus. Guy Tirolien may have been thinking of Baudelaire's *Bijoux* when he wrote *L'Ame du noir pays*, for the mistress of the author of *Fleurs du mal* was also a quadroon:

Tes seins de satin noir rebondis et luisants
tes bras souples et longs dont le lissé ondule
ce blanc sourire
des yeux
dans l'ombre du visage
éveillent en moi ce soir
les rythmes sourds
les mains frappées
les lentes mélopées
dont s'enivrent là-bas au pays de Guinée
nos sœurs
noires et nues
et font lever en moi
ce soir,
des crépuscules nègres lourds d'un sensuel émoi . . .

(Your round, shining breasts of black satin, your long and supple arms smoothly sinuous, that white smile, those eyes in the darkness of your face, awake in me this evening the dull beat, the tapping hands, the slow chanting on which our black and naked sisters back in Guinea become drunk; they arouse in me this evening the heavy black twilight of sensual excitement . . .)[18]

Senghor also sings of the Negro woman:

. . . Femme nue, femme obscure!
Fruit mûr à la chair ferme, sombres extases du vin noir,
bouche qui fais lyrique ma bouche
Savane aux horizons purs, savane qui frémis aux caresses
ferventes du Vent d'est
Tam-tam sculpté, tam-tam tendu qui grondes sous les doigts
du Vainqueur

Ta voix grave de contre-alto est le chant spirituel de l'Aimée.
Femme nue, femme obscure!
Huile que ne ride nul souffle, huile calme aux flancs
de l'athlète, aux flancs des princes du Mali
Gazelle aux attaches célestes, les perles sont étoiles
sur la nuit de ta peau
Délices des jeux de l'esprit, les reflets de l'or rouge
sur ta peau qui se moire.
A l'ombre de ta chevelure, s'éclaire mon angoisse aux
soleils prochains de tes yeux.

(. . . Naked woman, dusky woman! Ripe fruit with the firm flesh, dark ecstasy of black wine, mouth which makes mine lyrical; savanna of clear horizons, savanna that quivers under the hot caress of the east wind; sculpted tom-tom, tom-tom stretched out and sighing beneath the fingers of the victor, your deep contralto voice is the sacred song of the Loved One. Naked woman, dusky woman! Oil which no breeze ruffles, calm oil on the athlete's thighs, on the thighs of the princes of Mali; gazelle with heavenly leash, pearls are stars in the night of your skin, the pleasures of wit, the reflection of red gold on your clouded skin. In the shadow of your hair my anguish melts away before the nearby suns of your eyes.)[19]

Nevertheless, he is not indifferent to the white woman's beauty, which he extols in *Kaya Magan:*

Mon empire est celui d'Amour, et j'ai faiblesse pour toi femme
L'étrangère aux yeux de clairières, aux lèvres de pomme
cannelle, au sexe de buisson ardent.
Car je suis les deux battants de la porte rythme binaire
de l'espace, et le troisième temps
Car je suis le mouvement du tam-tam, force de l'Afrique future,
Dormez faons de mon flanc sous mon haut pschent de lune.

(My empire is the empire of love, and I have a weakness for you, woman, stranger with clear eyes, lips of cinnamon, and sex like the burning bush. For I am the two halves of the double rhythmic doors of space and the third time, for I am the beat of the tom-tom, the force of the future Africa; sleep, fawns of my thighs, beneath my high halo* of moonlight.)[20]

* Literally, coiffure of Egyptian God or Pharaoh.

Like Senghor, Lamine Diakhate is also eclectic, singer both of the 'girls of the northern mists' and the 'goddesses of Sangomar'.[21] Martial Sinda, on the other hand, is exclusive, like Damas:

> *Princesse-Noire*
> *Je te chante et te psalmodie*
> *Déesse de la beauté naturelle et que personne n'égale*
> *Statuette blanche aux lèvres rouges*
> *Non, ta beauté est vraiment trop factice.*

(Black princess, I sing of you and dedicate a psalm to you, goddess of natural beauty, without peer. White statuette with red lips, no, your beauty is really too contrived.)

The Ghanaian poetess, Efua Morgue, rebels on the other hand against racial prejudice which is poisoning her love for a white man:

> Tradition, race,
> Political snares,
> They formed a horrid cluster
> Us to part in twain
> To tear us bodily.[22]

The 'Redeemer'

This theme is also found of course in West Indian and African novels. In *Un Homme pareil aux autres*, René Maran tells how an African nearly had to give up his love for a European woman. In *The Path of Thunder*, the story of an affair between a half-caste, Lanny Swartz, and a Boer girl, Sarie Villiers, Peter Abrahams has set out to show apartheid in its true colours by using a personal drama. One of his characters says:

> The tragedy is not in Swartz and this girl. The tragedy is in this land and in our time. You must be first a native or a half-caste or a Jew or an Arab or an Englishman or a Chinaman or a Greek: that is the tragedy. You cannot be a human being first. That is the crime of our time, my friend. For that reason Swartz and this girl who have now become human beings will suffer. This love of theirs is a symbol of man's attempt to move forward beyond the chains that bind him. . . .[23]

However, the most striking aspect of the African novel on this subject is the vast difference between the picture it gives of the European woman and that found in Negro novels from the United States. In place of the criminally coquettish white woman of Gwendolyn Brooks or Chester Himes, we find the wife or mistress of a black man who is willing to brave racial prejudice for him. There is Solange who, as a child, is saved from drowning by little Mambeke, when she had fallen into the river bordering her father's estate in the Congo. The young Negro achieves brilliant results in his studies and Solange risks her father's anger to marry him.[24] There is Isabelle, wife of Oumar Faye, who follows him to Casamance, sharing his joys and sorrows with self-sacrifice in an African milieu which is difficult to enter and a European one which is frankly hostile. Two white men try to rape her since they think that the wife of a Negro must be easy game.[25] (This is an old prejudice: it is the first insult which comes to Othello's mind. In 1787, the boat which brought back freed Negro slaves to Sierra Leone for the first time carried, along with the 400 Negroes who founded Freetown, 60 white prostitutes picked up in the streets of London.) There is Lois, Udomo's mistress, who took him in when he was in London and supported him with her love and money. When Udomo became prime minister of his own country, he did not bring out the friend of his difficult days; but he was haunted by remorse for this desertion and it was Lois' name that he murmured when he fell assassinated.[26] There is Jacqueline, who married Fara, a black student, despite her father's curse.[27] There is Denise, a militant communist, who saved Kocoumbo from unemployment and hunger when the factory workers would not forgive his lukewarm attitude to the party.[28] There is Lucienne, a vicar's daughter and also a member of the communist party, who became the mistress of Samba Diallo.[29]

One characteristic is common to almost all these 'redeemers': like Desdemona, they come to a tragic end. Solange commits suicide after her father has wanted to kill his half-caste grandson at birth. Isabelle's husband is assassinated; Lois grows old, abandoned in London; Jacqueline dies in childbirth. Denise perishes in a senseless accident in the bus taking her to a communist demonstration. There is one exception among this gallery of exemplary women: Ginette Tontisane commits an intellectual theft by getting her Negro lover's manuscript published under her name. The latter kills her accidentally during a stormy scene about what she has done and he is condemned to forced labour for life. His trial gives the author an opportunity to tackle the subject of the murder of a white woman by a Negro in the American way: a professor from the faculty of medicine, called on to give evidence, gives a diatribe on the Negro's obsession with sex.[30]

Sembène Ousmane sought to make the clichés which swung the jury appear hateful and ridiculous. At the other end of the scale, Ferdinand Oyono was not afraid, in his last novel, *Chemins d'Europe*, to draw the portrait of a young Negro, Barnabas, who is haunted by desire for a lower middle-class Frenchwoman to such an extent that it becomes an obsession. The plot takes place in Africa, where the seduction is obviously more difficult to carry out than in Europe. Moreover, the hero is not in the least in love with the woman he wants to win; possessing her is just a sort of abstract wager for him. But Madame Gruchet, whose husband has left her for black prostitutes, is not at all interested in her daughter's young teacher. And when, one evening, this woman, lacking any great charm and yet so much desired, is weeping half-naked on his shoulder because her daughter is delirious with fever, Barnabas is not capable of seizing his opportunity. He stands there, glued to the spot. Oyono's tale is a vicious one: with the exception of the hero's mother, all the characters in the book are repugnant, ridiculous or imbecile, and everything gives an impression of unrest, even the choice of the obsessed young Negro's ridiculous name.

Negro novelists have not invariably presented this subject from the point of view of the difficulties facing the African man and European woman: the alternative couple, the European man with the African woman, has also held their attention. Sadji and Kane have both tackled the subject by choosing half-caste heroines. Nini, Sadji's heroine, is a mulatress from Dakar who repudiates the black race: she is the mistress of a European who leaves Africa without marrying her. Yet she is so sure of herself that she indignantly refuses the 'honourable' advances of an educated young Negro. Kane's heroine, Adele, on the other hand, who is Samba Diallo's West Indian friend in Paris, is rootless and she feels an awakening desire to go back to the Africa of her ancestors. Even the titles of Mayotte Capecia's two novels, *Je suis martiniquaise* and *La Négresse blanche* show the special nature of this 'dual loyalty' and the problems it poses for both men and women.

However, it is Camara Laye's second novel, *Le Regard du roi*, which offers the most interesting variation on this theme: it tells of a young European, Clarence, who lands in a rather mythical Africa. He looks for work without success, since he knows none of the trades of this traditional Africa where everything is thoroughly strange and inexplicable to him. In despair, he trusts his destiny to an old man, a beggar, who leads him after an interminable journey to a village where the king is due to pass. Clarence has set his last hope on a job at the king's court. He settles in a hut with a beautiful young black woman who each evening gives him a drink which is half-narcotic, half-aphrodisiac. It is only after many months when, by chance, he takes a walk around the old chief's compound and sees a whole crowd of half-caste children among the wives' huts, that he realises that each night his partner was different. All the impotent old man's harem had passed through Clarence's hut; he had finally been given the only job needing no training—that of a stud stallion. This time it was through the irony of fiction, and not by means of realist drama, that the Negro writer had freed himself from the complex of sexual humiliation that racism had sought to instil in him.

10

BEFORE THE REVOLT

LILYAN KESTELOOT has written the history of the negritude movement in her study, *Les Écrivains noirs de langue française: naissance d'une littérature*. Step by step, she follows the appearance of the various Negro intellectual periodicals in Paris between the wars; she analyses the influence of the American Negro writers of the period on French-speaking West Indians and Africans in France; and she underlines the profound attraction which communism and surrealism had for them before the birth of the negritude movement after the second world war. She went back to the grass roots to find its forerunners immediately after the first world war. It is not without interest to go even further back, although the works become very few and far between.

One can find writers whose viewpoint is very different from that of the poets and novelists of the negritude movement. Men such as James Africanus B. Horton and Léopold Panet were faithful servants of the colonial powers and devoted all their efforts to carrying out their missions successfully. Horton was a doctor in the British army and accompanied an expedition to the Gold Coast; his book, *Physical and Medical Climate and Meteorology of the West Coast of Africa* was primarily a collection of advice on hygiene for Europeans visiting this coast, often called 'the white man's grave'. He has no doubts about the purity of the colonialists' intentions. His dedication to Edward Cardwell, former secretary of state for the Colonies, announces the book as 'a tribute to his work for the promotion of the African race'.*

* For Horton, this promotion should lead the colonies of British West Africa, if not to independence, then at least to autonomy. This is made clear in another of his books, *West African Countries and People*. But Horton's nationalist sentiments did not go beyond a given limit. Thus, his plan for administrative reorganisation of the Gold Coast, drawn up in this book in 1868, foresaw the creation of a 'republic of Accra' and a 'Fanti kingdom' but did not seek to exclude British trusteeship. This, he thought, should be firmly fixed by the presence of Her Majesty's consuls who would act as advisers to the native authorities and would protect them from any outside intervention. Moreover, this attitude was common to most of the nationalist intellectuals in British West Africa. David Kimble

Léopold Panet, a Senegalese entrusted by the Department for the Navy and Colonies with an exploratory mission across the Sahara from Saint-Louis to Algiers, was just as eager to serve France. For his journey he had to disguise himself as a muslim. He contacted a Fulani from Massina to get himself taken for a deserter seeking conversion to Islam by Cidya, a marabout of the Trarza. The scheme failed. His disappointment is expressed with undeniable sincerity, despite the flowery style of the period. Such is his enthusiasm that the muslim baptism—which itself was a reprehensible deception—is transformed beneath his pen to a sort of party which he was eagerly anticipating: 'Oh what a cruel disappointment!—just as I was approaching Boutilimit and saying to myself: tomorrow as night throws its dark veil over the pale glow of dusk, I shall kneel at the feet of the venerable Cidya, who will shave my head with his *yataghan* and then declare me a muslim before all his students, and with this formality completed I shall be able to travel all over Africa without being troubled by anyone.'[1] This setback did not prevent his setting off in the end, but he was unable to reach Algiers and his journey ended at Es-Saouira (Mogador).

The Abbé Boilat, also from Senegal, was another ardent advocate of colonisation. When he founded the first French secondary school in Senegal in 1843, he described in the most attractive light in his inaugural speech the careers which would be open to the Negro students. The Abbé extolled military careers above all: Saint-Cyr and also 'the school of navigation or mechanics which they would soon leave to be in command of the colony's warships. You know very well that French officers cannot stand the heat on the river or the coast for long. It is for you, children of the tropics, that this noble work is reserved. If, as I do not doubt, you acquit yourselves honourably, Senegambia will one day see your decorations shining on your breast.'[2] But the Abbé Boilat assumed that the natives' promotion would be won by exemplary conduct. Hence he castigates in swinging terms the misconduct of the christians of Joal. The latter were converted to christianity by the Portuguese who founded the town in the sixteenth century but, according to him, had retained only a few of the external trappings of christianity and had fallen back into sinful ways:

---

says of *Towards Nationhood in West Africa* by J. W. de Graft-Johnson: 'In the tradition of Africanus Horton, James Brew, Mensah Sarbah, Casely-Hayford, and many others, de Graft-Johnson wished to preserve the British connexion. His ultimate goal was Dominion status.'

> Such polygamy allied to terrifying corruptions in their way of life is not the only defect afflicting this shadow of christianity at Joal. These so-called pure christians at Joal are the greatest drunkards on earth. . . . Although they are as black as the blackest Africans, they have the modest pretension to be pure white, and they take it as a great insult if they are treated as Negroes or Sereres. They want to be known as the white men of Joal, the christians of Joal, because they are direct descendants of the Portuguese and have been baptised. In a word, to be christian is to be white and free and to have the right and the wherewithal to drink.[3]

Another African writer, a contemporary of the Abbé Boilat and even harder on the Negroes, was Paul Holle, a half-caste soldier from Senegal, who defended Medina against al-Hajj Umar. He was very indignant that some black tribes in Senegal regarded themselves as the allies of France, questioned the orders of the colonial administration, and did not behave as colonial subjects held in uncomplaining obedience. He recommended a strange plan for the emancipation of slaves captured by African chiefs who were still engaged in the slave trade at the time. When they were delivered the French administration would send them to the West Indies where they would be offered for a fee to landed proprietors, for whom they would work for ten years. At the end of this period some, with their consent, would stay there, while others, who had learnt French and had been converted to christianity, would return to Senegal where the government would install them in reception villages. Holle wrote his book, *De la Sénégambie française*, in collaboration with a Frenchman, F. Carrère.

Fifty years later, in 1912, another Senegalese did not mince his words when addressing a governor-general who seemed to him to harbour prejudices against his race. This was Ahmadou Dugay Clédor (otherwise known as Ahmadou Ndiaye Clédor), vice-president of the Senegalese Union for the Propagation of French. In his preface to two short historical studies, *La Bataille de Guilé* and *De Faidherbe à Coppolani*, Clédor remarks that he wrote them in 1912 and 1913 when he 'had the honour to belong to that admirable band whom M. Ernest Roume has disdainfully enrolled under the name of teachers of the native cadre. . . . This governor-general, who showed himself a great administrator when it came to building ports and railways, had no real native policy at all. Badly advised by his secretary-general, M. Martial Merlin, he did not like the Negroes, who returned his feelings with interest.

Indeed, in 1904, he had just harshly disassociated us from our metropolitan colleagues.' This preface is a valuable document; it is far more than a minor problem of officialdom which the author is considering. This was a turning point in French colonial policy, when the true policy of assimilation was renounced and a distinction began to be drawn between native officials and French officials. In support of his demand to be treated as a French official, Clédor quotes 'the glorious feats of arms and the many acts of bloody sacrifice and French loyalty by our fathers during the stormy days of the French Revolution, the Consulate and the Empire, and by their descendants during the Senegalese epic under Faidherbe, Pinet-Laprade, Brière de l'Ile and Canard'.[4]

After the second world war, Africans were quoting the sacrifices of the former combatants in support of their demands; but soon they were claiming not French citizenship but independence itself. Thus the rare but valuable landmarks which the works of Léopold Panet, Abbé Boilat, James Africanus B. Horton and Ahmadou Dugay Clédor represent enable us to reconstruct the progression of events. The first three, writing before 1900, saw colonisation as an endeavour at human promotion, which they supported; the fourth, half-a-century later, was attempting to defend the rights conferred by the policy of assimilation proclaimed during the revolutions of 1789 and 1848.

All the same, a Negro literature of protest had already come to light a century before, with writers of the abolitionist movement. Was this faith in colonisation shown by nineteenth-century Africans—in contrast with the eighteenth-century Negro writers who had denounced slavery—due to the fact that the great powers, who were beginning to carve out empires in Africa, had in the meanwhile sided against the traffic in slaves? In his speech to the Rome Congress, the Reverend Mbiti commented on the importance of the abolition of slavery to the populations of East Africa. Muslims there were continuing the traffic at a time when English and Germans were freeing all their slaves.[5] On the west coast, Freetown and Libreville were founded, as their names suggest, to receive the freed slaves. The 'climate of confidence' engendered among the African elite in colonial establishments by the abolition of slavery was accompanied by a policy of social promotion. At last Negroes and half-castes could hold important posts: just two examples of this were General Dodds, a half-caste who conquered Dahomey for the French towards the end of the nineteenth century, and the first African (Anglican) bishop of Niger at the same period, the Right Reverend Ajayi Crowther, who had been a slave freed by the colonial conquest. Abolition, like some other concrete aspects of the great powers' colonial policies, gave the African elite of the time reasons to believe in the sincerity of European professions of humanitarian good faith.

For its part, Negro literature on slavery produced evidence of remarkable developments in the course of some fifty years. Jacobus-Elisa-Ioannes Capitein, a young African sold into slavery at the age of twelve to a Dutch sailor, entered Leyden University at twenty, and five years later, in 1742, 'believing, or pretending to believe that propagation of the faith would be promoted by the continuance of slavery, he composed a political and theological dissertation to show that slavery was not opposed to evangelical liberty'. The Abbé Grégoire's indignation shows through in this quotation. His 'betrayal' did not bring happiness to Capitein, either, reports de Graft-Johnson. Sent out as chaplain to the fort of Elmina in the Gold Coast, one of the Dutch centres of the slave trade at the time, 'the Europeans disregarded his office because of his colour and because he was an ex-slave; and his own people in turn ostracised him. He had a short and troubled career, and died at the early age of thirty.'[6]

The writings of Othello, Cugoana, Gustavus Vassa and Ignatius Sancho, less than fifty years later, are in a quite different vein. These Negro authors, all freed slaves, some of whom had been born in Africa, denounced the hypocrisy of a society which professed its christian faith yet tolerated slavery. In 1788, Othello published in Baltimore an essay against slavery. Here, reports the Abbé Grégoire, 'he paints in lines of fire the misery and weeping of children who have disappeared, and of friends who have been dragged far away from the land of their birth . . . a land which is always close to their hearts, so close in fact that one of the articles of their superstitious credulity is a belief that they will return there after death'. Ottobah Cugoana was born on the Fantim coast and married an English woman with whom he lived in London. He wrote *Thoughts and Sentiments on the Evil and Wicked Traffic of the Slavery and Commerce of the Human Species*, in which he called down divine judgement on slavery:

> In this Europe which claims to be civilised, we put men in chains, we hang thieves, we torture murderers, and if slave traders and settlers do not suffer this punishment it is because the people and the governments are their accomplices, for the laws encourage the slave trade and tolerate slavery. Sometimes Heaven sends down a national

> punishment for national crimes: in any case injustice is sooner or later fatal to its authors.

The tone of Ignatius Sancho, writing in 1783, is more measured, but just as firm:

> According to divine plan, trade should make the produce of each country equally available to the whole world, should unite the nations by their awareness of reciprocal needs and links of brotherly affection, and should speed the widespread diffusion of the benefits of the Gospels. But the poor Africans, to whom the Lord has granted a rich and 'luxuriant' land, are the most unhappy section of humanity on account of the horrible slave trade; and it is the christians who are responsible.

Gustavus Vassa's appeal to the British parliament in 1789, in which he produced his work pleading the cause of abolition, is drawn up in respectful language and appeals as much to christian morality as to British liberal traditions.

Clearly the distance separating Capitein's work from those which appeared thirty or forty years later coincides with a crisis in the European conscience. Capitein, isolated at Leyden, where one may legitimately imagine him to be the only black seminarist, was clearly the victim of his teachers. Liberal intellectuals in Britain, on the other hand, many of whom came from the aristocracy, encouraged the freed slaves to contribute to the abolitionist movement. Among the subscribers to Gustavus Vassa's book one finds the names of the Prince of Wales, and the dukes of York, Cumberland, Bedford and Marlborough. Ignatius Sancho was a protégé of Lord Montagu.

Signs of an evolution in Negro thought can also be distinguished between the end of the first world war and the present day. In his study on Algerian literature, Henri Kréa did not fail to remark on the 'three stages in the literature of the Maghrib': first 'the colonial and exotic' stage, mainly of European writers; then the period of 'evidence' which constituted a 'statement of misfortunes' but did not openly incite rebellion; and finally the moment when the writer threw himself into the battle and his works became frankly 'revolutionary'. An analogous classification of African literature might be attempted. There is no doubt that Negro writers also suffered the 'regionalist complex' decried by Kréa in the Maghrib literature of evidence. It would also be possible to follow the careers of some authors who started off as obedient pupils of the colonialists and only later joined the chorus denouncing colonialism. What is more interesting, however, is that an apparent paradox has led such widely different statesmen as Léopold Senghor and Sékou Touré to criticise the very elite who first raised the cry of revolt.

A significant episode in this respect was the plot discovered in Guinea in December 1961, in which the leaders of the Parti Démocratique de Guinée attacked the teachers. R. J. Guiton, specialist in Guinean affairs, gave an analysis of this plot in the Tunisian weekly, *Jeune Afrique*. He recalled that, some months previously, Sékou Touré had accused these same teachers of forming a 'caste of intellectuals'. And, indeed, it was intellectuals who were found guilty: among them the historian Djibril Tamsir Niane, author of a book on the Mandingo emperor, Sundiata, and of an historical manual in collaboration with the French marxist historian, Suret-Canale. Sékou Touré's warning to the intellectuals, which Guiton mentioned, was not the first. The president of Guinea had several times raised the problem of this intellectual elite. In his message to the second Congress of Negro Writers and Artists, he had (as we have seen earlier) stressed the need for this intelligentsia to grow intellectually 'decolonised' and recover contact with the people: 'Intellectuals or artists, thinkers or researchers, their ability is valid only if it coincides with the life of the people, if it is basically integrated into the activity, thinking and hopes of the populace.'[7]

Frantz Fanon was just as suspicious as Sékou Touré of middle-class intellectuals in colonial countries. Without underestimating their positive and progressive role in the fight for independence, he stresses in *Les Damnés de la terre* that 'the colonised intellectual has channelled his aggressiveness in a thinly-veiled desire for assimilation into the colonial world. He has put his aggressiveness at the service of his own individual interests. In this way, a sort of class of individually freed slaves can easily arise. What the intellectual demands is the chance to increase the number of freed men, to organise a veritable class of freed men.' The solution, Fanon concludes, is for the intellectual educated in colonial schools to recover contact with the masses.

Senghor also sees the intellectuals as an embryo class apart and underlines the dangers of this. He writes:

> In our Negro-Berber society there is no class warfare, but social groups striving for influence. Tomorrow they will be at war with

> each other if we are not careful, if we allow the intellectuals—of the liberal professions, officials, employees, even the workers—to create a class which oppresses the peasants, shepherds and artisans by deceiving them. Parties and governments must be on their guard to prevent this.[8]

Senghor's and Touré's definition of intellectual goes beyond the generally accepted meaning of the term, whereas Fanon remains close to its original signification. They are not thinking of exactly the same people, and Fanon goes on to specify that it is the colonised intellectual whom he has in mind. All the same, the three writers are directing their fire at a bourgeois caste, the very one from which the majority of the writers and thinkers of African nationalism has sprung. These are being clearly told that they must drop their class solidarity if they are to remain in the forefront of the revolution.

PART THREE

THE NEW AFRICA

Quamvis ille niger
quamvis tu candidus esses.
VIRGIL

II

THE SONS OF HAM

When the act separating church and state was passed in France in 1905, the colonies were exempted. It was recognised that the conversion of Africans undertaken by the missionaries was to the advantage of colonialism. The anti-clerical third republic thus adopted for itself the old formula of *gesta Dei per Francos*. This was true not only of France, however: all over Asia and Africa, missionaries from every European power had followed or preceded the colonial conquest—Livingstone is perhaps the best-known example. When the 1885 Treaty of Berlin, ratifying division of Africa by Europe, was revised in 1919 by the Convention of Saint-Germain-en-Laye, an article guaranteeing liberty of conscience and free profession of all sects affirmed the missionaries' right to enter, travel over and live in the African continent.

This collaboration in fact and in law between the colonial powers and the christian churches was bound, sooner or later, to arouse the suspicions of African nationalists, especially since the history of the slave trade revealed the concomitance of the two operations, baptism and slavery, from the sixteenth century onwards. Does not the Bible curse the sons of Ham; and have not the reformed churches in South Africa found justification for segregation in their churches in the negrophobia of the Scriptures outlined by Sheikh Anta Diop (and which is evident even in the 'but' of the famous line from the *Song of Songs*: 'I am black but comely')? Consequently the missionaries' work in Africa inevitably attracted the attention of Negro intellectuals, drawing very harsh criticism from some of them, particularly from those with communist associations. As for christian Negroes, the feeling that they were not always regarded as full catholics or protestants has frequently distressed them. As early as 1870, at the first Vatican Council, reports Marc Ela, 'a group of missionary bishops produced a document asking the pope to release the Negro race from the curse on it which, it seems, comes from Ham'.[1]

Anti-clerical negritude

In *African Glory*, the Ghanaian historian, Charles de Graft-Johnson, traces the problem back to its earliest origins. First he recalls how the Roman empire, converted to christianity, used missionaries to stabilise its dominion. This is one of the points emphasised by Professor C. P. Groves in *The Planting of Christianity in Africa*, from which de Graft-Johnson quotes the following two passages:

> The Church was recognised as a pillar of the State, so that to propagate the Christian faith was at the same time to consolidate the imperial power. Justinian pursued the policy in Africa of encouraging to become Christians all those chiefs and kings who sought his goodwill. He gave it as a definite instruction to his administrators that they should do all they could to incline the people to Christianity. In the case of native rulers, an investiture with robes of office and the bestowal of honorific titles went with the change. . . . Religious propaganda for imperial expansion was the policy. As Mesnage drily remarks, it was found more economical to make use of the Gospel than military power for the security of distant territories![2]

Then de Graft-Johnson turns his attention to the evangelisation which accompanied the slave trade. To give an idea of the state of mind of the first traders at the time of Henry the Navigator, he quotes a passage from a Portuguese chronicler, Eannes de Azurara, who witnessed the embarkation of one of the first cargoes of slaves in 1444. Without trying to hide his emotion, Azurara describes the heartrending farewells of slaves divided into various lots and separated from each other regardless of family relationship. He ends with these revealing lines:

> The Infante [Dom Henry], mounted on a powerful horse, disdained to take his share, some forty-six souls . . . taking pleasure only in the thought of so many souls being redeemed from perdition. And truly, his hope was not vain, since so soon as they learned the language, with very little trouble, these people became christians; and I who write this history saw afterward in the town of Lagos [in Portugal] young men and women, the offspring of these, born in the country, as good and genuine christians as if they had been descended from the generation first baptised under the dispensation of Christ. . . .[3]

The author of *African Glory* considers this ostentatious concern to save the souls of pagan Negroes pure hypocrisy; he sees it as a Portuguese endeavour to use christianity 'for imperial or commercial ends'.[4] He then remarks that:

> The Church accepted the slave trade, although it may be said that Pope Pius II in the fifteenth century, Pope Paul III in the sixteenth century, Pope Urban VIII in the seventeenth century, and Pope Benedict XIV in the eighteenth century, all protested against the slave trade; but these protests were ignored by both Catholics and Protestants. . . .[5]

De-Graft Johnson adds that, at that time, theologians were not unanimous on the Negro problem: J. A. J. Utting in *The Story of Sierra Leone* had written: 'I know that our divines and learned men cannot decide whether or not they [the Negroes] have souls. And, of course, if they have not, they are as well treated as other animals; but all the same I am sorry for them.'[6]

Finally, for the colonial period, de Graft-Johnson limits himself to this quotation from *The Rising Tide of Colour*, whose author, Lothrop Stoddard, writing in 1920, had said:

> Certainly, all white men, whether professing Christians or not, should welcome the success of missionary efforts in Africa. The degrading fetishism and demonology which sum up the native pagan cults cannot stand, and all Negroes will some day be either Christians or Moslems. In so far as he is christianised, the Negro's savage instincts will be restrained and he will be disposed to acquiesce in white tutelage.[7]

Assane Seck recalled the earliest days of Spanish and Portuguese colonisation in *Géographie, colonisation et culture*: 'So it was easy to justify the brutalities needed to civilise the savages to whom they were bringing the catholic faith. Hence, the missionaries followed the conquerors. . . .'[8]

The resolution presented by the West African delegates to the sixth Pan-African Congress in Manchester in 1945 stated unequivocally that organised christianity in West Africa 'is identified with the political and economic exploitation of the West African people by the foreign powers'.[9] The American Negro writer, James Baldwin, is just as critical of the christian church. In speaking of his loss of faith he wrote:

> I realised that the Bible had been written by white men. I knew that, according to many Christians, I was a descendant of Ham, who had

> been cursed, and that I was therefore predestined to be a slave. . . . I remembered the Italian priests and bishops blessing Italian boys who were on their way to Ethiopia . . . in the realm of morals the role of Christianity has been, at best, ambivalent. [He denounces] the remarkable arrogance that assumed the ways and morals of others were inferior to those of Christians, and that they therefore had every right, and could use any means to change them. . . . It is not too much to say that whoever wishes to become a truly moral human being . . . must first divorce himself from all the prohibitions, crimes, and hypocrisies of the Christian Church.[10]

Kenneth Kaunda, the son of a minister, has not lost faith as James Baldwin has. He has rejected the church yet continues to regard himself as a christian. He explains his position thus, in *Zambia Shall Be Free:*

> As I have already related, I was brought up in a Christian home and my Christian belief is part of me now. It is still my habit to turn to God in prayer asking for His guidance. I do not think I have ever seriously doubted the truth of the Gospel, but I seriously question sometimes whether God is really speaking to us in the voice of the organised churches as I see them in Northern Rhodesia today.[11]

The author is particularly hostile to the segregated religious services, separating whites from blacks, which the churches continue to hold, and to the fact that African priests are treated as inferior.[12] He concludes: 'Because the Christian Church in this country has so often failed to practise what it preaches in the matter of race and politics, thousands of my fellow Africans have rejected it.'[13]

Parmenas Githendu Mockerie also attacks segregation in the christian churches: 'Mohammedanism has taught the African converts that religious observances can bring races together and make them live as brothers. For instance, the Indian and Arab muslims did not encourage separate churches between races. . . . The [christian] missionaries, when their influence was felt in Africa, built separate churches for Africans and Europeans.'[14]

However, the missionaries' own evidence is even more revealing for Negro intellectuals seeking to prove collusion between christianity and colonialism. An article in *Présence Africaine* gives us a glimpse of the innermost thoughts of a catholic priest who made his career in Africa: 'Mgr Augouard, a simple priest at the time . . . asserted to his mother in one of his many letters that now he was living among

Negroes he was really certain that they were the descendants of Ham—a truly regrettable descent in the eyes of the prelate.'[15] Charles de Graft-Johnson draws on the Negro anthology by Raymond Michelet to show the impressions of a protestant missionary, Henri Junod, who wrote in his book, the *Ba-Ronga*: 'I speak with resignation. Despite all that has been written on the fundamental axiom of the absolute equality of mankind, the blacks are an inferior race, a race made to serve.'[16]

These severe judgements are echoed in the Negro poetry and prose of America and Africa. The American Negro, Langston Hughes, is particularly scathing:

> O, precious Name of Jesus in that day!
> That day is past.
> I know full well now
> Jesus could not die for me—
> That only my own hands,
> Dark as the earth,
> Can make my earth-dark body free.[17]

D. Mandessi is no kinder:

> *en ce temps-là*
> *à coups de gueule de civilisation*
> *à coups d'eau bénite sur les fronts domestiqués.*

(In those days, with shouts of civilisation, with blows of holy water on domesticated foreheads.)[18]

It is not so much Christ as the false christians who have betrayed His cause who arouse the cry of indignation which pierces through Tchicaya's recent collection, *Epitomé*. As Senghor remarks in the preface: 'There is but a step from despair to revolt: Tchicaya has taken it. In his most pathetic poems he blames Saint Anne (of the Congo) and Christ, and the religion of the poor which should have been the hope of the disinherited, instead of being appropriated by the bourgeoisie. His revolt itself shows the need for a faith; it is a religious cry:

> *Or face à Kinshasa*
> *Sainte-Anne à son heure critique*
> *hausse l'échine*
> *et n'a plus la chair fine du Messie*
> *ni le sang clair du Messie.*

And further on:

> *Christ je me ris de ta tristesse*
> *O mon doux Christ*
> *Épine pour épine*
> *nous avons commune couronne d'épines.*

(Now facing Kinshasa Saint Anne in her hour of trial raises her back, and no longer has the fine flesh of the Messiah nor the Messiah's clear blood. . . . Christ I laugh at your sorrow, O my gentle Christ. Thorn for thorn, we have the same crown of thorns.)[19]

This was also the subject of *Nouveau Sermon nègre* by the Haitian Jacques Roumain:

Oh Judas ricane:
Christ entre deux voleurs comme une flamme déchirée au sommet du Monde
Allumait la révolte des esclaves
Mais Christ aujourd'hui est dans la maison des voleurs
Et ses bras déploient dans les cathédrales l'ombre étendue du vautour
Et dans les caves des monastères le prêtre compte les intérêts des trente deniers
Et les clochers des églises crachent la mort sur les multitudes affamées.

(Ah, Judas smirks: Christ, between two thieves like a torn flame on the summit of the world, sparked off the slaves' revolt. But Christ today is in the house of the thieves, and in the cathedrals his arms cast the long shadow of the vulture; and in the cellars of the monasteries the priest counts the interest on the thirty pieces of silver, and the church bells spit death at the hungry multitudes.)[20]

Among the novelists, Mongo Beti has taken the failure of the missionaries' work as the theme for two of his books, *Le Pauvre Christ de Bomba* and *Le Roi miraculé*. In the first of these, the missionary of Bomba, after years in the apostolate, notices that all the girls in the *sixa* (the house which, in catholic missions in the Cameroon, shelters girls engaged to be married, during two to four months' preparation doing various tasks) have lovers. The Negro catechist has been making a profit by procuring them. The despairing priest, judging black lust to be beyond redemption, leaves Africa. In the second book, an obstinate missionary is determined to convert to christianity a polygamous Negro chief who always falls back into sin. The two books are written in ironic vein. The priest of Bomba's boy, after witnessing the confessions of the girls of the *sixa* and their penance of beating with clubs, exclaims: 'What a race! just as the Reverend Father Superior said. It's quite true, we are a funny race! And perhaps we are damned, as it says in the Bible. Certainly they don't have such goings-on as this in the Reverend Father Superior's homeland. . . .'[21]

Ferdinand Oyono presents the pious old Negro, who is persuaded to hand over his lands to the mission, as the prototype of the dupe.[22] The South African, Ezekiel Mphahlele, condemns the church out of hand: he considers it to be above all 'white', and to preach a false brotherhood: 'To us the church has become a symbol of the dishonesty of the West.'[23]

In the margin of these attacks on catholic and protestant churches there is a marked hostility among some African intellectuals towards a recent movement of anti-communist flavour, Moral Rearmament. Bakary Traoré reports his impressions of this movement, which has had a fairly wide reception in Africa:

> During the summer of 1955, Moral Rearmament presented an African play, *Freedom*, in the Cité Universitaire in Paris. The audience was largely made up of students, especially Africans. The play was attended by leading African figures, deputies, magistrates, trade union leaders and also student leaders. The subject of *Freedom* is the solution of the problem of colonial countries. The Nigerians, crushed by taxes, rise against yet another new tax. This gives the opportunity for a violent criticism of the colonial system and the christian missionaries. That is the first part. But dissension and jealousy raise their heads and set the parties against each other. Then a native comes back from a Moral Rearmament Conference where he had 'attained a state of grace'; he explains that the only revolution needed is that within oneself after examining one's conscience. That is the necessary condition to free mankind and assure peace between individuals, races and peoples. The play was greeted with disapproval by the public, especially the Africans, because it completely overlooked the determining political, economic and social factors and was based on emotionalism, or rather opportunism.[24]

Mphahlele considers that 'Moral Rearmament, with the millions of dollars put at its disposal by international liberalism, is ready to invest in Africa in order to break strikes and maintain the status quo between employers and workers there'. It is certainly Moral Rearmament which Ferdinand Oyono intends to castigate in the ironical last page of

Chemins d'Europe. The episode takes place as Barnabas flees from a night club, pursued by Europeans:

> I had fled headlong to the south of the town towards a pool of light cutting through the darkness which I had taken as my goal for the last two or three kilometres. 'It's only the Spiritual Renaissance', said a group of young people who turned round, attracted by my heavy breathing and the gusts of cold air which had accompanied my arrival. 'Another trick of the white men. All you have to do is confess your sins out loud in front of everyone. They love that. Our compatriots over there behind the white table have confessed so well that they are paraded everywhere in Asia and America, just for that! . . .' In Europe! My heart began to thud. I left the crowd and went to lean against a wall to recover, thinking that here at last was my chance! I approached and heard above the crowd a woman confessing. But she had no narrative talent. I looked at the well-fed Negroes behind the table; I was going to astonish this howling crowd with my story. What a novel my life had been! Spiritual Renaissance! I smiled and walked, illuminated, towards the crowd which separated spontaneously; and as I saw one of the four white organisers of the meeting coming towards me, the one whose face was so dilated that he seemed on the point of giving out something, the first sentence which was to set me on the road to Europe came to my mind. . . .[25]

The traditional binomial

Of course, the churches have found supporters among christian black intellectuals, often men who were also ardent nationalists. For these catholic or protestant Africans, the problem has been to show that christianity could in no way be equated with colonialism;[26] and on the contrary, that nationalism and christianity are at the least compatible. Thus, the Abbé Jean Zoa, currently archbishop of Yaoundé, in his brochure *Pour un nationalisme chrétien au Cameroun*, has set out to refute what he calls the traditional binomial: *nationalism equals communism; catholicism equals colonialism*. He points to the words of a bishop to the Congress of Kibusi in 1953:

> The colonial era is drawing rapidly to its close. The church will greet with satisfaction the moment when the colonial peoples are able to direct their own destinies. . . . Laymen should not abstain

> from patriotic movements aiming to increase political liberty. Their influence can be great and could avoid the irreparable harm which would result if such organisations were left solely in the hands of political agitators.[27]

Writers whose keen nationalism is no more in doubt than is their deep attachment to their respective churches, have dwelt at length on the problem of the missionaries. We may cite the Dahomean, Albert Tévoedjré in French-speaking Africa, and in English-speaking Africa the Rhodesian Ndabaningi Sithole—the former a catholic, the latter protestant. Although both are fervent christians—Sithole has been ordained—they are both well aware of the 'colonialist' spirit which animated, and still animates, some missionaries. 'There is a total antinomy between the colonial regime, which is above all oppression and lies built up into a system, and christianity, a universal religion of truth, love and fulfilment', Tévoedjré writes at the beginning of his chapter "L'Eglise et le problème colonial en Afrique noir". But immediately afterwards he goes on to analyse the 'colonial drama of the church'. He recalls the findings of the theological committee of Lyons, presided over by Cardinal Gerlier in 1955, which asserted that: 'The missionary movement and colonial expansion were independent of one another. It would be a mistake to connect the two in any way at all.' Tévoedjré comments: 'Unfortunately, there are thousands of examples of factual situations which could be quoted, even from recent times, which at the very least attenuate the thesis that the church is in no way connected with colonisation.' The author goes on to analyse the origins of such an attitude in the missions which he finds, among other sources, in Chateaubriand's *Génie du christianisme*. This, he says, 'gave the direction, and created a sort of collective mentality of which several missionary reviews still bear the stamp'. Another source was Lamennais who wrote: 'It was in the destiny of the human race that the white race should break out of their chains, bit by bit, while the ancient anathema pronounced on the heads of the descendants of Ham, according to the Scriptures, promised them only eternal slavery.' But Tévoedjré recalls in conclusion the encyclical letter of Pope Pius XII which in 1956 approved emancipation movements in the colonies.[28]

In his chapter on the christian church, Sithole writes: 'The Bible is redeeming the African individual from the power of superstition, individuality-crushing tradition, witch-craft and other forces that do not make for progress. The same Bible is helping the African individual to reassert himself above colonial powers!'[29] He gives equal emphasis to the fight of some churches against apartheid in South Africa (omitting from his list the Boer churches which support it*). He remarks, however, that some missionaries, working in a colonial atmosphere, have adopted a colonial attitude towards the African and have opposed his great dream of independence. In passing, Sithole also refutes the opinions of a great protestant whose work in Africa has aroused fervent admiration—Dr Schweitzer:

> Schweitzer . . . regards the African as a child. He plays the common role of the big 'white father', and if there is any blunder that most white people commit this is surely one. . . . Schweitzer deliberately reduces an adult African to a child so that he can justify the superimposition of European authority on the African. It is an insult for one man to regard another man as a child.[30]

Sithole refers in particular to the passages from Dr Schweitzer's book in which he says that the Negro is a child and that authority is essential in handling children. Schweitzer had therefore adopted the formula: 'I am your brother, it is true, but your older brother.'[31]

Sithole summarises the African's opposing views of the church in South Africa in the following conversation:

> Two South African natives were arguing one day over the unhealthy South African situation. One was inclined to censure the whole missionary enterprise in Africa in this strain, 'You see, the missionary came here and said, "Let us pray". And we closed our eyes. And when we responded "Amen" at the end of his prayer, we found the Bible in our hands. But lo! our land had gone!'
>
> To which the other replied, 'When Europeans took our country we fought them with our spears, but they defeated us because they had better weapons. And so colonial power was set up much against

* In November 1960, however, eleven leading members of the Nederduits Gereformeerde Kerk and other South African reformed churches announced their opposition to apartheid. The most important of them, Dr B. B. Keet, professor of theology at the Stellenbosch Seminary, wrote in *Delayed Action*, the collective work produced by these eleven religious leaders: 'It is well known that our Afrikaans churches are in favour of total apartheid, if by this division all groups are given the fullest rights. The fact is, however, that such a division is not possible at this period in our history. The advocates of apartheid have constantly claimed that only their policy is able to save white civilisation in South Africa. The opposite is true.' (*The Times*, London, November 21, 1960.)

our wish. But lo! the missionary came in time and laid explosives under colonialism. The Bible is now doing what we could not do with our spears.'[32]

Finally, Sithole concludes that African nationalism is strongly impregnated with christian principles, and he recalls that Gandhi admitted that he had been greatly influenced by Christ's sermon on the mount.

Tévoedjré and Sithole both praise the concrete work done by the church. Both underline the importance of the educational effort undertaken by the missions, and missionaries' major contribution to the study of African languages.

In the field of literature, the Negro novel denouncing the failure of missionary work finds its antithesis in that of frankly evangelical intent. This is particularly true of the first generation of South African novelists such as Thomas Mofolo or Arthur Nuthall Fula. Apart from his work on Shaka, in which the punishment of the Zulu conqueror was the ransom for his paganism, Mofolo wrote several other novels in which he extolled christianity. *The Traveller of the East*,[33] for instance, tells of a Sotho chief who sets off to find the land of God. He is saved from shipwreck by three white men who teach him the message of Christ's charity. Fula's novel (written in Cape Dutch) *Im goldenen Labyrinth*[34] recounts the hero's fight against the sins of modern civilisation, alcoholism, prostitution, etc., to promote the victory of an austere christian morality.

Janheinz Jahn, as we have seen, applies to this generation of South African writers in the service of missionary work the pejorative title of *Zöglingsliteratur:* the literature of good pupils. For Peter Sulzer, on the other hand, South African literature of the first quarter of the twentieth century—of which the great names for him were those of Mofolo and Plaatje—was '*das goldene Zeitalter des Bantuschriftums*': the golden age of Bantu literature. Its two sources of inspiration were christian proselytising and African folklore. Sulzer has collected a series of passages in praise of missionaries from Southern African writers such as A. C. Jordan, D. D. T. Jabavu, S. Y. Ntara* and S. M. Molema.

* Ntara writes in Nyanja, one of the main languages of Nyasaland (now Malawi). Literature in the vernacular received strong encouragement under the British administration from the Publications Departments in Northern Rhodesia (now Zambia) and Nyasaland. A similar institution—the East African Literature Office—functioning in Kenya, Uganda and Tanganyika, has made a notable contribution to the revival of Swahili literature. Swahili is one of the first African languages to have been given written form, using Arabic script. Swahili literature is remarkable for its poetry.

Ntara's novel *Man of Africa* is an edifying autobiography. The hero Nthondo exclaims when the Europeans first arrive in his village: 'Europeans mean strife. They have no brotherliness for us folk.'[35] But the Europeans build a school and Nthondo, who has become the chief of the village, 'showed anger when his own children strayed away from school and therefore it came about that the villagers began to get a real hold upon the value that schooling brings and also knowledge of Jesus Christ'.[36]

David Ananou, among the French-speaking novelists, denounced the stupidity and harmfulness of African pagan customs in his book, *Le Fils du fétiche*, in which he traces the misfortunes of a couple who fall victim to the swindling and frauds of the fetishists; they eventually find happiness through conversion to christianity. The novel *One Man, One Wife* by the Nigerian, T. M. Aluko, is in the same vein.

Black angel

The concomitance of colonisation and evangelisation could not fail to make christianity seem to some Africans a foreign religion which was being imposed on them. The fact that Christ, historically, was white, as were his apostles and saints, gave christianity a racial smell which was corroborated by the curse on the children of Ham. West Indian and African Negro poets have often echoed this 'suspicion'. For the West Indian, Paul Niger, *Dieu a oublié l'Afrique:*

Dieu, un jour descendu sur la terre, fut désolé de l'attitude des créatures envers la création. Il ordonna le déluge, et germa, de la terre, resurgie, une semence nouvelle.
L'arche peupla le monde et lentement
Lentement
L'humanité monta des âges sans lumière aux âges sans repos.
Il avait oublié l'Afrique.
Christ racheta l'homme mauvais et bâtit son Église à Rome.
Sa voix fut entendue dans le désert. L'Église sur la Société, la Société sur l'Église, l'une portant l'autre, fondèrent la civilisation où les hommes, dociles à l'antique sagesse, pour apaiser les anciens dieux, pas morts
Immolèrent tous les dix ans quelques millions de victimes.
Il avait oublié l'Afrique.
Mais quand on s'aperçut qu'une race (d'hommes?)
Devait encore à Dieu son tribut de sang noir, on lui fit un rappel.
Elle solda

Et solde encore, et lorsqu'elle demanda sa place au sein de l'oecumène, on lui désigna quelques bancs. Elle s'assit. Et s'endormit.
Jésus étendit les mains sur ces têtes frisées, et les nègres furent sauvés.
Pas ici-bas, bien sûr.
Mais le royaume du ciel aux simples étant ouvert, ils y entrèrent en foule, et la Parole rapporte que, pour achever le miracle et laver pour toujours les noirs de l'originel péché, ils sont là-haut transformés en blancs, pour quoi l'on ne voit pas (sauf dans les films américains) d'anges ni de saints noirs.

(One day God came down to earth and was dismayed by the creatures' attitude to creation. He ordered the flood, and a new crop sprang up from the land which rose again.

The ark peopled the world and slowly, slowly, humanity advanced from the dark ages to the restless ages. He had forgotten Africa. Christ redeemed man's wickness and built his church at Rome. His voice was heard in the desert. The church leaning on society, society leaning on the church, the one carrying the other, founded a civilisation where men, docile to the ancient teachings and to appease the ancient gods, still not dead, every ten years sacrified several million victims. He had forgotten Africa. But when it was noticed that a race (of men?) owed God the tribute of their Negro blood, it was brought to his attention. They paid and still pay, and when they asked for a place in the bosom of the church, they were offered a few benches. They sat down and went to sleep. Jesus placed his hands on those curly heads and the Negroes were saved. Not down here of course.

But since the kingdom of heaven is open to simple folk, they entered in droves; and the Word says that to achieve the miracle and wash away original sin for ever from the blacks they are transformed into whites up there and that is why one never sees black angels and saints—except in American films.)[37]

It was undoubtedly in order to mock this white paradise that R. E. G. Armattoe from Togo wrote of a black paradise:

That was there at the beginning,
When no bleaching was ever seen,
And angels black as Indian ink,
And dark saints blacker still did sing.
In that blissful heaven of blackness,
Will live the black men of today.[38]

Perhaps for different reasons, Jomo Kenyatta, shortly after his liberation, criticised the 'racism' of illustrators of the Bible and Scriptures. The political leader of Kenya, in a speech at Teveta on the borders of Tanganyika, complained that angels in holy pictures were always white whereas the devil was black with horns and a tail.[39]

Mistrust of the 'God of the whites' found an original expression among the African masses in contact with missionaries, who asked them to burn their idols and abandon their ancestral beliefs, in the proliferation of churches founded by black prophets. This sociological phenomenon has been the subject of numerous studies; those of B. G. M. Sundkler (*Bantu Prophets in South Africa*) and Georges Balandier ("Messianismes et nationalismes en Afrique noire") are particularly important. In the religious field these churches often preached a kind of inverted racism, proclaiming that heaven was henceforth reserved for black men. In the political field they favoured the demand for independence; hence the sentences sometimes passed on their leaders. These separatist churches were particularly prolific in South Africa, and Sundkler distinguishes between the churches called 'Ethiopian'—an allusion to their desire for independence from all European control, symbolised by the name of the only African kingdom to have escaped colonisation—and the so-called 'Zionist' churches. The latter were founded by black prophets who preached a wholesale apocalyptic upheaval leading to a fairer reconstruction of society. They practise a form of syncretism blending pagan ritual and christian belief. One of the best-known of these prophets is undoubtedly William Wase Harris from Liberia, who 'evangelised', according to very personal conceptions, many villages in his own country, the Ivory Coast and the Gold Coast, a little before 1920. In the Belgian Congo, there was an interval of twenty years between Simon Kimbangu, a prophet brought to justice in 1921, and Simon Mpadi. In the French Congo, there was André Matsua, arrested in 1930 and 1940 and eventually deported to Chad. In the Cameroon, Lotin Same founded a unified native church shortly after the first world war. The Watchtower Movement has had a lasting influence in East and Central Africa.

Jomo Kenyatta devoted a chapter of *Facing Mount Kenya* to these churches. According to him, they are the result of insufficient psychological training of missionaries who, he says, 'as far as religion was concerned, regarded the African as a clean slate on which anything could be written'.[40] He points out that Africans, on reading the Bible, noticed that many famous and saintly people had practised polygamy.

The need to create African churches arose, according to Kenyatta, from these gaps and contradictions in missionary teaching, which nevertheless was accepted since submission to it gave the Africans the right to send their children to school. Hence, in Kenya, the Watu Wa Mngu (the people of God) sect mixes Kikuyu and christian religious rites and, as well as other sources, draws its inspiration from this passage of the Bible, which is well suited to stimulate African religious nationalism: 'Princes shall come out of Africa, Ethiopia shall soon stretch out her hands to God.' Kenyatta considers their attitude 'symbolises their strong nationalistic feeling'.[41] He limits his conclusion simply to the remark that 'the sect is still in its infancy and its future growth and activities remain to be investigated by anthropological field-workers'.[42]

This proliferation of Christian sects seems in no danger of extinction; indeed, in some cases, it is even on the increase. In 1960 an 'African Church' was founded in Accra by the Reverend Mensah who, in 1961, canonised Patrice Lumumba, the assassinated Congolese leader, as a new saint—at about the same time as the USSR gave his name to the university which takes in African students.[43] Again, in Ghana also, the Anglican Archbishop Porter protested against the use of biblical language in the *Ghana Evening News*, which had compared Nkrumah to the Messiah. Two years later, the Ghanaian authorities expelled his successor Archbishop Roseveare. During a synod at Cape Coast, Archbishop Roseveare had violently criticised the cult surrounding President Nkrumah who, he said, 'takes himself for a God'.

An article published in the African students' review *Tam-Tam* in 1961 raised this whole problem of dissident churches. Under the title "Malaise de l'étudiant catholique africain", Paul Rouamba did not disguise his sympathies for the nationalist convictions of their founders, and his indignation at their repression:

> Do not take us for Whitsuntide visionaries when we want to be the forerunners and guarantors of Africa's cultural originality and integrity in face of the Europeans' invasion. Do not tax us with xenophobia and inverted racism (as though racism were a white prerogative) when we reject the silent complicity in the face of the cultural genocide linked with colonisation.
>
> I will take just three examples: André Matsua, who proposed to create an autonomous religious sect different from the 'white religion' and independent of it; Simon Kimbangu, and later his

> successor Simon Mpadi . . . who asked for the right to found a 'black church'; and finally, after 1890, the proliferation of separatist churches in Nigeria whose slogan was: 'Religious anti-imperialism must take its place in the anti-imperialist fight.' Here Edward Blyden's influence should be mentioned.[44] He was one of the first Negroes to underline the importance of cultural dispossession: he attacked the christian churches for their sin of cultural alienation and preached a christianity adapted to the African context.

But the writer does not want a schism:

> These are propositions which seem to bring a bit more grist to the mill than those which fear a future and inevitable premeditated separatism, a schism. They have no need to worry; if our concern to find an African dress for christianity in Africa sinks its roots in the politico-religious syncretism of the first manifestations of nationalism, it must for this reason evoke a favourable response in all who are not apathetic to the future of christianity in Africa. The necessary revolution will be carried out . . . with or without 'the christian West'.[45]

Contrary to the belief of most writers, the majority of new African churches in Ghana were founded independently of the nationalist movement, maintains Dr C. G. Baeta, director of the seminary of religious studies at the University of Ghana, and member of the International Missionary Council and the World Council of Churches, in *Prophetism in Ghana*. 'There is no evidence that anti-European or anti-Western feeling played a role' in their origin, asserts the author in the conclusion to his study.[46] 'Where reversions to African traditional practices have taken place (such as the restoration of taboos on women during their monthly courses), the reason has been the authority of the Old Testament rather than the fact that the customs were African.'[47] It is true that the Reverend Baeta has taken 'spiritual' churches as the object of his study, and they take the Bible as their sacred book; their principal deviation from orthodox teaching is in the practice of 'miraculous cures' carried out during seances with dancing, common prayer and veneration of contemporary prophets. Baeta has dwelt on their case with great understanding. Thus, after telling of the healing seances of the Church of the Twelve Apostles, which claims descent from the prophet Harris and uses the Bible to exorcise evil spirits, he adds: 'Although I was often tempted to do so, I did not have the heart to suggest to them that they were in fact using the Bible as a sort of ju-ju or fetish.'[48] And he concludes:

> When the Ghana churches are considered alongside similar bodies elsewhere, one cannot help noticing the modesty and sober reasonableness of their claims. It may be that this is due to the country's good fortune in having been spared the excessive political and other pressures to which the people in other parts have been subjected. In any case, no extravagant promises have been made here, e.g. of shiploads of rich consumer goods to arrive for the appropriation and free use of members, or of the latter being able to drive the Europeans into the sea, as such hopes have been held . . . in various sects of South, Central and Eastern Africa.[49]

Many religious movements, quite similar in a number of ways to the Ethiopian churches of Africa, have also sprung up in America. The Haitian voodoo is the best-known example, but there are others, such as Marcus Garvey's Orthodox African church which taught that angels were black and Satan white, or the 'Rastafarians' of Jamaica who claim descent from the kings of Ethiopia and also want to return to Africa. (The sect was founded in 1936 at the time of the Italian conquest of the kingdom of the Negus.) Voodoo specialists generally agree that the belief originally meant for Negro slaves a way of preserving their cultural identity, which is clearly one aspect of nationalism. Janheinz Jahn wrote: 'Voodoo also has a political aspect. Religious dances were the slaves' only way of re-creating the atmosphere of their homeland.'[50]

The Spanish writer, Juan Goytisolo, in a recent article on Cuba, "La Révolution qui danse", accompanied a description of a pagan festival with the following commentary:

> I had imagined that opposition from the catholic church would be very dangerous for the regime. I had read Cuba's future in the pasts of Spain and the Argentine. But I noticed that the Cuban crowds are indifferent to the church's orders. The people of Cuba are not catholic. They have never been. Beliefs of African origin have remained very much alive among the poorer classes. The 'Abakua' and 'Lucumies' sects, whose ceremonies are related to the voodoo rites, number more followers than the catholic church. These two sects originated among the Negro slaves. The survival of traditional beliefs was for them a means of defence against their white masters.

> The egalitarian, progressive character of the religious later attracted the 'poor whites'. . . . And indeed, after the abolition of slavery, many whites rallied to these dissident churches which from then on were identified not only with the oppressed race but also with the oppressed classes.[51]

The Vatican against colonial France

To come back to the African churches: their prophets were often former catechumens of European missions, without much education. Although this is not a general rule—it is undoubtedly truer of the 'Zionist' than the 'Ethiopian' churches—their followers were in general recruited from the more backward layers of the population. But, whatever the case may be, the European churches have been faced with nationalist demands from both the intellectuals and the comparatively uneducated prophets, and they could not remain indifferent to these if they were to continue their mission in Africa.

While some christian intellectuals were lingering over a 'theology of colonisation', as R. Codjo calls it in his article "Colonisation et conscience chrétienne",[52] a trend of thought going in the opposite direction became noticeable in ecclesiastical milieux, particularly among the catholics, as though preparing to face these claims. As Codjo showed, the protagonists of the movement in defence of colonisation had drawn their material from rather ancient authors; the doctrine of the 'common good' which they professed was in fact inspired largely by the works of a sixteenth-century Spanish Jesuit, Francis de Vitoria, a disciple of Saint Thomas Aquinas. According to this doctrine, which was taken into account very much later by Popes Leo XIII and Pius XII in several encyclical letters, the authority of a state was legitimate as long as it worked for the 'common good' of all its subjects. The use that can be made of this to justify colonisation is self-evident. In his thesis, *Le Droit de colonisation*, Joseph Folliet, a Catholic lawyer and sociologist, based a distinction between colonisation and colonialism on this criterion among others; he judged the former to be good while the latter was to be condemned. Folliet's doctrine is doubtless open to various interpretations. For Codjo, the distinction is too subtle and can too easily be used to uphold domination by the colonial powers. For the catholic journalist Robert Barrat, on the contrary, it contains the moral justification for the revolt of the colonised peoples when they are exploited.[53]

The movement in the opposite direction, towards African emancipation, was translated on to the political and theological planes. On the political plane, an ever-increasing number of Africans were raised to the highest ecclesiastical ranks. On the theological plane, European and African priests tried to find points of contact between Bantu ontologies and christian theodicy, which would allow for some adaptation of the catholic catechism and ritual in Africa. This development was consecrated in a sense by the encyclical letter, *Evangelii praecones*, of Pope Pius XII in 1953, which gave the missions the target of 'firmly and definitively establishing the church among the new nations, with a hierarchy of its own, chosen from among the inhabitants of the place'.* Henceforth, the 'foreign clergy' on African soil would not control the missions and would continue the evangelising campaign only as 'auxiliary troops'. This papal text aroused opposition among those who saw it as a call for colonial independence, against the interests of the colonial powers. This is one of François Méjean's arguments in his book with the significant title *Le Vatican contre la France d'Outremer*. 'It is because western civilisation has become secular that the catholic church is abandoning it',[54] asserts the author, who ends his book with this question: 'Is not the church relinquishing a certain good for a chimera by sacrificing France's overseas territories (and basically Europe's as well) to the daring views and hasty generalisations of the Congregation for the Propagation of the Faith which serves the interests of the Afro-Asians of the Bandung Conference?'[55]

François Méjean's book provided the basis for an editorial in *Présence Africaine* on the problems arising from the church's attitude to black nationalism. The writer was worried—contrary to what François Méjean believed—because for some European catholic intellectuals the West and christianity remain synonymous. *Présence Africaine* referred to *Civilisations et christianisme*, a special number of *Comprendre*, organ of the Société Européene de Culture. According to *Présence Africaine*, the authors' aim in this special number was to 'show that christianity cannot be dissociated from the vocation of the West which is a vocation to the Universal'. And on the same lines, the leader-writer was concerned to see that some catholic ecclesiastics, such as Father Ghedo in his book *L'Éveil des peuples de couleur*, subscribed to this identification. The editorial continued: 'One gets the impression that for [Ghedo]—who is a member of the Pontifical

* In 1962–3, at the second Vatican Council, there were one black cardinal and fifty-seven black bishops. In 1939, Pope Pius XII had consecrated the first two African bishops.

Institute for Foreign Missions—it is not so much a question of saving christianity as saving the West. The last pages seem to consider the awakening of the coloured peoples as the greatest danger of the twentieth century. The church has no mission as urgent as that of saving the West and missionary action would be reduced to strategy . . . vulgar and unacceptable.'[56]

At the time of the second Vatican Council, the *Présence Africaine* team was once again actively concerned with the 'African presence in catholic life'. The Society of African Culture launched an appeal to African catholics and laymen for studies on the Africans' place within the catholic church. Early in 1963, *Présence Africaine* published, under the title *Personnalité africaine et catholicisme*, the texts received from priests and laymen stating the claims of African catholics. The problem of the liturgy, and more especially of liturgical language, appears, from a study of this collection, to have been of primary concern. Hence, Marc Ela asks the question: 'Is it not because the church sought to Europeanise Africans that it is now in its present dilemma?', and replies by asserting the need to make the liturgy and theology more native. Abbé Nioka also wrote that christianity should not be chained to any one culture, while Engelbert Mveng, SJ, maintained that 'christian Africa is now adult and must speak to God in its own language'. The conciliar fathers acceded to the request of the African catholics: the constitution on the liturgy proclaimed in December 1963 gives space for 'use of the vernacular in public masses'.

Sign-posts

The same encyclical letter, *Evangelii praecones*, which established the principle of africanisation of the ecclesiastical hierarchy in Africa, also gave instructions on the attitude to be taken vis-à-vis pagan religions. 'The church has never treated pagan doctrines with scorn and disdain. Rather has she freed them from error and impurity, until complete and crowned with wisdom. . . . [She] is not like the man who, respecting nothing, cuts down a luxuriant forest, ransacks and ruins it. Rather does she imitate the gardener who grafts a bud on the wild shoot to make it produce better, sweeter fruit one day.'

Indeed, European missionaries in Africa had already done some research in this direction, to bring to light analogies between the African and christian religions. Foremost among them were Father Trilles, in his *L'Ame des Pygmées d'Afrique*, and Father Tempels, in his *La Philosophie bantoue*. In the first of the two books, Trilles affirms that the Pygmy has an idea of God which came to him through a revelation similar to that of the christian religions. An analysis of the legends on the origin of death leads him to the conclusion that, in Pygmy ontology, it is due to an 'initial fault', the conception of which is not totally alien to that of original sin. Trilles underlines the subordination of secondary divinities to the supreme being. In his study, Tempels attempts to establish the outlines of a philosophic system from the religious beliefs of tribes in the Belgian Congo. In analysing these, he points out the similarities between the 'vital force'—one of the fundamental concepts of Bantu ontology—and the doctrine of christian grace. Later he stresses that the Negroes of Central Africa have a conception of good and evil, etc., and concludes that the Bantu, with their spontaneous philosophy, are closer to christianity than to any other system of thought.

These books had a mixed reception from the African intelligentsia. Alioune Diop, director of *Présence Africaine*, wrote a glowing preface to the new edition of *La Philosophie bantoue* which he was publishing, and which had originally been published by the Catholic University of Louvain in 1945. Other African intellectuals, on the other hand, criticised the manifestly evangelistic aims of the book, sometimes at the expense, they claimed, of scientific accuracy. Indeed Tempels had not tried to hide this, and ended his book with these words: 'Bantu civilisation will be christian or will not be.'

The message of Pius XII's encyclical letter also urged African priests to study the religions of the black continent. Two examples of such a study are: the Abbé Vincent Mulago's doctorate thesis, *L'Union vitale bantu chez les Bashi, Banyarwanda et les Barundi face a l'unité vitale ecclésiale* at the Université de la Propagande in 1955; and that of the Abbé Alexis Kagame, *La Philosophie bantu-ruandaise de l'être*, at the Gregorian University in Rome in 1956.

Des Prêtres noirs s'interrogent, a special number of *Rencontres* published under the direction of *Présence Africaine*, was conceived in the same spirit. This was a collection of articles by Haitian and African priests which sought to show in African traditional beliefs concepts and rites which were 'valid' from a catholic viewpoint, and on which, if necessary, missionary work could be based. The most typical of these studies is probably Vincent Mulago's "Le Pacte de sang et la communion alimentaire, pierres d'attente de la communion eucharistique". Here the author brings out the analogies between traditional customs in the Congo and the christian communion. Mulago recalls that the blood pact is made between two people who wish to join in an irrevocable and sacred friendship by drinking a few drops of blood taken from a small incision in the breast and collected on the leaf of a tree. He then continues: 'The blood pact springs from a deep mystical sense. . . . [It is] the gift *par excellence* since it is the gift of oneself, fusion in the other person, entry and acceptance into the family of one's friend. . . . It is a part of me, a part of my vital essence that I am offering [my friend].' The Abbé Mulago gives a similar explanation of the communion through food, particularly with the dead. He concludes: 'This is enough for the apostle of the eucharist among our Bantu to make use of the communion meal and blood pact in his mission. Christianity was born in the mystery of the blood, and it is in the mystery of the blood that it is called on to live and spread; it is this mystery of the blood which creates and nourishes its solidarity and unity.'

The efforts of the young African catholic clergy, encouraged by the encyclical letter of Pius XII, often serve as a cross-check to the works of African ethnologists who had concluded that there was a belief in the existence of a Supreme Being in African religions. Their motives, however, were not the same. The ethnologists used this as evidence in their assertion that African cultures were not inferior to western culture, in so far as they identified christianity with the West. However, whatever the differences in their approach, there is no doubt that the research of both groups is inspired by a similar love for their ancestral African homeland; and also that it is an integral part, although to different degrees, of a current of nationalist thinking among the African intelligentsia.

Historically, the interesting thing in the catholic church's attitude to black nationalism is not just that it could foresee the inevitable independence of the colonies, but also that it understood that cultural needs lay behind the African's thirst for emancipation. And so, in its own domain, it tried to find a solution which would take into account both the political and the cultural aspects of African nationalism.

Islam

The conversion of Africa by christian missions has reached remarkable proportions, but Islam has remained an impressive competitor, and not only among the less advanced sectors of the population. There is a whole African elite attached to the beliefs of Islam, despite their European culture. Today a muslim 'revival' is finding expression in French in the works of Hampaté Ba from Mali and the Senegalese Sheikh Hamidou Kane, both of whom are Fulani.

Ahmadou Hampaté Ba dedicated his book, written in collaboration with a French islamist, Marcel Cardaire, to one of mohammedanism's saintly men. It tells of the life and teaching of *Tierno Bokar, le sage de Bandiagara*. (By concidence, Marcel Griaule also visited the same place, in Dogon territory, in his search for a pagan cosmogony—that of the Dogon—from the mouth of another venerable sage, Ogotemmêli.) Tierno Bokar spent his youth in the rather special context of the collapse of the Fulani empire of the Massina beneath the blows of the Tukuler conqueror, al-Hajj Umar. The Fulani belonged to the muslim Qadriya sect, the Tukuler to the Tidjaniya sect. Tierno Bokar was a descendant through his mother of a Qadriya family converted to Tidjaniya rites: thus the sage of Bandiagara had both Fulani and Tukuler ancestors. Perhaps it was this conglomeration of circumstances which gave him the bent for tolerence, even of the christian religion. That is one of the basic characteristics of the master's teaching, as Hampaté Ba points out, writing on the founding of koranic schools by his disciples after his death:

> The message of tolerance, charity and love spread across the countryside of the Sudan. At the very moment when in other parts of the Dar-ul-Islam messages of intolerance and hate flashed through politico-religious circles, muslim black Africa gave the world an example of serenity. The 'Saint Francis of Assisi' of Bandiagara was certainly born in the right place for his words to be heard and listened to. The golden jewel was rightly placed on the external ear and the lobe of the ear.
>
> Today this Word is breaking out of the narrow limits in which it has remained. We offer it to the public. The last paragraph of this chapter, devoted to the Message, cannot be from us. Once again we make way for Tierno Bokar: 'I look forward with all my heart to the era of reconciliation between all the creeds on earth, the era when these united faiths will support each other to form a moral canopy, the era when they will rest in God on three points of support: Love, Charity and Fraternity.
>
> There is only one God. There can only be one way to Him: one religion of which the others are merely variations. This religion can

> only be called Truth. Its dogmas can only be three: Love, Charity, and Fraternity. Why should this reconciliation, so often forecast, prepared and looked forward to, not be called the "True Alloy"?
>
> Certainly a combination of the essential truths of the different religions dividing the world would have a far wider and more universal religious appeal; and perhaps it would be closer to the Unity of God, the human spirit and the unity of creation in a unique world.'[57]

In his novel *L'Aventure ambiguë*, the Senegalese writer, Sheikh Hamidou Kane, has given the name Tierno to the koranic schoolteacher, the muslim sage who taught his hero. This choice does not seem to have been pure chance, in this story of mystical intent. Samba Diallo is the son of a Fulani nobleman who first entrusts him to Tierno. The teacher is distressed by the atheism which in his view characterises the West:

> I have learnt that in the land of the white men revolt against poverty is not distinguished from revolt against God. It is said that this is spreading and that soon throughout the world the great cry against poverty will also muffle the voice of the muezzins. How great must have been the fault of those who believe in God if, at the end of their rule in the world, the name of God arouses the resentment of the hungry? . . . [But] it is certain that their school is the best teacher of carpentry, and that men must learn to build homes which will last.[58]

Samba Diallo eventually leaves his old teacher for a European school and then he goes to Paris to study philosophy. This period is for him a break between the teachings of his parents and those of modern Europe, between the mysticism of muslim Africa, and the West devoured by materialism but temporarily superior because of its technical skill. The necessary fight against this materialism also comes into the colonial context. During a conversation in Paris with West Indian friends who have broken their links with the Negro world, Samba Diallo refutes the conviction that 'our great need of the West no longer leaves us the choice, and only allows submission, until we have acquired their skill'. This view is unacceptable to the young African student for 'if we accept it and accommodate ourselves, we shall never be in control of things. For we shall have no more dignity than things have. We shall not dominate them. And our failure would be the end of the last human being on this earth.'[59] But soon Samba Diallo fears God has abandoned him: he has lost his childhood faith.

His father recalls him. When he arrives in the village of his birth Tierno is dead. The village idiot—in the novelist's mind, obviously the symbol of destiny guarding over tradition—wants Samba Diallo to take his place. The young man refuses. The idiot then takes him on a night walk to the cemetery where the master is buried. He begs Samba Diallo to pray; the latter refuses a second time. Then the idiot ends the 'ambiguous adventure' by killing Samba. Despite the doubts which assailed him, Samba Diallo remained deeply imbued with his religion, and throughout the book Kane expresses a profound attachment to the muslim faith.

It is a return to islamic virtue which brings about the rehabilitation and consecration of an alcoholic African doctor in Mamadou Gologo's book, *Le Rescapé de l'Ethylos*. In the political field, some of the attitudes of the Sardauna of Sokoto (killed in the Nigerian military coup of January 1966) might be attributed to his religious convictions. A notable example of this was the 'fatalism', which some ascribe to Islam, shown in his attitude to the conquest of his country by British troops. 'Whatever may have been the rights and wrongs of the attack on Kano and Sokoto, the British were the instruments of fate and were carrying out the will of God.'[60] But this muslim stamp is not always to the advantage of the colonialists. Although Sir Ahmadu Bello, who had seven times made the pilgrimage to Mecca, devoted an enthusiastic chapter of his autobiography to Queen Elizabeth's visit to Nigeria in 1956, he also categorically criticised the British attack on Egypt in 1956, which he termed 'deplorable and completely unjustified', lacking even the 'merit of efficient preparation and determined execution'.[61]

The renaissance of Islam in French-speaking black Africa has also given rise to several muslim reviews which appear regularly in French in Dakar. Among these are *Le Réveil islamique*, organ of the Muslim Cultural Union, and *Vers l'Islam*, the Dakar periodical of African muslim students. These two publications both consider themselves progressive, and combat the prejudices of an over-strict orthodoxy, and even more an obscurantist marabout influence, which would be obstacles to the evolution which is needed.

12

THE AFRICAN PROLETARIAT

'SINCE THE END of the Second World War it has become notorious, both in the press and in certain political circles of the Western world, to ascribe every manifestation of political awakening in Africa to Communist inspiration.* This is gross hypocrisy, part of the cold war propaganda designed to discredit African Nationalists and to alienate from their movements the sympathy and support of anti-colonial elements within Labour and progressive organisations, which, while friendly towards the political aspiration of the colonial peoples, are hostile to Communism.'[1]

These lines by George Padmore clearly reflect the concern of many African nationalists at the accusations often made in colonialist circles that emancipation movements in the colonies are Russian-inspired.† Since all the colonial powers were in the western camp, it was particularly vital that non-communist African nationalist movements should keep their distance from the eastern bloc. This was all the more necessary since African nationalists could not fall back on violence in their struggle for freedom. Although they may have benefited indirectly from the open warfare in Indochina and Algeria (and Ferhat Abbas has maintained that France freed black Africa only under pressure of events in North Africa[2]), they were not able to follow the same path, for a number of reasons. The Malagasy uprising and the Mau Mau rebellion, in fact, both ended in defeat.

Many Africans saw as their greatest allies in the struggle the non-communist left and liberal opinion in Europe. To seek help from

* As an example the Suppression of Communism Act passed in 1950 in South Africa has been used principally against the black nationalists.

† At the end of Padmore's work, there is a harsh indictment of 'the opportunistic and cynical behaviour of the communists' (p. 289); he states that 'if ever the Africans turn to Communism, it will be due to the stupidity of the white settlers' (p. 378). In conclusion, he writes: 'Panafricanism offers an ideological alternative to Communism on the one side and Tribalism on the other.' (p. 379.) The English edition of his book is called *Panafricanism or Communism?*; the edition printed in Accra—from which the page numbers above and in the references are taken—is called simply *Panafricanism.*

Moscow under these circumstances would have meant forfeiting this support, which had proved of considerable importance. This is true both of Britain and of France. Padmore's ideas are directly echoed by Albert Tévoedjré. The Dahomean author wrote these lines in the last pages of his *L'Afrique révoltée:* 'When "patriotism" and "communism" are continually confused in our countries, a common judgement is perpetuated: as soon as a nationalist movement appears in Africa a few missionaries see the hand of communism at work. By this bias christians are forbidden to take part and the colonial administration can set "nationalist" Africans and "christian" Africans against each other at its leisure.'[3] Although Tévoedjré is as much aiming at missionaries who are too conservative for his liking as at the colonial authorities quick to play their game, his argument is basically identical with Padmore's. Just as the European churches felt obliged to guard themselves against their conservative and right-wing elements, so the non-communist African nationalist parties felt they had to be cautious towards the extreme left. Although the anti-communism of a devout catholic such as Tévoedjré is sincere, his attitude, like that of Padmore, is governed by tactical necessity. Indeed, metropolitan fear of increasing communist influence in Africa was such, in the view of African nationalists, that at times they found it convenient to brandish it as a bogey.

This procedure seemed perfectly legitimate to so fervent a protestant as Ndabaningi Sithole. In his chapter, on "Africa and Communism", his first step is to show that African nationalism is in no way communist. As part of his evidence, he quotes this statement by Nasser:

> There would not be any communist infiltration in any part of the Middle East and Africa if the United States could develop a courageous policy—and the only morally correct one—of supporting those who are anxious to get rid of foreign domination and exploitation. Real independence would be the greatest defence against communist—or any other type of—infiltration or aggression. Free men are the most fanatical defenders of their liberty, nor do they lightly forget those who have championed their struggle for independence.[4]

This contains the germ of the formal notice which Sithole addressed to the West a few pages later: 'We believe it is only an educated African imbecile who will trade the present European imperialism for Russian communism. . . . But, as we have already indicated, the African may take to communism as a desperate measure. He might use communism willingly as an instrument (though a very dangerous one) to get his full independence.'[5] This looks like a forecast of the policy of holding the balance between the two blocs which many underdeveloped countries have practised. There has been some dismay at this apparent appearance of a new machiavellianism, but the explanation seems rather too simple. It must not be forgotten that any foreign aid, even supposing it to be completely disinterested—and this hypothesis is as generous as it is untrue to life—constitutes a bond of dependence from the moment it becomes exclusive. It is difficult to imagine that any country which has just won its independence should not be very sensitive to this aspect of gift economies.

The marxist impress

The charge of collusion with communism brought against African nationalist movements cannot be explained merely by the historical chance which has made the USSR a non-colonial country. With Lenin's *Imperialism, the Highest Stage of Capitalism* and Stalin's *Marxism and the National and Colonial Question* as well as other works, marxism takes on the role of a doctrine of emancipation of colonial peoples. There is scarcely a newly independent African country today which does not practise some form or other of socialism. This has become virtually the general rule even in those countries—and they are the majority—which have stayed closer to the western than to the communist camp. This orientation is particularly noticeable in francophone countries, for obvious historical reasons: the existence in France of a strong communist party which has twice been associated with power—indirectly at the time of the Popular Front in 1936, and above all during the tripartism following the second world war. These two episodes gave the French Communist party the opportunity to exercise real influence in Africa, mainly through the intermediary of the Rassemblement Démocratique Africain, from its founding after the war to its alliance with the Union Démocratique et Socialiste de la Résistance (a French left-wing, non-communist party). The influence of the Confédération Générale du Travail, the communist workers' organisation, was even more decisive for the appearance of African militants imbued with marxist ideology.

In English-speaking Africa, dependent on Britain where the Communist party has always been very weak and the Labour party, which initiated decolonisation in India, has stayed resolutely anti-communist, the marxist impress is far less clear. Kwame Nkrumah has certainly expressed his admiration for communist theoretical analysis without any hedging: 'The most searching and penetrating analysis of economic imperialism has been given by Marx and Lenin', he writes in a brief chapter on "Colonial Economics" in *Towards Colonial Freedom.*[6] But Azikiwe, president of Nigeria, strikes a different note: 'Intellectual paternalism tends to emasculate Africans and it makes them spineless. I am aware of the pitfalls, fallacies and incongruencies of communism. But African society is essentially socialistic', he wrote in 1937.[7]

Although we may detect the clear influence of marxist thought in francophone Africa, many of the writers who refer to Marx are still far from being communists, or even orthodox marxists. On the contrary, it would seem that, with the exception of Maghemout Diop, they are all more or less 'free-lancers'—even Sékou Touré. The extreme cases are obviously Mamadou Dia and Senghor, who, in spite of borrowing from marxism, particularly by the former, are still very far from it on a number of fundamental issues. In fact, Senghor uses the adjective 'marxian' in preference to 'marxist'.

The class war

From the start, a major problem seems to have confronted those African intellectuals who, in varying degrees, adopted marxism. Is the concept of class and class warfare, fundamental to communism, also valid for Africa? The African context is, in fact, very different from the European one. Marxists are not unaware of this problem since they admit that the communist states should support bourgeois nationalist movements in dependent or developing countries. This is to anticipate in advance the theoretical obstacle arising from the lack of a genuine industrial proletariat in black Africa. But what should be the role of the peasant population, by far the poorest and least advanced class but making up practically the whole population?

The history of the movement for colonial emancipation shows that it started primarily in the towns, among social sectors more or less in contact with western civilisation. It was the war veterans who marched on the governor's palace in Accra in 1948, and who started the riots in Freetown in 1955. It was the trade unionists who so often took the initiative in the political battle. It was the middle-class cocoa planters who played a decisive political role in the Ivory Coast and the Gold

Coast. Finally, political leaders come almost exclusively from the educated class; there is virtually no example of an important African political leader who does not speak the European language of the colony and read and write his native tongue. Politicians find their main 'troops' in the detribalised proletariat of the shanty towns, among the unemployed and the 'verandah boys'. Usually the peasant stays on the sidelines, although frequently his annual income is scarcely higher than the monthly wage of a 'boy' in white service. He suffers periodic famine but he is 'officered' by traditional chiefs who have generally been zealous supporters of the colonial administration, the majority of them hostile to independence—to adventure—until the very last moment. But ninety per cent or more of the population are peasants and it is difficult to undertake anything without them.

These are the facts of the problem with which African intellectuals of marxist leanings are faced. Their answer has been qualified. It is remarkable, though, that both Sékou Touré and Senghor think the marxist analysis of class warfare is difficult to apply to Africa. Sékou Touré's speeches give the essence of the theoretical argument which, in 1957, led to his advocating a break with the extreme left-wing French trade union leadership and the rejection for Africa of one of the basic dogmas of international communism. Sékou Touré's two main points are, first: that, as there is no real class system in African society, the class struggle is not appropriate; and secondly: that metropolitan trade union interest, however favourable to African nationalism, cannot coincide exactly with those of African trade unions.

> Despite existing differences between various local levels of society, colonial domination makes any reference to class warfare inopportune and enables us to avoid dispersing our strength in doctrinal competitions. . . . In the independent countries of Europe, Asia and America, the working class is the productive class whose share in material wealth is minimal. A struggle ensues between this class and the exploiting class, whose interests are diametrically opposed. . . . In the colonised countries this is not the case. Differences between the various levels of the population are minor compared with the great difference between the interests of the population as a whole and the colonial system itself. . . . Class warfare in colonised countries merges into the fight against the colonial system, which, on a higher plane, is only the result of capitalist development outside the countries under this regime.[8]

Analysing the basic outlook of the three great trade union organisations—the Confédération Générale du Travail (CGT), the Force Ouvrière and the Confédération Française des Travailleurs Chrétiens (CFTC)—he concluded: 'The political views of these organisations are sufficiently well known for there to be no need for me to repeat them. I can assert that none of these trade unions—whether revolutionary, reformist or christian—corresponds exactly to the particular historical exigencies of the fight for emancipation in the colonies.'[9] This does not mean that Sékou Touré is unaware of the embryo class structure incipient in African society. On the contrary, he warns against the danger of its development, and at the fifth congress of the Parti Démocratique de Guinée he recalled that, before independence:

> Differences existed within the country. In the first place, the peasant strata, representing eighty per cent of the Guinean population, had different interests from those of their feudal overlords who, corrupted by the colonial power, had ceased to express faithfully the opinions of our whole nation. . . . There were other, less apparent, internal differences which had to be rapidly reduced in order to strengthen national unity. There was this incipient opposition between what I may call the intellectual elite and the peasant masses. Not only did our educational system tend to lead us to assimilation, depersonalisation and westernisation; it presented our civilisation to us, our culture and our own sociological and philosophical concepts, our very humanism in fact, as the expression of a barely conscious, primitive savagery. This was intended to instil in us the multiple complexes which would make us endeavour to be more French than the French. Moreover, this intellectual elite enjoyed a whole series of practical advantages and safeguards which were completely foreign to the life of the great majority of the people, and which represented a privileged way of life in comparison to that of the ordinary people. In this field, satisfaction of the demands of one group immediately became a new obligation, a new burden, for the others—and these others were not only the majority of the population, but the poorest section at that.[10]

In *Nation et voie africaine du socialisme*, Senghor wrote that rejection in Africa of 'the theory of class warfare, is a return from mere talk to Negro-African reality, from the clouds to *terra firma*'. And he added: 'The pretended solidarity of the European proletariat with the colonised peoples is a romantic myth propagated by Europe, but does not stand up to examination.'[11] In his long critical study of marxism, the president of Senegal showed that the predictions which Marx based on his analysis of the class struggle have not been realised. Marx, says Senghor, made two mistakes regarding the underdeveloped countries. In the first place, 'the peasants—whom Marx considered to be quasi-impermeable to revolutionary ferment and dedicated "to the stupidity of rural life"—have belied this judgement in the underdeveloped countries'. Secondly, 'socialism has not triumphed, as Marx forecast that it would, in the industrial countries of western Europe, but in the underdeveloped countries of Asia and Africa'.[12] Senghor thinks that Marx's mistakes can be explained by the fact that in his day 'colonisation was only just beginning'.

> He could not foresee the universal development which would take place in the second half of the nineteenth century. His almost blind confidence in proletarian awareness and generosity prevented him from seeing the struggle which would develop between the colonisers of the ruling countries and the proletariat of the colonised ones. It is a fact, to state which today has almost become banal, that the standard of living of the European masses was raised only at the expense of that of the masses in Asia and Africa. . . . The European proletariat has benefited from the colonial regime; therefore they have never really, and I mean effectively, opposed it.[13]

The revolutionary peasantry

Both Senghor and Sékou Touré have stressed the fundamental importance of the peasant masses in African society. Abdoulaye Ly also dwelt on their role in the African revolution in his book, *Les Masses africaines et l'actuelle condition humaine*, published in 1956. According to him, the two dangers threatening the African revolution, if directed by the urban element, are that it will lack the support of the peasant population, and that this urban element may appropriate all the benefits of the revolution.

To avoid these dangers, Ly gives a detailed analysis of peasant participation in the Russian revolution in his chapter, "On the fringes of the marxist conception of the proletariat: a rehabilitation of revolutionary peasantry". He first notes the similarities between Russia before the October revolution and black Africa today: an essentially rural economy, an embryo industry financed chiefly by foreign capital, largely illiterate peasant masses. Then he sets out to refute the theories of Plekhanov, 'a so-called marxist, who goes so far as to maintain that the progressive movement of the proletariat has been, and still is, shackled by the political inertia of the former peasant class'.[14] He stresses, on the contrary, 'the need to admit, with Trotsky—whose proletarian exaggerations are well-known—that the "deep-seated bases of the revolution lay in the agrarian question" '.[15] The Senegalese economist then attempts a rehabilitation of the Russian peasantry, recalling the importance of thc peasant troubles of 1905–6 and the part in the disorganisation of the tsarist regime played by the 'peasant revolt in the army'.[16] While admitting 'Lenin's genius . . . [in] paying the greatest attention to the Russian peasantry', he maintains that the great ideologist of the Russian revolution made one mistake: 'He sacrificed the authentic, radical, peasant revolution of modern times to the illusory proletarian revolution symbolised by the hammer and sickle.'[17] One of the most serious stumbling blocks for a conception of revolution which overlooks the importance of the peasant masses, in Ly's opinion, is the bureaucratisation which results from the very fact that the revolutionary legions—in this case the peasantry—are cut off from the intellegentsia leading them—in this case not only the intellectuals but also the militant workers. He remarks, still à propos of the Russian revolution, 'even the militant workers were bureaucrats in advance, convinced of their historic importance and their mission as a thinking and active elite among the muzhiks, of whom more than half were illiterate'.[18] And he continues: 'The same process of bureaucratisation is also taking place in black Africa . . . overshadowing a mass of agricultural workers.'[19]

With this preoccupation in mind, he draws up a chart of the social categories in the towns of black Africa, and assigns to each its task alongside the revolutionary peasantry. First, the minor bureaucracy is called on to play a considerable role because of its educational standards. Secondly, there is the 'nascent proletariat, that is, those workers with a permanent job'. Ly considers that the position of these two categories ensures in them 'a certain reformism', but a number of factors—and among them the discrimination to which they are subject and their opportunities for acquiring information—'fit them for the radical action of the poorest masses'. Thirdly, there are the 'most primitive' (the term is taken from a French sociologist): in this case the day labourers, 'a floating mass, who have permanently abandoned peasant life for the towns' and who live 'in instability and insecurity . . . fostering a capacity for agitation and social upheaval which can never be overestimated'. Finally, Abdoulaye Ly draws his conclusions from the example of the Chinese. 'The comparison between the two great periods of the Chinese revolution is very instructive: the ultraproletarian period—that of failure—and the period of peasant revolution led by Mao Tse-tung at the head of the Chinese Communist party—the period of victory.'[20]

Frantz Fanon expresses similar ideas to those of Abdoulaye Ly in *Les Damnés de la terre*, but does not mention marxist theory directly. As a result of his study of the native middle classes in colonial countries—classes which he thinks should be eliminated—Fanon concludes that the elements most apt for revolution will be found among the peasant masses.

Maghemout Diop, an orthodox communist, runs counter to Abdoulaye Ly's theories on the revolutionary role of the peasant masses. He attacks the 'anarcho-trotskyists, anti-leninists and knights of the contemporary peasant revolution' in the preface of his *Problèmes politiques en Afrique noire*. Like Abdoulaye Ly, Maghemout Diop draws up a chart of the different social categories, from the upper bourgeoisie to the semi-proletariat of small traders. When he comes to the peasants, it is to tell them they must accept proletarian leadership of the revolution. 'Subjected to all this exploitation, patriarcho-feudal as well as imperialist, it is to be expected that the great mass of peasantry should have remained disorganised, very poor and extremely ignorant.' Besides 'the dissemination of agricultural workers over wide areas cripples their power of resistance, while concentration increases that of urban workers. All these factors mean that the peasantry has advantages to gain from the liquidation of imperialism, but it must also accept the help and leadership of the proletariat, which is a more mature class, better educated and better organised.'[21]

The method to adopt, says Maghemout Diop, is that of Mao Tse-tung. An African proletarian party must be created—the Parti Africain de l'Indépendance—on a national basis, and the author quotes the Chinese leader: 'Without a bolshevik communist party, on national bases, this task [the democratic and socialist revolutions] cannot be accomplished. That is why every communist has a duty to build such a communist party.'[22] (Diop had previously stressed that 'it should not be thought that this task will be simple. Even if it were on the scale of French black Africa alone [his book was published in 1958], organising nearly half a million workers would be no easy matter.'[23]) It is to these workers, and not to the peasants, that direction of operations should be entrusted. Diop refers again here to Mao Tse-tung: 'If leadership of a common front in the anti-colonialist fight is not vested in the most politically conscious class, the logical one from the revolutionary point of view, there will obviously be no chance of success.' Mao had defined three characteristics of the Chinese proletariat: first, it was subjected to triple oppression by foreign imperialists, the middle class and the feudal rulers; secondly, it was led by a revolutionary party; and thirdly, it had a natural affinity with the peasantry. Maghemout Diop concludes: 'These are the characteristics which made the Chinese proletariat the conquering proletariat admired by the whole world.'

He is also convinced of a close alliance between the USSR and the French Communist party. 'It is easy to understand that our first foreign allies are the proletariat of the colonising nation, in our case the French proletariat and their party, the French Communist party. This is a completely natural alliance, within the framework of one state, of the oppressed against the oppressors.'[24] But Diop then quotes this warning from Lenin: 'Age-old oppression of weak colonial nations by imperialist powers has left among the labouring masses of the oppressed countries a feeling of hatred, and also of defiance, towards oppressor nations in general, including the proletariat of these nations. . . .' 'No neutralism', admonishes Diop. The African proletariat must seek alliance with the USSR, because: 'Stalin said the October revolution had cast a bridge between the socialist West and the enslaved East, by creating a new revolutionary front from the western proletariat, via the Russian revolution, to the oppressed peoples of the East.'[25] For Maghemout Diop these words apply to Africa and he quotes Mao Tse-tung again: 'If Soviet aid is rejected, the revolution will be defeated.'[26] A proposition which has at least a certain historic interest.

Proletarian expansionism

It was not just because of the primary revolutionary role he assigned to the African peasantry that Abdoulaye Ly aroused censure from orthodox marxists such as Maghemout Diop. He had also criticised some aspects of Soviet communism, both within and beyond its frontiers. Inside Russia, the peasants had been badly treated by the proletarian workers; outside, Soviet industrial power sometimes created the impression that the USSR was imperialist like the capitalist countries. For Ly, the capitalist countries and the middle classes did not have the monopoly in exploiting underdeveloped areas. The USSR could not escape this charge either. A highly industrialised country, the Soviet Union needs outlets just as much as the capitalist countries, and its 'proletarian expansionism' is akin to bourgeois imperalism. Moreover, continues Ly, the industrial power of the USSR is the result of tenacious planning of which the peasant masses too often footed the bill. He quotes one of Lenin's colleagues who deplored 'the solid wall of the shadowy peasant force which opposed all planned economic adjustments in accord with the needs of the proletariat and coinciding with historical necessity'. Ly then points out that the great peasant masses even had to suffer during the respite of the NEP period, 'handed over to exploitation by state monopolies' in conditions such that 'it is no exaggeration to draw a parallel between the conditions of the Russian peasantry and the poor agricultural workers in the United States or the peasants in underdeveloped countries dominated by imperialist monopolies'.[27]

After studying the results of planning inside Russia, Ly stresses the fact that Soviet plans had given priority to industrialisation. This meant that, in its dealings with underdeveloped countries, the USSR appeared increasingly in the role of an exporter of manufactured goods looking for outlets, and an importer of raw materials or foodstuffs. This is simply another edition of the colonial pact, operating particularly in the Far East. Such is the conclusion of the theory of proletarian expansionism; it goes hand in hand, as we have seen, with the rehabilitation of the revolutionary peasantry.

Senghor on Marx

At the very beginning of his essay, *Nation et voie africaine du socialisme*, Senghor defines his attitude to communist philosophy.

> Can we integrate Negro-African cultural values, and particularly religious values, into our socialism? To this we must definitely reply with an unequivocal 'Yes'. We shall see why. We are not marxist in the meaning given the word today, in that marxism is presented as a metaphysical atheism, a total or totalitarian view of the world, a *Weltanschauung*. Marx himself once said: 'For my part, I am not a marxist.' We are socialists. That means we do not exclude Marx or Engels from our sources; indeed we shall start off from their works. . . . Whatever their limitations, their insufficiencies or their mis-

> takes, it was they, more than any others, who revolutionised nineteenth-century political and economic thinking.[28]

Senghor systematically points out these limitations, insufficiencies and mistakes, particularly where they concern colonisation and the under-developed countries. But it is not Marx the economist whose teaching he wishes to perpetuate: it is Marx the sociologist and philosopher. Although the marxist economic system seems to him open to suspicion, its description of man, although materialist, reveals a certain humanism:

> The ambition—and the paradox—of Karl Marx was to express throughout his whole work the dignity of man and his spiritual needs; he sought to do this without ever having recourse to metaphysics, morals or religion, or even philosophy. He is a philosopher who refuses to be one—I do not say he is unaware of it—but a philosopher all the same. Moreover one has only to reread him carefully to notice that in his lyrical passages, which are many, his vocabulary is one of indignation because it has an underlying ethic. Because, in the end, in the name of whom or what does Marx dare to assert the dignity of man and his right to appropriate the fruits of his labours; in the name of whom or what does he condemn night work, child labour and the slave trade—if it is not in the name of some inner spirit in man, if not some spirit transcending man? Science reveals facts and their relationships: it explains, it makes no demands. It cannot pass from a factual judgement to a moral judgement.[29]

Thus, the theory of the alienation of the proletariat is infused with a moral, maintains Senghor: 'Marx's positive asset is his vision of man, which recalls that of Pascal.'[30] Moreover, in spite of appearances, atheism is not integral to the positive part of Marx's work, adds Senghor, who from then on can concentrate on reconciling the humanist aspect of Marx's thinking with his own religious convictions. He mentions Teilhard de Chardin, who was also thinking along these lines, and quotes a letter from the author of *Le Phénomène humain* in support of his argument: 'The synthesis of the [christian] God above and the [marxist] God in front is the only God which henceforth we should adore in spirit and in truth.' Senghor concludes with this point:

> The christian God, as you know, is also the God of the muslims. Obviously this is a postulate, but one of formidable revolutionary potential. It could revolutionise philosophy and the sciences. For

believers, as most of us are, it introduces freedom at the heart of the matter, along with the spirit—without abandoning the dialectical method. It allows us to keep the positive assets of socialism; it legitimises our faith. Muslims have now begun to make constructive criticisms of socialism, which some christians have already attempted. I shall quote only Sheikh Abdou, Al-Afghani and Mohammed Iqbal. Their aim is to open up Islam to the contemporary world without losing its spiritual flame. All these thinkers, whether christian or muslim, show us the way to follow.[31]

So Senghor's socialism sets out to achieve the synthesis of a high spirituality and a humanism which borrows from Marx a social ethic reconcilable with christian and muslim dogmas. But this humanistic socialism must be integrated into the African Negroes' universe. Is this possible? Senghor is in no doubt about it, for their society is socialist in structure and humanist in its beliefs. This is shown in the studies of ethnologists such as Father Tempels and Marcel Griaule, whose works should be on all our bookshelves, he says.

They would teach us that African philosophy is an existentialist and humanistic philosophy, like socialist philosophy, but also integrating spiritual values. For the African Negro, 'vital forces' make up the fabric of this world, and the world is animated by a dialectical movement. They would teach us that African Negro society is a collectivist society, or more precisely a community one, because it is made up of a community of spirits rather than a collection of individuals. They would teach us that we had already achieved socialism before the arrival of the Europeans. We should conclude that our vocation is to renew it and to help restore its spiritual character.[32]

Besides this 'coincidence' of African and European socialism, Senghor mentions another which should also lead to a harmonious fusion of African and European ways of thought: the similarity between twentieth-century methods of scientific thought and the traditional African manner of apprehending the world. The nineteenth-century marxist way of thought, the western objective method, is out-of-date today, observes Senghor. By this method the scientist became an observer, distinct from the object observed. Today, the most recent scientific discoveries—the quantum and relativity theories, for example —have revealed the limitations of modern science. The principles of discontinuity and indeterminacy have made their appearance. As a corollary, the European is abandoning the methods of observation which kept him at a distance from the object. Scientific knowledge is advancing more and more by means of confrontation and intuition, as Gaëtan Picon has said in his *Panorama des idées contemporaines*:

> We are witnessing a general ebb of the idea of objectivity. Everywhere we find the research worker involved in his own research, and only revealing this by attempting to hide it. The light of knowledge no longer has that unalterable brilliance which shines on an object without affecting it and without being affected by it. It is a blurred flash struck from their clasp, the blaze of contact, participation and communion. Modern philosophy seeks experience, a living identity of the world of knowledge and the known world, living and thinking, life and reality. The human sciences are opposed to explanation and understanding: to grasp the meaning of a human fact is to involve oneself in it and to find it in oneself.[33]

Now, Senghor says, this knowledge by confrontation, if you look closely at it, is the African way of knowledge,[34] which is 'intuitive through participation' and has 'more of the Greek *logos* than the Latin *ratio*'. After justifying himself before the reproach that he has 'reduced the African way of knowledge to pure emotion', he adds: 'Today we must go beyond materialist dialectics and draw our inspiration both from the modern European method and from the traditional African method which, by some strange chance, coincide.'[35]

What choices does he make on a more practical plane? Here are some of them. Although he judges the Yugoslav system to be an example of federalism worth following, he rejects nationalisation which is 'killing the goose which lays the golden egg'; he wants to use private capital because the 'early accumulation of capital is essential to the development of the modern state'. He believes in co-operatives on the Scandinavian model. In his choice of the sector of the economy which should have priority of investments, he refers to Mao Tse-tung:

> We shall insist on agricultural credits for training, mutual aid groups and co-operatives, modernisation of methods of cultivation, stock-rearing and fishing. Mao Tse-tung understood the problem and overtook Marx in this field. The Russian mistake was to neglect the peasants and farmers. Mao Tse-tung has not repeated this mistake. He has relied on the peasantry: his revolution was, above all, a

> peasant revolution. Even in developed countries, neglect of agriculture in favour of industry causes imbalance and checks the rise in the standard of living, without mentioning the dangers of a discontented peasantry, almost always the most numerous class.[36]

In short, Senghor's African socialism is that of the middle way and eclecticism.

For other African writers, the desire to create a specifically African socialism—if this means basing it on the structures of tribal society—is related even more clearly to the choice of non-alignment in the diplomatic field. This is true of the president of Tanzania, Julius Nyerere, who defines his choice in this way:

> The foundation, and the objective, of African socialism is the extended family. The true African socialist does not look on one class of men as his brethren and another as his natural enemies. He does not form an alliance with the 'brethren' for the extermination of the 'non-brethren'. He regards all men as his brethren—as members of his ever-extending family. *Ujamaa*, then, or 'familihood', describes our socialism. It is opposed to capitalism, which seeks to build a happy society on the basis of Exploitation of Man by Man. And it is equally opposed to doctrinaire socialism, which seeks to build its happy society on a philosophy of Inevitable Conflict between Man and Man.[37]

Equally interesting are Sékou Touré's views on Islam. His also is a tolerant attitude, for the Guinean leader believes that any doctrine must take into account the concrete circumstances into which it is to fit. The following passage from one of his speeches is significant in this respect:

> Didn't the party decide to organise mass demonstrations on the occasion of a muslim feast? Some comrades cried shame. They did not understand that revolutionary activity is made not against the people, but through the people and for the people. Wasn't the party right to adapt to the economic, social and cultural characteristics of the country and to set its activity in the context of existing circumstances and opportunities for mobilisation and general action? Some comrades did not see that if an anti-muslim taint weighed on our party, there would be extensive areas (the Fouta, Upper Guinea and the Lower Coast) unable to adhere basically and unanimously to the party. All these were only means to attain the end of mobilising the

> nation, to give an active content to the national group, to educate it in order to free it from reactionary customs.[38]

On the fringes of doctrinal works on marxism by African intellectuals, mention should be made of the anti-communist stand of two young writers, Aké Loba and Sheikh Hamidou Kane. The heroes of their books are two young African students whose mistresses are communist party militants. In Loba's novel, Kocoumbo's mistress, Denise, is employed at the factory where he works, but where he is in perpetual danger of losing his job through his lukewarm attitude to the party. Denise takes him in hand and he joins the cell to keep his job; henceforward he will be left in peace. But he preserves his convictions intact. In this novel, we find the literary corollary of Senghor's ideas on the divergence of interests between the European proletariat and the colonised peoples. The hero of Kane's *L'Aventure ambiguë*, Samba Diallo, also has a communist girl friend, Lucienne, but his muslim faith excludes the possibility of any conversion to her beliefs. He tells her:

> My struggle goes beyond yours in every way. You have not only raised yourself from the natural state: you have turned the blade of your mind against it. Your struggle is to subjugate it. Isn't that so? Whereas I have not yet cut the umbilical cord linking me with nature. The supreme dignity to which I still aspire is to be its most sensitive, filial member. I do not dare to fight it, since I belong to it. . . . You yourself have admitted that when you have freed the last proletarian from his poverty and invested him with dignity, you will consider your work done. You even say that your tools, useless then, will perish, so that nothing will separate man's naked body from liberty. But I do not fight for liberty: I fight for God.[39]

The single party

Gradually, but inevitably, the formula of a single-party system has taken hold in black Africa. Madeira Keita, minister of the Interior in Mali, thinks this choice stems, in French Africa, from the experience of the *loi-cadre* which, in effect, gave rise to governmental councils throughout the French colonial territories. In countries where one party held all the seats on the local assembly, everything went well, remarks Keita; but where it was necessary to form coalitions, crisis followed crisis. Moreover, a plurality of parties is not considered essential in Africa, since the African population is not divided in its interests by the existence of a clearly differential class system. Hence, the problem of determining whether democracy presupposes a number of political organisations is a false problem. To the question 'Does democracy necessarily imply a plurality of parties?' Keita replies without hesitation: 'We say no. We believe there have been forms of democracy without political parties. . . . Naturally, we cannot claim that black African society is a classless society. But we do say that the differentiation between classes in Africa does not imply a diversification of interests, nor above all a clash of interests.'[40]

Sékou Touré justifies the single-party system less for reasons, like Keita's, of historical opportunism than because it allows valid democratic action. Nevertheless, he too takes the need for unity among the people as the determining factor. This unity implies hostility to all tribalism and regionalism, as well as to all class distinctions. The practice of democracy within the party will spring from the application of principles of 'democratic centralism' which he defines as follows:

> (*i*) All party officers are directly elected by democratic methods by party members who all enjoy complete freedom of conscience and speech within the party.
>
> (*ii*) Guinean affairs of state are the concern of all Guineans. The party programme is discussed democratically. As long as a decision has not yet been taken everyone is free to say what he thinks or what he wants. But once a decision has been taken unanimously or by a majority, after lengthy discussions in congress or assembly, the party members and officers are under obligation to apply it correctly.
>
> (iii) Responsibility for leadership is not shared. Only responsibility for decisions is shared. In this way there should be no infringement of discipline.[41]

The views of Tom Mboya, the Kenyan political leader, are not based on marxism, from which he is far removed, and have a frank simplicity: a single party is necessary before independence because the fight for liberation does not allow dispersal of forces. It is still necessary after independence because it is the best factor for cohesion in the new nation.[42] Senghor's views are more subtle. He rejects the single party on the grounds that 'opposition at first sight is necessary'. But the role of an opposition party must be 'to follow the same end as the majority party. It should prevent the crystallisation of social groups into antagonistic classes. Its role is very precisely to be the conscience of the majority party.' And although he 'proscribes the single-party system', that does not mean that one should 'renounce a unified party, that is, rallying the opposition in the service of the national ideal'.

The whole of black Africa has not yet agreed to the single or unified party system. Immediately after independence, Dr Azikiwe, later president of Nigeria, declared himself an ardent partisan of parliamentary democracy in an article published in *Présence Africaine*.

> We should not hesitate to have our governmental administration put to the test by an organised public opinion. We must be tolerant and accept close scrutiny of our official activities, no matter what the cost. Not tolerating the existence of an opposition party could be a disaster for a democracy. This is the readiest path to dictatorship, and we must avoid autocracy in any form. We must not give the impression that we have eliminated British colonial rule merely to replace it by its Nigerian counterpart.[43]

Frantz Fanon also criticises the single-party system, but he draws on an analysis which is very different from Azikiwe's. Throughout *Les Damnés de la terre*, this West Indian writer criticises the 'nationalist bourgeoisie' and the political parties under their influence. The meaning which Fanon gives to these terms should not be misunderstood. His primary objection is to the single party system where the party is dominated by the bourgeoisie. According to him, 'the great mistake, the congenital vice of most political parties in underdeveloped areas, has been to appeal, in the accepted, classical fashion, first and foremost to the most politically conscious elements: the urban proletariat, the artisans and the officials. In other words, to an infinitesimal portion of the population, representing as much as one per cent.' As the most politically conscious elements among the colonised peoples are in fact 'the bourgeois fraction', it is therefore not surprising that 'the immense majority of nationalist parties show a great distrust of the rural masses'.[44]

Up to this point, Fanon's study parallels those of Ly, Senghor and Sékou Touré. But he diverges from them when he tackles the problem of the single party. 'In some underdeveloped countries, parliamentary activity is fundamentally falsified. The bourgeoisie, economically impotent, unable to produce coherent social relationships based on the principle of its domination as a class, has chosen the solution which seemed easiest, the single-party system . . . [which] is the modern form of a bourgeois dictatorship, undisguised, unscrupulous and cynical.'[45]

He continues his exposé with an attack on the 'popular leader' whom the bourgeoisie, cut off from the peasant masses, soon 'finds indispensable'. However sincere a nationalist before independence, the double role of stabilising the regime and perpetuating middle-class rule will fall to him. 'Far from being the concrete incarnation of the people's needs, and promoting their true dignity—which comes from bread, land and restoring the country to the sacred ownership of the people—the leader will reveal his real function: to be the general president of the society of profiteers impatient for wealth—the national bourgeoisie'.[46] (On rereading these lines one sees how far they influenced Ben Bella's government in its campaign against the bourgeoisie and the profiteers from the war. This campaign opened in March 1963, when the estates confiscated from great European landlords were placed under the management of workers' committees; but a similar fate also befell those Algerian speculators who had bought hotels, restaurants and cinemas cheaply from Frenchmen in a hurry to leave Algeria.)

Writing of his own country, Ghana, in *The Challenge of Africa*, Professor K. A. Busia mentions several original aspects in the expansion of the single-party system in the new states of Africa. He underlines, in the first place, the fact that the former colonial administration, which brooked no institutional opposition, had in a way bequeathed to Africans an authoritarian tradition in line with the methods of the single-party system. Secondly, he points out that foreign investors, who trust only so-called strong and stable governments, have provided an unexpected and indirect prop to regimes which do not tolerate any parliamentary opposition. (The exceptionally moderate tone of Busia's book should be noted: although he condemns single-party and dictatorship regimes, he does so in very measured terms; not once does he attack President Nkrumah, against whom he, as leader of the opposition, waged a relentless battle before choosing exile, while several of his colleagues were imprisoned.)

Eurafrica

Before the continent's accession to independence, some African nationalists' fears of a continuing European hold on Africa were reinforced by the so-called 'Eurafrican' policies advocated in certain European circles. Albert Tévoedjré gave a very clear 'No' to Eurafrica in his *L'Afrique révoltée;* he saw in it a glaring form of neo-colonialism.

> For some time, the 'dazzling' prospects of an intercontinental federation, between a united Europe and an Africa whose future is as yet undecided, have been dangled before our eyes. Europe would help us through its banks and its technical experience, and thus would rapidly raise our standards of living. The tasks before Africa are such that, to save this continent from death, it would be necessary to create what M. Pierre Moussa has called a 'cosmic tax'. Presented in this way, Eurafrica is very enticing and shows great generosity on the part of its authors. But *timeo Danaos et dona ferentes;* once again reality differs from propaganda.
>
> The Eurafrican idea is not new. It comes, first, from the inability of some European countries to exploit all the raw materials of the colonies they control; and secondly from the desire to create a third world bloc under European hegemony, to stand up to the Russian and American blocs.[47]

The author asks the question whether it is in the African interest 'to associate, in an as yet ill-defined intercontinental federation, a dependent and divided Africa, and a technically more advanced Europe, mistress of its own destiny' but he puts the question only to reply in the negative. He answers in these terms: 'It will easily be understood that our first task today is to build an African community, and not to take part in some doubtful crusade in defending a civilisation and interests of which we have been the victims rather than the beneficiaries.'[48]

Sékou Touré is no less categorical. In 1961, in the report on doctrine and orientation of the political office of his party, he declared:

> The African nations realise, from one day to the next, that if they are to resolve the urgent and important social problems facing their people, they must undertake as quickly as possible the necessary reconversion of their trading economy. Obviously, if our economic and social problems have to be solved by the industrialisation of our countries, this cannot be done within the micro-economies of the individual states. But unconditional integration in a multinational market consisting of highly developed nations and underdeveloped nations would represent at the outset a refusal of this industrial promotion. In fact, such integration could only be an association of the jockey and his horse.[49]

Kwame Nkrumah wrote in *Africa Must Unite*: 'It is significant that the word "Eurafrica" has come into use in connection with the European

Common Market negotiations. It sums up the dangerous conception of a close, continuing link between Europe and Africa on neo-colonialist terms.'[50] In contrast to this, he favoured the creation of an African Common Market.[51] Mamadou Dia, in his *Nations africaines et solidarité mondiale*, approaches the question of relations between 'proletarian nations' and industrialised countries with rather less distrust. For the Senegalese writer, 'the way out of the conflict between the Third World and the rich countries lies neither in a levelling-off, nor in open or secret competition composed of hatred, but in frank and faithful co-operation which will assure reciprocal and harmonious development'.[52]

African unity

Before launching into organic co-operation with Europe, African unity must first be established, wrote Albert Tévoedjré. African unity has been in the forefront of the minds of African statesmen, even before their countries gained independence. Their efforts in this direction have met with varying degrees of success. The Ghana-Guinea Union, later joined by Mali, did not get past the stage of a temporary, loose confederal alliance. But the British and Italian Somalilands did unite, and British Cameroon federated with the former French Cameroon. The Federation of Mali had only an ephemeral existence, while the association of the Ivory Coast, Niger, Upper Volta and Dahomey within the Conseil de l'Entente, and that of the four former French Equatorial African territories, have barely gone further than the consultation stage. The proposed Federation of East Africa—Kenya, Uganda and Tanganyika—has, so far, come to nothing. The balance sheet for panafricanism seems a little disappointing.

However, the idea is constantly present in the minds of African statesmen. Sékou Touré's attack on the balkanisation of Africa by the *loi-cadre* and the 1958 Constitution found its counterpart after independence in the assertion of the need for African unity. The Guinean politician conceived of it in these terms:

> It is our good fortune that the factors uniting us are more important than those which separate us. The present division of Africa is both arbitrary and illusory. In the economic, social and cultural fields our present conditions, means and objectives are identical. We should denounce the complex of apparent differences by an objective

> analysis in each sector. . . . A given part of Africa may produce some crop more and better, but what influence can it have if the market for this product is settled in London, Le Havre or New York, based on an offer in which the Africans are not represented? Political unity is the only answer to the economic colonisation which has become established on the foreign exchanges and to which Africa is subject even after independence.[53]

We find a similar exposition by President Nkrumah, in the collection of his speeches published under the title *I Speak of Freedom*: 'Africa being a source of riches to the outside world, while grinding poverty continues at home, there is a real danger that the same old colonial type of economic organisation continues long after independence has been achieved.'[54] On this point also Senghor is more cautious. The United States of Africa are a good thing, but they are not for tomorrow, he says in substance in the preface to *Nation et voie africaine du socialism*. But this reflects a recent disappointment; the preface was written just after the collapse of the Federation of Mali.

> We have underestimated the present strength in Africa of territorialism, micro-nationalism. We have failed to analyse and understand the sociological differences between the territories of the former French West Africa, differences reinforced by the colonial administration. That goes beyond personal ambition and the states' race for leadership. Does this mean that good cannot come from evil, that we must abandon all idea of regrouping, and of African unity? I do not think so. Let us meditate on the lesson and become more modest, more circumspect and more realistic.[55]

Gabriel d'Arboussier, former secretary-general of the RDA,* (one of the great undertakings of the African unity movement) and later Senegalese ambassador in Paris, wrote—also after the failure of the Mali Federation—that the formula for the future should be 'the federation of states' and not 'the federal state'. Although the author of *L'Afrique vers l'unité* underlines the need to take into account 'territorial awareness', which is opposed to the movement of unity, he also stresses the present 'unequal economic development' of the territories and calls for solidarity between the rich and the poor. Indeed, it was the Ivory

* The Rassemblement Démocratique Africain (RDA) was the most important political party in black French Africa; it had regional branches in almost all the territories of the former federations of French West Africa and French Equatorial Africa.

Coast and Gabon, the 'rich' countries of the former French West Africa and French Equatorial Africa, which were most clearly opposed to maintaining the federal structures after the emancipation of the former French colonies. The secession of Katanga was later to offer a glaring example of 'financial egoism'.

Azikiwe, in an article for *Présence Africaine*, "The future of pan-africanism", draws up a fairly impressive list of obstacles in the path of African unity. Not the least of these are the widely differing influences to which French and British territories were subject, and the disputes between neighbouring states. All the same, he says, the challenge must be accepted; panafricanism has roots which go deep in the African consciousness. He ends his exposé on an encouraging note: 'In conclusion, I firmly believe that an African Leviathan is bound to appear in the end; it may take the form of an association of African states, or a council of African states, but the essential thing is that . . . the dream of panafricanism is destined to come true.'[56]

Furtherance of the ideal of African unity is not confined to the works of politicians. The whole of Sheikh Anta Diop's historical, sociological and ethnological work is underlaid with the notion of the common Egyptian origin of the Negro peoples, the cultural unity of a matriarchal society, and the memories of the great empires of the Soudan. This writer's first three books, in which he presents his ideas, lead on naturally to the fourth which is oriented not to the past, but to the future. This African future should be marked with the seal of its underlying unity which has survived the colonial divisions, and it should provide the basis for federalism. This is the concrete solution chosen by Anta Diop; he expresses it from the title onwards in his work, *Les Fondements culturels, techniques et industriels d'un futur état fédéral de l'Afrique noire.*

13

THE COLONIAL CONSCIENCE

'It is no mere chance that French colonialism boomed at the time of the famous, now obsolete, theory of "primitive" and "prelogical mentality" ', said Sékou Touré in a message to the second Congress of Negro writers and Artists.[1] The campaign for the abolition of slavery is also a good example of the metamorphosis which may overtake intellectual theories concocted to meet both moral and political demands. The evolution of theological thought on the problem is most revealing. The two reasons advanced in ecclesiastical circles to justify slavery were absolutely contradictory. Prince Dom Henry of Portugal baptised slaves and so saved their souls; on the other hand, some theologians were still questioning whether Negroes really had a soul, and on the whole were inclined to think not. (Montesquieu ridicules the latter in his famous page on Negroes, but by his day it is probable that this theological justification of slavery had few serious adherents.) Whatever the case may be, the Bull of Pope Nicholas V of 1452, declaring that any slave who was baptised became *ipso facto* a free man, remained a dead letter. Despite the efforts of those who refused to consider baptism as a kind of compensation for loss of liberty, and who tried to make it a means of emancipation, the conception never became law. Even as late as 1729, the attorney-general of England issued an edict stating that the baptised slave should not be considered a free man. Moreover, at that time, philosophy in the British Isles was still impregnated with racism, and David Hume wrote in his essay "Of national characteristics": 'I am apt to suspect the Negroes . . . to be naturally inferior to white men. There never was a civilized nation of any other complexion than white, nor even any individual eminent either in action or speculation.'[2]

But the anti-slavery movement gained ground, with devout christians at its head. It was in the name of christian morality that Granville Sharpe and William Wilberforce led the abolitionist campaign in England. The development of this campaign is well known. In 1772, Granville Sharpe obtained from Lord Justice Mansfield a judgement which set a precedent, and which meant that any slave setting foot in Britain became *ipso facto* a free man. In 1807, Wilberforce got through parliament an act forbidding the slave trade. Finally, in 1833, slavery was abolished in the British colonies. In France, the two decisive measures for the abolition of slavery came under two republican regimes. Yet the Abbé Grégoire, who prompted the decree of 6 *Pluviôse* of the year II (January 1795) which abolished slavery for the first time in France, was a devout christian as well as a good republican. Napoleon annulled the Abbé Grégoire's efforts with a stroke of the pen, and it was not until 1848 that Schoelcher obtained the abolition of slavery in the French colonies for the second and final time.

Although the abolition of slavery was a heavy blow to racism it was, of course, far from eliminating it. During the nineteenth century, racial theorists appeared, such as Count Gobineau with his well known *Essai sur l'inégalité des races humaines*. Others, such as the Englishman Houston Stewart Chamberlain and the American Lothrop Stoddard, were to follow throughout that century and the early decades of the next, which was the period of the great colonial expansion in Africa and Asia. These authors developed, in particular, the theme of the Negro's intellectual inferiority. African intellectuals have not neglected to quote widely the passages from these works most likely to arouse indignation in liberal Europe and nationalist Africa. Sheikh Anta Diop, for example, quotes the famous passage by Count Gobineau on the Negro's artistic emotivity:

> If we admit with the Greeks, and those most competent to judge in this matter, that exaltation and enthusiasm are the life of the arts, and that this gift—when carried to a high degree—borders on madness, we shall not look to the wise, administrative ability of our own character for its creative origins; rather shall we look to the sensual disturbances, to those ambitious outbursts which lead to a marrying of spirit and appearance to produce something more pleasing than reality. . . . Thus we are faced with the inescapable conclusion that the source of the arts is foreign to civilising instincts. It lies hidden in Negro blood. . . . The Negro possesses to the highest possible degree the sensual faculty without which no art is possible. On the other hand, the absence of any intellectual aptitude makes him completely incapable of cultivating this art or appreciating the heights to which this noble application of human intelligence may rise. For his faculties to be exploited, they must be allied with those of a race

> differently endowed. . . . The artistic genius, lacking in the three great races, has flowered only as a result of the marriage of black and white.[3]

C. S. Tidiany summarises Lévy-Bruhl's theories in this way: 'There is a sort of primitive, social, ideological concept, and a scientific and experimental evolution; the latter is a European privilege. The discord between these two methods of thought is radical and stems from different but successive stages of civilisation; the word primitive is convenient to indicate the lower level. Everything takes place as though there were one evolution of thought for the whole of mankind.'[4] Professor Mohamed Aziz Lahbabi, doyen of the faculty of arts at Rabat, comments on the way the French ethnologist later rejected his early opinions:

> How can we explain the flagrant differences between the two peoples? First these differences are never specific, so that Lucien Lévy-Bruhl, with admirable objectivity and probity, at the end of his career was forced to jettison the distinction, which he himself had promoted, between the 'logical' mentality of 'civilised' societies and the 'prelogical' mentality of 'primitive' societies. Perhaps he had been led to this preconceived contrast by the desire for symmetry which the European tries to find in everything, at all costs, even in the psychic sphere. But over twenty-eight years Lévy-Bruhl had the time to examine reality closely; this led him to a better interpretation of the facts in the various documents.[5]

This quotation game—which English-speaking African intellectuals, like de Graft-Johnson, have also taken up—has not been one-sided. The African nationalist movement has had recourse to quotations from its defenders as often as from its detractors. And in this respect, they have been able to draw on an extensive anti-colonialist literature which has come into being since the second world war. Names like those of Father Tempels, author of *La Philosophie bantoue*, and Marcel Griaule, with his *Dieu d'eau*, have become as familiar to readers of African reviews as that of Lévy-Bruhl. No doubt because the field of contemporary science seemed the most important to African intellectuals, the latter have given pride of place to the opinions of European ethnologists: they refer constantly to the works of Tempels and Griaule. Men as different as Prince Dika Akwa, who appeared as the chief of staff of the national liberation army of the Cameroon at the Conference of African Peoples at Accra in 1958, and Léopold Senghor, the poet of catholic reconciliation, both refer to the Flemish missionary and to the exegete of Dogon cosmogony. Dika Akwa considered Tempels and Griaule to be the first scholars really to have explored Negro thought; and Senghor, as we have seen, thought their works were so important that they should be found on every cultivated African's bookshelf.

Indeed, the swing of opinion in the twentieth century in favour of colonial emancipation is comparable to the earlier intellectual movement for abolition of the slave trade. The twentieth century has also had its Beecher Stowes, its Lincolns, its Abbé Grégoires and its Schoelchers, its Granville Sharpes and its Wilberforces: a pleiad of intellectuals, writers, scientists and politicians who have stripped the humbug from the official picture of colonisation. This evolution has been a phenomenon of the first importance. It is probable that the emancipation of black Africa would not have been so rapid without the support of a European intellectual elite (even taking into account such decisive factors as Gandhi's activities, the fight of Ho Chi Minh and Sukarno, Tunisian and Moroccan nationalism and the war in Algeria). It was undoubtedly an outstanding development in the history of twentieth-century political thought. Naturally, this wave of anti-colonialism gained considerable moral support from the colonial powers' fight against Hitler's racism; similarly, the liberal promises which these same powers, weakened by five years of warfare, had made during the second world war to the colonial peoples were an ideal platform for the fight for liberation.

Hence, European anti-colonialist thinking developed in a wider historical setting, and the 'wind of change', to which the British prime minister, Harold Macmillan, referred in his famous speech in South Africa in 1960, was blowing across Africa and outside Africa as well. Even before Tempels and Griaule, Frobenius—one of the greatest ethnologists of Africa—had already disputed current views and proclaimed the great interest of African civilisations. He saw in the Yoruba civilisation of the time of the Ife bronzes a memento of the mythical Atlantis. Lilyan Kesteloot has emphasised the enthusiasm with which young Negro students between the two wars devoured the works of the German scientist, together with those of Delafosse who introduced them to Ibn Batuta, Ibn Haukal, Ibn Khaldun, and Al Bekri, from whose writings they gained an impression of the grandeur of the medieval African empires. In a different perspective, Mannoni drew portraits of the coloniser and the colonial subject in his *Prospero and Caliban*. He pointed out that the first settlers were taken as demi-gods whose arrival had been foretold in legend; for example, they were welcomed and given a place beside the ancestors in the Malagasy system of 'dependence'. But he also lays bare the mentality of the coloniser who projects on to the colonial subject, of whom he makes a scapegoat, all his guilt complexes, especially sexual ones. In these same ethnological circles, theses on African tribal belief in a creative God, employed to refute the picture of polytheistic fetishism, are also worthy of note. In Britain, two collections of studies have been devoted to the subject: *African World* and *African Ideas of God*. A Belgian, Jules Chomé, has taken up the defence of the Negro prophets. Writing indignantly against the treatment to which the authorities of his country subjected Simon Kimbangu, he condemns the harsh judgement (the prophet was condemned to death) and the irregularities of his trial. 'The Reverend Father Van Wing SJ said in 1958 that this trial took place "according to all the rules of law". I am convinced that if the Reverend Father Van Wing were to study the documents which I have assembled, he would reverse his opinion, and would admit that this trial violated all the most rudimentary notions of human rights.'[6]

Although some ecclesiastics are in the dock alongside colonialism, others are in the forefront of the fight for African emancipation. Among Anglican priests, one notes in particular the Reverend Michael Scott, who was spokesman for the Hereros of South West Africa at the United Nations, and Father (now Bishop) Trevor Huddleston, who wrote the preface to Muga Gicaru's book on Kenya, *Land of Sunshine*, and is celebrated for his indictment of racialism in South Africa in *Naught For Your Comfort*. Some of the catholic missionaries in French-speaking Africa have shown similar zeal: the weekly *Afrique nouvelle*, directed by Father de Benoist in Dakar, was the mouthpiece of African nationalism during the 'fifties. In Madagascar, European bishops took a particularly energetic stand in favour of the Malagasy nationalist movement shortly after the 1947 revolt.

Among the historians, one of the works most frequently quoted by English-speaking Negro intellectuals from West Africa is *African Empires and Civilisations*, the little booklet by Raymond Michelet—a direct descendant of Jules Michelet, the French historian. It was published by the Socialist Book Centre in London in 1945, in a collection of pamphlets of the panafrican movement. Raymond Michelet traces the outlines of the history of countries such as Ghana and Mali, and warmly supports Frobenius' theory on Atlantis. The preface to this little book is by George Padmore, and there is an introduction by Nancy Cunard, one of the most eminent figures of the anti-colonialist left-wing in Britain. The English journalist and writer, Basil Davidson, with his two books, *African Awakening* and *Old Africa Rediscovered*, is another pioneer of African history seen in the perspective of the nationalist movement; his works have had considerable repercussions among the Negro intelligentsia.

Linguistic specialists on Africa have also come forward to attack preconceived notions on the poverty of vocabulary in African languages. Théodore Monod, director of the Institut Français d'Afrique Noire, wrote in the preface to a French-Wolof manual:

> The first navigators regarded Hottentot speech as barely different to the barking of dogs. We are making an equally elementary mistake when we class African Negro languages as 'primitive', taking this adjective as synonymous to 'simple'. Is a language simple when, like Nama, it has ten words for our pronoun 'us', four verbs meaning 'to eat' according to what one is eating, and forty expressions for man's various gaits, as in Ewe? Is a language simple when, like Wolof, it has a verb meaning 'pour out the contents of the sack' and quite a different one for 'pour a liquid into a narrow-necked receptacle', or when in place of our adjective 'big' it has 123 words as in Nupe or 311 as in Hausa?'

Time has wrought its work at the Sorbonne also. The chair of colonial history passed from Georges Hardy, chronicler of the European epic, to Charles-André Julien, a specialist on the Maghrib, dedicated to the study of the North African nationalist movement. His *L'Afrique du Nord en marche*, published in 1952, was as prophetic for this region as Davidson's *African Awakening* was for black Africa. Sociology and geography are also involved in these developments. *Présence Africaine* has regularly published articles by Georges Balandier, professor of African sociology at the Sorbonne, which are very critical of the colonial powers; it also devoted a special number to the work of Richard-Mollard, whose research in human geography had called attention to the precarious plight of African populations.

As a result of the efforts of various scholars, a phrase appeared in the ethnologists' vocabulary: 'cultural relativism'. It meant that no culture is essentially superior to any other. Claude Lévi-Strauss made the notion academically reputable; J. J. Maquet defined it thus:

1. Any value judgement on a foreign culture is devoid of an objective basis and should be avoided;

2. One's own culture does not have an absolute value, any more than any other one;

3. Imposition of one culture is as unjustifiable as restraining the diffusion of another.[7]

To measure the importance of the evolution in contemporary thought which African emancipation has brought about, one probably ought to take account of a whole range of exotic colonial literature expressing an impenitent racism, often under cover of the picturesque. Negro intellectuals have not failed to denounce this. Ezekiel Mphahlele, in *African Image*, devotes several pages to scrutinising the picture given of Africa in the English novel. He does not restrain his sarcasm for writers like Charles Scully or Sarah Gertrude Millin, whose racial prejudices reached hair-raising depths at times; on the other hand, he welcomes the attitude of writers like Olive Schreiner, William Plomer, Laurens van der Post and Nadine Gordimer who dwelt sympathetically on the fate of the oppressed Negro. What is more interesting, however, is that the author of *African Image* is somewhat resentful of some other novelists, such as Alan Paton, who are themselves engaged in the fight for African emancipation. What is it that Mphahlele reproaches in the author of *Cry, the Beloved Country*? In a word, it is the passivity of the Africans depicted by Paton; Mphahlele finds them too resigned, too ready to accept their suffering and humiliation without reacting. Richard Wright has also attacked this sort of sentimental paternalism of which he considers *Uncle Tom's Cabin* to have been one of the first examples. It was in reply to this pitying literature, which exasperated him, that he wrote *Uncle Tom's Children*, a collection of short stories whose characters give a fighting picture of the American Negro. Indeed, the character of Harriet Beecher Stowe's old slave has become so odious to African nationalists that 'Uncle Tom' is now used as an insult meaning 'imperialist valet'. It is used in this new sense in an editorial of the *West African Pilot*, the organ of Dr Azikiwe's party in Nigeria, and also by the Algerian Henri Kréa in the preface to his *Panorama de la nouvelle littérature maghrebine*.[8]

Decolonisation and the press

This pricking of the colonial conscience was very sensitive to public opinion in Europe. Above all, it was echoed in the British and French press in whose columns, after the second world war, decolonisation was a recurrent subject of controversy. In Britain, papers like the *Observer*, and in France—besides the communist press—papers such as *L'Express* and *France Observateur*, were in the forefront of liberal or left-wing opinion calling for emancipation of the former colonies. In the columns of the *Observer*, journalists like Colin Legum, and in those of *L'Express*, leader-writers such as Jean Daniel, were among the people who contributed most to bring home the importance of the interests at stake in Africa.*

The European press had long since established its interests in Africa, and the controversies in the metropolitan papers were often reflected even more virulently in publications overseas. These frequently showed a hostile attitude to Negro emancipation: the viewpoint of the European community which provided most of their readers. There were, however, newspapers under European direction which followed the liberal line without waiting for the great turning point of the 'sixties, when decolonisation appeared inevitable. This was particularly the case in British West Africa where, from 1950 on, the *Daily Mirror* (London) chain, consisting of the *Daily Graphic* of Accra, the *Daily Times* of Lagos, and the *Daily Mail* of Freetown, took up the cry. These papers also followed a consistent policy of africanisation of personnel which has produced such highly talented journalists as Tai Solarin, leader-writer of the *Daily Times*, and Timothy Bankole of the *Daily Graphic*, author of one of the first books on Nkrumah. However, the advent of independence did not always leave intact the links between these papers and the parent company in Europe. The *Daily Graphic*, for instance, came under the control of the Ghanaian government, but smoothly and with no expropriation. This government also launched its own press after 1957, and successively founded or restarted the *Ghana Times*, *The Evening News* and *The Spark*, all more or less dependent on the party in power, the Convention People's Party. *The Spark* has been noteworthy for the passionate tone of its articles in support of the panafrican theories of the Osagyefo—the official title, meaning 'Redeemer', which Nkrumah took at his installation as president of Ghana in July 1960. Its aim was the propagation of his views beyond the frontiers of Ghana, as evidenced by the French edition, *L'Étincelle*.

In Nigeria, where independence did not produce the single-party system chiefly because of the federal structure of the state, decolonisa-

* Colin Legum was born in South Africa, and Jean Daniel in Algeria.

tion brought new newspapers in the service of regional governments; these spelt competition for the *Daily Times* and Azikiwe's long-established *West African Pilot*. The Action Group, the party in power in the Western Region, created the Amalgamated Press, whose principal paper, the *Daily Service*, came out in Lagos; in the Northern Region, there was the Gaskiya Press, of Northern People's Congress convictions, whose various publications are for the most part in the vernacular.

While in many colonial territories the approach of independence was heralded by a more or less marked retreat of the metropolitan press, British East Africa furnished the paradoxical, and certainly exceptional, example of new investments. A group financed by the Aga Khan and the British newspaper magnate, Lord Thomson, launched a new chain of papers of liberal leanings shortly after 1960. They were in both English and the vernacular; the *Daily Nation* of Nairobi is the best-known.* These papers brought competition to the existing chain which owned the *East African Standard* of Nairobi. Papers in these groups had long reflected white settler opinion, but when the time came they managed to adapt to the new circumstances, and they still appear today.

It is in South Africa that a European-directed press has most clearly taken sides with the black nationalist movement. Apart from the communist *New Age*, we should note *Contact*, founded by Peter Duncan, son of a British governor-general of the Union of South Africa, *Africa South*, edited by Ronald Segal, and *Drum* under Jim Bailey. *Contact* and *Africa South* both took an openly hostile stand on apartheid as a result of which both Segal and Duncan—who were militant activists in the African National Congress and the Panafricanist Congress respectively—had to leave the country. However, the publications of these three liberal Europeans were only reviews or magazines. The daily press in South Africa, which is also European, belongs to powerful combines linked to one or other of the two parties which share the European vote. The United Party has a firm hold on most of the English-language press (that of the *Argus* group which extends to the neighbouring Rhodesia); this is often critical of

* The Aga Khan's 'adventure' in British East Africa was due in part to the presence of a colony of the minority muslim sect of which he is the spiritual head, the Ismaelites, most of whom live in the Indian peninsula. Moreover, a fairly substantial Indian press has long existed in this region, in both Gujerati and Hindustani. It is mostly in the hands of non-muslim elements and is often hostile to Arab influence.

the government but is not against white hegemony. Beside the *Argus* group, there are several important English-language dailies, like the *Rand Daily Mail*, which support the Progressive Party, a small breakaway group from the United Party with more liberal leanings. The Afrikaans papers are closely tied to the Nationalist Party and uphold government views. An important newspaper chain in the vernacular, the *Bantu Press*, was founded in 1931 by Europeans. The director in the journalistic field was, for a long time, J. M. Nhlapo, an African who waged a battle in the columns of his papers against both communism and apartheid. But for many years now there have been virtually no African-directed papers, even of low circulation, to support the programme of the black nationalist parties.

In French-speaking Africa, independence saw the disappearance of some European newspapers. Guinea banned *La Presse de Guinée* in 1958. It had belonged to the chain owned by the Marquis de Breteuil, the most important in French Africa; the other papers of the group, *Paris-Dakar* (later *Dakar-Matin*), *Abidjan-Matin* and *La Presse du Cameroun*, all survived, as well as the illustrated monthly, *Bingo*, which for a long time was printed in Tangiers. A notable loss was that of the *Echos d'Afrique noire*, a weekly published in Dakar. It was directed by Maurice Voisin and for years enjoyed some notoriety for its virulent attacks on the colonial administration and equally lively defence of European private interests. The *Echos d'Afrique noire* aroused little appreciation from the governments in office under the *loi-cadre*; it was soon banned in the Ivory Coast and frequently seized in Upper Volta.

As was to be expected, the catholic church played an important role in the development of the press in francophone black Africa. Its chief organ was *Afrique nouvelle*, founded at Dakar in 1947; this paper is still published but is now directed by an African, Simon Kimba. In Brazzaville, *La Semaine de l'AEF*, directed by Father le Gall, has filled a role similar to that of its contemporary in Dakar, and has supported nationalist claims, but the catholic press also suffered some setbacks with independence, despite having experienced considerable difficulties under the colonial administration. Although *Afrique nouvelle* gained a moral victory from the case brought against it in 1951 by the government of French West Africa, other catholic publications were destined to feel the rigours of the independent African governments a few years later. In 1962, the government of Cameroon expelled the director of *L'Effort Camerounais*, Father Pierre Fertin, and the same year the government of Togo seized *Présence Chrétienne* (formerly *Mia Holo*).

The Ghana government, for its part, had imprisoned an African priest for an article which appeared in *The Standard*. In the former Belgian Congo, the *Courrier d'Afrique*, which the Fathers de Scheut had helped found, saw its mainspring, Gabriel Makosso, imprisoned. Also in 1962, the staff of *Les Temps nouveaux d'Afrique*, which came out in Usumbura, 'scuttled' the paper rather than betray their convictions. The protestant church was just as active as the catholic church in the field of journalism in Africa. The nationalist intellectual, Attoh Ahuma, made his journalistic debut in the *Gold Coast Methodist Times* shortly before 1900. Among current successes in the protestant press there is the illustrated monthly of the Soudan Interior Mission at Lagos, *Challenge*.

Alongside the private press, there was an 'administrative' press in many territories in Africa before independence. This was especially so in small colonial territories with a limited clientele and little advertising revenue; these included Niger, Mali and several British East African territories, where such papers were in the vernacular, like *Mutende* in Northern Rhodesia, and *Mamboleo* in Tanganyika.

In contrast with this European press, private, missionary and administrative, the African press before independence was generally poor and badly organised, except in British West Africa. With a few rare exceptions, African papers were never dailies and their existence was as short as their appearance was irregular. They ranged from the clandestine, roneographed bulletin to the rather rough and ready news-sheet printed on a flat-bed press in some artisan's workshop. Nevertheless, this press was amazingly vital, and never discouraged by frequent proceedings from the colonial administration. It often fulfilled an important political role. For example, it was *Conscience Africaine* with its 1956 manifesto, and *Kongo Dia Ngunga*, organ of the Abako, with its counter-manifesto the same year, that really gave the signal for the political demands of the then Belgian Congo. (The former claimed eventual independence, the latter wanted it immediately.) It is extremely difficult to give a complete survey of the African press before independence. For Dahomey alone, in the years between 1930 and 1959, Father de Benoist's study of the press in francophone Africa lists more than fifty different African publications. Many of these were party political and trade union organs which appeared irregularly. An example of such papers was *La Bataille*, supporting the Parti de l'Union Progressiste Dahoméenne, and appearing spasmodically, with long intervals in between, first in 1936, then in 1948 and finally in 1952. There was also *Travail*, organ of the local section of the French communist trade union organisation, the Confédération Générale du Travail. Others were the result of more or less individual initiative and took their names from local mythology: for example, *Aziza*, which appeared episodically from 1954–8 and was named after a monster with terrifying appearance but supernatural second sight.

Journalism was just as active in the other French territories as in Dahomey. The 'weightiest' of these publications were those depending on a major political party, such as the Rassemblement Démocratique Africain (RDA) which founded *L'Essor* in French Soudan as a roneographed bulletin; this has now developed into a real newspaper. The advent of independence, which caused various newspapers owned and directed by Europeans to close down, obviously also sounded the knell for the press of the colonial administrations. At the same time, new publications appeared, linked to the parties in power, while those already in existence found their precarious existence reinforced by government support. These included *Horaya* in Guinea, organ of the Parti Démocratique de Guinée; *L'Essor* in Mali; *Fraternité* in the Ivory Coast, organ of the Parti Démocratique de la Côte d'Ivoire; *L'Unité africaine*, in Senegal, organ of the Union Progressiste Sénégalaise; and *The Nationalist* in Tanganyika, organ of the Tanganyika African National Union.

In most cases, the single-party system spelt death to independent or opposition newspapers. Thus, the *Ashanti Pioneer* in Ghana, activated by Dr Busia and Dr Danquah, and the *Sawaba* in Niger, named after the exiled Djibo Bakari's party, have both disappeared. In the Belgian Congo, 1960 saw the start of a major transformation of the press which until then had been almost entirely in European hands. Although the *Courrier d'Afrique* survived, its rival in Leopoldville, *L'Avenir Colonial Belge*, whose tendency was akin to the Belgian Socialist party, had soon to close its doors. Then a whole crop of new papers was brought out, representing the many new political parties. Among those which have shown the greatest endurance, relatively speaking, are the *Présence Congolaise*, a weekly with Mouvement National Congolais-Kalonji sympathies, and the daily *Le Progrès*, with close affinities with Cyrille Adoula's government.

However, the governments of the newly independent African states were not slow to realise that their sources of information beyond their borders were still largely the great international press agencies;

only these could supply them both with world news and also with news of the rest of Africa. Moreover, the lack of trained African journalists was painfully apparent, for the cultured elite was too much in demand most of the time to be able to devote itself to journalism. Consequently, the creation of African national press agencies was soon followed by the formation of inter-African news organisations—such as the Union des Agences de Presse Africaine, and the Union of National Radio and Television Organisations of Africa—to promote a co-operation which would free them from what they regard as foreign tutelage. A scheme for a major African news agency is under study. The appearance of a press in the service of a single-party government, and the difficulties of independent newspapers, European or otherwise, was bound to cause apprehension in countries devoted to freedom of the press. In 1964, the International Press Institute, with headquarters in Zürich, remarked in its annual report that Africa was a continent where this freedom was in the greatest danger. The Institute's reproach was not only addressed to countries with a single-party system and to black African governments; it also put in the dock, by the side of Zanzibar, the Republic of South Africa and Rhodesia, where Ian Smith's government had just banned the Salisbury *Daily News* which, according to the report, 'was the only spokesman for a population which is in majority African'. (The *Daily News* was another African venture of Lord Thomson.)[9]

14

LIMITATIONS OF THE REVOLUTION

THE NATIONALIST slogans were 'independence' and 'unity'. 'Socialism' and 'neutrality' also featured among the driving principles of panafricanism. To measure the impact of thought on action, we must compare the results achieved with the theoretical objectives. The conference of Addis Ababa, which brought together in May 1963 practically all the heads of the thirty-two independent African states, provided valuable evidence for a survey of this kind.

The fight for independence had produced results. Apart from South Africa, the Portuguese colonies, a few Spanish enclaves and the Central African Federation of Northern and Southern Rhodesia and Nyasaland, by 1963—only six years after the emancipation of Ghana—the whole of Africa was independent, and the last bastions of colonialism were under pressure. By creating a co-ordinating committee to help liberation movements, the Addis Ababa conference gave a powerful impetus to decolonisation; it also facilitated a concerted diplomatic boycott by African countries, particularly within the international organisations, of South Africa and Portugal.

At first sight, therefore, the results have been gratifying for African nationalists. But one wonders just how real this independence is. Apart from the great mass of Nigeria's 55 million inhabitants and the 15 million in Congo-Leopoldville, none of the twenty-five or so independent African states south of the Sahara has more than a few million citizens. Certainly, the strength of a nation is not to be measured only by this criterion, but, in terms of economic strength, the newcomers to the concert of nations are very weak, and the factors of dependence characteristic of the colonial pact economy are still largely operative today. Of course, here and there, independence has already brought a salutary stimulus to development, and the 'gift economy' advocated by François Perroux has become a reality. Nevertheless, even if the manna dispensed from New York, Brussels and elsewhere were to continue for a long time to come to prop up the staggering economies, it would be years before these little countries managed to reduce the scale of this aid; and, despite all precautions, it cannot fail to weave a web of dependence.

But undoubtedly the most serious problem is that, at the very moment when leaders of the Third World were striving to emerge from underdevelopment, a combination of world economic forces diminished their resources. Sékou Touré pointed out in 1961 that 'in the last ten years alone the price of industrial products in international trade has risen by 24 per cent while that of raw materials has dropped by 5 per cent.'[1] The GATT report for 1961 also showed this trend, and remarked that prices of raw materials and tropical products had shown a marked and regular fall over the previous few years. The first conclusion to be drawn from this information, commented *Jeune Afrique* in December 1962, is that 'the trade deficit of underdeveloped countries is rapidly increasing'. The new states of Africa are perfectly well aware of the dangers of such a situation. Particular proofs of this are their efforts to obtain a stabilisation of coffee and cocoa prices by a world agreement between the producer and consumer countries. And the idea of economic unity for Africa still plods along. At Cairo in July 1962, the Casablanca group had sketched out the organisation of an African common market. But at Addis Ababa, the resolution on economic problems merely advocated the setting up of a committee to study 'the possibility of a free trade area' and establishing 'a common external tariff'; it did not mention an 'African common market'. However, the heads of state did decide at Addis Ababa to create an African development bank—evidence of the African politicians' keenness to free themselves, as far as possible, from the hold of foreign capital. All the same, the disproportion between African needs and the resources immediately exploitable is worrying; one way of measuring it is by looking at the volume of economic aid promised to the eighteen African countries which are associate members of the European Economic Community: $800 million in five years. The dispute in Brussels in the winter of 1962–3 over Britain's entry into the Common Market brought the extent of their dependence sharply home to Africa.

In the political field, the balkanisation of Africa is not without tactical advantages, from one point of view: it has given the Afro-Asian group a large number of votes in the United Nations. Even so, it is more often a source of weakness. Unity of action, except on very general points such as colonialism, is very difficult to arrange. Indeed, a division soon appeared between states of the Monrovia group (the most numerous and closest to the West, and consisting mainly of the former French colonies of the Afro-Malagasy Union) and those of the Casablanca group, who were more intransigent in their attachment to panafricanism and several of whose leaders did not disguise their marxist sympathies.

However, the rivalry between the two groups did not outlive the Addis Ababa conference of 1963, where they were brought together in the new Organisation of African Unity. Without lingering over the events leading to this new-found unity (Guinea's position vis-à-vis the USSR, Algerian independence, end of the secession of Katanga, etc.), we should note that the warmest supporters of African unity were lined up against the least enthusiastic. President Nkrumah's draft African charter, providing for an African continental government with a parliament on the continental scale, was abandoned in favour of an Ethiopian project which did little more than institutionalise periodic meetings of African heads of state and foreign ministers. Yet the Ghanaian president had not spared his efforts to make his point of view prevail. His book, *Africa Must Unite*, had been published shortly before the conference, and copies of it were circulated in the corridors. In it he wrote: 'The greatest danger at present facing Africa is neo-colonialism and its major instrument, balkanisation.'[2] He also expressed his lack of confidence in regional unions of African states[3]—which, indeed, are not mentioned in the charter as one of the stages towards African unity, although such regional groupings had many supporters, Senghor among them. At the first conference for foreign ministers of the Organisation of African Unity, held at Dakar in July 1963, several states expressed reservations concerning regional groupings and foreign aid. President Sékou Touré was in the vanguard of an attack on countries of the Afro-Malagasy Union. In this context, the Algerian weekly, *Révolution Africaine*, reported in August 1963 the setback, at least temporarily, of this offensive: 'Although subjected to attack, the Afro-Malagasy Union is still today a firm entity.' It recalled 'the considerable French aid' to the member states, both direct from France itself and via the European Economic Community, and added: 'Thus the idea of Eurafrica has materialised in the Afro-Malagasy Union which is the very personification of France in Africa.'

One should not underestimate the achievements of the conference of Addis Ababa. To get unanimity from some thirty states is an amazing achievement of which history provides few examples; and the most ardent panafricanists can hope that the charter of African unity will prove to be, not the end, but the point of departure.

However, balkanisation continues to weigh on the black continent in the new era of independence. It is remarkable that the two great geographical blocks—that of the fourteen territories of the former French West Africa and the former French Equatorial Africa, and that of British East Africa and the Central African Federation—both disintegrated at the moment of emancipation. Many people would say that this balkanisation was a carefully calculated measure on the part of the former colonial powers. Sékou Touré has insisted that his opposition to the *loi-cadre* and the 1958 constitution was derived from the disintegration which the first of these texts prepared and the second consummated. When Mali was being planned, Léopold Senghor had expressed concern at the fragmentary state of Africa. There is no doubt that, for the African nationalists to whom the unity of the black continent was an indispensable complement to emancipation, the *loi-cadre* and the French Community were both tarred with the same brush. Similarly, the attitude of Macmillan's government, despite its stand over apartheid, remained suspect in the eyes of these same nationalists. They can maintain that everything has come about 'as though' the British government had deliberately staggered the granting of independence to Tanganyika, Uganda and Kenya, so that each should become set in its own particularism. They can assert that the United Kingdom was careful to see that the power of the European minority in Central Africa was eroded, not by frontal attack on the federal institutions in Salisbury, but by successive dismantling of the federation giving rise to three separate states.*

But at the time of the disintegration of the ephemeral Federation of Mali, the Senegalese leaders admitted that they had underestimated the extent of 'micro-nationalism'. It is only natural that any attempts at unity should come up against territorial chauvinism expressed not only through diplomatic channels. One remembers the forced exodus of Togolese and Dahomeans living in the Ivory Coast, after the rioting;

* Nevertheless Britain, before Tanganyika's independence, took steps to preserve the economic unity of the East African territories by organising East African common services which would assure co-ordination in this field. Moreover, shortly after the Addis Ababa conference, Jomo Kenyatta, Milton Obote and Julius Nyerere joined together to lay the foundations of a federation corresponding to the objectives drawn up some years ago by the Panafrican Freedom Movement for East and Central Africa (PAFMECA). Julius Nyerere had even considered delaying the independence of Tanganyika so that an East African Federation could be formed. (See Tom Mboya, *Freedom and After*, p. 212.)

a football match once provoked a veritable crisis between two states of the former French Equatorial Africa. While the colonial structures were still extant, Frantz Fanon explained intertribal hostility and outbreaks as 'escapist' behaviour. He thought the colonial world suffocated its subjects and stimulated rancour, the desire for vengence and a thirst for liberty which boiled up but found no outlet. Then, wrote Fanon, 'with all this aggression stored up in his muscles, the colonial subject will turn it first against his own people. It was the period when Negroes scrapped with each other, and the police and examining magistrates, confronted with the astonishing North African crime rate, did not know where to turn.'[4] After independence, Frantz Fanon threw the blame for intertribal or interterritorial rivalry on the use of power by the national bourgeoisie. Wherever the national bourgeoisie had gained power,

> We witness a withdrawal to tribalist positions, we witness, with rage in our hearts, the triumph of exacerbated racial differences. The only policy of the bourgeoisie is to replace the foreigners and, in all sectors, to step into their shoes as quickly as possible and take the law into their own hands; of course the little jingoists, taxi drivers, bakers and bootblacks, are also going to insist that the Dahomeans go home, or worse still that the Foulbes and the Fulani return to the bush or the mountains.[5]

At Addis Ababa, the African heads of state tacitly acknowledged the artificial frontiers inherited from colonialism by writing into the charter that one of its objectives was to defend 'the sovereignty, territorial integrity and independence' of the member states. This was an effort to shut out fratricidal warfare; in a way it was also the consecration of balkanisation.

Panafricanism's third objective was neutrality. Here again there was often a considerable lag between the policies of the newly independent states of black Africa and the ideal of non-engagement promulgated by the ideologists of panafricanism. A list of African states which recognised the Formosa regime would illustrate the influence of American diplomacy, and another list of those which recognised East Germany would indicate their chances of obtaining aid from the Common Market. One has only to review the voting of francophone Africa in the UN debates on the Algerian question to estimate their confidence in General de Gaulle's France, and the voting on the

Congo to appreciate the extent to which Britain is still able to bring pressure on her former colonies. But this analysis would also show that the great powers have had to temper their steel. The ever-present threat that an African capital may veer towards the other bloc when faced with refusal has at least given the Third World and black Africa room to manoeuvre. This has been formidable enough for the United States to come round to admitting—and this was a fundamental change—that neutrality is not necessarily synonymous with communism. This was undoubtedly a victory for the active diplomacy of the underdeveloped states. There are also many countries in the Third World today where technicians from the East are operating side by side with those from the West.

We should also consider whether the meaning of the terms 'positive neutrality', 'non-engagement' and 'non-alignment'—from Bandung to Addis Ababa via Belgrade—has not altered, from two points of view. For one thing, the thaw between Moscow and Washington and the crisis between Moscow and Peking have somewhat blurred the traditional frontiers between East and West. But, above all, the underdeveloped countries are increasingly worried by the possibility of an alignment quite other than that of capitalist against socialist regimes: namely, a split between their world—the Third World of the underdeveloped countries—and that of the northern hemisphere, the white race and industrialisation. 'We affirm that the greatest and most dangerous imbalance in the world today results from its division into rich and poor nations. . . . Our international activities should constantly aim to reduce this imbalance.' So spoke Sékou Touré, long before the Addis Ababa conference.[6]

There are very few countries in black Africa whose leaders do not regard themselves as socialists.* But the formulas they practice, or even only preach, vary considerably:† even the countries which claim

* It is tempting—and probably justifiable—to see the concern to preserve the African personality and culture, or to find an 'African way' of socialism, as a cultural attribute of diplomatic neutrality. This desire for specificity is not limited to Africa: it also occurs among Arab and Asian nationalists. And it is sometimes found in unexpected fields—strategy, for instance, such as Mao Tse-tung's, which endeavoured to define the particular characteristics of revolutionary war in China. The first pages of his mémoire of December 1936 to the assembled officers of the Red Army Academy are striking. The leader of the 'Long March' insists that it is not enough to know the rules of war in géneral, or even those of revolutionary war, to defeat the enemy. The rules of the revolutionary war *in China* are essential for this purpose. (Mao Tse-tung, *Revolutionary War*, pp. 14 f.)

† Cf. President Ben Bella's well-known dictum: 'We have chosen between the socialism of the Abbé Fulbert Youlou and that of Fidel Castro.'

most distinctly to be ready to apply the principles of marxism-leninism often hesitate to nationalise the means of production, and great foreign companies continue to exploit mineral resources there. But strict control of foreign trade, a planned national economy, and so on, have nevertheless given the state so strict and detailed a control of the whole economy that private initiative is left little more than a tightly supervised freedom. Such countries are a long way from liberal capitalism, even if some foreign trust does continue to extract a given mineral. In other countries, the socialism they proclaim has yet to be defined, let alone applied. Apart from three or four countries resolutely set on a more or less African path of socialism, decolonisation has not notably modified the economic structure except on one point: the new state has taken over the shares of the former colonial power in companies in which there was a government shareholding. These companies were particularly common in francophone Africa. The social structure, if one is to believe the majority of writers from Fanon to Senghor, does not seem to have been greatly modified. Politicians, tradesmen, officials and clerical staff continue, after the end of colonial rule, as a privileged class by comparision with the peasant masses.

The single-party system has become virtually universal in black Africa. Sociologists have tried to discover the deep-seated reasons for this quasi-unanimity in the black continent; sometimes they have found echoes of the various clan systems. In any case the 'charismatic' nature of some African leaders seems to correspond to that 'father complex' (to use the expression coined by Jean Lacouture and Jean Baumier[7]) which Tom Mboya echoes when he asserts the cohesive value of an 'heroic father-figure' leader of the single party.[8] Can one say that the Africa of the single-party system is also the Africa of plots? The explanation inherent in such a suggestion may at first sight appear tempting to opponents of totalitarian regimes. However, it does not take account of all the factors. Morocco, with its constitution favouring party plurality, had a plot in 1963; the Cameroon likewise before the regrouping in 1962. At all events, the problem was sufficiently worrying to African heads of state for them to introduce into the charter a clause unreservedly condemning political assassination and subversive activities in neighbouring states or any other states.

Thus, between African nationalism's objectives—independence, unity, neutrality and socialism—and the results achieved so far (or the policies adopted), the gap is still wide. However, not all the African statesmen now in control of their countries had subscribed entirely to these objectives, not even to the first and least controversial: independence. Houphouet-Boigny had challenged Nkrumah when the latter chose independence. The Ivory Coast leader maintained that continued French presence would be more advantageous to his country than emancipation similar to Ghana's. The Fulani emirs of Northern Nigeria were in less of a hurry than the political leaders of the Eastern and Western Regions to see the federation freed from British trusteeship. But it would have been extraordinary to see realised in only a few years so vast and complex a programme—and that is what it was, this economic and social transformation linked with the gigantic task of unification—especially since the whole of Africa was not yet free from colonisation.

Finally, in the interdependent world of today, where Africa on its own does not carry much weight,* it would be very unfair to judge it as solely and uniquely responsible for its destiny. The great powers, ex-colonial or no, have played and still play a major role in sculpting the face of the new Africa. This face has not been fashioned by Africans alone, and a thousand influences and contingencies will continue to shape it. 'Neo-colonialism' is by no means always a mere slogan. But, although Africa may perhaps be more affected by the world around it than other continents are, it also exerts an influence on it. African emancipation was undeniably one of the causes of a major social revolution in one of the great world powers—the United States. As Africa gained its freedom the descendants of Negro slaves in North America took up the fight against racial segregation. This awakening was in a way repayment of a debt, for it was American Negro intellectuals such as Marcus Garvey, Booker T. Washington and W. E. B. DuBois who had brought panafricanism to the baptismal font. George Padmore came originally from Trinidad, and the negritude movement started in the French West Indies and Guiana, with the works of Césaire and Damas. In the eddies of the great streams of history, there is always a significant little detail: it is to a Nigerian Negro student, studying in Chicago, that we owe one of the very first analyses of the Black Muslim movement in the United States.[9]

* A paraphrase of the titles of Charles-Henri Favrod's two books, *L'Afrique seule* and *Le Poids de l'Afrique*.

15

NEGRITUDE AND THE FUTURE

IF ONE ACCEPTS the definition of negritude as an ideological movement, the expression in literature and the human sciences (particularly ethnology and history) of African nationalism, one must ask what will be its role now that independence has been achieved. The leading specialists in contemporary Negro literature, science and art—Sartre, Jahn and Kesteloot—have not overlooked this problem. Sartre saw Negro poetry in the first place as a splendid weapon against colonial rule for writers rediscovering pride in their own race. But, for Sartre, the negritude movement was only one stage. Basing his conclusions on the marxist convictions of many Negro poets, their urge to transcend racial concepts and merge with the proletarian fight, the author of "Orphée noir" considered Negro protest poetry a temporary phase.

> Negritude is the low ebb in a dialectic progression. The theoretical and practical assertion of white supremacy is the thesis; negritude's role as an antithetical value is the negative stage. But this negative stage will not satisfy the Negroes who are using it, and they are well aware of this. They know that they are aiming for human synthesis or fulfilment in a raceless society. Negritude is destined to destroy itself; it is the path and not the goal, the means but not the end.[1]

Sartre concluded his study with the following words:

> What will happen if the Negro despoils his negritude for the sake of the revolution and only wishes to be taken for a member of the proletariat? What will happen if he allows himself to be defined only by his objective condition; if he forces himself to assimilate white techniques to fight against white capitalism? Will the source of his poetry run dry? Or will the great Negro river colour the sea into which it flows? No matter: to each age its own poetry; in each period a nation, race or class is singled out by historical circumstances to take up the torch, because its situation can only be expressed or

> mastered through poetry. Sometimes poetic inspiration and the revolutionary urge coincide, sometimes they diverge. Let us welcome today the historical chance which has enabled the Negroes 'to utter such a great Negro cry that it will shake the very foundations of the world'.[2]

Lilyan Kesteloot rebukes Sartre for the 'no matter', and above all for appearing to think that the day will come when there is no longer any need for the exaltation of negritude. For her, it has a permanent value.

> Survival of their own cultural values in writers using a foreign language is not exclusive to the Negro race. The poems of Rabindranath Tagore have retained all the grace and wisdom of India, and *The Prophet* of Khalil Gibran is full of eastern mysticism. So much so that these works, written in English or French, belong in style to the literature of their countries and not ours. The Negro soul revealed here belongs to all time, and will not be superseded, as Sartre and his followers have maintained, any more than will the Slav or Arab souls or the French spirit!

She ends with this quotation from Alioune Diop's inaugural speech to the conference at Rome: 'Since we cannot let ourselves be assimilated by the English, French, Belgian or Portuguese, or allow the original aspects of our talent to be eliminated in favour of a hypertrophied western vocation, we shall struggle to give this talent means of expression suited to its vocation in the twentieth century.'[3]

Janheinz Jahn, who barely touches on the political aspects of contemporary Negro literature, has set out to define the criteria of 'neo-African culture'. He maintains that it should be a contribution to universal culture, but he assigns to it a more precise and important role than the mere offering of its originality to the world. Because it is essentially different from western culture—not just another culture among other peoples—African culture will provide a steadying factor intellectually and morally. Indeed, Jahn sees the western world as rather 'dried up' by a mechanical civilisation which sacrifices everything to the object for its own sake. In African philosophy, on the other hand, the important thing is the meaning which the creator gives his object, this having a significance only in so far as man gives it one. Such a conception is necessary for the western mind as a kind of antidote to materialism. 'Only the Negro', asserts Jahn, quoting

Senghor, 'can teach rhythm and joy to our world subjugated by machines.'[4]

As we have seen, independence has come to practically the whole of Africa, but it is a tenuous independence, especially in the economic field. Unity has still to come. Neutrality has suffered many compromises. Socialism—in most cases—has yet to be built. Although the foundations have been laid, there is still a lot to do. In these circumstances, one might imagine that literature and scientific research would set their sights on completing the first conquests of emancipation, and that this would determine the literary themes and direction of scientific research for the second generation of African intelligentsia. The cause of unity could be decisively upheld by the ethnologists who would uncover the common ground in the beliefs and institutions particular to each African tribe. Historians could also take up the work by drawing the military conquerors, empire-builders and outstanding figures of African history as the forerunners of a future United States of Africa. Every war gives rise after the event to a whole literature recounting the exploits and sufferings of those involved, so one might expect Negro historical novels exalting the memory of the fight for independence. In the construction of socialism, an aggressive literature might be developed, criticising the go-getting of some, the opportunism of others, abusive profits, and customs shackling economic development. Ethnologists could find in the customs of their countries community habits which would forecast the institution of collectivism; they could hunt out the traditions which could best be adapted to the needs of modern Africa.

A few writers have already started on this work. Sheikh Anta Diop has tried to find characteristics common to the different African societies; Sembène Ousmane has traced the story of one of the historic strikes in French West Africa; Frantz Fanon has discovered in the 'African palaver' a custom close to self-criticism;[5] Mamadou Dia has attempted to sketch out a type of co-operative based on clan property;[6] Niane has resurrected the epic of Sundiata, and Babikir has revived that of Rabah.

There is still a vast field to explore, but pioneers have already pointed the way. There remains the work of the second wave. Sartre predicted that the Negro struggle would give way to a proletarian struggle; the fight of African intellectuals has so far not always tended to go in this direction. This is not because some of them have become resolutely anti-communist. The striking thing, even among marxist sympathisers, has been their concern to build an African version of socialism. Georges Balandier summarises this desire for a specific brand of socialism when he stresses that African marxists have accepted Soviet ideology only with reservations.[7] African christians have also tried to give their faith a special stamp. This is the whole reason for the black messiahs and the 'Ethiopian' churches. But this preoccupation with the African personality is just as marked among strict catholics and protestants, if only in their efforts to find echoes of Christ's teaching in their ancestral beliefs. The Kampala meeting, in 1963, of representatives of Anglican, Protestant and Orthodox churches to create a 'panafrican conference of churches' which would give 'a renovated church to young Africa', was a clear illustration of this concern.

African intellectuals should bring the 'Negro emotion', mentioned by Senghor, to modern society, which has been levelled off by a mechanical, dehumanised civilisation; the interest of their message should outlive the historical situation which has revived Negro philosophy. But once the spur of a cultural renaissance, brought into being by political claims, is lacking, will the spirit which animated the first surge of negritude survive? Jahn's suggestion of the need for an African contribution towards a more balanced world seems far less compelling than one which would lead to political combat arising from a statement of the wrong doings of the colonial regime.

When Césaire takes for granted the Negro's non-technical nature in his famous lines, it is to boast that suffering has made him more human than other people. Jahn considers that the source of this warmer Negro humanity lies in his ancestral traditions; Césaire thinks it comes from his past as a slave and a colonial subject; for Kane it is the muslim faith. But all three agree that the Negro has a better feeling for humanity than other people, and a message to give the world. This message counterbalances the white man's technical contributions and is a step towards cultural miscegenation, which Alioune Diop and Senghor have also advocated.

Such are the reflexions to which a study of the future of negritude give rise.

A controlled negritude

It is surprising that Sartre, Jahn and Kesteloot have not considered the possible courses opened, or closed, to Negro literature by political regimes placing scientific thought and artistic endeavour under state control. Such a situation clearly cannot be ignored, especially since it is already a reality in a number of states. This second phase of the negritude movement would differ in several essential ways from the preceding one, yet still be inspired by the same themes. It would lack one dimension essential up till now—that of the pioneer and combatant. Negro intellectuals in the service of the African state will no longer need to fear repression or pressure from the colonial administrations; they will receive official encouragement. Although their work may be inspired by convictions as strong as those of politically committed intellectuals before independence, they will have lost the freedom fighter's halo. Must one assume that their work will be less interesting, their contribution to the building of a new Africa less important?

Mphahlele maintains that the cultured elite in Ghana and Nigeria is becoming middle class because the diplomas of its members give them access to positions of responsibility, whereas in South Africa the Negro intellectual is still a member of the proletariat because the policy of racial segregation prevents his obtaining any of the better jobs reserved for white people.[8] In West Africa, devoid of settlers, negritude could become a game for aesthetes, finding their *raison d'être* in a complacent narcissism, while in the detribalised southern part of Africa 'a rugged proletarian literature' could develop, as Fanon has suggested.

Whether this be so or not, and although we may miss the spontaneity and taste of danger characteristic of a literature which fights against the established order, we may look forward to more productive scientific research, unshackled from the prejudices of a foreign power.

The rebel intellectual's works may suffer from his precarious situation, just as that of the cosseted intellectual may be impaired by his security. In any case, it would be going too far to presuppose the African intellectuals' docility in his independent homeland. On the contrary, we can imagine that not all the intellectuals of the next generation will be satisfied with the path that is laid down for them. It is probable that their critical faculties will be sharpened by the choice between the various ways open to the newly independent states of Africa. The controversies already in full swing among politicians will doubtless be extended into literature and scientific research. As far as one can tell from the first indications, the dividing line will be drawn less by geographical criteria than by ideological dictates. The latest collection of Sembène Ousmane's short stories, *Voltaïque*, is an indictment of the new coloured bourgeoisie which has come to power.[9]

The new wave in Africa

An enquiry carried out recently among African students in France by Jean-Pierre Ndiaye provides some answers to these questions on the future of the negritude movement.[10] The young Senegalese sociologist questioned a sample of over 300 black students, in Paris and the provincial towns, out of a total of nearly 5,000 African students in France in 1961–2. A first questionnaire set out to discover whether the new generation of African intellectuals feels that the fight is virtually over when independence is granted. Far from it. Indeed, to the question 'Do you feel that there is a conflict between your leaders and yourself?', 63 per cent of students answered 'Yes'. And the causes of this discontent? For 27 per cent of the students who felt themselves in conflict with their leaders, it was because 'they are betraying independence, endorsing the policy of neo-capitalism and rejecting African solidarity and unity'. For 18 per cent it was because 'they are favouring the establishment of a middle class and carrying out a class policy against the people and progress.'*

If today's students remain faithful to their youthful convictions, we may expect the literary and scientific work of the new wave in Africa to be scarcely less politically committed than that of their predecessors. As with the work of the first authors of the negritude movement, it is likely to be militant literature and research—unless, that is, the blackguard politicians of today mend their ways or are replaced by others who can do better.

What will be the aims of this young generation, in the light of the weakness which they are denouncing in the African statesmen of today? The ideals of unity and socialism are still in the forefront of their minds. To the question, 'Do you think the African states of tomorrow

* The conflict between expatriate African students and the governments of their countries has become a common phenomenon, sparked off, it sometimes seems, by the fairly unbridled competition between western and communist countries to win them over. Negro student demonstrations in several eastern countries have attracted attention to the problem. President Houphouet-Boigny's comment on this is well known: 'Send your students to Paris and they will come home communists. Send them to Moscow and they will come back capitalists.' Two Ghananian students have tackled the question: the first, Jilly Osei, in a little booklet *Un Africain à Moscou* published in the *Etudes Soviétiques* collection in Paris, attacks the propaganda which tends to give credence to the tale that African students are victims of racial discrimination in the USSR; the second, Emmanuel John Hevi, in his book *An African Student in China*, draws up an indictment of Chinese communism.

should be split up as now, federally united or confederally united?' only 3 per cent opted for the first solution, 34 per cent for the second and 53 per cent for the third. Similarly, very few Negro students advocated a capitalist-type economy: only 7 per cent of those questioned would like to see a liberal economy with a preponderence of private business established in their own country. Although most of them favour socialism, their views are divided more or less equally between its different aspects: 38 per cent prefer 'integral socialism' on Soviet or Chinese lines, 30 per cent 'personal or community socialism', and 20 per cent the 'liberal socialism' of the Scandinavian countries.

Other equally clear signs of the reflection of marxist ideologies in the thinking of African students emerge from Ndiaye's questionnaires. The USSR and the Chinese People's Republic head the list of the most-admired countries. The writers who have had the greatest influence on the students questioned are revolutionary and marxist writers. It is interesting to note that 52 per cent class themselves as christian (catholic or protestant) and 32 per cent as muslim. Opinions on religion are nevertheless extremely divided, and their stay in France has generally resulted in students practising their religion far less than before.

Replies to Ndiaye's enquiry give the impression, therefore, that the two major slogans of African nationalism—independence and unity—have kept their validity for the next generation of Africans. Socialism also has widespread support, but interpretations of it vary. The questions asked do not throw any clear light on the popularity of neutrality and non-engagement. It is also difficult to know (the question was not asked) whether the students think the exaltation of negritude should continue to be a weapon in the fight. The only indications here are the order of preference of Negro writers 'who have contributed most to knowledge about and rehabilitation of African Negro culture'. Césaire comes top (42 per cent), followed by Senghor (38 per cent) and Sheikh Anta Diop (31 per cent). Ndiaye's questionnaire also throws light on the African students' attitudes to the former colonial power now that decolonisation is complete. On the whole, this is not unfavourable, and France is held to be maintaining friendly relations at government level with its former colonies.

Under the circumstances, and as the wounds are closing fast, should we conclude that, after all, they were not so deep? That would be a very hasty judgement. The works I have quoted in this study testify to the deep humiliations experienced. Of course, some of the African nationalists' exaggerations have been dictated, not purely by conviction, but by tactical considerations also. From the moment battle was engaged, it was no longer possible to give the enemy the benefit of the doubt. The colonial world had to be painted in black and white, with no shades of grey: the black was for Europe and the white for Africa. Exaggeration, however, was not exclusively the privilege of African intellectuals. It was a reply to other extravagances, which were felt all the more keenly since they came from the stronger side. Moreover, it is unusual for a writer of the negritude movement not to have expressed, at some time or another, his rejection of all anti-white racialism and his desire for the brotherhood of man.

Today, when most of Africa is free or, more precisely, freed from direct colonisation, the movement's often aggressive attitude to the white world at the height of battle, when exaltation of Negro values was but an aspect of the dominated people's protest, has rather lost its point. The generation of Africans who have not known colonisation should be able to adopt a calmer attitude towards the white world. But—and this is an important qualification—this new generation has been nourished on the literature of its predecessors. Their recent fight will be the pride and inspiration of their successors for years to come.

We should not forget this as we try to establish a new friendship. A sudden interest in Africa runs the risk of seeming like a tardy conversion to the cause of African freedom. Conspicuous solicitude, hasty to offer advice from centuries of experience, may be interpreted as the expression of egoistic interests or tenacious paternalism. Such attitudes are sure to arouse latent susceptibilities. The people of the former colonies, and particularly those where blood was shed, are slowly recovering from a profoundly traumatic experience. Only Europe could believe it easy to make a clean sweep of memories such as these.[11]

BIBLIOGRAPHY

Note: In both this bibliography and the notes and references, *PA* stands for the review *Présence Africaine*. Two series were published successively: the first from number 1 to number 16, the second from number I onwards. The first four numbers of the first series were published in Paris and Dakar; all other numbers of both series were published in Paris only. The abbreviation *IFAN* stands for the Institut Français d'Afrique Noire.

Abbas, Ferhat, *La Nuit coloniale*, Paris 1962.

Abrahams, Peter, *Dark Testament*, London 1942; *Song of the City*, London 1945; *Mine Boy*, London 1946, New York 1955; *The Path of Thunder*, New York 1948, London 1952; *Wild Conquest*, New York 1950, London 1951; *Return to Goli*, London 1953; *Tell Freedom*, London and New York 1954; *A Wreath for Udomo*, London and New York 1956.

Achebe, Chinua, *Things Fall Apart*, London 1958; *No Longer at Ease*, London 1960, New York 1961; *Arrow of God*, London 1964.

Adandé, Alexandre, "La Tradition gnomique", *PA* 8–9 1950; "L'Impérieuse nécessité des musées africains", *PA* 10–11 1951.

Adiko, Assoi, *Histoire des peuples noirs*, Abidjan 1962.

Ahuma, Attoh, *Memoirs of West African Celebrities*, Liverpool 1905.

Ajao, Aderogba, *On the Tiger's Back*, London and Cleveland 1962.

Ajisafe, A. K., *The Laws and Customs of the Yoruba People*, London 1924.

Akindélé, Adolphe, and Aguessy, Cyrille, "Contribution à l'étude de l'ancien royaume de Porto Novo", *Mémoire IFAN* no. 25; *Le Dahomey*, Paris 1955.

Akpan, Ntieyong U., *Epitaph to Indirect Rule*, London 1956.

Akwa, Dika, *Bible de la sagesse bantoue*, Paris 1955.

Alapini, Julien, *Les Initiés*, Avignon 1953.

Aluko, T. M., *One Man, One Wife*, Lagos 1959; *One Man, One Matchet*, London 1964.

Amamoo, J. Godson, *The New Ghana*, London 1958.

Amo, Antonius Guilielmus, *De jure Maurorum* (see Grégoire, below).

Amon d'Aby, F. J., *Croyances religieuses et coutumes juridiques des Agni de la Côte d'Ivoire*, Paris 1960.

Ananou, David, *Le Fils du fétiche*, Paris 1955.

Andriantsilaniarivo, E., "Le Malgache du XXe siècle", *PA* VII–IX–X 1956.

Arboussier, Gabriel d', *L'Afrique vers l'unité*, Paris 1961.

Armattoe, R. E. G., *The Swiss Contribution to Western Civilization*, Londonderry 1945; *Deep Down the Blackman's Mind*, Ilfracombe 1954.

Armistead, Wilson, *A Tribute for the Negro: Being a Vindication of the Moral, Intellectual and Religious Capacities of the Coloured Portion of Mankind*, Manchester 1848.

Assane, Sylla, "Une République africaine du XIXe siècle", *PA* I–II 1955.

Awolowo, Obafemi, *Path to Nigerian Freedom*, London 1947; *Awo: The Autobiography of Chief Obafemi Awolowo*, Cambridge and New York 1960.

Azikiwe, Nnamdi, *Renascent Africa*, Accra 1937; *The Development of Political Parties in Nigeria*, London 1957; "La Part du Nigéria dans la politique mondiale", *PA* XXXIV–XXXV 1961; *Zik: A Selection from the Speeches of Dr Nnamdi Azikiwe*, Cambridge and New York 1961; "L'Avenir du pan-africanisme", *PA* XL 1962.

Ba, Ahmadou Hampaté, and Cardaire, Marcel, *Tierno Bokar, le sage de Bandiagara*, Paris 1957.

Ba, Ahmadou Hampaté, and Daget, J., "Empire peul du Macina", *IFAN* 1956.

Ba, Ahmadou Hampaté, and Dieterlen, Germaine, *Koumen*, Paris 1961.

Babikir, Arbab Djama, *L'Empire de Rabeh*, Paris 1950.

Badian, Seydou Couyate, *Sous l'orage*, Avignon 1957; *La Mort de Chaka*, Paris 1962.

Baeta, C. G., *Prophetism in Ghana*, London 1962.

Balandier, Georges, "La Littérature noire de langue française", *PA* 8–9 1950; "Nationalismes et messianismes en Afrique noire", *Cahiers internationaux de sociologie*, Paris 1953.

Baldwin, James, *The Fire Next Time*, New York and London 1963.

Bamboté, Pierre, *La Poésie est dans l'histoire*, Paris 1960; *Chant funèbre pour un héros d'Afrique*, Tunis 1962.

Barrat, Robert, "L'Église contre le colonialisme", *L'Express* (Paris), February 5, 1955.

Bastide, Roger, *A Poesia Afro-Brasileira*, São Paulo 1943; "Naissance de la poésie nègre au Brésil", *PA* 7 1949.

Bate, H. Maclear, *South Africa Without Prejudice*, London 1956.

Bello, Alhaji Sir Ahmadu, *My Life*, Cambridge and New York 1962.

Beti, Mongo, *Ville cruelle* (under the pseudonym of Eza Boto), Paris 1954; *Le Pauvre Christ de Bomba*, Paris 1956; *Mission terminée*, Paris 1957; published in USA as *Mission Accomplished*, New York 1958, in Britain as *Mission to Kala*, London 1958; *Le Roi miraculé*, Paris 1958; published in English as *King Lazarus*, London 1961.

Bhely-Quenum, Olympe, *Un Piège sans fin*, Paris 1960.

Biobaku, Saburi O., *The Egbas and Their Neighbours, 1842–1872*, Oxford and New York 1957.

Bognini, Joseph Miezan, *Ce dur appel de l'espoir*, Paris 1960.

Boilat, Abbé P. D., *Esquisses Sénégalaises*, Paris 1853.

Bolamba, Antoine-Roger, *Esanzo: chants pour mon pays*, Paris 1955.

Boni, Nazi, *Crépuscule des temps anciens*, Paris 1962.

Brawley, Benjamin, *Early Negro American Writers*, Chapel Hill, North Carolina, 1935.

Brooks, Gwendolyn, *Ballad of Pearl May Lee*, *PA* 1 1947.

Busia, K. A., *The Position of the Chief in the Modern Political System of Ashanti*, London 1951; *The Challenge of Africa*, London and New York 1962.

Capecia, Mayotte, *Je suis martiniquaise*, Paris 1948; *La Négresse blanche*, Paris 1950.

Capitein, Jacobus-Elisa-Ioannes, *De vocatione Ethnicorum* (see Grégoire below).

Casely-Hayford, Joseph Ephraim, *Gold Coast Native Institutions*, London 1903; *Ethiopia Unbound*, London 1911.

Césaire, Aimé, *Cahier d'un retour au pays natal*, *Volonté*, no. 20, Paris 1939; revised, Paris 1947 and 1956; *Les Armes miraculeuses*, Paris 1946; *Discours sur le colonialisme*, Paris 1950 and 1958; "Culture et colonisation", *PA* VIII–IX–X 1956.

Chomé, Jules, *La Passion de Simon Kimbangu*, Paris 1959.

Clark, John Pepper, *Poems*, Ibadan 1951; *Song of a Goat*, Ibadan 1961; *The Raft*, Ibadan 1964; *America, Their America*, London 1964.

Clédor, Ahmadou Dugay, *La Bataille de Guilé*, Dakar 1931; *De Faidherbe à Coppolani*, Dakar 1931.

Codjo, R., "Colonisation et conscience chrétienne", *PA* VI 1956.

Cole, Robert Wellesley, *Kossoh Town Boy*, Cambridge 1960.

Conton, William, *The African*, London and Boston, Mass., 1960; *West Africa in History*, London 1961, New York 1963.

Cornevin, Robert, *Histoire des peuples de l'Afrique noire*, Paris 1960.

Coyssi, Anatole, "La Honte plus meurtrière que le couteau", *PA* 3 1948.

Cugoana, Ottobah, *Thoughts and Sentiments on the Evil and Wicked Traffic of the Slavery and Commerce of the Human Species*, London 1787.

Dadié, Bernard, *Le Pagne noir: Légendes africaines*, Paris 1955; *Climbié*, Paris 1956; "Le Rôle de la légende dans la culture populaire des noirs d'Afrique", *PA* XIV–XV 1957.

Damas, Léon-Gontran, *Pigment*, Paris 1937 and 1961; *Black Label*, Paris 1956; published in English as *African Songs of Love, War, Grief, & Shame*, Ibadan 1961.

Danquah, J. B., *Akan Laws and Customs*, London 1928; *The Akan Doctrine of God*, London 1944.

Davidson, Basil, *The African Awakening*, London and New York 1955; *Old Africa Rediscovered*, London 1959; published in USA as *Lost Cities of Africa*, Boston 1959.

Decraene, Philippe, *Le Panafricanisme*, Paris 1959.

Dei-Anang, Michael Francis, *Africa Speaks: A Collection of Original Verse*, Accra 1959; *Ghana Semi-tones*, Accra 1962; *Two Faces of Africa: A Collection of Poems*, Accra 1965.

Delavignette, Robert, *Christianisme et colonialisme*, Paris 1960.

Delobsom, Dim, *Les Secrets des sorciers noirs*, Paris 1934.

Dembele, Sidiki, *Les Inutiles*, Dakar 1960.

Depestre, René, "Réponse à Aimé Césaire", *PA* IV 1955.

Dhlomo, Herbert I. E., *Shaka*, Pietermaritzburg 1938; *Valley of a Thousand Hills*, Durban 1941.

Dhlomo, R. R. R., *An African Tragedy*, Lovedale 1928.

Dia, Mamadou, *Réflexions sur l'économie de l'Afrique noire*, Paris 1953; *Contribution à l'étude du mouvement coopératif en Afrique noire*, Paris 1958; *Nations africaines et solidarité mondiale*, Paris 1960; published in English as *The African Nations and World Solidarity*, New York 1961.

Diakhate, Lamine, *Primordiale du sixième jour*, Paris 1963.

Diallo, Bakari, *Force et Bonté*, Paris 1926.

Dike, K. Onwuka, *Trade and Politics in the Niger Delta, 1830–1885*, Oxford and New York 1959.

Diop, Birago, *Les Contes d'Amadou Koumba*, Paris 1947; *Les Nouveaux Contes d'Amadou Koumba*, Paris 1958; *Leurres et lueurs*, Paris 1960; *Contes et lavanes*, Paris 1963.

Diop, David, *Coups de pilon*, Paris 1956; "Contribution au débat sur la poésie nationale", *PA* VI 1956.

Diop, Maghemout, "L'Unique Issue: l'indépendance totale", *PA* 14 1953; *Contribution à l'étude des problèmes politiques en Afrique noire*, Paris 1958.

Diop, Sheikh Anta, *Nations nègres et culture*, Paris 1954; *L'Unité culturelle de l'Afrique noire*, Paris 1959; *L'Afrique noire pré-coloniale*, Paris 1960; *Les Fondements culturels, techniques et industriels d'un futur état fédéral d'Afrique noire*, Paris 1960.

Dorsainvil, J. C., *Vodou et névrose*, Port-au-Prince 1931.

Douteo, Sertin B., *La Maison isolée*, Monte-Carlo 1963.

DuBois, W. E. Burghardt and Johnson, Guy B., *Encyclopedia of the Negro*, New York 1946.

Dugast, J., and Jeffreys, M. D. W., "L'Écriture des Bamoun", *Mémoires de l'IFAN*, Centre du Cameroun, série Populations, no. 4, 1950.

Ekodo-Nkoulou-Essama, Fabien, "La Médecine par les plantes en Afrique noire", *PA* XXVII–XXVIII 1959.

Ekwensi, Cyprian, *Peoples of the City*, London 1954 and 1963; *Jagua Nana*, London 1961; *Burning Grass*, London 1962; *Beautiful Feathers*, London 1963.

Ela, Marc, "L'Église, le monde noir et le concile", *Personnalité africaine et catholicisme* Paris 1963.

Elias, T. Olawale, *The Nature of African Customary Law*, Manchester 1956.

Ellis, George W., *Negro Culture in West Africa*, New York 1914.

Equiano, Olaudah, *Equiano's Travels: The Interesting Narrative of the Life of Olaudah Equiano or Gustavus Vassa the African*, London and New York 1966; originally published London 1789.

Essien-Udom, E. U., *Black Nationalism: A Search for Identity in America*, Chicago 1962.

Ezera, Kalu, *Constitutional Developments in Nigeria*, Cambridge and New York 1960.

Fanon, Frantz, *Peau noire, masques blancs*, Paris 1952; *Les Damnés de la terre*, Paris 1961 published in English as *The Wretched of the Earth*, London and New York 1965.

Favrod, Charles-Henri, *Le Poids de l'Afrique*, Paris 1958; *L'Afrique seule*, Paris 1961.

Fodeba, Keita, *Poèmes africains*, Paris 1950.

Folliet, Joseph, *Le Droit de colonisation*, Paris 1933.

Fula, Arthur Nuthal, *Jôhannie giet die Beeld*, Johannesburg 1954; published in German as *Im goldenen Labyrinth*, Basel and Stuttgart 1956.

Gibirila, Bazou, *Rencontres et passions*, Bordeaux 1961.

Gicaru, Muga, *Land of Sunshine: Scenes of Life in Kenya Before Mau Mau*, London 1958.

Gobineau, Joseph Arthur, comte de, *Essai sur l'inégalité des races humaines*, Paris 1853–5.

Gologo, Mamadou, *Le Rescapé de l'Ethylos*, Paris 1963.

Gosset, Pierre and Renée, *L'Afrique, les Africains*, Paris 1958.

Graft-Johnson, Charles de, *African Glory*, London 1954.

Graft-Johnson, J. W. de, *Towards Nationhood in West Africa*, London 1928.

Gras, Jacqueline, *Situation de la presse dans les états de l'Union Africaine et Malgache, en Guinée, au Mali, au Togo*, Paris 1963.

Gratiant, Gilbert, "D'une Poésie martiniquaise dite nationale", *PA* V 1956.

Grégoire, Abbé, *De la littérature des nègres*, Paris 1808.

Griaule, Marcel, *Dieu d'eau*, Paris 1948.

Guerin, Daniel, *Front populaire, révolution manquée*, Paris 1962.

Gueye, Lamine, *De la situation politique des Sénégalais originaires des Communes de plein exercice—telle qu'elle résulte des lois des 19 oct. 1915, 29 sept. 1916 et de la jurisprudence antérieure*, doctoral thesis, Paris 1922; *Etapes et perspectives de l'Union française*, Paris 1955.

Hailey, Lord, *An African Survey*, rev. edn., London and New York 1957.

Hama, Boubou, and Boulnois, Jean, *Empire de Goa, histoire, coutumes et magie des Sonrhai*, Paris 1954.

Hazoumé, Paul, *Doguicimi*, Paris 1937; "Le Pacte de sang au Dahomey", *Travaux et mémoires de l'Institut d'ethnologie*, Paris 1956; "L'Humanisme occidental et l'humanisme africain", *PA* XIV–XV 1957; "L'Ame du Dahoméen révélée par sa religion", *PA* XIV–XV 1957.

Hendriks, Katie (pseud.), *The Bend in the Road*, Cape Town 1953.

Hevi, Emmanuel John, *An African Student in China*, London and New York 1963.

Himes, Chester, *If He Hollers, Let Him Go*, Garden City, N.Y., 1945.

Hodgkin, Thomas, *Nationalism in Colonial Africa*, New York 1957, London 1958.

Holle, Paul, and Carrére, F., *De la Sénégambie française*, Paris 1855.

Horton, James Africanus B., *Physical and Medical Climate and Meteorology of the West Coast of Africa*, Edinburgh 1867; *West African Countries and People . . . and a Vindication of the African Race*, London 1868.

Hutchinson, Alfred, *Road to Ghana*, London and New York 1960.

Ikelle-Matiba, Jean, *Cette Afrique-là*, Paris 1963.

Issa, Ibrahim, *Grandes Eaux noires*, Paris 1959.

Ivy, James W., "Le Fait d'être nègre dans les Amériques", *PA* xxiv–xxv 1959.

Jabavu, Noni, *Drawn in Colour*, London 1960, New York 1962; *The Ochre People*, London and New York 1963.

Jacson, William, *Les Noirs sauveront les blancs*, Paris 1961.

Jahn, Janheinz, *Muntu*, Düsseldorf 1958; English language editions, London and New York 1961.

Johnson, Samuel, *The History of the Yorubas*, London 1921.

Jordan, Archibald, *Ingqumbo Yeminyana*, Alice, South Africa, 1940.

Joy, Charles R., *Albert Schweitzer: An Anthology*, New York 1947.

Julien, Charles-André, *L'Afrique du Nord en marche*, Paris 1952.

Kagame, Alexis, *La Divine pastorale*, Brussels 1952–5, 2 vols.; *La Philosophie bantu, ruandaise de l'être*, Brussels 1956; "La Poésie guerrière", *PA* xi 1957.

Kagwa, Sir Apolo, *The Tales of Sir Apolo*, London 1927.

Kalanda, Mabika, *Baluba et Lulua, une ethnie à la recherche d'un nouvel équilibre*, Brussels 1959.

Kane, Sheikh Hamidou, *L'Aventure ambiguë*, Paris 1961; published in English as *Ambiguous Adventure*, New York 1963.

Kariuki, Josiah Mwangi, *Mau Mau Detainee*, London and New York 1963.

Kaunda, Kenneth, *Zambia Shall Be Free*, London 1962, New York 1963.

Keatley, Patrick, *The Politics of Partnership: The Federation of Rhodesia and Nyasaland*, Harmondsworth and Baltimore, Md., 1963.

Keita, Madeira, "Le Parti unique en Afrique", *PA* xxx 1960.

Kenyatta, Jomo, *Facing Mount Kenya*, London 1938, New York 1962.

Kesteloot, Lilyan, *Les Écrivains noirs de langue française: naissance d'une littérature*, Brussels 1963.

Khan, Ras, "The Poetry of Dr R. E. G. Armattoe", *PA* xii 1957.

Kitchen, Helen, *The Press in Africa*, Washington, D.C., 1956.

Ki Zerbo, Joseph, "Histoire et conscience nègre", *PA* xvi 1957; "L'Économie de traite en Afrique noire ou le pillage organisé", *PA* xi 1957.

Koinange, Mbiyu, *The People of Kenya Speak for Themselves*, Detroit 1955.

Kréa, Henri, *La Révolution et la poésie sont une même chose*, Paris 1960.

Lacouture, Jean, and Baumier, Jean, *Le Poids du Tiers Monde*, Paris 1962.

La Guma, Alex, *A Walk in the Night*, Ibadan 1962.

Lahbabi, Mohamed Aziz, "Propos sur la civilisation et les cultures", *PA* xvi 1957.

Lavergne de Tressan, "Inventaire linguistique de l'AOF et du Togo", *Mémoires de l'IFAN*, no. 30, Dakar 1953.

Laye, Camara, *L'Enfant noir*, Paris 1953; published in English as *The Dark Child*, New

York 1954, London 1955 (reissued as *The African Child*, London 1959); *Le Regard du roi*, Paris 1954; published in English as *The Radiance of the King*, London 1956.

Legum, Colin, *Congo Disaster*, Harmondsworth and Baltimore, Md., 1961; *Pan-Africanism*, London and New York, rev. edn. 1965.

Legum, Colin and Margaret, *South Africa: Crisis for the West*, London and New York, 1964.

Leiris, Michel, *L'Afrique fantôme*, Paris 1951.

Lévy-Bruhl, Lucien, *Les Fonctions mentales dans les sociétés inférieures*, Paris 1910; *Carnets*, Paris 1949.

Loba, Aké, *Kocoumbo, l'étudiant noir*, Paris 1960.

Lobagola, *An African Savage's Own Story*, London and New York 1930.

Luthuli, Albert John, *Let My People Go*, London and New York 1962.

Ly, Abdoulaye, *Les Masses africaines et l'actuelle condition humaine*, Paris 1956; *La Force noire, mercenaires noirs: notes sur une forme de l'exploitation des Africains*, Paris 1957; *La Compagnie du Sénégal*, Paris 1958.

Malonga, Jean, *La Légende de M'Pfoumou Ma Mazono*, Paris 1954; *Coeur d'Aryenne*, *PA* 16 1954.

Mannoni, O., *Psychologie de la colonisation*, Paris 1950; published in English as *Prospero and Caliban: The Psychology of Colonization*, New York 1964.

Maran, René, *Patouala*, Paris 1921, New York 1922; *Un Homme pareil aux autres*, Paris 1947.

Maquet, J. J., "Le Relativisme culturel", *PA* XXIII 1959.

Matip, Benjamin, *Afrique, nous t'ignorons!*, Paris 1956; *A la belle Étoile*, Paris 1962.

Mauny, Raymond, "Le Judaïsme, les Juifs et l'Afrique occidentale", *Bulletin de l'IFAN*, vol. XI, Dakar 1949.

Mbiti, John Samuel, "Christianisme et religions indigènes au Kenya", *PA* XXVII–XXVIII 1959.

Mboya, Tom, *Freedom and After*, London and New York 1963.

Méjean, François, *Le Vatican contre la France d'Outremer*, Paris 1957.

Mélone, Thomas, *La Négritude dans la littérature négro-africaine*, Paris 1962.

Michel, Serge, *Uhuru Lumumba*, Paris 1962.

Michelet, Raymond, *African Empires and Civilisations*, London 1945.

Mockerie, Parmenas Githendu, *An African Speaks for his Own People*, London 1934.

Modisane, Bloke, *Blame Me on History*, London and New York 1963.

Mofolo, Thomas, *Shaka: An Historical Romance*, London 1931; *The Traveller of the East*, London 1934.

Molema, S. M., *Bantu Past and Present*, Edinburgh 1920.

Moore, Gerald, *Seven African Writers*, London and New York 1962.

Mopeli-Paulus, A. S., and Lanham, Peter, *Blanket Boy's Moon*, London 1953.

Mopila, Francesco Jose, *Memórias de un Congoles*, Madrid 1949.

Moreau de Saint Mery (Mederic Louis Elie), *Description topographique, physique, civile, politique, et historique de la partie française de l'isle de Saint-Dominque*, Philadelphia 1797–8.

Morisseau-Leroy, F., "Littérature haïtienne d'expression créole", *PA* XVII 1958.

Mphahlele, Ezekiel, *Man Must Live, and Other Stories*, Cape Town, 1947; *Down Second Avenue*, London 1959; *The Living Dead, and Other Stories*, Ibadan 1961; *The African Image*, London and New York 1962.

Mulago, Vincent, *L'Union vitale bantu chez les Bashi, Banyarwanda et les Barundi face à l'unité vitale ecclésiale*, Brussels 1955; "Le Pacte de sang et la communion alimentaire, pierres d'attente de la communion eucharistique" (in "Les Prêtres noirs s'interrogent"), *Rencontres*, Paris 1956.

Ndiaye, Jean-Pierre, *Enquête sur les étudiants noirs en France*, Paris 1962.

Nditsouna, Francesco, *Fleurs de latérite*, Monte-Carlo 1954.

Ngugi, James, *Weep Not, Child*, London 1964; *The River Between*, London 1965.

Niane, Djibril Tamsir, *Soundjata ou l'épopée mandingue*, Paris 1960; published in English as *Sundiata: An Epic of Old Mali*, London 1965.

Niane, Djibril Tamsir, and Suret-Canale, Jean, *Histoire de l'Afrique occidentale*, Paris 1962.

Nkili Abessolo, Martin Dieudonné, *Famille, dot et mariage dans le droit coutumier des Boulous*, doctoral thesis, Aix-en-Provence 1954.

Nkosi, Lewis, *Rhythm of Violence*, London 1964.

Nkrumah, Kwame, *Towards Colonial Freedom*, London 1947; *The Autobiography of Kwame Nkrumah*, Edinburgh 1957; published in the USA as *Ghana: The Autobiography of Kwame Nkrumah*, New York 1957; *I Speak of Freedom*, London and New York 1961; *Africa Must Unite*, London and New York 1963.

Ntara, Samuel Yosia, *Man of Africa*, London 1934; *Headman's Enterprise*, London 1949.

Nyerere, Julius K., *Ujamaa: The Basis of African Socialism*, Dar es Salaam 1962.

Nzekwu, Onoura, *Wand of Noble Wood*, London 1961; *Blade Among the Boys*, London 1962.

Ojike, Mbonu, *My Africa*, New York 1946, London 1955; *I Have Two Countries*, New York 1947.

Okara, Gabriel, *The Voice*, London 1964.

Okigbo, Christopher, *Heavensgate*, Ibadan 1962; *Limits*, Ibadan 1964.

Orizu, A. A. Nwafor, *Without Bitterness*, New York 1944.

Ortiz, Fernando, *El engaño de las razas*, Havana 1946.

Osei, Jilly, *Un Africain à Moscou*, Paris 1962.

Othello, *Essay Against Negro Slavery*, Baltimore 1788 (see Grégoire).

Ouane, Ibrahima-Mamadou, *L'Énigme du Macina*, Monte Carlo 1952; *Fâdimâtâ, la princesse du désert, suivi du Drame de Déguembéré*, Avignon 1955; *Le Collier de coquillages*, Andrézieux 1957; *Les Filles de la reine Cléopatre*, Paris 1961.

Ousmane, Sembène, *Le Docker noir*, Paris 1956; *O pays, mon beau peuple*, Paris 1957; *Les Bouts de bois de Dieu*, Paris 1961; published in English as *God's Bit of Wood*, Garden City, N.Y., 1962; *Voltaïques*, Paris 1962; *L'Harmattan*, Paris 1964.

Ouzegane, Amar, *Le Meilleur Combat*, Paris 1962.

Owono, Joseph, *Tante Bella*, Yaoundé, Cameroon, 1959.

Oyono, Ferdinand, *Une Vie de boy*, Paris 1956—published in English as *Houseboy*, London 1966; *Le vieux Nègre et la médaille*, Paris 1956; *Chemins d'Europe*, Paris 1960.

Padmore, George, *Panafricanism or Communism?*, London 1956 (issued as *Panafricanism*, Accra 1956).

Panet, Léopold, "Rélation d'un voyage du Sénégal à Soueira", *Revue Coloniale*, Paris November 1850.

Panikkar, K. M., *Asia and Western Dominance*, rev. edn., London and New York 1959.

Paton, Alan, *Cry, the Beloved Country*, New York 1948, London 1950.

Paul, Emmanuel C., "L'Ethnologie et les cultures noires", *PA* VIII–IX–X 1956.

Perham, Margery, *Ten Africans*, London 1936, Evanston, Ill., 1964.

Plaatje, Sol. T., *Native Life in South Africa*, London 1916; *Mhudi: An Epic of South African Native Life a Hundred Years Ago*, Lovedale 1930.

Quenum, Maximilien, *Au Pays des Fons: us et coutumes du Dahomey*, Paris 1938; *Trois*

Légendes africaines, Paris 1946; *L'Afrique noire: Rencontre avec l'Occident*. Paris 1958.

Rabearivelo, Jean-Joseph, *La Coupe de cendres*, Tananarive 1924; *Sylves*, Tananarive 1927; *Volumes*, Tananarive 1928; *Imaitsoanala—Fille d'oiseau—Cantate*, Tananarive 1935; *Traduit de la nuit*, Tunis 1935; *Poèmes*, Tananarive 1960; *Presque-songes*, Tananarive 1960; *24 Poems*, Ibadan 1962.

Rabemananjara, Jacques, *Sur les Marches du soir*, Gap 1942; *Les Dieux malgaches*, Paris 1947; *Antsa*, Paris 1948 and 1956; *Rites millénaires*, Paris 1955; *Lamba*, Paris 1956; *Témoignage malgache et colonialisme*, Paris 1956; *Les Boutriers de l'aurore*, Paris 1957; *Nationalisme et problèmes malgaches*, Paris 1958; "Les Fondements de notre unité tirés de l'époque coloniale", *PA* XXIV–XXV 1959; *Antidote*, Paris 1961; *Agapes des Dieux—Tritriva*, Paris 1962.

Ranaivo, Flavien, *L'Ombre et le vent*, Tananarive 1947; *Mes Chansons de toujours*, Paris 1955; *Le Retour au Bercail*, Tananarive 1962.

Raponda-Walker, André, *Notes d'histoire du Gabon*, Montpellier 1960.

Raponda-Walker, André, and Sillans, Roger, *Rites et croyances des peuples du Gabon*, Paris 1962.

Rive, Richard, *African Songs*, Berlin 1963.

Rouamba, Paul, "Malaise de l'étudiant catholique africain", *Tam-Tam*, nos. 1–2, Paris 1961.

Rousseau-Nadir, Henri, *Les Colonisés devant l'Union française*, Paris 1953.

Sadji, Abdoulaye, "Nini, mulatresse du Sénégal", *PA* 16 1954; *Maïmouna*, Paris 1958.

Sakiliba, F. D., "Présent et futur des langues africaines", *PA* XII–XIII 1957.

Sancho, Ignatius, *Letters of the Late Ignatius Sancho, an African*, London 1782, 2 vols.

Santos, Anani, *L'Option des indigènes en faveur de l'application de la loi française en AOF et au Togo*, doctoral thesis, Paris 1943.

Sartre, Jean-Paul, "Orphée noir", in *Anthologie de la nouvelle poésie nègre et malgache*, Paris 1948.

Seck, Assane, "Géographie, colonisation et culture", *PA* XIV–XV 1957.

Seid, Joseph Brahim, *Au Tchad sous les étoiles*, Paris 1962.

Selormey, Francis, *The Narrow Path*, London and New York 1966.

Senghor, Léopold Sédar, *Chants d'ombre*, Paris 1945; *Hosties noires*, Paris 1948; *Chants pour Naëtt*, Paris 1949; *Ethiopiques*, Paris 1956; "L'Esprit de la civilisation ou les lois de la culture négro-africaine", *PA* VIII–X 1956; *Nocturnes*, Paris 1961; *Nation et voie africaine du socialisme*, Paris 1961; published in English as *Nationhood and the African Road to Socialism*, Paris 1962; *On African Socialism*, New York and London 1964; *Liberté I: Négritude et humanisme*, Paris 1964; *Selected Poems*, London 1964.

Sidibe, Mamby, "Contes de la savane", *PA* 8–9 1950.

Sinda, Martial, *Premier Chant du départ*, Paris 1955.

Sissoko, Fily Dabo, *Les Noirs et la culture*, New York 1950; *Sagesse noire*, Paris 1953; *Crayons et portraits*, Mulhouse 1953; *Harmakhis*, Paris 1955; *La Savane rouge*, Avignon 1962; *Poèmes d'Afrique noire*, Paris 1963.

Sithole, Ndabaningi, *African Nationalism*, London 1959.

Socé, Ousmane [i.e., O. S. Diop], *Karim*, Paris 1935; *Mirages de Paris*, Paris 1937; *Contes et légendes d'Afrique noire*, Paris 1962; *Rhythmes du khalam*, Paris 1962.

Soga, John Henderson, *The Ama-Xosa: Life and Customs*, London 1932.

Soyinka, Wole, *A Dance of the Forests*, London 1963; *The Lion and the Jewel*, London 1963; *Three Plays*, Ibadan 1963; *The Interpreters*, London 1965.

Sulzer, Peter, *Schwarze Intelligenz*, Zürich 1955.

Sundkler, B. G. M., *Bantu Prophets in South Africa*, London 1948.

Suret-Canale, Jean, *Afrique noire*, Paris 1961.

Syad, William J. F., *Khamsine*, Paris 1959.

Tchibamba, Paul Lumani, *Ngando*, Brussels 1948.

Tchicaya U'Tamsi, Gérald Félix, *Le mauvais Sang*, Paris 1955; *Feu de brousse*, Paris 1957; published in English as *Brush Fire*, Ibadan 1964; *A Triche-coeur*, Paris 1958; *Epitomé*, Tunis 1962.

Tchidimbo, R., "L'Etudiant africain face à la culture latine", *PA* 14 1952.

Tempels, Fr Placide, *La Philosophie bantoue*, Elisabethville 1945.

Tévoedjré, Albert, *L'Afrique révoltée*, Paris 1958.

Thiam, "Des Contes et des fables en Afrique noire", *PA* 4 1948.

Thiam, Doudou, *La Portée de la citoyenneté française dans les territoires d'Outremer*, doctoral thesis, Paris 1953.

Tidiany, C. S., "Noir africain et culture latine", *PA* 14 1952.

Touré, Mamadou, "Responsabilité de l'économiste africain", *PA* XXVII–XXVIII 1959.

Touré, Sékou, *Guinée: Prélude à l'indépendance*, Paris 1959; "Le Leader politique considéré comme le représentant d'une culture", *PA* XXIV–XXV 1959; *L'Action démocratique du PDG pour l'émancipation africain*, vols. I & II, Conakry n.d.; *La Lutte du PDG pour l'émancipation africaine*, vol. IV, Conakry n.d.; *La Révolution guinéene et le progrès social*, vol. VI, Conakry n.d.; *L'Action du PDG et la lutte pour l'émancipation africaine*, Paris 1959.

Traoré, Bakary, *Le Théâtre négro-africain*, Paris 1958.

Trilles, R. P., *L'Âme des Pygmées d'Afrique*, Paris 1945.

Tutuola, Amos, *The Palm-Wine Drinkard*, London 1952, New York 1953; *My Life in the Bush of Ghosts*, London and New York 1954; *Simbi and the Satyr of the Dark Jungle*, London 1956; *The Brave African Huntress*, London 1958; *Feather Woman of the Jungle*, London 1962.

Tyam, Mohammadou Aliou, "Livre d'El Hadj Omar", *Travaux et mémoires de l'Institut d'ethnologie*, vol. XXI, Paris 1931.

Verger, Pierre, *Dieux d'Afrique*, Paris 1954.

Vigné d'Octon, P., *La Gloire du sabre*, Paris 1900.

Vilakazi, Benedict Wallet, *Zulu Horizons*, Cape Town 1962.

Wade, Abdoulaye, "Afrique noire et Union française", *PA* 14 1953.

Westermann, Dietrich, *Afrikaner erzaehlen ihr Leben*, Essen 1938.

Williams, Eric, "Le Leader politique considéré comme un homme de culture", *PA* XXIV–XXV 1959.

Williams, Garth, *The Rabbits' Wedding*, New York 1958.

Williams, J. J., *Hebrewisms of West Africa*, London 1930.

Wright, Richard, *Uncle Tom's Children*, New York 1938, London 1939; *Native Son*, New York and London 1940; *Black Power*, New York 1954, London 1956.

Yondo, Epanya Elelongué, *Kamerun! Kamerun!*, Paris 1960.

Youlou, Fulbert, "Le Rêve, le sorcier, le devin et le féticheur en Afrique centrale", *Communauté France-Afrique*, no. 133, Paris 1962.

Zoa, Abbé Jean, *Pour un nationalisme chrétien au Cameroun*, Yaoundé 1957.

ANTHOLOGIES AND COLLECTIVE WORKS

African World, Oxford 1954.

Andrade, Mario de, *Letteratura negra: I Poeti*, Rome 1961.

"Aspects de la culture noire: recherches et débats", *Cahiers du Centre catholique des intellectuels français*, no. 24, Paris 1958.
Ballagas, Emilio, *Mapa de la poesía negra americana*, Buenos Aires 1946.
Bassir, Olumbe, *An Anthology of West African Verse*, Ibadan 1957.
Cook, David, *Origin East Africa: A Makerere Anthology*, London, 1965.
Couffon, Claude, trans., *Chansons cubaines et autres poèmes*, Paris 1955.
Damas, Léon-Gontran, *Poètes d'expression française*, Paris 1947.
Drachler, Jacob, *African Heritage*, New York 1964.
Hughes, Langston, *An African Treasury*, New York 1960, London 1961; *Poems from Black Africa*, Bloomington, Ind., 1963.
Hughes, Langston, and Reygnault, Christiane, *Anthologie africaine et malgache*, Paris 1962.
Justin, Andrée, *Anthologie africaine des écrivains noirs d'expression française*, Paris 1962.
Komey, Ellis Ayitey, and Mphahlele, Ezekiel, *Modern African Stories*, London 1964.
Le Dossier Afrique, Verviers 1962.
Les plus beaux écrits de l'Union française, Paris 1947.
Moore, Gerald, and Beier, Ulli, *Modern Poetry from Africa*, Harmondsworth 1963.
Poètes d'Afrique, vol. 1, La Courneuve, 1956.
"Poètes noirs d'expression portugaise", *Europe*, Paris 1956.
"Des Prêtres noirs s'interrogent", *Rencontre*, Paris 1956.
Personnalité africaine et catholicisme, Paris 1963.
Reed, John, and Wake, Clive, *A Book of African Verse*, London 1964.
Rive, Richard, *Modern African Prose*, London 1964.
Rive, Richard, et al., *Quartet*, London and New York 1963.
Rutherfoord, Peggy, *Darkness and Light: An Anthology of African Writing*, London and Johannesburg 1958; published in USA as *African Voices: An Anthology of Native African Writing*, New York 1960.
Sainville, Leonard, *Letteratura negra: I Narratori*, Rome 1961.
Senghor, Léopold Sédar, *Anthologie de la nouvelle poésie nègre et malgache*, Paris 1940.
Smith, E. W. and Parrinder, E. G. *African Ideas of God*, 2nd edn., London 1961.
Tibble, Anne, *African English Literature: A Survey and Anthology*, London 1965.
Valdès, Ildefonso Pereda, *Antología de la poesía negra americana*, Montevideo 1936.
Whiteley, W. H., *A Selection of African Prose*, Oxford 1964, 2 vols.
Young, T. Cullen, *African New Writing: Short Stories by African Writers*, London 1947.

NOTES AND REFERENCES

INTRODUCTION

1 In *La Négritude dans la littérature négro-africaine* Thomas Mélone from Cameroon compares the origins of African and German literature. The latter stemmed, according to him, from a reaction against French cultural supremacy in seventeenth and eighteenth century Europe. This had reached such a pass that French had become the language of the cultured European. Similarly the African cultural renaissance, although expressed in French, is due—in his opinion—to the refusal to be culturally assimilated, the demand for a black African personality completely distinct from that of the coloniser.

2 *Présence Africaine* (henceforth abbreviated to *PA*), XI, p. 4.

3 *PA*, XXIV–XXV, p. 385.

4 Agence France Presse, *Africa South of the Sahara*, no. 495, October 13, 1958.

5 *Le Petit Matin* (Tunis), February 20, 1962.

6 Agence France Presse, North African Service, February 16, 1962.

7 *Ibid*, February 15, 1962.

8 Kesteloot, Lilyan, *Les Écrivains noirs de langue française*, p. 22.

9 Among the most recent are Mario de Andrade and Léonard Sainville's anthology in Italian, and Chimchon Inbal's in Hebrew. Africa must also have been one of the first continents to have an anthology of radio programmes, *Voices of Ghana, Literary Contributions to the Ghana Broadcasting Corporation*, published from 1958 on. It is a pity that similar publications have not appeared in other African capitals. The dramatic work of Abdou Anta Ka of Senegal is still unpublished, so far as I know.

10 Similarly Damas in *Le Dossier Afrique*, a collective work introducing European and African writers to the black continent, has assembled oral legends collected by Frobenius, a story by Birago Diop, extracts from the works of Kwame Nkrumah, Sékou Touré and Jomo Kenyatta, South African novelist Peter Abrahams' recollections of the presidents of Ghana and Kenya, and a striking indictment of the social consequences of apartheid by Phyllis Ntantala.

11 Diop, Sheikh Anta, *L'Afrique noire pré-coloniale*, pp. 199–200.

12 Ras Khan, a Ghanaian writer, has devoted an article to R. E. G. Armattoe's work in *PA*, XII.

PART ONE: RETURN TO ORIGINS

CHAPTER 1: LINGUA FRANCA

1 From Senghor, Léopold Sédar (ed.), *Anthologie de la nouvelle poésie nègre et malgache*, p. 108.

2 *PA*, XXIV–XXV, p. 70.

3 *Ibid*, XII and XIII.

4 Gandhi, *Collected Works*, vol. X, p. 156.

5 Agence France Presse, North African Service, November 17, 1962.

6 See Ojike, Mbonu, *My Africa*, p. 218.

7 See Ellis, George W., *Negro Culture in West Africa*, and Dugast, J., and Jeffreys, M. D. W., "L'Écriture des Bamoun", on this subject.

8 *PA*, XII, p. 135.

9 *Inventaire linguistique d'AOF-Togo*, p. 21.

10 *PA*, 8–9, p. 394.

11 Sissoko, Fily Dabo, *Les Noirs et la culture*, p. 28.

12 Hailey, Lord, *An African Survey*, p. 79.

13 *PA*, XIV–XV, p. 43.

14 *PA*, XII, p. 136.

15 Hailey, p. 80.

16 Tévoedjré, Albert, *L'Afrique révoltée*, p. 70.

17 *PA*, 14.

18 Mockerie, Parmenas Githendu, *An African Speaks for his Own People*, p. 15. Mockerie's autobiography appears in *Ten Africans*, by Margery Perham.

19 Extract from a speech by Damas in Brazzaville, 1954.
20 Sakiliba, F. D., "Présent et futur des langues africaines", *PA*, XII and XIII, p. 140. The *West African Pilot*, which has played a considerable role in the history of Nigeria, is one of the oldest papers in Africa and also dates from this period. Dr Azikiwe started his journalistic career in 1934 in the Gold Coast, where he launched the *African Morning Post*. He was editor-in-chief when he was sentenced to six months' imprisonment for incitement and sedition. The early success of the *West African Pilot* was largely due to the column by 'Zik' called "Inside Stuff".
21 "Débat sur les conditions d'une poésie nationale chez les peuples noirs", *PA*, IV, V, VI and XI.
22 *PA*, VI, p. 115.
23 Jahn, Janheinz, *Muntu*, p. 157.
24 Morisseau-Leroy, F., "Littérature haïtienne d'expression créole", *PA*, XVII.
25 *PA*, IV.
26 *PA*, XIV–XV, p. 255.
27 From Bassir, Olumbe (ed.), *An Anthology of West African Verse*, p. 17.
28 Armattoe, R. E. G., *Deep Down the Blackman's Mind*, p. 17.
29 Quoted by Dike, K. Onwuka, *Trade and Politics in the Niger Delta*, p. 17.
30 Boilat, Abbé P. D., *Esquisses Sénégalaises*, p. XIV.
31 Diop, Sheikh A., *Nations nègres et culture*, p. 262.
32 *PA*, 14, p. 169.
33 *PA*, VIII–IX–X, p. 74.
34 Senghor, "Le Message" in *Chants d'ombre*, p. 25.
35 *PA*, VIII–IX–X, pp. 215–17.
36 Tchidimbo, R., "L'étudiant africain face à la culture latine", *PA*, 14 p. 61.
37 *PA*, XIV–XV, p. 42.
38 *Ibid*, p. 43.
39 Hailey, p. 80.
40 See Guy Sitbon's article in *Le Monde*, April 19–20, 1959.
41 *PA*, XXIV–XXV, p. 397.

CHAPTER 2: CUSTOMS AND TRADITIONS

1 Ojike, p. 192.
2 Tidiany, C. S., "Noir africain et culture latine", *PA*, 14.
3 Paul, Emmanuel C., "L'Ethnologie et les cultures noires", *PA*, VIII–IX–X.
4 Kenyatta, Jomo, *Facing Mount Kenya*, p. 133.
5 *Ibid*, p. 153.
6 *Ibid*, p. 317.
7 Paul, p. 146.
8 Johnson, Samuel, *The History of the Yorubas*, p. 26.
9 Kenyatta, p. 233.
10 Raponda-Walker, André, and Sillians, Roger, *Rites et croyances des peuples du Gabon*, p. 16.
11 Ojike, p. 149.
12 Hama, Boubou, and Boulnois, Jean, *Empire de Goa*, p. 73.
13 Hazoumé, Paul, "L'Âme du Dahoméen révélée par sa religion", *PA*, XIV–XV, p. 236.
14 *Ibid*, p. 243.

15 Quenum, Maximilien, *Au Pays des Fons*, p. 64.
16 *Ibid*, p. 122.
17 Danquah, J. B., *The Akan Doctrine of God*, p. 49.
18 Quenum, *Au Pays*, p. 61.
19 Hazoumé, "L'Âme", p. 245.
20 Quenum, *Au Pays*, p. 125.
21 Hama and Boulnois, p. 180.
22 Ojike, p. 131.
23 Kenyatta, p. 186.
24 Ojike, p.193.
25 Kenyatta, p. 196.
26 Mockerie, p. 36.
27 Assane, Sylla, "Une République africaine au xix siècle", *PA*, I–II.
28 Sithole, Ndabaningi, *African Nationalism*, p. 86.
29 Kenyatta, p. 290.
30 Hama and Boulnois, p. 127.
31 Youlou, Fulbert, "Le Rêve, le sorcier, le devin et le féticheur en Afrique centrale", *Communauté France-Afrique*, no 133, 1962.
32 *PA*, XXVII–XXVIII.
33 Ekodo-Nkoulou-Essama, Fabien, "La Médecine par les plantes en Afrique noire", *PA*, XXVII–XXVIII, p. 257.
34 Kenyatta, p. 305.
35 *Ibid*, p. 290.
36 *Ibid*, p. 295.
37 Ojike, p. 133.
38 Quenum, *Au Pays*, p. 80 f.
39 Hama and Boulnois, *op. cit.*, p. 135.
40 Fanon, Frantz, *Les Damnés de la terre*, p. 44.
41 Ojike, p. 145.
42 Kenyatta, p. 176.
43 Quenum, *Au Pays*, p. 109.
44 Hazoumé, "L'Âme", Introduction, p. v.
45 Raponda-Walker, André, *Notes d'histoire du Gabon*.
46 Ajisafe, A. K., *The Laws and Customs of the Yoruba People*, p. 94.
47 Quenum, *L'Afrique noire: rencontre avec l'Occident*, p. 15.
48 Alapini, Julien, *Les Initiés*, p. 10.
49 *Ibid*, p. 94.
50 Hazoumé, "L'Âme", p. 141.
51 Amon d'Aby, F. J., *Croyances religieuses et coutumes juridiques des Angi de la Côte d'Ivoire*, p. 61.
52 *Ibid*, p. 121.
53 *Ibid*, pp. 121–3.
54 Diop, Sheikh Anta, *L'Unité culturelle de l'Afrique noire*, p. 185.
55 *Ibid*, p. 23.
56 *Ibid*, p. 18.
57 *Ibid*, pp. 91–2.

58 See Abbé Grégoire, *De la littérature des nègres*, ch. VIII. Amo also wrote a philosophical work, *De humanae mentis apatheia*.
59 Elias, T. Olawale, *The Nature of African Customary Law*, p. 25.

CHAPTER 3: BACK TO THE SOIL

1 *PA*, XIV–XV, p. 173.
2 Thiam, "Des contes et des fables en Afrique noire", *PA*, 4, p. 667.
3 Dadié, Bernard, "Le Rôle de la légende dans la culture populaire des noirs d'Afrique", *PA*, XIV–XV, p. 165.
4 *Black Orpheus*, No. 2, January 1958, p. 5.
5 Sissoko, *Sagesse noire*, p. XVI.
6 *PA*, 8–9, p. 331.
7 Dadié, "Le Rôle de la légende", p. 167.
8 Thiam, p. 669.
9 Dadié, "Le Rôle de la légende", p. 168.
10 *Ibid*, p. 167.
11 *PA*, 10–11, p. 195.
12 Sissoko, *Sagesse*, preface.
13 Seid, Joseph Brahim, *Au Tchad sous les étoiles*, p. 12.
14 *PA*, XXVII–XXVIII, p. 79.
15 Laye, Camara, *L'Enfant noir*, p. 91. (English edition, pp. 62–3.)
16 Laye, *Le Regard du roi*, p. 37. (English edition, pp. 39–40.)
17 Jahn, p. 218.
18 Laye, *L'Enfant*, p. 35. (English edition, p. 27.)
19 Jahn, pp. 160–1.
20 Laye, *Le Regard*, p. 189. (English edition, pp. 210–11.)
21 Jahn, p. 181.
22 *PA*, 7, pp. 315–16.
23 Boni, Nazi, *Crépuscule des temps anciens*, p. 16 f.
24 Malonga, Jean, *La Légende de M'Pfoumou Ma Mazono*, p. 99.
25 *Ibid*, p. 152.
26 *PA*, 8–9, p. 196.

CHAPTER 4: TO EACH HIS OWN TRUTH

1 Ki Zerbo, J., "Histoire et conscience nègre", *PA*, XVI, p. 53.
2 Wade, Abdoulaye, "Afrique noire et Union française", *PA*, 14, p. 118.
3 Diop, Sheikh Anta, *Nations nègres*, p. 253.
4 *Ibid*, p. 8.
5 Andriantsilaniarivo, E., "Le Malgache du xx Siècle", *PA*, VIII–IX–X, p. 98.
6 Johnson, p. 6.
7 Niane, Djibril Tamsir, *Soundjata ou l'épopée mandingue*, p. 8.
8 Ki Zerbo, "Histoire et conscience nègre", p. 55.
9 *PA*, XI, p. 119.
10 Biobaku, Saburi O., *The Egbas and Their Neighbours 1842–1872*, preface.

11 Diop, Sheikh Anta, *Nations nègres*, pp. 27–8.
12 *Ibid*, p. 28.
13 *Ibid*, p. 38.
14 *Ibid*, p. 41.
15 *Ibid*, p. 127.
16 *Ibid*, pp. 21–2.
17 *Ibid*, p. 35.
18 *Ibid*, p. 38.
19 *Ibid*, p. 71.
20 *Ibid*, p. 89.
21 *Ibid*, p. 117.
22 *Ibid*, p. 253.
23 Suret-Canale, Jean, *Afrique noire*, p. 59 f.
24 Conton, William, *West Africa in History*, introduction.
25 Graft-Johnson, Charles de, *African Glory*, pp. 117–18.
26 *Ibid*, fn. p. 118.
27 *Ibid*, p. 3.
28 Wade, p. 118.
29 de Graft-Johnson, p. 8.
30 *Ibid*, p. 7.
31 *Ibid*, p. 34.
32 *Ibid*, p. 153.
33 Padmore, George, *Panafricanism*, p. 32.
34 Nkrumah, Kwame, *The Autobiography of Kwame Nkrumah*, p. 199.
35 *PA*, XI.
36 *PA*, XVI.
37 Diop, Sheikh Anta, *L'Afrique*, p. 101 f.
38 *Ibid*, p. 38.
39 *Ibid*, p. 16.
40 *Ibid*, p. 17.
41 *Ibid*, p. 18.
42 *Ibid*, pp. 20–1.
43 *Ibid*, p. 27.
44 *Ibid*, p. 112.
45 *Ibid*, p. 109.
46 *Ibid*, p. 79.
47 *Ibid*, p. 114.
48 Ouane, Ibrahima-Mamadou, *L'Énigme du Macina*, p. 150.
49 *Ibid*, p 82.
50 Babikir, Arbab Djama, *L'Empire de Rabeh*, foreword.
51 *Ibid*, p. 70.
52 *Ibid*, p. 72.
53 *Ibid*, p. 80.
54 Sissoko, *Les Noirs*, p. 40.
55 Wade, p. 124.
56 Mofolo, Thomas, *Shaka*, translator's preface.
57 *Ibid*, p. 198.
58 *Ibid*, p. 268.

59 Jahn, p. 203.
60 Senghor, *Ethiopiques*, p. 31 f.
61 Sithole, pp. 78–9.
62 Molema, S. M., *Bantu Past and Present*, p. 120.
63 Yondo, Epanya Elelongué, *Kamerun! Kamerun!*, p. 40.
64 Ahuma, Attoh, *Memoirs of West African Celebrities*, preface.
65 Sissoko, *Les Noirs*, p. 13.
66 Abbé Grégoire also mentions him.
67 Hazoumé, *Doguicimi*, p. 509.
68 Azikiwe, Nnamdi, *Renascent Africa*, p. 9.
69 Cited by David Kimble in *A Political History of Ghana*, p. 525.
70 Nkrumah, quoted in *Darkness and Light* by Peggy Rutherfoord, p. 180–1.
71 "L'Afrique noir devant les lois historiques de l'évolution" in *L'Action démocratique de Parti démocratique de Guinée pour l'emancipation africaine*, vol. 1, p. 178. This is a collection of speeches by President Sékou Touré in 1958.
72 Syad, William J. F., *Khamsine*, poem entitled "Hier", p. 44.

CHAPTER 5: THE RETURN REVIEWED

1 Césaire, Aimé, "Culture et colonisation", *PA*, VIII–IX–X, p. 204.
2 Senghor, *Anthologie de la nouvelle poésie nègre et malgache*, p. 57.
3 *PA*, VIII–IX–X, p. 216.
4 Touré, Sékou, *L'Action du PDG et la lutte pour l'émancipation africaine*, p. 165. This book, published by *Présence Africaine*, is a choice of speeches by President Sékou Touré. The title is almost identical to that of the collection of his speeches published in Conakry by the Guinean government in several volumes, from which *Présence Africaine* made their selection.

PART TWO: REVOLT

CHAPTER 6: THE POLITICAL KINGDOM

1 Quoted by Amamoo, J. Godson, *The New Ghana*, p. 73.
2 Kalu Ezera, a Nigerian lawyer, has devoted a book to the subject, *Constitutional Developments in Nigeria*.
3 Nkrumah, *Towards Colonial Freedom*, pp. 27–8.
4 Touré, *L'Action démocratique du PDG*, vol. 1, p. 183.
5 Tévoedjré, pp. 33 and 37.
6 Sithole, pp. 20–1.
7 Ly, Abdoulaye, *La Force noire, mercenaires noirs*, p. 51.
8 Touré, *L'Action du PDG et la lutte*, p. 148.
9 *Ibid*, p. 148.
10 Senghor in *Chants d'ombre*, p. 81.
11 Kaunda, Kenneth, *Zambia Shall Be Free*, pp. 41 f.
12 Delobsom, Dim, *Les Secrets des sorciers noirs*, pp. 154 and 158.

13 *PA*, XI, p. 25.
14 Hodgkin, Thomas, *Nationalism in Colonial Africa*, p. 36.
15 Santos, Anani, *L'Option des indigènes en faveur de l'application de la loi française en AOF et au Togo*, p. 106.
16 Diop, Maghemout, "L'Unique Issue: l'independance totale", *PA*, 14.
17 Wade, pp. 144 and 133.
18 Tévoedjré, p. 17. This was a warning by Henri Culmann, quoted by Henri Rousseau-Nadir in *Les Colonisés devant l'Union française*.
19 Gueye, Lamine, *Etapes et perspectives de l'Union française*, p. 120.
20 *Ibid*, p. 132.
21 Thiam, Doudou, *La Portée de la citoyenneté française dans les territoires d'Outremer*, p. 10.
22 *Ibid*, pp. 97–8.
23 Tévoedjré, pp. 19–20.
24 *Ibid*, pp. 22–3.
25 Touré, *L'Action démocratique du PGD*, vol. 1, p. 21.
26 *Ibid*, pp. 93–4.
27 *Le Monde*, April 12, 1961.
28 Senghor, *Nation et voie africaine du socialisme*, pp. 27–9.
29 Molema, p. 366.
30 Padmore, p. 276.
31 Akpan, Ntieyong, *Epitaph to Indirect Rule*, p. 29.
32 Amamoo, p. 9.
33 *Ibid*, p. 99.
34 Kaunda, p. 58.
35 *Ibid*, p. 87.
36 Bello, Sir Ahmadu, *My Life*, p. 98.
37 Nkrumah, *Africa Must Unite*, p. 191.
38 Ouzegane, Amar, *Le Meilleur Combat*, p. 56.
39 Awolowo, Obafemi, *Awo: The Autobiography of Chief Obafemi Awolowo*, p. 200.
40 *Ibid*, p. 206.
41 *Ibid*, pp. 261–2.
42 Nkrumah, *Autobiography*, pp. vii–viii.
43 Kaunda, p. 140.
44 *Ibid*, p. 155.
45 Casely-Hayford, *Gold Coast Native Institutions*, p. 220.
46 Koinange, Mbiyu, *The People of Kenya Speak for Themselves*, p. 72.
47 Mboya, Tom, *Freedom and After*, p. 50.
48 *Les étudiants noirs parlent*, *PA*, 14, p. 184.
49 Sithole, p. 160.

CHAPTER 7: THE COLONIAL PACT

1 Nkrumah, *Towards Colonial Freedom*, p. 7.
2 Ly, *La Compagnie du Sénégal*, p. 31.
3 *Ibid*, p. 296.
4 Dike, p. 3.
5 Abbas, Ferhat, *La Nuit coloniale*, pp. 16–17.
6 Panikkar, K. M., *Asia and Western Dominance*.

7 Dia, Mamadou, *Réflexions sur l'économie de l'Afrique noire*, p. 27.
8 Nkrumah, *Towards Colonial Freedom*, p. 36.
9 Dia, *Réflexions*, p. 28.
10 Tévoedjré, p. 92.
11 *Ibid*, p. 90.
12 Nkrumah, *Towards Colonial Freedom*, p. 19.
13 Ly, *Les Masses africaines et l'actuelle condition humaine*, p. 164.
14 *Ibid*, p. 125.
15 Nkrumah, *Towards Colonial Freedom*, p. 16.
16 *Ibid*, p. 19.
17 Tévoedjré, p. 86.
18 Gologo, Mamadou, *Le Rescapé de l'Ethylos*, p. 378.
19 Dia, *Réflexions*, p. 30.
20 Nkrumah, *Towards Colonial Freedom*, pp. 20–1.
21 *Ibid*, p. 21, fn.
22 *Ibid*, p. 18.
23 Ly, *Les Masses africaines*, pp. 214–15.
24 *Ibid*, p. 222–3.
25 Dia, *Réflexions*, p. 35.
26 *Ibid*, p. 39.
27 *Ibid*, p. 41.
28 *Ibid*, pp. 49–50.
29 *Ibid*, pp. 49–50.
30 Touré, Mamadou, "Responsabilities de l'économiste africain", *PA*, XXVII–XXVIII, p. 246. The author of this article, who is Senegalese, should not be confused with his namesake, the Mauritanian diplomatist.

CHAPTER 8: POLITICALLY COMMITTED LITERATURE

1 Damas, Léon-Gontran, *Poètes d'expression française*, p. 13.
2 *Ibid*, p. 10.
3 *Ibid*, p. 16.
4 Andrade, Mario de, "Poètes noirs d'expression portugaise", in *Europe*, January 1961, no. 381, p. 3.
5 Quoted by Mélone, p. 65.
6 See Brawley, Benjamin, *Early Negro American Writers*.
7 Quoted by Roger Bastide, *A Poesia Afro-Brasileira*, p. 55.
8 Nicolàs Guillén, *La paloma de vuelo popular*, Buenos Aires, 1948.
9 "Orphée noir", in Senghor, *Anthologie de la nouvelle poésie*, p. XXXVI.
10 Tchicaya U'Tamsi, F., *Epitomé*, p. 27.
11 Senghor, *Anthologie de la nouvelle poésie*, p. 183.
12 From *La Ronde des jours*.
13 From *Europe*, January 1961.
14 From Senghor, *Anthologie de la nouvelle poésie*, p. 175.
15 *Ibid*, p. 114.
16 *Ibid*, p. 126.
17 From Bamboté, Pierre, *La Poésie est dans l'histoire*.
18 From *PA*, 14, p. 201.

19 Armattoe, *Deep Down the Blackman's Mind.*

20 From *Modern Poetry from Africa* by Gerald Moore and Ulli Beier.

21 From Bassir, *An Anthology of West African Verse.*

22 Dei-Anang, Michael, *Africa Speaks*, p. 35.

23 *PA*, XXXII–XXXIII, pp. 141–2.

24 From *An African Treasury*, anthology by Langston Hughes.

25 From Senghor, *Anthologie de la nouvelle poésie.*

26 From Bassir, *An Anthology of West African Verse.*

27 *PA*, III, p. 79.

28 From Rutherfoord, *Darkness and Light*, p. 90.

29 Dei-Anang, p. 50.

30 Tchicaya U'Tamsi, *Epitomé.*

31 Senghor, *Hosties noires.*

32 Dadié, *Climbié*, p. 182.

33 Mopila, Francesco Jose, *Memòrias de un Congoles*, p. 25. This is one of the very few if not the only books, by a Spanish-speaking African author. He is an Azande from the eastern province of the former Belgian Congo. I should also mention here one of the rare works by a German-speaking African writer, the autobiography of Martin Akan from Togo in Diedrich Westermann's work *Afrikaner erzachlen ihr Leben.*

34 Fanon, *Peau noire, masques blancs*, pp. 118–19.

35 Lobagola, *An African Savage's Own Story*, p. 42.

36 Ba, Ahmadou Hampaté and Dieterlen, Germaine, *Koumen*, p. 95.

37 In *Bulletin de l'IFAN*, Dakar, nos. 3–4, July–October, 1949.

38 Fanon asserts in *Peau noire*, p. 124, that 'an anti-semite is inevitably a negrophobe'.

39 Kane, Sheikh Hamadou, *L'Aventure ambiguë*, p. 183.

40 Fanon, *Peau noire*, pp. 219–20.

41 Sissoko, *La Savane rouge*, p. 125.

42 Bognini, Joseph Miezan, *Ce dur appel de l'espoir*, preface, p. 10.

43 Gologo, pp. 43 and 368.

44 Orizu, N., *Without Bitterness*, p. 377.

45 Sissoko, *Crayons et portraits*, p. 75. (This dates from 1937.)

46 Socé, Ousmane, *Karim.*

47 *PA*, I–II, p. 144 and *PA*, 16, p. 420.

48 Sartre, Jean-Paul, "Orphée noir", p. XL.

49 *Ibid.*, p. XXV.

50 *Ibid*, p. XXVIII.

51 *Ibid*, p. XXXIX.

52 Jahn, pp. 112–13, 117–18.

53 *Ibid*, pp. 123–4.

54 *Ibid*, chapter headed "Nommo".

55 Wright, Richard, *Black Power*, p. 237.

56 Jahn, p. 146.

57 *PA*, XXIV–XXV, pp. 109–10.

58 Fanon, *Les Damnés*, p. 159.

59 *Ibid*, p. 161.

60 *Ibid*, p. 162.

61 *Ibid*, p. 162.

62 *Ibid*, p. 165.

63 Mphahlele, Ezekiel, *The African Image*, pp. 27–8.
64 *Ibid*, pp. 22–3.
65 *Ibid*, p. 25.
66 *Ibid*, p. 22.
67 *Ibid*, p. 66.
68 *Ibid*, p. 83.

CHAPTER 9: THE NEW DESDEMONA

1 *PA*, XXVI, p. 114. The children's book was *The Rabbits' Wedding*, written and illustrated by Garth Williams.
2 Andrade, Mario de, "Poètes noirs d'expression portugaise", in *Europe*, no. 381, p. 4. He, of course, does not share all of Freyre's ideas.
3 Keatley, Patrick, *The Politics of Partnership*, p. 245.
4 Brooks, Gwendolyn, *Ballad of Pearl May Lee*, *PA*, I, pp. 112–13.
5 Padmore, p. 89–91.
6 Soares' *Dicionario brasileiro da lingua portuguesa* was published in 1954.
7 Ivy, James W., "Le Fait d'être nègre dans les Amériques", *PA*, XXIV–XXV, p. 130.
8 From Senghor, *Anthologie de la nouvelle poésie*, p. 108.
9 *Ibid*, pp. 124–5.
10 Fanon, *Peau noire*, pp. 162–3.
11 *Ibid*, p. 72. Apparently, Fanon does not believe this anecdote, but he considers its very existence significant.
12 From Senghor, *Anthologie de la nouvelle poésie*, pp. 8–9.
13 *PA*, IV, p. 63.
14 Tchicaya U'Tamsi, *Epitomé*, p. 91.
15 Senghor, *Anthologie de la nouvelle poésie*, p. 93.
16 Diop, David, *Coups de Pilon*, p. 174.
17 *Ibid*, p. 25.
18 From Senghor, *Anthologie de la nouvelle poésie*, p. 87.
19 *Ibid*, p. 151.
20 *Ibid*, p. 171.
21 Diakhate, Lamine, *Primordiale du sixième jour*.
22 From Bassir, *An Anthology of West African Verse*, p. 45.
23 Quoted by Mphahlele, *African Image*, p. 180.
24 Malonga, *Coeur d'Aryenne*.
25 Ousmane, Sembène, *O pays, mon beau peuple*.
26 Abrahams, Peter, *A Wreath for Udomo*.
27 Socé, *Mirages de Paris*.
28 Loba, Aké, *Kocoumbo, l'étudiant noir*.
29 Kane, *L'Aventure ambiguë*.
30 Ousmane, *Le Docker noir*.

CHAPTER 10: BEFORE THE REVOLT

1 "Relation d'un voyage du Sénégal à Es-Saouira", *Revue Coloniale*, November 1850 pp. 379–445.

2 Boilat, p. 237.
3 *Ibid*, p. 106.
4 The two books mentioned here were apparently first published separately in 1912 and 1913. They appeared together in a second edition in 1931 (with an introduction by Blaise Diagne), and a third time under a different author's name, Ahmadou Mahmadou Ba, if we are to believe M. Joucla's general bibliography of French West Africa. I have seen only the 1931 edition, printed by the government printing press in Senegal.
5 *PA*, XXVII–XXVIII, p. 133 f.
6 Graft-Johnson, Charles de, p. 159.
7 *PA*, XXIV–XXV, p. 110.
8 Senghor, *Nation et voie*, p. 116.

PART THREE: THE NEW AFRICA

CHAPTER 11: THE SONS OF HAM

1 Ela, Marc, "L'Église, la monde noir et le concile", from the *PA* anthology, *Personnalité africaine et Catholicisme.*
2 Graft-Johnson, Charles de, p. 49.
3 *Ibid*, p. 157.
4 *Ibid*, p. 132.
5 *Ibid*, p. 157.
6 *Ibid*, p. 158.
7 *Ibid*, p. 50.
8 *PA*, XIV–XV, p. 47.
9 See the appendix of Nkrumah's *Towards Colonial Freedom.*
10 Baldwin, James, *The Fire Next Time*, pp. 46–56. However several of the most prominent Negro leaders in the anti-segregationist fight in the United States are ministers in particular the Reverend Martin Luther King.
11 Kaunda, p. 146.
12 *Ibid*, p. 146.
13 *Ibid*, p. 150.
14 Mockerie, pp. 33–4.
15 "Afrique noire, littérature rose", *PA*, I–II, p. 133.
16 Graft-Johnson, Charles de, p. 51. The Ba-Ronga are a tribe in South Africa.
17 *PA*, VI, p. 165.
18 *PA*, 12, p. 182, *Les Vautours.*
19 Tchicaya U'Tamsi, *Epitomé*, pp. 11–12. Saint Anne's is the cathedral in the African quarter of Poto-Poto in Brazzaville.
20 From Senghor, *Anthologie de la nouvelle poésie*, p. 120.
21 Beti, Mongo, *Le Pauvre Christ de Bomba*, p. 322.
22 Oyono, Ferdinand, *Le vieux Nègre et la médaille.*
23 Mphahlele, *Down Second Avenue*, p. 221.
24 Traoré, Bakary, *Le Théâtre négro-africain*, p. 59.
25 Oyono, *Chemins d'Europe*, pp. 195–6.

26 Robert Delavignette, former colonial governor-general, devoted a book to the subject, called *Christianisme et colonialisme*.
27 Zoa, Abbé Jean, *Pour un nationalisme chrétien au Cameroun*, p. 16.
28 Tévoedjré, pp. 109 f.
29 Sithole, p. 53.
30 *Ibid*, p. 122.
31 Joy, Charles, *Albert Schweitzer: An Anthology*, p. 85. Dr Schweitzer's medical work has also been severely criticised by Pierre and Renée Gosset in *L'Afrique, les Africains*, pp. 160 f.
32 Sithole, pp. 53–4.
33 This is the title of the English translation.
34 Title of the German translation.
35 Ntara, S. Y., *Man of Africa*, p. 158.
36 *Ibid*, pp. 180–1.
37 From Senghor, *Anthologie de la nouvelle poésie*, pp. 94–5. Niger is undoubtedly referring to the American film *Green Pastures*.
38 Armattoe, *Deep Down the Blackman's Mind*, p. 13.
39 *Le Monde*, January 31, 1962.
40 Kenyatta, p. 269.
41 *Ibid*, p. 275.
42 *Ibid*, p. 279.
43 *Le Monde*, February 25, 1961.
44 Although a native of Sierra Leone, Dr Blyden was the first Liberian ambassador to London in the nineteenth century. He wrote several books, including *Christianity, Islam and the Negro Race*.
45 *Tam-Tam*, nos. 1–2, 1961, pp. 18–19.
46 Baeta, C. G., *Prophetism in Ghana*, p. 128.
47 *Ibid*, p. 128.
48 *Ibid*, p. 25.
49 *Ibid*, p. 130. The author is making an allusion to the 'cargo cult', which is widely prevalent in the islands of the Pacific also.
50 Jahn, p. 54.
51 From *France Observateur*, August 9, 1962.
52 *PA*, VI.
53 *L'Express*, "L'Eglise contre le colonialisme", February 5, 1955.
54 Méjean, François, *Le Vatican contre la France d'Outremer*, p. 73.
55 *Ibid*, p. 197.
56 *PA*, XVI. Alioune Diop, director of *Présence Africaine*, is a catholic.
57 Ba, Ahmadou Hampaté, and Cardaire, Marcel, *Tierno Bokar, le sage de Bandiagara*, p. 93.
58 Kane, pp. 23–4.
59 *Ibid*, pp. 178–9.
60 Bello, p. 19. The Algerian, Amar Ouzegane, in *Le Meilleur Combat* has indignantly denounced this supposed fatalism, and especially the use made of it by some writers as a justification for continued colonial domination. The Algerian war obviously provided him with a weighty argument.
61. Bello, p. 197.

CHAPTER 12: THE AFRICAN PROLETARIAT

1 Padmore, p. 15.
2 Abbas, p. 13.
3 Tévoedjré, p. 123.
4 Sithole, p. 133.
5 *Ibid*, pp. 143–4.
6 Nkrumah, *Towards Colonial Freedom*, p. 15.
7 Azikiwe, *Renascent Africa*, p. 131.
8 Touré, *L'Action du PDG et la lutte*, p. 16.
9 *Ibid*, p. 21.
10 Touré, *La lutte du PDG pour l'émancipation africaine*, vol. IV, pp. 27–8.
11 Senghor, *Nation et voie*, p. 78.
12 *Ibid*, p. 50.
13 *Ibid*, p. 51. It is interesting to compare the opinions of Sékou Touré and Senghor on the vested interest of the European proletariat with Daniel Guérin's virulent indictment of left-wing French attitudes to colonial matters before the war in *Front populaire, révolution manquée*.
14 Ly, *Les Masses africaines*, p. 116.
15 *Ibid*, p. 109.
16 *Ibid*, p. 112.
17 *Ibid*, p. 120.
18 *Ibid*, p. 45.
19 *Ibid*, p. 46.
20 *Ibid*, p. 121.
21 Diop, Maghemout, *Contribution à l'étude*, pp. 119–20.
22 *Ibid*, p. 154.
23 *Ibid*, p. 153.
24 *Ibid*, pp. 226–7.
25 *Ibid*, p. 134.
26 *Ibid*, p. 235.
27 Ly, *Les Masses africaines*, p. 70.
28 Senghor, *Nation et voie*, pp. 42–3.
29 *Ibid*, p. 55.
30 *Ibid*, p. 53.
31 *Ibid*, p. 66.
32 *Ibid*, p. 71.
33 *Ibid*, pp. 97–8.
34 *Ibid*, p. 99.
35 *Ibid*, p. 103.
36 *Ibid*, p. 85.
37 Nyerere, Julius, *Ujamaa: The Basis of African Socialism.*
38 Touré, *L'Action du PDG et la lutte*, p. 221.
39 Kane, p. 163 f.
40 Keita, Madeira, "Le Parti unique en Afrique", *PA*, XXX, p. 7.
41 Touré, *L'Action du PDG et la lutte*, vol. IV, p. 131.

42 Mboya, Tom, *Freedom and After*, p. 88.
43 Azikiwe, "La Part du Nigéria dans la politique mondiale", *PA*, XXXIV–XXXV, p. 9.
44 Fanon, *Les Damnés*, p. 84.
45 *Ibid*, p. 124.
46 *Ibid*, p. 125.
47 Tévoedjré, pp. 26–7.
48 *Ibid*, pp. 30–1.
49 Touré, *La Révolution guinéenne et le progrès social*, p. 187.
50 Nkrumah, *Africa Must Unite*, p. 187.
51 *Ibid*, ch. XXI.
52 Dia, Mamadou, *Nations africaines et solidarité mondiale*, p. 100.
53 Touré, *L'Action du PDG et la lutte*, pp. 79–80.
54 Nkrumah, *I Speak of Freedom*, p. 255.
55 Senghor, *Nation et voie*, pp. 9–10.
56 *PA*, XL, p. 31.

CHAPTER 13: THE COLONIAL CONSCIENCE

1 *PA*, XXIV–XXV, p. 106.
2 Quoted by Eric Williams, *PA*, XXIV–XXV, p. 93. Dr Williams is now prime minister of Trinidad and Tobago.
3 Diop, Sheikh Anta, *Nations nègres*, pp. 33–4.
4 Tidiany, C. S., "Noir africain et culture latine", *PA*, 14, p. 43.
5 Lahbabi, Mohamed Aziz, "Propos sur la civilisation et cultures", *PA*, XVI, pp. 100–110. *Les Fonctions mentales dans les sociétés inférieures*, in which Lévy-Bruhl gives his ideas on the prelogical mentality of the primitive peoples, was written in 1910. The notes of his posthumous *Carnets*, in which he corrects these opinions, were written in 1938 and published in 1949.
6 Chomé, Jules, *La Passion de Simon Kimbangu*, pp. 64–5.
7 Maquet, J. J., "Le Relativism culturel", *PA*, XXIII, p. 60.
8 See Awolowo, *Awo*, p. 137 and *PA*, XXXIV–XXXV, p. 171.
9 Here is a list of the few books on the history of the press in Africa:

Kitchen, Helen, *The Press in Africa*, Washington, 1956.

Gras, Jacqueline, *Situation de la presse dans les états de l'Union Africaine et Malgache, en Guinée, au Mali, au Togo*, Paris, 1963.

Vivante Afrique, a special number devoted to the catholic press in black Africa, May–June 1964, Paris.

de Benoist, Father Joseph-Roger, "Report on the Position of the Press in French-Speaking West Africa": a report presented to the Dakar conference in June 1960 on the subject of "Press and progress in West Africa"; it appeared in *Afrique documents*, a review published in Dakar.

I have also consulted a manuscript by Tom Hopkinson, director of the International Press Institute, University College, Nairobi, which appears in the second edition of *Africa, a Handbook of the Continent*, published under the direction of Colin Legum; also a study by Manuel Brindier who is responsible for African trainees at the Centre de Formation des Journalistes in Paris. Lord Hailey's encyclopedic work, *An African Survey*, has several interesting pages on the history of the African press. Finally there is a study of the press in the former Belgian Congo in the journal of the Institut

Politique Congolais, Leopoldville, number II/5, 1962. Furthermore, most numbers of this journal give a report on the Congolese press.

CHAPTER 14: LIMITATIONS OF THE REVOLUTION

1 Touré, *La Révolution guinéenne*, p. 184.
2 Nkrumah, *Africa Must Unite*, p. 173.
3 *Ibid*, p. 214.
4 Fanon, *Les Damnés*, pp. 40–1.
5 *Ibid*, p. 120.
6 Touré, *La Révolution guinéenne*, p. 19.
7 Lacouture, J., and Baumier, J., *Le Poids du Tiers Monde*.
8 Mboya, p. 62.
9 Essien-Udom, E. U., *Black Nationalism: A Search for Identity in America*.

CHAPTER 15: NEGRITUDE AND THE FUTURE

1 Sartre, p. XL–XLI.
2 *Ibid*, p. XLIV. Sartre quotes Césaire, *Les Armes miraculeuses*, p. 156.
3 Kesteloot, pp. 115–16.
4 Jahn, p. 242.
5 Fanon, *Les Damnés*.
6 Dia, Mamadou, *Contribution à l'étude du mouvement coopératif en Afrique Noire*.
7 From *Jeune Afrique*, December 3–9, 1962.
8 Mphahlele, *African Image*.
9 As was pointed out by the critic in *Révolution africaine* (March 30, 1963).
10 Ndiaye, Jean-Pierre, *Enquête sur les étudiants noirs en France*, 1962. (*Réalité Africaine* Publication).
11 This was the essence of Patrice Lumumba's speech in reply to that of King Baudouin on the day independence was proclaimed for his country. See *Uhuru Lumumba* by Serge Michel, p. 175.

INDEX OF NAMES

The country of origin of African and American Negro and Coloured intellectuals cited is, where possible, given in brackets after the name.

INDEX OF SUBJECTS AND TITLES OF WORKS